W9-ACY-253

THE GROUND WE STAND ON

Also by John Dos Passos

THREE SOLDIERS

MANHATTAN TRANSFER

THREE PLAYS

JOURNEYS BETWEEN WARS

U. S. A.

one volume containing

1. THE 42ND PARALLEL
2. NINETEEN NINETEEN
3. THE BIG MONEY

ADVENTURES OF A YOUNG MAN

THE GROUND WE STAND ON

SOME EXAMPLES FROM THE HISTORY OF A POLITICAL CREED

BY JOHN DOS PASSOS

HARCOURT, BRACE AND COMPANY, NEW YORK

KRAUS REPRINT CO.
New York
1970

first edition

Reprinted from the original edition in the
Wesleyan University Library

LC 41-16286

PRINTED IN THE UNITED STATES OF AMERICA

Reprinted with the permission of the author
KRAUS REPRINT CO.
A U.S. Division of Kraus-Thomson Organization Limited

For

K. D. P.

Acknowledgments

Chapters from this book were first printed in *The New Republic*, *The American Mercury*, and *Accent* and are reprinted by permission.

I want to thank Mr. H. S. Brockunier for his kindness in reading over the Roger Williams section and making several valuable suggestions about it, and the Harvard College Library for promptness in mailing me books when I asked for them, and the Library of Congress for the use of a study and for valuable pointers from the research staff, and Edith Shay for her hard work in helping edit the manuscript. Quotations from Gouverneur Morris' Paris diary are by permission of Beatrix Cary Davenport who edited the latest edition, and of the Houghton Mifflin Company. Especially I want to thank my friend Sam Barlow of New York for his thoughtfulness in bringing to my attention and letting me use his collection of his greatuncle Joel's letters and notebooks and for letting me print some unpublished material out of it.

A grant from the Guggenheim Foundation was a great help to me during the preparatory work.

"My object is altogether of a moral and political nature. I wish to encourage and strengthen, in the rising generation, a sense of the importance of republican institutions; as being the great foundation of public and private happiness, the necessary aliment of future and permanent ameliorations in the condition of human nature.

"This is the moment in America to give such a direction to poetry, painting and the other fine arts, that true and useful ideas of glory may be implanted in the minds of men here, to take the place of the false and destructive ones that have degraded the species in other countries; impressions that have become so wrought into their sacred institutions, that it is there thought impious to detect them and dangerous to root them out, tho acknowledged to be false. Wo be to the republican principle, and to all the institutions it supports when once the pernicious doctrine of the holiness of error shall creep into the creed of our schools and distort the intellect of our citizens."

JOEL BARLOW, IN THE PREFACE TO THE PHILADELPHIA EDITION OF THE Columbiad, 1807

Contents

I

THE USE OF THE PAST

"I am sensible that there are defects in our federal government, yet they are so much lighter than those of monarchies, that I view them with much indulgence. I rely too, on the good sense of the people for remedy, whereas the evils of monarchical government are beyond remedy. If any of our countrymen wish for a King, give them Aesop's fable of the frogs who asked a King; if this does not cure them, send them to Europe. They will go back good republicans."

FROM JEFFERSON'S LETTER TO DR. RAMSAY
Paris, August 4, 1787

The Use of the Past

EVERY generation rewrites the past. In easy times history is more or less of an ornamental art, but in times of danger we are driven to the written record by a pressing need to find answers to the riddles of today. We need to know what kind of firm ground other men, belonging to generations before us, have found to stand on. In spite of changing conditions of life they were not very different from ourselves, their thoughts were the grandfathers of our thoughts, they managed to meet situations as difficult as those we have to face, to meet them sometimes lightheartedly, and in some measure to make their hopes prevail. We need to know how they did it.

In times of change and danger when there is a quicksand of fear under men's reasoning, a sense of continuity with generations gone before can stretch like a lifeline across the scary present and get us past that idiot delusion of the exceptional Now that blocks good thinking. That is why, in times like ours, when old institutions are caving in and being replaced by new institutions not necessarily in accord with most men's preconceived hopes, political thought has to look backwards as well as forwards.

In spite of the ritual invocation of the names of the Founding Fathers round election time, Americans as a people notably lack a sense of history. We have taken the accomplishments in statebuilding of the seventeenth century colonists and of the thirteen states for granted as we took the rich forest loam and the coal and the iron and the oil and the buffalo. We have wasted and exploited our political heritage with the same childish lack of foresight that has wrecked our forests and eroded our farmlands and ruined the grazing on the great plains. Now that we are caught up short at the edge of the precipice, face to face with the crowded servitude from which our fathers fled to a new world, the question is how much is left; how much of their past achievement is still part of our lives? It is not a question of what we want; it is a question of what is. Our history, the successes and failures of the men who went before us, is only alive in so far as some seeds and shoots of it are still stirring and growing in us today.

The Americans of our time who have put their minds to work in this direction have come late, on the whole, to understanding the actuality of the American past. They had to get a lot of callow debunking off their chests first. Right from the beginning the line of American thinking has been twisted off the straight course by periods of backsliding into a provincial tone towards Europe. One of those periods has come to an abrupt end right now.

Young men were set from childhood against looking with fresh eyes into our history by the lackluster almost apologetic tone of the voices that taught it in school. From the beginning romantic schoolteachers had insinuated that proper history was something that had happened to lords and ladies and knights in armor in a cultivated never never land across the sea. In the colleges, instructors full of the unconscious yearning of the underpaid for an upperclass viewpoint told of the vulgarity and corruption of the American system and couldn't wait to unveil the fashionable beauties of the British Constitution. In the towns and cities they knew young men found the phraseology of our political heritage dribbling greasily from the mouths of wardheelers spellbinding the greenhorns, or else polished smooth and meaningless in the afterdinner speeches of the respectable starchedshirt candidates for office. Election time and the Fourth of July they saw the old bunting brought out and tacked on the political booths the politicians operated with the open and cynical geniality of gamblers getting their shell-games and three-card tricks ready for the yokels at a country fair. It was inevitable that the first impulse of any fresh young intelligence was to throw the whole business overboard lock stock and barrel.

In a rebellious frame of mind the young men listened to Woodrow Wilson. From the business of reforming America they were distracted by the dream of making the world safe for democracy. They had hardly time to get a deep sniff of the New Freedom before the first great disillusion came. In the face of the electoral mandate to stay out, they found the country at war and themselves conscripted into the army. Wilson's failure to pull anything worth while for America or for the world out of the peace finished the business. To the minds of angry young men, and we mustn't forget that they were right to be angry, the American republic was just another piece of stage scenery, so crudely painted as to deceive only the rankest suckers, that masked a slaughterhouse of industrial exploitation. They had seen the physical power of lies to kill and destroy. To men who still had the smell of blood and rotting flesh in their nostrils any chance seemed worth taking that might lead to a better world.

It was against this stale murk of massacre and plague and famine that, just as the early Christians had under somewhat similar circumstances painted in the mind's eye a shining City of God above the clouds, the social revolutionists began to project their magic lantern slides of a future of peaceful just brotherhood, if only the bosses of the present could be overthrown. While the bulk of the American population settled back to the wisecracks and the bootlegging and the cheerful moral disintegration of Normalcy and the New Era, angry young men whose careers lay outside of the world of buying cheap and selling dear, swallowed the millennial gospel of Marx in one great gulp.

Marx was a mighty historical critic of the society he knew and his voice had the ethical assurance of the old Bible prophets, but the trouble with Marxism as a religion was that its principles had to be carried out on earth. Once the Russian experiment got under way it was perfectly possible to go see for yourself how it was working out in terms of misery or happiness. The history of the political notions of American intellectuals during the past twenty years is largely a record of how far the fervor of their hopes of a better world could blind them to the realities under their noses. Conversion was followed sooner or later by disillusion; the process was useful in so far as it turned disinterested people to the study of our own frame of society in pursuit of the deadly pressing question: how to make the industrial setup fit for a man to live in.

Meanwhile, right from 1917 on, the gulf between Europe and America, that had seemed so narrow and bridgeable then, widened and widened. In Europe the police state the Bolsheviks had called into being under the delusion that they could use it to force men into the mold of a good society, ran its normal course towards tyranny bloodshed and despair. In Italy and Germany the fascist and nazi regimes, after dumping the humanitarian baggage overboard, took over and improved the efficient machinery for driving the mass which the Bolsheviks had invented in their one party system. The businessmen and politicians of the oligarchic and even of the approximately selfgoverning states of Europe proved helpless to hold their divided nations together in the face of an incomparable industrial machine so skillfully rigged for the purposes of destruction.

In contrast to the agony of Europe, it began to be apparent that our poor old provincial American order, whatever it was, was standing up fairly well. Maybe the republic was something more than a painted dropcurtain hiding the babyeating Moloch of monopoly capital. Maybe there was something more than campaign oratory and pokerplaying and pork and dummy bankaccounts behind those Greco-Roman colonnades.

While we can't get away from the fact that most everybody

in the world today believes in his heart that life is more worth living for the average man in North America than anywhere else, we still don't feel secure. Indeed we feel we lack that minimum of security necessary to keep a human institution a going concern. Too many Americans have let in among their basic and secret beliefs the sour postulate that American democracy is rotten. In spite of the ritual phrases and the campaign slogans out of our national folklore, like the frogs in Aesop's fable, many of us are croaking that we are sick of King Log and that we want to be ruled by King Stork. "When fascism comes to America," said Huey Long, one of the smartest aspirants for the position of King Stork that ever stuck his head out of our frogpond, "it will come as antifascism." It won't matter what name we call King Stork by, if we let him in he'll eat us up just the same. Under the verbal pieties of democratic phraseology the state of mind of a good deal of the country is summed up by a man I heard cap a long irate political argument by shouting: "This man Roosevelt's got too much power: what we need's a dictator."

How are these doubts to be answered? I myself believe that we are going to stick to our old King Log, that our peculiar institutions have a future, and that this country is getting to be a better place for men to live in instead of a worse; but unfortunately just putting the statement down on paper does not make it true. How are we to answer the angry young men of today? How are we going to reassure the great mob of secret subjects of King Stork? Are we sure that King Log isn't as rotten as they say?

The answer is not in speeches or in popular songs, but in the nature of our political habits.

One reason why the communist cure in Russia has proved worse than the disease of an outrageously decrepit and brutal social order, is that the only political habits the Bolsheviks had to work with were those of serfdom and subjection to a despot. In Germany the republic failed for much the same reason. German history has been politically the opposite of English history: it has been the history of the successive subjugation of the more western and selfgoverning aspects of Germany by the despotism of the Prussian drillmaster. None of the Russian or German Marxists had any idea of politics as an art. The Englishspeaking peoples are heirs to the largest heritage of the habits and traditions and skills of selfgovernment there has ever been in the world. Politics is our whole history. If we fail to cope with the problem of adjusting the industrial machine to human needs it won't be for lack of the political tradition.

By politics I mean simply the art of inducing people to behave in groups with a minimum of force and bloodshed. That was the purpose of the tribal traditions on which our Common Law is based: the patching up of private and public rows without violence by the opinion of a jury or the counting of heads at a meeting.

Under the stresses of the last years we have seen nation after nation sink to its lowest common denominator. Naturally it's easy for us to see the mote in our brother's eye. The question we have to face is: What is the content of *our* lowest common denominator?

If, in the bedrock habits of Americans, the selfgoverning tradition is dead or has been too much diluted by the demands of the industrial setup or the diverse habits of the stream of newcomers from Europe during the last century, no amount of speechifying of politicians or of breastbeating by men of letters will bring it back to life. We so easily take the word for the thing anyway, that even if what we consider our way of life were gone, we wouldn't quite know it. It's part of the way the human mind works that the verbal trappings of institutions linger on long after the institutions they referred to have faded away. We can study the past but about the present there are times when we can only state our hope and our faith.

What we can do is give that cantilever bridge into the future that we call hope a firm foundation in what has been. We can, without adding to the cloudy masses of unattached verbiage that make any present moment in political life so difficult to see clear in, at least point out that, so far in our history, the habits of selfgovernment and the use of the art of politics towards increasing rather than decreasing the stature of each individual man, have survived.

Often it's been nip and tuck. Our history has been a contest between the selfgoverning habits of the mass and various special groups that have sought to dominate it for their own purposes. So long as that contest continues the nation will remain a growing organism.

On the whole the struggle has been carried on thus far without destroying the fabric of society. In any cross section of our history you can find the political instinct running a binding thread through the welter of interests, inertias, impulses, greeds, fears, and heroisms that make up any event. Without overconfidence we can say that our people and the people of England, in their long career, first embracing and later supplementing and paralleling our own, have used the art of politics with more skill and have upheld the dignity of the citizen as a man better than the peoples of continental Europe, who at frequent intervals have gotten sick of King Log and called in King Stork and have been properly eaten up by him for their pains.

When we wake up in the night cold and sweating with nightmare fear for the future of our country we can settle back with the reassuring thought that the Englishspeaking peoples have these habits engrained in them. The reason so many angry young men were all for calling in King Stork in the form of the socalled dictatorship of the working class (we know now whose dictatorship it really is) was that they confused selfgovernment as a political method with a particular phase of the economic setup of production. It is fairly easy to demonstrate that uncontrolled government of monopolized industry by irresponsible men is headed for ruin, and that that ruin might carry a good deal of the social fabric down with it; but it doesn't follow that the selfgoverning republic, as a method of enabling people to live together in groups without conking each other on the head every minute, would necessarily go by the board too.

If all the monopolies folded up over night, or if their bosses converged on Washington and seized the government, as they've occasionally been on the edge of doing in one way or another, the next morning we would still face the problem of politics. Would the men who held power want to induce the others to behave in groups with a minimum rather than a maximum expenditure of force? At the minimum end of the scale would still be selfgovernment and the need to argue, cajole, and bribe their fellowcitizens into doing what they wanted them to; at the maximum end would be the sort of military bureaucracy and personal despotism that has so often been the style of government of the world outside of the Anglo-Saxon family of nations.

In the last analysis, to be sure, the continuance of selfgovernment will always depend on how much the people who exercize that liberty will be willing to sacrifice to retain it. A man in power will push his subjects around just as much as they'll let him. But even in a riot the members of the mob and the members of the police force will behave as they have been brought up to behave.

We must never forget that men don't make up much of their own behavior: they behave within limits laid down by their upbringing and group background. That is why individual men feel so helpless in the face of social changes. Modifications in the structure of any organization of men can't ever really take effect till the next generation. A revolution can keep people from behaving in the old way but it can't make them behave effectively in the new way. That is why a political system elastic enough to allow drastic changes inside of its fabric is one of the greatest boons any people can possess. Our occasionally selfgoverning republic has proved itself capable of bending without breaking under the terrific strains of the last ten years. The question is whether there is enough will to freedom in the country to make it keep on working. Social machinery, no matter how traditional, left to itself runs down; men have to work it.

Our history is full of answers to the question: How shall we make selfgovernment work? People like ourselves have been making it work with more or less success for centuries. And history is only dead when people think of the present in terms of the past instead of the other way round. The minute we get the idea that the records can be of use to us now, they become alive. They become the basis of a worldpicture into which we can fit our present lives, however painful they may be, and our hopes for the future. We have never been told enough about the worldpicture which the founders of the American republic held up to the men who followed them.

We need to look into that worldpicture to see how it has changed with the years and whether enough of its brilliance is left to outshine the dazzling hopes which are at present leading millions to conquest and destruction in Europe. We consider these hopes lying and false, but there is no denying their enormous energizing force. Lenin and Trotski, backed only by a few bookish enthusiasts and some starving and ragged partisans, managed to establish their system over one sixth of the globe against all the armies and the dead weight of the old order. There is something more than a magnificent chemical industry behind the immense explosive force of Hitler's Reich.

In our past we have whatever hope it was that kept Washington's army together the winter at Valley Forge; but today in the nineteen forties, have we anything left of that worldpicture of 1776? Fascists and Communists alike tell us that we have only the Almighty Dollar and the degradation and sluggishness that comes from too much property on top and too much poverty below. To answer them we don't need to fill ourselves up with the hop of another historical illusion like theirs, but we do need to know which realities of our life yesterday and our life today we can believe in and work for. We must never forget that we are heirs to one of the grandest and most nearly realized worldpictures in all history.

If we can counter the deathdealing illusions of Europe with practical schemes for applying the selfgoverning habit more fully to our disorganized social structure, to the factories, unions, employers' associations, chains of stores, armies that are imposed upon us by today's methods of production and destruction, then the croaking doubts will be quiet. Even if it means reversing the trend of our whole society in order to make it continually more selfgoverning instead of less so, the trend will have to be reversed. The alternative is destruction.

If, then, what we aim to do is to work towards increasing the happiness and dignity of every man, just because he is a man, that is what the founders of this country wanted too; in their lives and writings is a great storehouse of practical information on how to go about it. Our machinery has changed, but the men who run it have changed very little. That the republicans of the seventeenth and eighteenth centuries succeeded in starting something mighty in the world I don't think even the most despairing black advocate of tyranny can deny. If the first builders succeeded against great odds, why should we who have their foundations to build on, necessarily fail?

It's worth trying to imagine, to take an example, how the problem the little group of Virginians round Jefferson and young Madison had to face at the beginning of the Revolutionary War must have seemed to them, to imagine it without any of the assurance of hindsight.

They had first of all a war to carry on against the most powerful nation on earth. To do that they had to induce the scattered farmers and plantation owners and country gentlemen of

English origin, and the wild Irish and Scotch pioneers of the region beyond the Blue Ridge to work together and to risk their lives and property in the enterprise of independence, to forget their religious bigotries with the disestablishment of the Anglican church, to drop their local prejudices and interests for the sake of co-operating with the states to the north and south, and at the same time to concur in a radical rationalization of legal and governmental procedure: all that sounds easy when you read it in a history book, but imagine how hard it must have seemed to the men of the time, continually hampered as they were by the difficulty of communication and of transporting themselves and their goods across a country that had only muddy tracks for roads.

In spite of the immense increase in the complexity of organization, our problem is not so very different now: again in order to survive in a warring and hostile world we have to induce the weak and the powerful of all sections of our population to drop prejudices and bigotries and to pool their efforts in the common cause. We have probably to fight a war and to carry on at the same time stringent rationalization and reorganization at home. In some ways the problem is more difficult, in some ways easier. What we must have in order to tackle it is what those men had; besides the selfgoverning habit: the will.

But will and energy cannot be directed without an aim. The aim that moved them was the attainment of a world that could be pictured fairly sharply in the mind's eye. Of all the great mass of material that has come down to us from that day, the letters and notes Jefferson wrote and particularly the buildings he designed, which we can still see and walk around in, are of paramount interest because he had this worldpicture so clearly in his mind that the imprint of it was sharp on everything he did. It was as if his clear musing mind had reduced the main conformations of the thought of his time to a design as plain as a seal on a ring.

When Jefferson as a young man used to scramble up the

steep trail among the oaks that took him up in half an hour to the top of the hill he was later to name affectionately Monticello, what kind of a world was it that he saw, looking thoughtfully at the densepacked trees of the valley of the Rivanna and the little raw village of Charlottesville and the long ranges of the Blue Ridge beyond?

What he saw depended on what he was. He was a frontiersman, first, and always felt the great continent, stretching ridge after ridge to the west, opening out into the grasslands, rivers, plains, a boundless store for the generations growing up, the promise of a future that like a great convex mirror magnified every act and gesture of the men working their fields and building their farms in the tiny settlements along the eastern seaboard. Then he was a Virginian who shared the traditions of the highflown gentry that came to him through his mother's family, and, through his father's, of the pushing country stock forced westward by the hardening stratification of British society. He had had the best eighteenth century education, through his good luck in finding in Williamsburg, when he went to study law there as a boy, a small group of brilliant men, from whom he had eagerly absorbed the vanguard intellectual outlooks of Europe. His philosophic and religious bent was impressed on him by early and thorough training in the Greek and Roman classics; it was the stoicism of Cicero and Seneca, strained through the *noblesse oblige* imperative that the English gentry had inherited from the chivalry of the feudal landlords, combined in the best Englishmen of the century with an intensely practical flair for experimental knowledge, the heritage of Newton and the Royal Society. Although he never went abroad until middle life he somehow managed to absorb even the literary fads and accomplishments that were the trimming on the sound broadcloth of the age, the taste for Ossian, the Gothic sensibility to landscape, the fondness for Italian music. Somewhat unique, because those were the directions in which his mind pushed out towards original discoveries, was his sense of the Common Law as a code of human rights rather than as a code for the protection of privilege, and his intense and inventive interest in architecture. Already as a young man he was planning with the help of a volume of Palladio to build on that very hill above Charlottesville a homestead that would make manifest in brick and stucco his own adaptation to the Virginia frontier of an antique Roman sense of the dignity of free men.

There was more than a trace of Ralegh in the background of the Virginia planters Jefferson grew up among, although Ralegh's colony had vanished into the wilderness. It is a common thing for states of mind to linger on in a distant province long after they have matured and died in the metropolis; among the Virginia gentry there remained up into the eighteenth century much of the independent and overweening self-importance which had driven Ralegh and the great westcountry explorers on their garish careers, and which, in the generation that followed, had formed the characters of such ardent republicans as the younger Vane and Harry Marten and Algernon Sidney. The Randolphs were a crazy crew who felt they were equal to and better than any man on earth, or king for that matter. The knowledge, on the other hand, that his father had risen from the ranks tended to give young Jefferson the feeling that he was kin, as well as to the noblest, to the humblest of men. His was the leveling cast of mind of the man who feels, not that he's one of the groveling mob of mankind, but that he is a free nobleman with only the sky over his head and so takes it for granted other men must be as good as he. Jefferson, although his education was very similar to that of the sons of the foxhunters and placeholders of Walpole's squirarchy, had more in common with the great country gentlemen of the period of the civil wars in England than with the portsodden authoritarians of George Third's ministries.

A set of ideas, a point of view, a frame of reference is in space only an intersection, the state of affairs at some given moment in the consciousness of one man or many men, but in time it has evolving form, virtually organic extension. In time ideas can be thought of as sprouting, growing, maturing, bringing forth seed and dying like plants. To make sense of the tangled jungle of men's thoughts and impulses that makes up the history of a culture we have continually to invent sequences which we can follow like footpaths through the thickets of what was.

Into the antecedents of the American republic, I think it is useful, at the moment, to trace two main trails. One is the trail I have been speaking of that leads back through the Low Church and the traditions of the plantation families of Virginia to the country gentleman republicanism of the seventeenth century in England. The other leads back to the roundhead townspeople and the protestant sects. While the gentlefolk and parvenu planters and the country lawyers of Virginia were quite unconsciously laying the foundations of Monticello and of *The Federalist,* the New England towns, each one a little City of God, were developing townmeeting, building public schools and town homes and libraries and volunteer fire departments and perfecting that intense municipal organization that made it possible for the Englishspeaking settlements out in the great riversystem of the Mississippi and in the west to stick fast where the French and Spaniards who had preceded them had lasted no longer than the buffalohide villages of the wandering Indians.

In the seventeenth century Commonwealth of England these two currents had merged and fused, but after its collapse the English social system had become stratified and set under the pressure of reaction, and the setup we think of as characteristically English in distinction to American, had come into being. But in New England, on a small provincial scale, the English republic went on. The political and religious life of Boston, Plymouth, Hartford, New Haven, Providence, Newport had much more in common with the life of the British Isles under Elizabeth and James and Cromwell than it had with the various transformations of the developing maritime empire. During the High Church reaction and the counterreaction that brought in the house of Orange and saw the beginnings of the Old Lady of Threadneedle Street and of the plundering of India, the settlements of Englishspeaking peoples on the east and west coasts of the Atlantic were already drawing apart. In England social stratifications were setting hard: in America they continually tended to break up.

In distinction to the absolute liberty of the Virginia planter, who had only to pay his tithes in tobacco to the local clergyman to be undisputed king of his acres and his bondservants and his slaves, the New England townsman was walled up in the exact limits of a theocracy. But the New England towns stayed alive and kept breaking out of the narrow shells their clergy kept tracing for them; first, because there were vast open lands to the west to which energetic men who couldn't stand the tyranny of the local pulpit could move with some certainty of bettering their condition; and, second, because protestant theocracy rested on the conscience of every man alone, instead of being vested in an organized priesthood.

Continually the divines tried to organize themselves into a ruling caste, but they never entirely succeeded on account of this fundamentally libertarian bias of protestant Christianity. Almost from the first moment of the first puritan settlement the conflict between the clergy and the consciences of their churchmembers began. As the towns developed it became complicated by the long struggle between the proprietors of the lands and the voting inhabitants of the towns that foreshadowed the later social history of the United States as the federal arrangements of the New Englanders foreshadowed the form of political organization for the nation.

Of all the men who stood boldly up to the denunciations of

the pulpit, and so helped keep the towns alive, and made possible their growth into the singularly beautiful and successful social units they became, Roger Williams stood tallest. He best exemplified the fruitful side of English protestantism, the side from which grew the Quakers and all the rational and irrational sects and humanitarian movements that we think of as peculiarly American. As Jefferson was the second, Roger Williams was the first great leader of the tendency in American life that has striven to keep the roads open instead of to close them, that has fought for selfgovernment instead of for government by a privileged group, and that has defended liberty against the oligarchy of one of the various privileged groups who have at one time or another tried to impose themselves upon the country. Without his influence and the success of his rash enterprise at Providence Plantations, other men in New England would hardly have had the courage to call their souls their own in the face of the convinced autocrats of the pulpit and the bench, and the New England towns, instead of being the seedbed of the nation, would have shriveled into grim little lamaseries in the granite inlets of their chilly coast.

Like Jefferson's, Roger Williams' mind was the ancestor of the mind we, for want of a better word, call liberal in America today. With the drift of western Europe back into an epoch of wars and savage persecutions, we suddenly find ourselves very near the seventeenth century. Twentyfive years ago we could not have understood the fervors or the ideological jargon of the Cavaliers and Roundheads. Our time has in common with theirs the manly revolt that is behind the labor movement, the fanaticism of the Marxist and nationalist cults and the sullen hatred that people of property and privilege, who fear that everything they own is slipping out from under their feet, feel towards people without property. Accustomed to the doubletalk of Marxist ideology it is easy for us to translate into our own terms the religious jargon of the Roundheads. We too have seen men and women dying for righteousness' sake. As they did, we live in a time of danger when life is cheap. Then as now a man who writes has to weigh his words. They had to train themselves not to be afraid of the scaffold and the brandingiron; even in America with the great oceans between us and the worst of it, we can feel across our windows as we write a shadow of barbed wire.

The men of those times lived through and brought through with them the bundle of notions that is the culture of the western world; what has been done once can be done again.

If ever a man crossed the ocean bringing the seeds of a whole civilization in his head, like the culture heroes of the old legends, it was that preacher explorer trader negotiator linguist Roger Williams. Just as it's hard to imagine the Democratic Republican party overthrowing the special interests of the Federalists who had grabbed hold of the machinery of the young republic for their own purposes, without Jefferson's broadminded leadership and the rich variety and dignity of his life, so it is impossible to see how toleration of religion and thought, or indeed selfgovernment at all, could have taken root on this continent without the long life of fiery preaching and canny negotiating and the goodnatured hardihood of Roger Williams.

The side they fought and worked and lived for hasn't won by a long shot. Perhaps it never can win. But to let the other side win we know means death. It has been the struggle between privileged men who have managed to get hold of the levers of power and the people in general with their vague and changing aspirations for equality, for justice, for some kind of gentler brotherhood and peace, which has kept that balance of forces we call our system of government in equilibrium. Sometimes one scale is up and sometimes another. Sometimes the conflict is acute and at other times barely visible under the prosperous surface of eras of good feeling. Now that we feel that the struggle is sharp and violent, waged in the difficult and unfamiliar terrain of a new system of production, when we rack our brains for hope and understanding for the future, it does us good, I think, to remind ourselves that in spite of hell and high water men in the past managed to live for and to establish some few liberties.

II

ROGER WILLIAMS AND THE PLANTING OF THE COMMONWEALTH IN AMERICA

". . . I know what it is to study, to preach, to be an elder, to be applauded and yet also what it is to tug at the oar, to dig with the spade, and plow, and to labor and travel day and night amongst the English and amongst the barbarians."

ROGER WILLIAMS

1. So Hopeful a Youth

ROGER WILLIAMS was born in London about the year Queen Elizabeth died, very likely in one of the new houses with tall gables facing the street that were building through the early years of the seventeenth century in the boom section round Smithfield outside the ancient cramping city walls. The records of his parish church, St. Sepulchre's outside Newgate, were lost in the great fire of 1666, so the exact year of his birth is not known; but it is known that his father, James Williams, was a member of the Merchant Taylors' Company, and that his mother came of a rising family of shopkeepers and small gentry, the Pembertons of St. Albans. She owned a lease on the tenement called The Harrow, across Cow Lane from James Williams' shop. The chances are that the family lived and the children were raised in the dwelling above the shop, where the tailors worked crosslegged and the apprentices spread out bolts of goods for customers to appraise with thumb and forefinger.

The family fortunes were on the way up. Roger Pemberton, Roger Williams' uncle and godfather, served a year in the post, that only a man of some wealth could afford to hold, of High Sheriff of Hertfordshire. Another Pemberton, a grocer, was Lord Mayor of London. When their father died, Roger Williams' elder brother Sydrack, who with the growth of trade with the East in the middle years of James Stuart's reign, had gone to Leghorn as a Turkey merchant, inherited the family business, the membership in the guild, and freedom of the City, and thereafter in legal documents signed himself 'Citizen and

Gentleman.' In spite of his otherworldliness Roger Williams himself was all his life a successful trader.

The London Roger Williams grew up in was Elizabeth's London, the city of great fairs and stinking crowded lanes and fulldress executions on Tower Hill, and taverns where court wits and gentlemen returned from the wars went to drink canary sack and to hear the quips and fancies of dramatists and poets and 'such trash,' and to smoke the novel weed, tobacco, that Walter Ralegh, still arbiter of elegances as Ben Jonson was prince of poets, had brought home from Roanoke.

Under Elizabeth a certain hale unanimity of feeling had grouped most Englishmen behind the great Queen's policies. The feudal nobles skulked, it is true, in their country mansions and continued, many of them, to hold popish ceremonies in secret; and among artisans and small traders the sharp leaven of lollardry and nonconformism was quietly at work; but on the whole all classes held together against the Pope and the Spaniards. Englishmen of every walk of life felt a patriotic glow over the exploits and the brisk seamanship of the west-country explorers and navigators who were nibbling their way through the inert vast overseas empire of Philip of Spain, clogged as it was by superstition, bureaucracy and oppression, like mice though a cheese. The variety and energy of the work in the theaters was the mirror of the time.

Under James the form of Tudor life continued, but a sour autumnal tone began to be heard. Plays began to be about the inside of people's minds. Doubt got on the boards, spoiling the old easy madrigals and taking the heart out of the cheerful blood and thunder. Rifts appeared between various classes of society. James Stuart's reign was a period of plots, suspicions and scandals.

James Stuart himself was a Scotchman and his court was crowded with lean Scots on the make who the English felt had come south to eat up the profits of their hard work. He was a man of intelligence and considerable learning, but he was full of theories and pedantries that rubbed against the grain of his English subjects. He drank too much. He had little personal dignity and lacked the good horsesense that had endeared the Tudors to their people even in their most brutal and selfseeking moments.

James' policy of playing up to Spain was unpopular. People felt that England and the protestant cause in Europe were being sacrificed to the interests of the house of Stuart, and that they were victims of shady intrigues they didn't understand, but which, they suspected, tended towards popery and despotism. Especially Londoners were getting every day more suspicious of the court. It was natural that an impressionable youngster growing up in a shopkeeper's family should feel this stirring of revolt and disgust at the doings of the winey disreputable and impecunious courtiers, and the foreboding of change that stewed in men's minds.

The first form revolt took was religious. Roger Williams was converted to puritanism early and got into hot water at home on account of it. This violent emotional upset set him out of key, for the rest of his life, with his humdrum family and with the whole dying world of courtly show and foppery and fashion to which a tailor's shop must have in some humble measure belonged.

Conversion, a sudden exalting switch of outlook that changes heaven and earth for a man, is so common in all societies we know anything about that it can almost be set down as a type human experience; but the terminology of puritanism has become so distant to us, where its sense hasn't been worn out by ceremonial repetition in the churches, that it takes as great an effort for an American of the twentieth century to understand the mind of an American of the seventeenth as it would to understand the totem feelings of an Ojibway.

The English Bible, which is only now ceasing to be the heart of our language, was then a compelling novelty. The King James version was first published in 1611. The return to the study of Greek and Latin texts two centuries before had touched off among limited groups of nobles and scholars that great explosion of intellectual life that has been labeled the Renaissance; but now the cheapness of printed books set fire to the aspirations of a new and more numerous class of men, the businessmen, the farmers, the trading country gentry, the merchants and shopkeepers and artisans of the manufacturing towns and seaports. The Bible was the word of God. In it resided all the magic power the Reformation had stripped from the hierarchy of the Roman Church. With the King James version the old texts were skillfully reworded into English at its highest moment of energy. The magnificent conductor of the new prose brought men immediate contact with the intense religious and tribal feelings of the ancient Hebrews. Trammeled on every side by the stale debris of the feudal order, the middle classes of England, daily growing richer and more powerful, felt instant kinship with the Chosen People of God. They too were in bondage in Egypt, all about them were the abominations of Moab, they were eager to spoil the weakening Amalekites that dwelt in the promised land.

It was one of those times when new men demand a new world to live in. The rules for the new world had been laid down in the stony laws of Moses and in the gospels. The feudal world of master and man relation, already wormeaten at the top by the humane subtleties of aristocratic classical thought, no longer in any way corresponded with the reality that tailors and drapers and glovers and wheelwrights and gentlemen adventurers of their own and their friends' money, saw about them. The hardheaded tooth for a tooth monotheism of the Old Testament fitted in remarkably well with the emotional needs of businessmen whose energy and brains were challenging status and birth as a source of power. Riches in this life were the reward for faithful obedience to Jehovah's laws. On the other side the romantic humaneness of Jesus' sayings answered their need for order and gentleness and thrift in the savage and already obsolete world of swordsmen and hangmen and torture and filth and agony and waste all about them. Conversion in the England of the early seventeenth century was as much social and political as it was religious. The Puritans believed in the hereafter, but especially they wanted a godly life in England now.

As a child Roger Williams read the new Bible fresh from the press, and felt himself part of the surge of revulsion against the disorder and cruelty of the throngs in the streets crowding towards the gallows where godly men were dying, and against the scandalous stories old women whispered around the house about the court of the drunken Scotchman. He must have felt that he, too, although a younger brother in a tradesman's family, was great and powerful as one of the chosen people of God. Conversion gave him that conviction of the sublime importance of any one man's thoughts and feelings at every separate moment of his life that has been the mark of protestant politics and protestant religion since the day of Luther's cry of 'Ich kann nichts anders.'

This conversion is about all his biographers have been able to dig up about his childhood. One other thing is known, and is extraordinarily characteristic of the man: he learned shorthand 'as well as any in England,' so well indeed that as a youngster he acted as stenographer for Chief Justice Coke in the court of the Star Chamber.

This we know from the note on a packet of correspondence in the handwriting of Mrs. Anne Sadlier, one of Coke's daughters, with whom Williams, years later under the Commonwealth, got into one of his many fiery arguments by letter. She had remained a royalist and had inherited her father's sharp tongue if not his pro-parliament opinions. What she wrote was this:

This Roger Williams, when he was a youth, would, in a short hand, take sermons and speeches in the Star Chamber and present them to my dear father. He, seeing so hopeful a youth, took such liking to him that he sent him in to Sutton's Hospital, and he was second that was placed there; full little did he think that he would have proved such a rebel to God, the king, and his country. I leave his letters, that, if ever he has the face to return to his native country, Tyburn may give him welcome!

Sir Edward Coke, the commentator of Littleton, and one of the great influences on English law, was, as were the Williamses, a parishioner of St. Sepulchre's without Newgate. The son of an obscure Norfolkshire barrister, he had become, in the course of a career that skyrocketed through the reigns of Elizabeth and James, one of the richest men in England. His had been one of the toughest legal minds at Elizabeth's disposal. A past master of the art of the frameup, so indispensable to authority under the Anglo-Saxon system, he had had the heads of Essex and Southampton for the Crown. He was a savagely biased prosecuting attorney and an indomitable social climber; at the same time he had one of the most energetic and merriest brains the English people have ever produced, and basic independence of judgment. He never lost his plain country sense and his flair for the living as against the dead and formal sides of a case. His life was a long struggle to establish the pre-eminence of the Common Law instead of the Civil or Roman Law of the Court of Chancery that his great antagonist, Francis Bacon, advocated, and on the whole he won.

It was into Coke's great town house, very much the center of all the storms of the time, where the great lawyer lived in state and in lavish plenty of food and drink that quite put the King to shame, that Roger Williams, still a gangling boy in his teens, found himself as secretary and stenographer in direct attendance on the old man.

In his lifelong struggle with Bacon, Sir Edward Coke had represented the native English ideas of the upstart businessmen and small gentry as against the more European cast of mind of the great empiricist, who, like Ralegh and Shakespeare, thought of government in the terms of authoritarian monarchy. Bacon, whose intelligence was one of the most curious and subtle we know, more or less consciously gave only part of himself to the law business and to the tricky infighting of a court career; but Coke's singleminded drive never flagged. The race the two men ran covered every phase of their lives; they were even both suitors for the hand of the same woman. When Coke's first wife, the mother of the testy Anne Sadlier, who had been Lady Paston and had brought him great connections, died, the fashionable catch around the court was a niece of Robert Cecil's, Lady Hatton. Both Bacon and Coke set out to marry her. Coke won, although the hoitytoity lady refused to take his name or to give up her independent household. The crowning of his career in a social way had been their gaudy entertaining of Queen Elizabeth at his great country mansion, Stoke House, in 1601. He is said to have presented the aged virgin at that time with jewels and knicknacks worth twelve hundred pounds. He evidently knew the way to her heart. So long as Elizabeth lived she was smart enough to keep both Coke and Bacon in her service.

With James it was different. Coke conducted, with his customary rancor and savagery, the trials of the Gunpowder plotters and helped frame Ralegh in connection with another flimsy conspiracy against the Stuarts, but in the long wrangle about the jurisdiction of ecclesiastical courts that occupied so much of James' time, he and the King, who fancied himself as a bit of a lawyer too, found themselves on opposite sides of the fence. He so far forgot himself as to tell James Stuart that the King was subject to the Common Law as much as anybody. That remark put James into such a fury that Coke had to fall down on all fours and apologize. After that it became evident that Coke's days at court would be few.

During the years that young Williams was growing up in Coke's household, this somewhat technical contest about court jurisdiction was gradually turning into the battle that was to split the kingdom in two. Williams was already a Puritan.

There was no question of which side he was on. Taking down Coke's speeches in shorthand was the greatest education in the spirit and practice of the Common Law, on which the revolutionary upsurge of England was to be based, that could possibly be imagined. To the end of his life that ruthless, hardheaded, practical old man was the living embodiment of the Common Law and the spirit of individual liberty that permeated it, and of the new men that were springing up all over England to take the place of the courtly soldiers and sailors of Queen Bess's day.

In Coke's house everything was vivid, rambunctious, full of fresh ozone as if a window were open on the future years of the century; but, on the whole, the London Williams grew up in was enervating with the decay of a great age.

When Williams was a small boy one last survivor of the Elizabethan breed could still be seen by strolling Londoners fine afternoons taking his exercise with his outlandish Indian attendants on a bastion of the Tower. Sir Walter Ralegh had been held a prisoner under suspended sentence ever since his conviction for conspiracy against the Stuarts the first year of James' reign. James had many reasons for hating him, but at first he did not dare destroy so great a vestige of the great Elizabeth. The Queen, and James' heir, the young Prince Henry, who was immensely popular with the English, loved him, too. So Ralegh was allowed to live on in the Tower. There he passed the time making chemical experiments in a little laboratory they let him set up, and in putting into words the concepts of the duties and methods of authority which he had learned from Machiavelli, in an essay called *The Cabinet Council* he wrote for the young prince's education. When all else failed he kept his restless spirit quiet molding the resounding longcadenced prose of his *History of the World.*

When young Henry died it was the end of Stuart popularity in England. The people had thought of him as a prince on the model of Shakespeare's young Henry Fifth, hearty and decorous, with a taste for seafaring and a proper hatred for Spain and popery, the makings of a monarch in the grand Elizabethan style. If he came to the throne Ralegh would be himself again. Among other projects Ralegh had invented a cordial or universal elixir, which he distilled out of Indian herbs and simples. It was supposed to cure all diseases. When the doctors gave the young man up, his mother sent a messenger desperately to Ralegh for some of this elixir he had talked so glowingly about. It was no use, the elixir didn't help, the prince died and with him any hope that Ralegh may have had of reinstatement at court. In the mode of the time, gossip ran round London that Prince Henry had died poisoned by a love potion sent him by the pretty young Countess of Essex. His untimely passing was one more reason Londoners had for hating the court and all its works.

When Roger Williams was thirteen or fourteen, Ralegh managed to get himself out of the Tower by bribing one of the newly arrived Villiers family, and was grudgingly permitted by King James to fit out one more expedition in search of the gold mines up the Orinoco he had talked and dreamed and written so much about. The condition was that he should on no account get into a fight with the Spaniards. Peace with Spain was the cornerstone of James' continental policy. Ralegh pledged his head on it, and the stores and the soldiers were put on board and he sailed away west.

Meanwhile Coke was conducting his last case for the Crown in connection with that same Lady Frances, Countess of Essex no longer, but of Somerset, about whose love philters the tongues of gossip had so wagged when Prince Henry died. There seems to be no way of knowing whether Williams took down his patron's speeches in shorthand in this trial or not; but he must have heard a good deal about it, as it was the *cause célèbre* of the period. It became one of those public shows from which nobody comes out with any credit. Whether Coke intended to or not, in the course of the prosecution he turned all the petty shady doings of the court inside out in the public eye and helped to make ridiculous, to say the least, the King's pretensions to absolute rule by divine right.

James Stuart, beside his taste for legal and theological argument, had the taste for disreputable young men that had been regarded as an amiable weakness in Elizabeth; with the difference that the Virgin Queen's relations with her favorites had been on a high platonic plane, and that she had had the sense to pick youngsters with brains. When James hurried down from Scotland to occupy the throne of England he brought a boy named Preston with him whom he made Lord Dingwill. It seems to have been Lord Dingwill himself who, feeling perhaps that his own charms were fading, produced at court a well-built yellowhaired young Scot named Robert Carr. During a tilting this young man managed to get himself thrown off his horse at His Majesty's feet. His Majesty was stirred to the depths by his good looks and his broken leg and had him carried off to his own rooms in the palace, where he nursed him until the bones knitted, and read Latin texts with him in an effort to give him a little of the schooling he very much lacked.

This Damon had a Pythias, a man of respectable county family named Sir Thomas Overbury, who had also been interested in the education of so likely a lad. As he rose, Sir Thomas rose too, until no business could be done with the Crown except through Carr, soon Lord Rochester, and his mentor Sir Thomas. Much of their business was the sale of baronetcies, monopolies and wardships to fill King James' always empty till and their own pockets.

Meanwhile the real government of the kingdom was in the hands of Robert Cecil, the hunchback son of Elizabeth's Burleigh, an astute and able man whom James liked to call his little beagle. So long as he lived the court kept a semblance of dignity. When he died the high offices fell into the hands of the raffish heads of the great house of Howard.

The Howards got the idea that they could consolidate their

power by capturing the favorite by a marriage. A certain casting of sheepseyes back and forth had been noticed between Carr and the beautiful young Frances Howard, the old admiral's daughter. The only thing that stood in true love's way was the unfortunate fact that the girl had been married at thirteen to the weakly successor of Elizabeth's brilliant and beloved and decapitated Essex. Soon after the marriage the young Earl, who seems to have been not very bright, had been sent abroad in the hope that a grand tour would furbish him up a bit.

Frances, left on her own at court, had first stirred the Howards' ambitious hopes by flirting with shortlived Prince Henry, whose death had first set tongues wagging on the subject of potions. But now she fell hard for the yellowhaired Scot. Carr had already risen to her own rank as Earl of Somerset. Her brothers and cousins did everything to encourage the guilty pair to go to bed together. There was more talk of magic and philters. The earl and the countess slipped away wherever they could to meet in lonely farmhouses. The Howards were determined to push the match through.

There was the little difficulty of the marriage with Essex; but James couldn't think of crossing his favorite's slightest whim. A roomful of bishops was collected to annul the marriage. James organized the whole thing himself; he had a special taste for the subtleties of ecclesiastical law. Essex, back from his travels, was induced to swear that, although not impotent with other women, with the fair Frances he was. A jury of twelve midwives examined a much veiled young woman who they were eager to believe was the countess and announced triumphantly that she was *virgo intacta*.

So Frances Howard and the Earl of Somerset were married amid damask draperies, illuminations and toasts in canary sack. Ben Jonson wrote the masque for the wedding and Inigo Jones arranged the sets. A certain Mrs. Turner, the inventor of a yellow starch for ruffs very fashionable at court, was wardrobe mistress. In the City of London the Merchant Taylors'

Company, the guild of which Roger Williams' father was a fairly obscure member, capped the festivities with a lordly spread at Guildhall. The only sour notes were some low mutterings from puritan divines. They didn't count much. They hadn't raised their voices since the execution, a couple of years before, of a certain Legate who had argued out his private heresy to the end with the royal theologian, and lost, and had been burned alive at Smithfield, the great fairground adjoining Roger Williams' own house. And the abstention of old Abbott, Archbishop of Canterbury, who would have nothing to do with the business. And the cries of Sir Thomas Overbury.

Sir Thomas raised the roof. Nothing would pacify him. He vowed he'd stop the marriage, threatened all kinds of disclosures, made his dear Robin nasty scenes in the presence of menials in palace corridors. The new earl, who seems to have been somewhat proud of his anatomy, was heard answering shrilly that he was on his own now, his own legs were straight enough to carry him.

To keep Sir Thomas from spoiling the young people's honeymoon, James was induced to offer him the job of ambassador to Russia. With extraordinary treachery, because after all Overbury had been the brains of the combination that had made him, Carr induced the exasperated knight to refuse to go, telling him he had better things in store. James went into a passion and sent Sir Thomas to the Tower. Perhaps it was that he had begun to notice that Carr and the Howards were making a monkey of him; but, if the truth must be told, there had already appeared at court a highly educated young Englishman named George Villiers at whose every step His Majesty felt a fluttering of the heart.

In the Tower Sir Thomas took sick, lingered and, in spite of the ministrations of a series of physicians, among them the King's own doctor, died. The friends of the Somersets said he'd died of the French pox; but the Overburys and the Puritans and the new court party fawning ever more numerous about Villiers, shook their heads in corners and whispered poison. The King took fright and allowed Coke, then his Lord Chief Justice, to make an investigation.

Coke, as I have said, showed in this case more energy than tact. As a publicspirited man of business he must have felt that it was time the court and its favorites were given a thorough airing. But it also happened that he had just managed to arrange for the marriage of his own daughter Frances, much against the poor girl's and her mother's will, to Villiers' penniless brother John. Coke was a champion of the rights of Englishmen, but he was also one of the great careerists of his time.

It was *fiat justitia* with a vengeance. Londoners crowded to the trial of the poisoners of Sir Thomas Overbury at Guildhall in such numbers that one day the stands fell and a number of people were hurt. Among the accused was Mrs. Turner, the wardrobe mistress for the masque at the Somersets' wedding, who, it turned out, had been the go-between and confidant of the Somersets during their adulterous courtship.

A story was unfolded that reads like one of the tragedies of blood so popular then at the playhouses over on Bankside. Mrs. Turner had been under the thumb of an astrologer and sorcerer known as Dr. Forman, who had the good luck to die before the trial. Mrs. Forman, his widow, evidently had it in for the goodlooking Mrs. Turner and came eagerly to court bringing the astrologer's trunk and a little book that contained the list of his customers.

The Chief Justice reached over and took the small parchmentbound volume, glanced at it for a moment and slipped it in his pocket. The story went around that one of the first names he saw listed was that of his wife, the highspirited and flighty Lady Hatton, mother of the daughter he was having such a hard time marrying into the waxing clan of Villiers. There was plenty of evidence without it.

Coke opened the case by making poor Mrs. Turner take off

her becoming bonnet and by yelling at her that she was 'a whore, a bawd, a sorcerer, a witch, a papist, a felon, a murderer, the daughter of the devil Forman.' She was found guilty of poisoning, sentenced and hanged. At the gallows the executioner wore yellow starched cuffs. The famous yellow starch became suddenly unfashionable at court.

Among Forman's papers were pathetically illiterate letters from the Lady Frances to Mrs. Turner that told everything. She had sent Carr love philters and had hired Forman to perform magic rites with a set of obscene little figurines in wax that caused great stretching of necks when they were produced in the courtroom. Mrs. Turner had helped her catch her lover and had helped her get rid of her lover's boyfriend. An elderly serving man named Weston had been sent to the Tower to wait on Sir Thomas, and had fed him arsenic in tarts and jellies. When Sir Thomas didn't die fast enough an apothecary was bribed to give him sublimate of mercury in a clyster; that finished the business. The Chief Justice roared at the prisoners, threatened them with the *peine forte et dure* and didn't let one of them go until he had incriminated the earl and the Lady Frances. Coke was out for bigger game than the miserable assassins.

The last man hanged was Sir Gervaise Elwes, a lieutenant at the Tower, who had gotten wind of the plot and tried to block it by substituting fresh tarts and jellies for those sent in to satisfy poor Sir Thomas's insatiable sweet tooth. In the account of the trial Sir Gervaise sounds like a simpleminded fellow. He didn't dare report the goings-on because he didn't know from what high quarters the tarts and jellies might have come. In fact the suspicion that the whole thing was arranged by James himself has never quite been downed. Sir Gervaise met his end rather cheerfully, sitting on the top of the hangman's ladder to make the usual speech of repentance of his sins. The worst crime he was able to remember was gambling. He had been a great waster round the gaming tables on Bankside and sincerely repented of it. He caught sight of some of his cronies among the crowd that had come to see him die and called on them to give up the vice, and then he gave away his silk cloak and the money in his purse and put his head in the noose, and the hangman and his servant grabbed hold of his legs and he died.

The small fry were all tried in Guildhall; after the hangman had done his work on them at Tyburn, it was the turn of the people of quality, and the pageant moved to Westminster. There Bacon conducted the proceedings in his high style. Westminster Hall was hung in black, and the peers met in all the pomp of ermine and coronets for the indictment and trial of the Somersets.

The arrest of the earl was full of false drama. A royal messenger appeared at Coke's house in the middle of the night to get a warrant sworn out. The King, slobbering drunk, hung on the waning favorite's neck all down the great stairway at Hampton Court, kissing him, so the courtiers said, at every step. The lords found both Somersets guilty of murder, but the King didn't want to go to extremes. The Lady Frances was not sent to the Tower until her child, a little girl, was born. Then she was placed in the elegant apartment Ralegh had recently vacated to go off on his last expedition in search of the golden Manoa. When the talk had blown over a little, Somerset was pardoned and retired to an estate in the country. It was said that the love between the Somersets turned to bitter hatred. The Lady Frances died without being allowed to see her child, who grew up to become the ancestress of the great English family of Russell.

So the headsman was cheated of the Somersets. But he had his way with Ralegh. Ralegh had come back to England a failure. He hadn't found the mines, he had fought the Spaniards. The expedition had been dogged by ill luck from the first. Time and money had been frittered away, the ships had lost half their crews from fever. Against orders Sir Walter's hothead son had tried to assault a Spanish town in the mouth of the Orinoco, his force had been beaten off and he had been killed. The fever never let up on the ships. The pilot who had claimed to know the road to the mines broke down and confessed he knew nothing and killed himself. Some of the ships' crews mutinied.

Ralegh had put in all his fortune, all the money he could raise from his friends, all he had left of hope in the world, on the expedition. As when he'd planned the colony at Roanoke that remained so strangely lost, every detail had been put down on paper. Everything had been thought of with all the subtle energy of his mind, everything had been explained in clear English prose; on paper. Perhaps his schemes were too perfectly planned to come true. Perhaps he had always been more a writer than a practical organizer. Back in England the great promoter, the great schemer, the great adventurer was at the end of his tether. When he heard that James was going to exact the penalty he made a halfhearted effort to get onto a barge on the Thames to slip down the river to a ship that would spirit him away to France, but nothing went well any more. When the arrangements broke down he waited quietly and allowed himself to be arrested.

James had always hated him. With grim satisfaction in the success of the sly manipulation of events he liked to call kingcraft, which this time at least had brought a gaudy bird into his springes, he dragged out the old sentence of death. It was a chance, by one blow of the ax, to get rid of a troublesome reminder of the Tudors and to prove to the court of Madrid, by offering up the head of his most eminent subject, that he was willing to pay the price of peace.

The scaffold was put up on Tower Hill; and the rabble Ralegh scorned with Shakespeare's scorn saw for the last time the erect elegant figure, the long yellow face with twirled mustaches and pointed beard already gray; and heard, until the trumpets drowned him out, the shrill voice that had never lost, in all the years of travels and courts and armies, the broad Devonshire drawl of his boyhood; and the last of the Virgin Queen's lovers knelt on the rough boards of the scaffold and laid his head down on the block.

Meanwhile Coke had been suddenly dismissed from his post as Chief Justice. He went back to his writing and his law-books at Stoke House, where he lived in state, like Chaucer's Franklin, famous for the oldtime country abundance of his table and for his immense legal learning, the intellectual backbone, more and more, of the puritan and parliamentary parties. It was Bacon's day of revenge. After a lifetime's service to the Crown, in which he had seen so many lesser men push on ahead of him, at last his great abilities were recognized. He was made Privy Councilor. He was reaching the peak of his career, but he wasn't yet making enough money to keep up with the debts he ran up building his country houses and his great gardens.

One of Coke's many contests with Bacon was over education. Bacon's views were aristocratic and somewhat lost in the platonic cloud, while Coke's were down to earth and popular. In the course of it he managed to get out from under Bacon's influence the new school for commoners' sons established by a bequest at Sutton's Hospital in Westminster. When he retired from the bench and had no further need for a stenographer, it was natural that he should place Roger Williams, a lad whose brains he felt were worth training, in that school to be prepared for Cambridge. The school's name was soon changed to Charterhouse: young Williams was entered in 1621 and studied there two years until he managed to get himself a scholarship to Pembroke Hall at Cambridge.

In the Parliament of that year Bacon, now Lord Verulam, sat on the woolsack as Lord Chancellor, but he wasn't free of his old enemy. Coke had been elected to the Commons and immediately became the leader of the party that was for clipping the wings of royal prerogative. Instead of voting subsidies to the King, the Commons had questions to ask. That ruinous chain of marches, countermarches, murders, massacres and sieges, the Thirty Years' War between Protestants and Papists that was permanently to maim the culture of the peoples of Germany, had begun with defeat for the Protestants. The complicated and lackadaisical Stuart foreign policy was bearing fruit in the misfortunes of James' daughter Elizabeth who had been chased not only out of the Kingdom of Bohemia, but out of her husband's own Palatinate, without a blow being struck by the English to help her. The Commons wanted to know the reason why. As always the King needed money; before they would grant him any subsidy the Commons began to call into question the whole system of authoritarian rule. To affirm their rights as representatives of the people of England they passed a motion, which Coke worded: ". . . that the liberties, franchises, privileges and jurisdictions of Parliament are the ancient and undoubted birthright and inheritance of the subjects of England; and that the arduous and urgent affairs concerning the king, state and defense of the realm and of the church of England, and the making and maintenance of laws, and redress of grievances which daily happen within the realm, are proper subjects of council and debate in Parliament, and that in the handling and proceeding of these businesses every member of the house hath, and of right ought to have, freedom of speech."

The King was in such a pet that he tore the motion out of the record himself. A week after the houses adjourned Coke was sent to the Tower, where he entertained himself for seven months writing Latin doggerel. After his release he was banished to Stoke House; there he lived busy with his revision of Lyttleton's Institutes, the hero and animator of the puritan parliamentary party.

In the next session the parliament men, as they were beginning to be called, came back by impeaching the Lord Chancellor. They had the goods on Bacon in twentytwo cases of bribery. Bacon, a man of too fine sensibilities to brazen it out, fell into a strange fit of selfaccusation, admitted that he had received presents (indeed it was the custom at the time for all great officers, judicial and otherwise, to pocket anything anybody offered them); he admitted he had done wrong; his only defense was that the bribes had never influenced his decisions. He was removed from all his offices and retired to St. Albans in deep disgrace. The King did nothing to help him in spite of his devoted service to the building up of the scheme of authoritarian kingship that was James' dream. The Stuarts didn't have the Tudors' knack for keeping firstrate men working for them.

The rift was widening between the puritan party and the court. James Stuart died in 1625, dutifully, to put down rumors that he was a Papist, surrounded by the sacraments and the bishops of the Church of England; but when the people crowded into the streets to see Charles, the new young King, drive in his coach through London and Westminster, the man they saw sitting beside him, lolling back against the brocaded seat in his frills and silks, with his beard and his mustaches pomaded to a point and jewels in his ears, was George Villiers, Duke of Buckingham. There were few cheers. A silent chill of hatred froze the City at the sight of the indestructible favorite.

The accession of Charles First in 1625 found Roger Williams studying at Pembroke Hall, a Cambridge college in which his patron Coke held the office of Lord Steward. He had obtained his scholarship, and was studying Latin, Greek and Hebrew in fervent preparation for the ministry. He felt he had a call to serve God and to help in the coming purification of the English church of worldly and popish vestiges. In the great rift between King's men and parliament men that was beginning to divide all classes, the University of Cambridge was becoming a nucleus of popular thought and of the trend of opinion that aimed at completing the reformation of the church and restoring the authority of Parliament.

Oxford on the other hand was drifting into the other camp and becoming the center of a new tendency, much favored by the Duke of Buckingham, that its enemies labeled Arminianism, and that was soon to find a tireless leader in Laud, Bishop of Bath and Wells. The aim of the Arminians was to restore in England the Catholic Church of the Fathers, in which the King and the Archbishop of Canterbury would take the place of the Pope. Obedience to the royal authority was their first tenet. For the more logical thinkers of this group it was only the bad morals of the papacy that hindered a reconciliation with Rome. During the last years of James' life these two parties in the church had been more or less kept at a balance, first by the tolerant Archbishop Abbott, and after his death, by the really liberal good sense of John Williams (so far as I know, no relation to Roger), Bishop of Lincoln and Lord Keeper of the Privy Seal. Laud hated this Bishop Williams so much that he noted naïve dreams about him in his diary, that he was dead, or that he'd seen him led away loaded with chains. As soon as Charles came to the throne he sent John Williams back to his bishopric and, completely under the influence of Buckingham, threw the weight of the royal authority behind the Arminians.

Since, consequently, he found himself at a stalemate with his first Parliament, Charles dissolved it and called a new one. Buckingham had hit on the trick of appointing the leading reformers High Sheriffs of the shires, to a position that made them ineligible for Parliament and forced them to spend a lot of money in overseeing the elections. Coke, who had successfully dodged an ornamental appointment to Ireland by announcing that he knew of many abuses in the government there that it would give him pleasure to uncover and correct, was forced to take the office of High Sheriff of Buckinghamshire.

The only result was that the Commons found new spokesmen, among them John Eliot, a vice-Admiral of Devonshire, whom Buckingham had let in because he was a personal friend. The second Parliament was dissolved and another elected, more determined and calvinist than the last. A gentleman writing to friends in the country described the House of Commons of 1628 as 'the most noble magnanimous assembly that ever these walls contained; and I heard a lord estimate that they were able to buy the upper house (his majesty only excepted) thrice over.'

The sessions opened in March 1628 in an atmosphere of conciliation. Coke, now a hale sharptongued old man of seventynine, had been appointed Secretary of State to weight a hopedfor compromise between the Crown and Parliament with his great prestige. The summer before Buckingham, in an effort to curry favor with the puritan party, had put through an expedition to relieve the Huguenots, besieged by Richelieu in La Rochelle. He had to do something to prove his enthusiasm for the protestant cause to a nation that considered him a secret Papist and that remembered bitterly how, in the last reign, he'd been regularly in the pay of Gondomar, ambassador of the Spanish King. He had come back desperate from the expedition's failure and now needed funds to get a new army ready. The King made it known that if the Commons granted him the necessary subsidies, he would take up the matter of reform. The Commons promptly voted the subsidies, but Charles began to hem and to haw, to consult judges, and to temporize about assenting to the Petition of Right the parliamentary lawyers had drawn up.

Meade, Master of Christ's College, Cambridge, where John Milton was studying at the time, was in London and wrote to a friend in Suffolk:

"I know you have heard of that black and doleful Thursday, the day I arrived in London. Which was by degrees occasioned, first by his Majesty's unsatisfactory answer on Monday, increased by a message delivered afterward, that his Majesty had resolved neither to add to nor alter the answer he had given them. Hereupon they fall to recount the miscarriages of our Government, and the disasters of all our designs these later years; representing everything to the life, but the first day glancing only at the Duke, not naming him. On Wednesday they procede further to the naming of him, Sir Edward Coke breaking the ice and the rest following. So that on Thursday, they growing more vehement and ready to fall right upon him, a message was sent from his Majesty absolutely forbidding them to meddle with the government or any of his ministers, but, if they meant to have this a session, forthwith to finish what they had begun; otherwise his Majesty would dismiss them. Then appeared such a spectacle of passions as the like hath seldom been seen in any assembly; some weeping, some expostulating, some prophesying of the fatal ruin of our kingdom; some playing the divines in confessing their own and their country's sins which drew these judgments upon us; some finding as it were, fault with them that wept, and courageous resolutions against the enemies of the king and kingdom. I have been told by Parliament-men that there were above a hundred weeping eyes, many who offered to speak being interrupted and silenced with their own passions. But they stayed not here; but as grieved men are wont, all this doleful distemper showered down upon the Duke of Buckingham, as the cause and author of all their misery."

Two days later the King appeared before Parliament and gave his assent to the Petition of Right with the ancient Norman formula: '*Soit fait comme il est desiré.*' Churchbells rang, bonfires were lighted in open spaces in the City. Every day the Londoners expected the impeachment of Buckingham. They were not acquainted yet with Charles Stuart's peculiar catlike obstinacy. In the end of June, as soon as the supplies the Commons had voted began to come in, to avoid a new set of remonstrances brewing, he prorogued Parliament until the next January.

It was during this period of somewhat deceptive lull, when it still seemed that a compromise could be reached, that Roger Williams took his degree of Bachelor of Arts and signed the thirtynine articles of belief in the creed of the Church of England in order to be ordained a minister. He had already some idea of going to Massachusetts Bay, where there was an opening for bright young preachers without family prospects in the pulpits of the puritan colonists. For some months he stayed on in the accustomed monastic quiet of his college. His exhibition still supported him there. Events outside had begun to move fast.

Buckingham had determined to stake everything on breaking the siege of La Rochelle. He had hopelessly underestimated the military ability of his opponent, Richelieu, that least churchly of cardinals. The second expedition was to turn out a worse fizzle than the first, but before the troops sailed from Portsmouth, Buckingham was dead. He was stabbed as he was walking across the camp among his officers by a redheaded soldier named Felton, who instead of escaping in the confusion when Buckingham fell bleeding to the ground stood still and gave himself up, saying, "No villain did this, but an honorable man. I am the man." The crews of the ships getting ready to sail burst into a Hip Hip Hooray when they heard the exquisite duke had been murdered. Parliament men drank Felton's health all over England, and the crowds cheered him and old women came out to bless him on the London road on his way to trial and execution.

The death of Buckingham left Charles in the hands of Bishop Laud, who had recently stepped up a notch, through the duke's favor, into the diocese of London. Immediately the repression of the parliament men began. One of Laud's first acts was to prosecute before the Star Chamber a somewhat bibulous scholar who exchanged many Latin epistles with Milton, Alexander Gill, the son of the poet's old schoolmaster at St. Paul's School. His crime was a set of drunken remarks disrespectful of the King, his royal father and the late lamented duke, overheard in the buttery of Trinity College, Oxford. Young Gill was ousted from the ministry, and the intercession at court of his father's many friends just barely saved his ears, which he had been condemned to lose. For eleven years there was to be no more free speech in England. The system of Thorough was beginning.

Lingering on in Cambridge, like a swimmer on the bank not quite ready to take the plunge, Roger Williams must have felt that Laud's rise meant the closing of any good church livings to any man who thought and felt as he did, if indeed it did not portend worse things.

By the time Parliament reconvened the two parties were dug into their positions. The Commons insisted that the King had no right to levy taxes and that popish and Arminian tendencies must be weeded out of the church. The court party, under Laud's careful leadership, set out deliberately to create, through the machinery of the authoritarian church, the sort of police state Richelieu was building up so effectively in France. The Cardinal had crushed the Huguenots and was stamping the French people into a mold so cleverly constructed that it wasn't broken for a hundred and fifty years. If the French court had succeeded, why shouldn't the English? There was no further ground left for compromise.

This session of Parliament that was Coke's last appearance in public life was the first of a redfaced young countryman in a dirty neckband and illfitting clothes newly elected from Huntingdon, who got to his feet one day to stammer a few incoherent words to the effect that if preaching flat popery were the steps to church preferment, what were we to expect? His name was Oliver Cromwell.

Laud had the medicine ready but the Commons wouldn't take it. The session had not gone very far before they got completely out of hand. Three men held the Speaker down in his chair when he tried to adjourn the sitting. The doors were locked and resolutions were passed by acclamation to the effect that whoever should encourage popery or Arminianism, or advise the levying of tonnage and poundage by the King without the authority of Parliament, or who should pay these taxes if they were levied, should be accounted an enemy to the kingdom and state of England. Then the doors were opened and the members filed out. Holles, Selden, Eliot, Strode, and the rest of the leaders were indicted in the Star Chamber and packed off to the Tower. The King sent down a bitter message to dissolve Parliament. After that he would rule by military power, in the hands of artists in repression like Strafford, and by the subtler methods of the smallminded painstaking Laud, who always was ready to hand a fat living over to an obedient divine or to crop the ears of the unruly, and in the end turned the church into a vast spying organization in support of the monarchy.

Probably it was Coke's extreme old age that saved him from going back to the Tower himself. He went down to Stoke House and spent the rest of his life revising his commentaries on the Common Law. His mind remained extraordinarily vigorous, and his last years were full of hard study in spite of occasional descents on his house by Laud's agents, who ransacked his library and annoyed him by carrying away papers and documents he needed in his work. He wrote rather ruefully in those days about the irksomeness of the writing life: "Whilst we were in hand with these four parts of the Institutes, we often having occasion to go into the city, and then into the country, did in some sort envy the state of the honest ploughman and other mechanics; for one, while at his work would merrily sing, and the ploughman whistle some self-pleasing tune, and yet this work proceeded and succeeded; but he that takes it upon him to write doth captivate all the faculties and powers, both of his mind and body, and must only be attentive to that which he collecteth, without any expression of joy or cheerfulness whilst he is at work." If he didn't like writing, it meant he liked everything else on the face of the globe. He clung, hale and vigorous, to this life of cheerful retirement until he died at eightyfour.

Meanwhile his protégé, the ambitious and earnest young parson, Roger Williams, found himself ready to begin his ministry, but with no church to preach to. Laud's system of Thorough blocked every avenue of advance for him, as it did for his fellowstudent at Cambridge, John Milton. For a young man with a profound belief in the sacredness of his calling, and in the deep necessity of his own convictions, lipservice to Laud's church was impossible. Keeping silent on the issues involved couldn't help him much, because Laud demanded active participation in his campaign, and his familiars and poursuivants were spreading over the country, listening to the talk in taverns and the gossip around the church door after service, opening letters and listening at keyholes to check on the orthodoxy of the Cloth. As a temporary refuge Williams got hold of the job of chaplain at Otes in Essex.

Otes was the seat of a staunch Puritan and parliament man, Sir William Masham, who had been one of the members of the House of Commons imprisoned a few years before for refusing to pay shipmoney. His wife, Lady Masham, was the granddaughter of Sir Henry Cromwell, of Hitchinbroke, and so a cousin of Oliver Cromwell's and related to most of the great puritan families of the eastern counties. A few miles away, at Hatfield Priory, lived her mother, Lady Joan Barrington, a lady of great influence on her widely scattered family, at whose house at that time was Lady Joan's niece, Jane Whalley, the sister of the Edward Whalley who was later to write his name on Charles Stuart's deathwarrant. The first thing Roger Williams did at Otes was to fall in love with Jane Whalley. There still exists a letter of the young parson's to Lady Joan asking for her niece's hand, in which he speaks of ". . . fears for her present condition, it being some Indecorum for her to condescend to my low ebb—there I somewhat stick.

But were all this cleared, there is one bar not likely to be broken and that is the present estate of us both. That portion it hath pleased God to allot to her, as I hear, is not for the present and, happily as things stand now in England shall never be by us enjoyed. For my own part, it is well-known, though I would gladly conceal myself, how a gracious God and a tender conscience, as Balak said to Balaam, hath kept me back from honor and preferment. . . . Nor do I seek, nor shall I be drawn on any terms to part, even to my last parting, from Otes, so long as any competence can be raised or liberty afforded . . . After the death of my aged loving mother, amongst some other children, I may expect, though for the present she be close and will not promise, some twenty pounds or marks per annum. At hand undisposed of I have some seven score pieces and a little yet costly study of books . . . Poor yet as I am, I have some few offers at present; one put into my hand, person and present portion worthy. Yet stand they still at the door, and shall, until the fairest end the Lord shall please to give to this shall come to light. I have been told to open to your Ladyship the whole anatomy of this business. To wrong your precious name and answer her kind love with want would be like gall to all the honey of my life and my marriage joys."

The family didn't consider him a good enough match for Jane Whalley. To them he was a penniless parson without prospects or connections, although a lively godly fellow. He was bitterly disappointed. He wrote testily to Lady Joan that as they couldn't be joined in this world perhaps they would be in the next, and then proceeded to give the old lady a thorough ministerial raking over the coals, reminding her that there was 'but the breadth of a few grey hairs' between her and her everlasting home, and ending with the pious hope that she would forego her evil ways and seek 'a blessing of a heart softened and trembling, of a soul gasping after Jesus Christ.'

Roger Williams was not a man to let a rich dowager have the last word. Naturally Lady Joan was furious.

That summer of 1629 Williams went to a meeting of the Massachusetts Bay Company, which had been newly chartered by the Crown, at Sempringham. The meeting was under the protection of the liberal John Williams, Bishop of Lincoln. Sir William Masham was an investor in the company, and his stiffnecked young chaplain had already received a call from them to a New England pulpit. With Williams when he rode up into Lincolnshire went another clergyman named Thomas Hooker. On the way they stopped at Boston to eat dinner with John Cotton, who was already very much the famous preacher of St. Botolph's Church. He went along with them the next day. Possibly it is at this meeting at Sempringham, too, that Williams first met John Winthrop, the Suffolk country gentleman who was packing up his family to take them to America. In spite of many disagreements about politics and religion, John Winthrop and his son were to be Williams' friends for many years.

When Williams got home to Otes at harvest time he fell sick of a fever. The Mashams, who were devoted to their fiery young chaplain, used his sickness to patch up a reconciliation for him with Lady Joan. Sir William wrote her: "Mr. Williams hath been ill of a fever, though now, God be praised, he is on the mending again. In the depth of his sickness, when he and we all took him for a man of another world, he desired me to remember his humble and affectionate service to you . . . A kind word from you would much refresh him in this his weak state."

All the while he was recovering from his fever under the tender nursing of the ladies of the family and making up his mind for a complete break with the Church of England amid his 'little yet costly study of books,' the Mashams were arranging the engagement of Jug Altham, Lady Masham's daughter by a previous marriage, to Oliver St. John, later to be one of the Commonwealth's great lawyers. This was probably the Mrs. St. John to whom, eight years later, when she was again staying at Otes, her cousin Oliver Cromwell wrote the dark selfdeprecatory letter . . . 'O I lived in and loved darkness, and hated the light; I have been the chief, the chief of sinners . . .' that so teased Carlyle.

Jug Altham's maid was a girl named Mary Barnard. Marriage was in the air at Otes that fall, and evidently Williams had been in a marrying mood for some time. In December he married Mary Barnard at the parish church of High Laver not far away. Their life together seems to have been thoroughly happy. Now that there was no danger of the plausible young parson's carrying off her niece, Lady Joan relented, and was willing to see him. There is a letter of Lady Masham's to her mother on which Sir William scrawled a note: "I am right glad to hear of your inclination to Mr. Williams, who as to his own soul is a good friend and a good man."

Roger Williams and his wife spent one more summer quietly at Otes; but Laud was methodically weeding Puritans of whatever complexion from out of the church livings, and, as Otes was under his direct supervision as Bishop of London, it had become a dangerous place for a preacher of unorthodox opinions, no matter how carefully phrased. Laud was for his time a humane man; his weapons were dismissals, fines and imprisonment, in extreme cases branding or the cropping of ears in the pillory, rather than burning and hanging; but the system of Thorough was demanding more than silence from churchmen. It was demanding enthusiastic partisanship of the reorganized church with its kingworship and its popish ceremonies. Eventually Thorough caught up with Roger Williams, even protected by warm and powerful friends deep in the secluded Essex countryside, and he had to run for it. Though he passed by Stoke House on his way he didn't dare show himself there to say good-by to his old patron.

He wrote describing his flight, years later to Coke's daughter, Mrs. Sadlier: "My much honored friend, that man of honor and wisdom and piety, your dear father, was often pleased to call me his son; and truly it was bitter as death to me when Bishop Laud pursued me out of his land, and my conscience was persuaded against the national church and ceremonies, and bishops, beyond the conscience of your dear father. I say it was bitter as death to me, when I rode Windsor way, to take ship at Bristow, and saw Stoke House where the blessed man was; and I then durst not acquaint him with my conscience and flight. But how many times since then have I had honorable and precious remembrance of his person, and the life, the writings, the speeches, and the examples of that glorious light. And I may truly say, that besides my natural inclination to study and activity, his example, instruction, and encouragement, have spurred me on to a more than ordinary industrious and patient course in my whole course hitherto." At Bristol he met John Winthrop the younger; years later he reminded him in a letter of how they had drunk the west country metheglin, mead that is, together there. On the first of December of 1630 Roger Williams and his wife, Mary, sailed for Massachusetts Bay on the ship *Lyon*.

2. The Country Free Before Me

AMERICA was very much in the minds of Londoners during the years Roger Williams was growing up. The stories of the westcountry navigators were part of the bright myth of Elizabeth's reign: Drake and Cavendish rounding the globe, the search for the Northwest Passage, Hawkins' crossing with his first load of kidnapped blacks, Grenville's end on the *Revenge* that Ralegh himself wrote up, the burning of the Spanish fleet and shipyards at Philip's own base at Cadiz, Ralegh's colonists lost on Roanoke, the last glimpse of Sir Humphrey Gilbert quietly reading his book at the helm of the tiny *Squirrel* before she swamped in the gale coming back from Newfoundland. In taverns old sailors still sat over their ale telling of the bloody scramble of boarding parties, the gold bars hoisted out of the deep holds of treasureships, the fresh ripple under English prows breaking the stillness of harbors not yet named, the crowding on shipboard and the scurvy and the fevers and the moldy biscuit and the foul water, and the nightmare fear of the Inquisition and arrest by its hooded familiars and the strain on English ears of the gibberish of foreign speech. Successive editions of Hakluyt's *Voyages* and Ralegh's and Captain John Smith's promotional tracts were keeping bright the afterglow of the first great age of British seamanship.

Meanwhile, hardly spoken of in the limited circle of royal palaces, country noblemen's mansions and London taverns that the Elizabethans thought of as the World, hundreds of captains of small vessels, traders, masters of fishing boats, were making yearly trips to the American coast for salt fish and furs. Basques and Portuguese fished the Grand Banks and set up their flakes along the shores of sheltered bays for drying *bacalao*, as cod was still called even in England. The French had trading posts in Maine. The Dutch were planting themselves at the mouth of the great river Hudson had hoped would lead him to the Isles of Spices.

Indeed, in the years after the defeat of the great armada, the Dutch, who had themselves just shaken off the Spanish incubus, had been forging ahead and had captured the bulk of the European carrying trade. The British were losing out. The improved sailing qualities of the fore and aft rig, and the businesslike toleration of merchants of all countries and religions in their many convenient ports, were giving the Dutch the advantage. The big efficient Dutch fishingsmacks called 'busses' were even taking the North Sea fisheries away from the English. James Stuart's reign, on the sea as in everything else, was a period of ebb and slackwater between two great tides of English energy.

But at last Englishmen at Jamestown had managed to get back the foothold on the American coast they had lost with the wiping out of the Roanoke settlement. Soon the planters on the James and the York and the Rappahannock began to thrive off the tobacco the Indians had taught them how to cultivate. In England new companies of investors were organizing to exploit and colonize the great stretch of northeast coast that was still all known as Virginia. These companies were to prove the hope of a new world for Englishmen whose religious beliefs rendered them liable to continual harassment by the magistrates if not to a worse fate. In England no nonconformist could make a living, even if by some chance he managed to keep out of jail.

The first people who had to leave were the Brownists and Separatists, whose freedom of worship in England had always been precarious; as early as the middle of Elizabeth's reign congregations of them had been going to Holland where the trading and manufacturing towns allowed them to work and to listen to their preachers in peace. James' categorical Scotch mind was keenly suspicious of the political implications that from the time of the Lollards had been latent in independence in religion; but he seems to have been willing to let them go try out their theories in America. So in the fall of 1620 the first shipload, part from Holland, but most from England direct, had dropped anchor in the *Mayflower* behind the sandy hook of Cape Cod and gone ashore to give thanks to God and do their washing on the beach.

Speaking to the group that had collected at Delfthaven to sail to Plymouth to meet the *Mayflower*, John Robinson, their pastor, who like Moses was not to see the promised land, had said to them: "If God reveal anything to you by any other instrument of his, be as ready to receive it as ever you were to receive any truth by my ministry; for I cannot sufficiently bewail the condition of the Reformed Churches, who are come to a period in religion, and will go at present no farther than the instruments of their reformation. The Lutherans cannot be drawn to go beyond what Luther saw, and the Calvinists, you see, stick fast where they were left by that great man of God, who yet saw not all things. This is a misery much to be lamented; for, though they were burning and shining lights in their times, yet they penetrated not into the whole counsel of God, but, were they now living, would be as willing to embrace further light as that which they first received. I beseech you to remember it a first article of your Church covenant that you be ready to receive whatever truth shall be made known to you from the written Word of God."

It was with such seeds of the heady doctrine of progress in their minds that Robinson sent the Pilgrims on shipboard. Very different had been the instructions Ralegh had meticulously set down to help the colonists at Roanoke establish a model of the rural hierarchy of the England of his day. The tradesmen the Elizabethans scorned, that the courtly English church they believed in, at least as good discipline for the vulgar, had persecuted out of the land, these craftsmen and artisans and small businessmen Shakespeare and Jonson had loved to make fools of in their plays, had the molding of a century in their hands; and they knew it. They were to succeed where the brilliant Ralegh had failed. Twenty years later all Britain would know what was meant by the New England way.

After James' death and the ascendancy of Laud, even the puritan country gentlemen who were firm for the organized church as an instrument of governmental control, but who stuck at the ceremonial and royal despotism of the system of Thorough, found their lives in England blocked on every hand. It was men of that type with their pastors and divines who had gone to the meeting Roger Williams attended at Sempringham to reorganize the Massachusetts Bay Company. Their attitude of mind has been admirably preserved for us in John Winthrop's writings. This Winthrop group was already established in Boston and had already taken the center of the Massachusetts Bay settlements away from Salem when Roger Williams and his wife landed.

According to John Winthrop's journal their ship, *Lyon,* with twenty passengers and two hundred tons of goods on board, dropped anchor off Nantasket February 5, 1631, after a very rough passage. The General Court promptly proclaimed a day of thanksgiving. The chances are that there was snow on the ground and on the hills back of the tiny town, and soggy ice in the tidal inlets. The new steely sharpness in the wintry light of New England must have seemed dazzling to the eyes of the immigrants climbing stiffly with their bundles and chests over the sides of the ship they had been cooped up in for nine weeks between pitchy creaking decks, in the smell of moldy goods and bilge and puke and unwashed bodies and charcoal fumes and cookery. It was four days more before the ship could pick its way through the unmarked reefs and the sprinkling of rocky snowcrusted islands full of strange seabirds, while white familiar gulls circled overhead, into Boston harbor.

Roger Williams was very well received. He was well connected among puritan families, he was well read in the scriptures in their original tongues. He evidently had an open ingenuousness of manner that charmed even those most shocked by his frank nerve in blurting out every change in the interpretation of religious doctrine that rose to the restless surface of his mind. He was one man who would take old John Robinson's admonition literally.

The first thing he did was to refuse the call to the Boston church, the best preaching job in New England, because the congregation was not separated from the Church of England, and to accept a lesser post as teacher at Salem. Presumably he had brought some tradegoods with him, because instead of letting his parishioners support him he immediately set up shop to trade in furs and wampum with the Indians.

By the next fall he had moved to Plymouth where, still under the liberal influence of John Robinson of Leyden, the church was more Congregationalist and the government was nearer a democracy. In Massachusetts the leading citizens never tired of laying down the law on the peculiar powers of ministers and magistrates to govern their flock.

In Plymouth Williams made his living, planted and hoed corn with the rest of the ablebodied men and started in earnest studying the Algonquin dialects. From his early skill at shorthand it may be inferred that he had a natural ear for languages. The strangeness of Indian life filled his curious and elastic spirit with enthusiasm. A 'constant zealous desire to dive into the native language . . . so burned' in him that he spent more and more time with them 'in their filthy smokeholes.' From the first he seems to have known how to win the Indians' friendship and respect, although, as he said in one of his letters, he had continually to remind himself that they were 'as wolves with the brains of men.' In fact all his long life he got along with the Indians much better than with his own people.

Winthrop tells of a visit to Plymouth on a fine October day in 1632. He and a friend had been set down in the cove where Weymouth is now by a shallop from the *Lyon,* anchored off Nantasket ready to sail on what proved to be the last of many yearly crossings; she was wrecked soon after off the Virginia Capes. They followed the Indian trail through the forest until they reached the clearings of Plymouth and saw through the last trees the flickering lights of the settlers' houses.

"Mr. William Bradford, a very discreet and grave man, with Mr. Brewster the Elder, and some others, came forth and met them without the town and conducted them to the governor's house where they were very kindly entertained and feasted every day at several houses . . . On the Lord's day there was a sacrament which they did partake in; and in the afternoon, Mr. Roger Williams, according to their custom, propounded a question, to which the pastor Mr. Smith spoke briefly; then Mr. Williams prophesied; and after, the governor of Plymouth spoke to the question; and after him the elder; then some two or three of the congregation. Then the elder desired the governor of Massachusetts and Mr. Wilson to speak to it, which they did. When this was ended the deacon, Mr. Fuller, put the congregation in mind of their duty to contribution; whereupon the governor and all the rest went down to the deacon's seat and put into the box and then returned."

All the colonists who wrote about Williams concur in admiration for his eloquence and fervent religion and his modesty and good humor. Personal liking for the man was always struggling in them with pious horror at the unseasonable extremes to which he let the logical development of puritan ideas take him.

"Mr. Williams," wrote Governor Bradford in his *History,* "a man godly and zealous, having many precious parts, but very unsettled in judgment, came first over to Massachusetts but upon some discontent, left the place and came hither where he was friendly entertained according to their poor ability and exercised his gifts among them, and after some time was admitted a member of the church; and his teaching well approved, for the benefit whereof I still bless God and am thankful to him even for his sharpest admonitions and reproofs, so far as they agreed with the Truth. He this year began to fall into some strange opinions and from opinions to practice which caused some controversy between the church and him, and in the end some discontent on his part, by occasion whereof he left them something abruptly."

"At Plymouth," wrote Roger Williams himself years later, "I spake on the Lord's day and weekdays, and wrought hard at the hoe for my bread, and so afterwards at Salem, until I found them both professing to be an unseparated people in New England, not yet admitting the most godly to communion without covenant, and yet communicating with the parishes in Old by their members repairing on frequent occasions thither."

Back in Salem, after finding things too tight for him at Plymouth, he acted as informal assistant to Mr. Skelton, the minister there, and began to have a considerable personal following. People even moved from Plymouth to join his church in Salem.

Meanwhile colonists from England, not all of them godly, were pouring into the Bay shipload after shipload. John Winthrop and his group of unseparated puritan ministers were hard put to it to keep hold of the reins. On the one hand they had to keep down the democrats and extreme protestants, whose theories they considered rank anarchy in their own flocks; on the other they had to contend with the ungodly of the court party who, like Sir Christopher Gardiner and Morton of Merrymount, not only observed Christmas and set up maypoles but sold guns and liquor to the Indians, and carried on intrigues with Laud, now all powerful as Archbishop of Canterbury, to get the charter away from the Puritans.

By 1634, when the people of the new settlement of Watertown staged a sort of revolt of the plebs and won a limited franchise for all owners of townlots, even Winthrop, a moderate man with the rural authoritarian ideas of a wellbred English country squire, who had jotted down as a truism in his journal that 'democracy is amongst civil nations accounted the meanest and worst of all forms of government,' was being nagged by the ministers, every day more powerful in the colony, for lenience towards the unorthodox.

Roger Williams' preaching at Salem, that was continually attracting a wider following, became a scandal to the small group of men of substance who were beginning to think of themselves as the Elect, ordained of God to keep the government of New England in their own hands. "He who is willing to tolerate any religion or decrepit way of religion beside his own," wrote Nathaniel Ward, the codifier of the first set of laws for the commonwealth, "unless it be in matters merely indifferent, either doubts his own or is not sincere in it."

For one thing Williams had begun to preach that the grant from the King didn't give the colonists the right to take the Indians' lands without paying for them. He even prepared a pamphlet on the subject which John Cotton, who had just landed, and Winthrop and other friends induced him not to publish. That matter had hardly been patched up when he got into a row about the oaths of subservience to the dictates of the General Court that the magistrates were beginning to exact from all freemen and even all residents. Williams had so many of the ministers and people with him that at first the magistrates had to back down on this point. But his plain speaking was getting to be too much even for his friend Winthrop.

Another argument was about John Endecott's cutting the cross, as an idolatrous symbol, out of the corner of the colors of the Salem trainband. The magistrates in Boston were just as ready as Endecott to defend themselves against an invasion of the agents of Thorough, but they felt that his fuss about the flag was untimely. The cutting out of the cross had followed Williams' Fast Day sermon in Salem in which he had dusted the jackets of the magistrates for sins to the number of eleven, among which probably the taking of the Indians' lands, the subjecting of the people to oaths, the exaction of tithes, and the punishment of unorthodox opinions loomed large. He was hauled up before the General Court and induced to promise to abstain from further offensive teachings.

Meanwhile news came that the patent of the colony had been rescinded. The General Court prepared to resist a royal governor and took as its flag the crossless standard Endecott had been so scolded for making. The attack never came because Laud was soon too busy putting down opposition in England to worry about matters overseas; until near the end of the century the New England settlements were virtually independent of the Crown.

While defending their own independence the Boston magistrates were busy bringing the people of Salem to submission. In spite of every warning the Salem church formally elected Williams teacher. Members of the General Court argued with Williams and Endecott privately, and held out to the Salem people the bait of ceding them a piece of land on Marblehead Neck 'between the Clifte and the Forest Ryver,' if they would give up all this defiance of authority.

"At the General Court Mr. Williams of Salem was summoned and did appear," wrote Winthrop in his Journal under July 8, 1635. "It was laid to his charge that, being under question before the churches and magistracy for divers dangerous opinions: viz. (1) that the magistrates ought not to punish the breach of the First Table [that is the Commandments dealing with man's duty to God], otherwise than in such cases as did disturb the civil peace; (2) that they ought not to tender an oath to an unregenerate man; (3) that a man ought not to pray with such, though his wife, his child, etc.; (4) that a man ought not to give thanks after the sacraments nor after meat, etc. [Williams denied that the last two charges expressed his meaning.] And that the other churches were about to write to the church of Salem to admonish him of these errors; notwithstanding the church had since called him to office of a teacher. Much debate was had about these things. The said opinions were adjudged by all magistrates (who were desired to be present) to be erroneous and very dangerous, and the calling of him to office at that time, was adjudged a great contempt of authority. So, in fine, time was given him and the church of Salem to consider of these things till next General Court and then either to give satisfaction or else expect the sentence; it being professedly declared he who should obstinately maintain such opinions (whereby the church might run into heresy, apostacy or tyranny, and yet the civil magistrates could not intermeddle) were to be removed and the other churches ought to request the magistrates so to do."

After a vast amount of argument the Salem people gave in and the land on Marblehead Neck was granted them. Roger Williams, as had happened back at Otes when he couldn't marry Jane Whalley, got sick and took to his bed. "It pleased God," he said, "by excessive labors on the Lord's days and thrice a week at Salem, and labors day and night in the field with my own hands for the maintenance of my charge, by travels also Day and Night to go and return from their Court . . . to bring me near unto death."

He resigned from the Salem church and formally withdrew from the communion of the churches of the Bay and thereafter only preached in his own house. His opponents, the magistrates, claimed that his illness was an act of God to warn him of the stiffnecked wickedness of his opinions. From his sickbed he wrote letters to all the churches of New England vehemently restating his position.

In October he was tried at the session of the General Court held in Hooker's church at Newtown, that was soon to be renamed Cambridge, and was solemnly sentenced to be banished.

"At this General Court, Mr. Williams, the Teacher at Salem was again convented and all the ministers of the Bay being desired to be present, he was charged with the said two letters —that to the churches complaining of the magistrates for injustice, extreme oppression, etc., and the other to his own church to renounce communion with all the churches in the Bay as full of anti-Christian pollution, etc. He justified both these letters and maintained all his opinions and being offered further conference or disputation and a month's respite he chose to dispute presently. Mr. Hooker [with whom he had ridden to dine with John Cotton at Boston in Lincolnshire some years before] was appointed to dispute with him but could not reduce him from any of his errors."

The court ordered him to leave the jurisdiction of the Bay within six weeks, but later extended the time till spring on account of his ill health and his wife's pregnancy. The baby born soon after turned out a girl and they named her Freeborne.

Late that fall young Sir Harry Vane arrived in Boston. He was already famous for his good looks and his charming manners. He had had to leave England because of his radical opinions, in spite of the Vanes' high standing and his father's position at court as one of Charles' most trusted officers. He landed in New England full of youthful enthusiasm for freedom in religion and in everything else.

He had traveled in Germany and the Low Countries on his own, and as his father's secretary on diplomatic missions, and had picked up many of the liberal ideas floating about learned aristocratic circles on the Continent. In spite of his long hair and his cavalier ways he seems to have swept the dour magistrates of the General Court off their feet. Almost immediately they elected him Governor for the following year. They probably thought his election would have a good effect at court in the matter of the charter. Then too he was so softspoken and so sincerely godly that it must have been felt that, if anybody could smooth down the partisan rows, which along with the heavy work of planting and grubbing and the constant fear of the Indians beyond the edges of the forest clearings, were getting on everybody's nerves, young Sir Harry was the man. Vane and Williams hit it off immediately, and remained fast friends the rest of their lives.

For some time Williams had been talking with the chiefs of the Narragansets about going to live among them to trade and to study their language. Vane and John Winthrop were evidently all for his plan to start a trading and missionary settlement in one of the great inlets to the westward. Williams was no man to keep any new light under a bushel, so his house at Salem soon became the center of all the restless freedom-seeking spirits in the colony.

Haynes, whose year of governorship had not yet expired, and the majority of the court were convinced, largely by John Cotton, who was already the pillar of orthodox intolerance he was to remain while he had breath in him, that now was the time to get this 'minter of exorbitant novelties' out of the way for keeps, and that the thing to do was to ship him home to England. When Williams refused to come to Boston to be shipped, they sent Captain John Underhill with fourteen men in a pinnace to Salem to arrest him and to put him on board a vessel that was waiting off Nantasket for a fair wind to sail.

They had just passed a vote of censure on John Winthrop himself for 'his too much lenience to disaffected souls' and had forced him to take a back seat for the time being, so he was helpless to do more than send a warning word to Salem. By the time the pinnace got there, Williams was nowhere to be found. He was walking through snowy trails in the winter woods to Sowams, an Indian town to the westward, where the sachem put him up kindly in his 'filthy smoke hole.' He wrote about the trip to John Mason towards the end of his life: "First: When I was unkindly and unchristianly, as I believe, driven from my house and land and wife and children (in the midst of a New England winter, now about thirtyfive years past,) at Salem, that ever honored governor Mr. Winthrop privately wrote to me to steer my course to Narragansett Bay and Indians, for many high and heavenly and public ends, encouraging me, from the freeness of the place from any English claims or patents. I took his prudent notion as a hint and voice from God, and waving all other thoughts and motions, I steered my course from Salem (though in winter snow, which I feel yet) unto these parts, wherein I may say, Peniel, that is, I have seen the face of God."

The Massachusetts settlers, snug in their new tight houses, huddling round their great hardwood fires, were far from easy in their minds that winter. Haynes and Hooker and their friends were getting ready to move to the richer farmland of the Connecticut valley in the spring, where they hoped to found a church and government exactly to their own strict taste. John Winthrop, who liked to keep religion subordinate to the practical problems of running the colony, had lost control of his own enterprise and was on the edge of moving to Mystic, as his son actually did.

Even in the flock of the unctuous John Cotton, due, some claimed, to doctrines he had preached himself, discord had broken out. When he came to America from Boston in Lincolnshire an energetic lady named Anne Hutchinson had felt she couldn't live without his pious homilies and had uprooted her husband and a whole family of relatives and friends to emigrate with him. Already on the boat the spirit had moved her to utterances that gave offense to respectable Calvinists. Now in Boston she began to hold meetings of women to discuss Mr. Cotton's sermons and to comment, not always favorably, on them. At these meetings she elaborated the revivalist doctrine of grace into a special mystical dogma of her own. Her followers affectionately called her 'the Nonsuch.' No man, except occasionally the handsome and gentlemannered Sir Harry Vane, was allowed to sit in on the meetings. The wives came home much excited. In every household wives and daughters began to toss their heads in the air and lecture the menfolk on fine points of doctrine.

For a year the colony was in an uproar over Antinomianism, which was the name applied to the Nonsuch's special brand of heresy. Nobody could help taking sides. In the end partisanship became so violent and bitter that, worn to a frazzle by the effort to get some idea of toleration into the hard heads of the colonists, Sir Harry Vane burst into tears at a meeting of the General Court. The parsons were too much for him; especially Hugh Peters, a harsh moneyloving individual who had taken over the church at Salem and whose daughter had married young Winthrop. Peters probably felt that this mystical moonshine and idealistic talk of Vane's were interfering with his organizing the New England fisheries, and had lectured him like a Dutch uncle.

In the end the holy men of Massachusetts Bay were too much for Peters himself, and he went back to England to become one of Cromwell's chaplains. American farmers and traders were beginning to want religion organized and set, like the multiplication table, so that they could go about their business weekdays and be edified on the Lord's day, without being thrown into confusion and terror for their soul's salvation every time the minister opened his mouth. The work of making a living out of a new land took all their energy. The ministers seized the opportunity to get into the saddle, and ride them, and they rode them hard. When young Vane's year was over he went back to England despairing of building the kingdom of God in America.

John Winthrop was chosen Governor once more, but he never again dared stand up to the Elect. Something dour and spiteful comes into the so admirably worded entries of his journal after this. Eventually Mrs. Hutchinson and her friends were banished as Williams and his friends had been, and Boston and Salem settled down under the strict oligarchy of men of substance who were in turn ruled by their ministers gathered in their synod. As the first leaders, who had certainly been men of brains, grew old and lost their influence, a general intellectual shrinking occurred. The people of the Bay had started on that process of narrowing of the mind that was to culminate in the raving madness of the witchcraft trials forty years later: the stamp of it is still on Boston to this day.

3. The Coming Reformation

"SECOND, I first pitched, and began to build and plant at Seekonk, now Rehoboth," wrote Roger Williams in the letter to Mason I have quoted before, "but I received a letter from my ancient friend, Mr. Winslow, then Governor of Plymouth, professing his own and others' love and respect to me, yet lovingly advising me, since I was fallen into the edge of their bounds, and they were loath to displease the Bay, to remove but to the other side of the water, and then, he said, I had the country free before me, and might be as free as themselves, and we should be loving neighbors together. These were the joint understandings of these two eminently wise and Christian Governors, and others, in their day, together with their counsel and advice as to the freedom and vacancy of this place, which in this respect and many other Providences of the Most Holy and Only Wise, I called *Providence*.

"Third, sometime after the Plymouth great Sachem (Ousamaquin) upon occasion affirming that Providence was his land, and therefore Plymouth's land, and some resenting it, the then prudent and godly Governor, Mr. Bradford, and others of his godly council answered that if after due examination it should be found true what the barbarians said; yet, having to my loss of a harvest that year, been now (though by their gentle advice) as good as banished from Plymouth as from Massachusetts, and I had quietly and patiently departed from them, at their motion, to the place where I now was, I should not be molested and tossed up and down again, while they had breath in their bodies; and surely between those my friends of the Bay and Plymouth, I was sorely tossed for one fourteen weeks in a bitter winter season, not knowing what bread or bed did mean, beside the yearly loss of no small matter in my trading with English and natives, being barred from Boston the chief port and mart of New England. God knows that many thousand pounds cannot repay the very temporary losses I have sustained. It lies upon the Massachusetts and me, yea and other colonies joining with them, to examine with fear and trembling before the eyes of flaming fire the true cause of all my sorrows and sufferings. It pleased the Father of spirits to touch many hearts dear to him with some relentings; amongst which that great and pious soul Mr. Winslow melted and kindly visited me at Providence, and put a piece of gold into the hands of my wife for our supply."

At Seekonk, as soon as the abandoned Indian cornfields were dry enough to hoe in the spring, Roger Williams, with the help of William Harris, and John Smith, the miller, and young Angell and another young man, Francis Wicks, had set to work to plant a crop and build a house. When the message from Winslow came they packed up their tools and their trade-goods and put them into a canoe and paddled down the river out into the great bay again, rounded two rocky points and then pushed northwest up the broad tidal inlet then known as the Great Salt River, till they came, on the western shore, in the territory of the Narragansets, to a patch of meadowland watered by a big spring and by two little fresh streams. There they landed and made camp.

Williams had been a friend of the old chief Canonicus for some time. Indeed, that very spring he had patched up a truce between Ousamaquin of Sowams, who had put himself under the protection of Plymouth and hoped to make himself independent with English help, and his old overlords Canonicus and Miantonomo, the head sachems of the whole Narraganset tribe . . . 'When the hearts of my countrymen and friends failed me the Most High stirred up the barbarous heart of Canonicus to love me as his son to the last gasp . . .' Evidently, by his ingenuous shrewdness about people, his frank and fiery way of speaking, his utter lack of fear, and his daily increasing understanding of their language, he had already won the ascendancy over the Indians that he was to retain all his life. He was to remain the one white man the Narragansets trusted to interpret for them and whose word they believed.

The land Williams took up by gift from Canonicus he named New Providence. Most of it was abandoned Indian cornfields and clearings. The Indian method of cultivation, sowing corn beans and squash in small hills the women piled up with clamshells over a dead fish for manure in patches cleared by burning off the trees and the underbrush, was so wasteful that they had to move their plantations every couple of years to get a decent crop. These rough clearings were the first places the English tilled. Once the land was spaded and hoed in European style it began to yield much bigger crops. The Indians soon caught on and iron hoes became a staple article of trade.

Roger Williams chose wisely the location for his settlement. It was a country of great tidal inlets pushing up between rocky hills to the first falls of the short swift rivers. Wide salt marshes full of ducks and geese and cranes and shorebirds merged gradually into grasslands in the rivervalleys, where the fires the Indians continually set in their wars and their hunting or to clear new cornfields, had ruined the forest. There were acres and acres of wild strawberries in the thinner woods that the Indians pounded up into a sort of cake, and huckleberries made a dense scrub over the stony uplands. Williams speaks in his *Key* of wild turkeys and geese and cranes eating the acorns under the great forest oaks. Further up in the woods, through deerpaths, up streams cluttered by the felled logs of beaverdams, was a rolling hilly section, so full of the cooing and fluttering of wild pigeons that the Indians called it the pigeon country. The rivers were full of fish, alewives running up into the fresh ponds in the spring in packed dark masses; cod, sturgeon, bass churning the bays in great schools that the Indians caught by spearing or in weirnets at the rivers' mouths. On the flats at low tide there were endless beds of clams to be had for the digging and further out oysters and scallops. The many fresh ponds inland were full of beaver and otter, and fish to be caught with hook and line through the ice in winter, and on the edges of the clearings there were deer and moose for meat all year around. Songbirds were so numerous the Indians kept tame owls to drive them off their freshsown patches of corn. Of preying animals, wolves, bear and wildcat were more scary to children than really dangerous to man.

Immediately the Indians became dependent on European tradegoods: hoes, hatchets, needles, awls for piercing the seashells they strung into wampumpeague, iron pots and kettles to cook in instead of their fragile pottery and closewoven baskets, lookingglasses and colored beads and, when they could get hold of it, the desire of desires, a musket with powder and shot, or a sip of distilled spirits. Williams says they liked 'sad colors' in the English cloth they bought for clothes to wear instead of the fine furs that had suddenly become currency to be exchanged for English and Dutch export goods. It's not surprising that Williams, with his knowledge of the language, his curiosity about the innermost minds of the Indians and his endless traveling about the wilderness, by boat, canoe, and on foot on the risky forest trails, where he immediately seems to have felt as much at home as between Essex hedgerows, throve mightily as a trader and by the time another year had come around was accounted one of the most successful in New England.

With the good weather new settlers straggled into Providence. As they came a street was laid out along the shore and each head of a family admitted as a freeman was given a tenacre houselot and a sixacre woodlot back of the town. The first houses were oneroom structures with a steep roof and a big loft reached by a ladder, built of clapboards sawed on the spot, with chimneys of logs chinked with mud. Later the settlers started to work a stonequarry and built huge chimneys of squared stone that filled the entire gable end of the house. Williams' own house must have been large from the first, because he held services there and entertained Indian sachems with all their attendant braves and squaws.

In a letter written to the elder Winthrop either in the first or second summer of the settlement Williams outlined the system of government:

The condition of myself and those few families here planting with me, you know full well; we have no Patent, nor doth the face of Magistracy suit with our present condition. Hitherto the masters of families have met once a fortnight and consulted about our common peace, watch and planting, and mutual consent have finished all matters with speed and ease.

Now of late some young men, single persons (of whom we had much need) being admitted to freedom of inhabitation and promising to be subject to the orders made by consent of the householders, are discontented with their estate and seek the freedom of vote also, and equality, etc.

Beside, our dangers (in the midst of these dens of lyons) now especially call upon us to be compact in a civil way and power.

I have had therefore thoughts of propounding to my neighbors a double subscription concerning which I shall humbly crave your help.

The first concerning ourselves, the masters of families, this:

We whose names are hereunder written, late inhabitants of Massachusetts, (upon occasion of some difference of conscience) being permitted to depart from the limits of that Patent, under which we came over into these parts, and being cast by the Providence of the God of Heaven, remote from others of our countrymen, among the barbarians in this town of New Providence, do with free and joint consent promise each one to other, that, for our common peace and welfare (until we hear further of the King's royal pleasure concerning ourselves) we will from time to time subject ourselves in active or passive obedience to such orders and agreements as shall be made by the greater number of the present householders, and such as shall be hereafter admitted by their consent into the same privilege and covenant in our ordinary meeting. In witness whereof we hereunto subscribe, etc.

Concerning those few young men and any who shall hereafter (by your favorable connivance) desire to plant with us, this:

We whose names are hereunder written, being anxious to inhabit this Town of New Providence, do promise to subject ourselves in active or passive obedience to such orders and agreements as shall be made from time to time by the greater number of the present householders of this Town, and such as they shall admit into the same fellowship and privilege. In witness whereof etc. . . .

Hitherto we choose one (named the officer) to call the meeting at the appointed time: now it is desired by some of us that the householders by course perform that work and also gather votes and see the watch go on, etc.

I have not yet mentioned these things to my neighbors but shall as I see cause upon your loving counsel.

As also, since the place I have purchased, secondly, at my own charge and engagements, the inhabitants paying (by consent thirty shillings a piece) as they come until my charge be out for their particular lots: and thirdly, that I never made any other covenant with any person but that if I got a place he should plant there with me: my query is this:—

Whether I may not lawfully desire this of my neighbors, that as I freely subject myself to common consent, and shall not bring any person into the town without their consent: so also that against my consent no person be violently brought in and received.

I desire not to sleep in security and dream of a nest no hand can reach. I cannot but expect changes and the change of that last enemy death, yet dare I not despise a liberty which the Lord seemeth to offer me, if for mine own or other's peace: and therefore have I been this bold to present my thoughts unto you. . . .

As more settlers came and all the stresses and tangles of group life piled up, the town government became more complicated. The first permanent officer was a town clerk. Then it was found necessary to elect five 'disposers' to arbitrate disputes. The disposers gradually became the board of selectmen of the typical New England town. Regulations accumulated: you were fined for being absent from townmeeting or for leaving without permission, you couldn't sell your land to an outsider without permission of townmeeting; you were fined if you left your land uncultivated; any timber felled and not carted away became property of the town after a year.

Soon after settling in Providence Williams was baptized by a Baptist preacher, but his mind was too restless to stay long within the limits of any special sect. At first many settlers followed him in his informal seeking after the true religion, which as he got older developed into the sort of fervent mysticism without dogmas that was to be labeled 'Transcendentalism' in New England two centuries later, but eventually the organized churches in the colony took many of his parishioners away. Although he preached to the Indians, he never overcame his scruples sufficiently to form them into an Indian church as John Eliot did his praying Indians in Massachusetts.

As orthodoxy became more and more entrenched in Massachusetts, first Mrs. Hutchinson's Antinomians and then various new types of Baptists took refuge in Rhode Island, all finding themselves free to found their special churches and to conduct their preachings to their hearts' content. Orthodox Congregationalists looked upon Baptists with particular horror at that time because many of them were nonresisters who denied the authority of magistrates and the law over man's conscience, and because complete toleration, even of infidels and Papists, was one of their basic tenets.

The sects tended to try to preach one another down, and sorely tried the patience of Roger Williams and his friends, who became less interested in religious specifications and more in humane behavior and civil liberty as time went on; but everyone was allowed to say his say. Without Roger Williams' innocent breadth of mind, his complete lack of selfseeking combined with his practical sense, and his breathless activity that made him the town's most enterprising citizen, the colony would have fallen to pieces a dozen times.

As the Massachusetts Bay colony got richer and more straitlaced, and especially after the destruction of the Pequots had made Long Island Sound and the islands safe for settlers and fishermen, and so had enormously increased the value of the Providence land and of the two new towns of Portsmouth and Newport that were taking root on Rhode Island, the Elect became more and more anxious to extend their authority over these disgraceful libertarians who lived in slackness and sin in the Narragansett country, where every man did what was right in his own eyes. Especially they envied their rousing trade with the Dutch.

Shrewdly and genially as his way was, Williams had induced Winthrop the elder to take up half the 'spectaclewise' island in the middle of the bay which he had bought from Canonicus and named Prudence. His house was always open to men from Massachusetts and Connecticut traveling through. He was always ready to undertake the most dangerous missions to Indian chiefs. He understood better than any other white man the complicated net of connivings of the sachems of the Narragansets and the Pequots, the Mohegans and the Wampanoags and the Massachusetts, who were all trying to use the whites to put it over one another, but who were all, if they were given a chance, ready to come down with fire and scalping knife on the fastspreading settlements they knew too well were ruining their huntinggrounds and cutting them off from their cornfields and their fishweirs. They complained to Williams that even their clambeds were being rooted up by the white men's pigs.

Williams made himself indispensable to young Winthrop in Connecticut and to Winslow and Brewster in Plymouth and to old Winthrop who controlled the thriving towns round the port of Boston. He wrote them and lectured them and preached at them for their intolerance and inhumanity, managing all the while to keep personally on good terms with them, even while officially, from the pulpit, he was ranted at for an outlaw. Still Providence men were liable to be fined and beaten if they were found in the jurisdiction of the General Court; it was with the greatest difficulty that they collected debts due them in Massachusetts, they couldn't ship their furs out to England through the port of Boston. On the other hand they were in a better position to trade with the Indians and with the Dutch at New Amsterdam. There too Roger Williams was always the man to call on in a pinch. Along with the Indian languages, somehow he had found time to learn Dutch.

In the Providence town records there is in the form of an affidavit an account of a typical trip of Williams and his friends in 1646 to settle a dispute with Ousamaquin over some cornfields. (It was after Williams' return from England with his brother Robert and Gregory Dexter, the London printer who settled in the colony and opened up a stonequarry and was town clerk for many years.)

We Gregory Dexter, Tho. Olney, Roger and Robert Williams in a word of truth and faithfulness declare that being requested in our own and their behalf [to purchase] the right which Ousamaquin pretendeth to a parcel of land which lies between our bounds at Pawtucket and an Indian plantation northwest from thence . . . so making a journey to Ousamaquin's house, offered him but fifteen fathom of white wampum (it being a Time when white wampum only was current; and which we knew he only would accept); but he desired to have commodities and wampum, and at last we agreed upon ten fathom of white wampum, four coates of English cloth, six of the best English howes [hoes] and English axes and twelve great knives. . . . We brought him the wampum which he accepted; of the coates allso, which he accepted and received the cloth, chosing out of two parcels; but of twelve knives he chose eight; out of six howes he chose one, we promising to procure the rest of the howes and hatchets and knives to his liking, which he was fully content. Afterward going to sleepe he begged two coates of us, which we promised to give him; yet in the morning, some of us refusing to sell him shot, as also our refusing to give him four coates more, he took forth our money and goods again to us; which we refused, not being willing to countenance such dealings in the barbarians . . . and so unreasonably to raise the price of such parcels of land in this barbarous wilderness, and therefore we declare that the said land according to a fair and righteous bargain belongs to the town of Providence.

We can conclude that Roger Williams, in spite of his liking for the Indians, didn't let them get away with anything.

The more you read his letters the more impressive seems the practical skill with which he handled people. Keeping his settlement together, in spite of all the wrangling of the motley crew of honest men who wanted to build up their homes in freedom, fanatics who wanted to impose their own notions on the rest, and plain rascals and loose livers who took refuge in the Narragansett country from the straitlacedness of the other colonies, was a job that took endless watchfulness and tact. He kept his end up with the Indians easily enough: but the landhunger and intolerance of his friends and fellowcountrymen in Massachusetts were a continual threat.

Toleration became more and more the basic tenet of his creed. Given the peculiar formation of the human mind which automatically responds badly to unfamiliar sets of words, or to sets of words to which it has been adversely conditioned, tolerance is the most difficult of social habits to implant. Roger Williams would never have succeeded if he hadn't been able to couch these repugnant teachings in godly language, in language so impregnated with righteous feeling that it produced an unthinking approval in his listeners. The tremendous religious verbiage of the time so infused liberal ideas with the magic of God's word that simple men accepted them in spite of themselves.

". . . I commend that man whether Jew or Turk or Papist," he wrote John Whipple, "or whoever, that steers no otherwise than his conscience dares, till his conscience tells him that God gives him a greater latitude. For, neighbor, you shall find it rare to meet with men of conscience, men that for fear and love of God dare not lie, nor be drunk, nor be contentious, nor steal, nor be covetous, nor voluptuous, nor ambitious, nor lazybodies, nor busybodies, nor dare displease God by omitting either service or suffering, though of reproach, imprisonment, banishment and death, because of the fear and love of God."

Looking back from the vantage of the still shaky scaffold of scientific thinking, we today can begin to see how certain tendencies in the Christian religion, and especially in the more radical types of protestantism, made way for the slowly formed habit of the comparatively free use of the reasoning faculty even in the dangerhaunted regions of religion and government, where grim taboos have always held sway. Toleration in religion was the first step towards liberty in other directions.

Toleration was a tenet of obscure sects of Baptists even before Roger Williams' day when, through his influence and Vane's and Cromwell's, it became the cardinal principle of English Independency. In England it was lost in the hysteria of the Restoration and only came back much later when money had begun to oust religion as the ruling center of consciousness. But in America the habit hung on in spite of all odds against it.

By the end of his long life Roger Williams had managed to accustom the settlers of the whole Narragansett region to living in towns where various religious practices were tolerated. Gradually, as the early fervor of Massachusetts and Connecticut subsided into formalism, liberal ideas from Rhode Island seeped back in, and the Quaker magnate, William Penn, had time to establish the principle on a much larger scale and over a much wider area in his great proprietary domain of Pennsylvania.

During the eighteenth century, due to different causes and influences coming from another sector of the English Church (the liberal country square sector, the gentlemen who read Montaigne and, in religious matters, Chillingworth and Jeremy Taylor and the later Sir Thomas Browne) a similar state of mind was to start up in Maryland and Virginia; so that by the time the colonies united to form the thirteen states it was possible without much opposition to make the notion of complete separation of church and state part of the fundamental law of the Union, if not of all of the component states.

Meanwhile, on May 19, 1643, after two years of discussion, there was drawn up that agreement of 'consociation' between the governments of New Haven, Connecticut, Massachusetts and Plymouth that is of such immense historical importance as the first model for the federal Union. In the early seventeenth century intelligent Englishmen of all political colors from Ralegh to Milton and Cromwell admired above anything the breadth of mind and the excellent commercial organization of the United Provinces of the Netherlands. Left on their own by the collapse of government in England during the Civil War, the leaders of the orthodox colonists tried to emulate the orderly civil processes of the Dutch in organizing their too scattered settlements into the United Colonies.

Like many great steps ahead in social organization the institution of the United Colonies had also its reactionary effects. The Narragansett country and the scattered hamlets on the Maine and New Hampshire coast were left out, and heretics had every reason to fear a concerted assault on their liberties. In a panic the three towns of Newport, Portsmouth and Providence appointed Williams their agent to go to England to get a charter for the colony that would protect them from the encroachments of the orthodox. So strong was the feeling against him that the General Court would not allow him to ship from Boston; so he had to sail up the Sound to Manhattan to take passage on a Dutchman.

Williams reached the Dutch colony just in time to help Governor Krieft talk some of the neighboring tribes out of an Indian war that was scaring his people out of their wits, and that was to drag on all summer in a series of raids, and burnings of outlying boweries, like the raid in September in which poor Mrs. Hutchinson, who had moved west again from the refuge Williams had helped arrange for her on Rhode Island, to farm a tract of land near Hell Gate, was to lose her life.

The Massachusetts magistrates who controlled the United Colonies were proving that they were in earnest in their plans to clean out opposition, by their alliance with Uncas and his Mohegans against the Narraganset Indians. It was at their request that Uncas executed Williams' friend Miantonomo, the war chief of the Narragansets, who had fallen into his hands. Later that fall the General Court sent a detachment to help a local faction attack Samuel Gorton's settlement at Shawomet, now Warwick, Rhode Island. Houses were burned and the women and children were left to shift for themselves in the November woods, while the nine Gortonists the Massachusetts men laid hold of were marched to Boston and indicted as blasphemers and tried for their lives. It was high time that Roger Williams got help from his powerful connections among the parliament men in England.

He kept himself busy during the crossing getting up his *Key into the Language of America,* the singularly charming little Algonquin phrasebook which is the first book of its kind in English, and in working up his ideas on toleration, a subject on which he had been conducting a polemic with his erstwhile friend John Cotton. John Cotton had a tough time talking himself out of an accusation of Antinomianism and was trying to show the world that he was a right thinker by a series of blasts against the anarchists and innovators of Rhode Island. In the course of the argument, he dragged out the old Inquisition sophistry that heretics were not punished for acting according to their conscience, but for sinning against their conscience in refusing out of wicked pride to see the true light.

As his ship wallowed eastward through the gray Atlantic

seas, Williams must have thought deeply and passionately about these things, marshaling to his help all his practical experience in trying to get narrowminded men to live together without cutting each other's throats. In religion by this time he was definitely a Seeker, a kind of mystical agnostic, believing that his duty was patiently to seek further light on the truth revealed and about to be revealed. This new revelation was to come soon. All the preacher could do was tell his hearers to seek the truth and to tolerate the faulty truths others believed in. This was the train of thought which finally found expression in *The Bloudy Tenent of Persecution for Cause of Conscience*, that lyrically fervid pamphlet in defense of toleration which he left, with his usual worldly wisdom, to be published just before he left England to go home after his mission was accomplished.

The Bloudy Tenent came out in the summer of 1644, just at the moment when it was needed to focus similar trains of thought in other Englishmen. The book had great immediate influence, in spite of the fact that the Presbyterians in Parliament were still strong enough to order it burned by the hangman. But outside of Parliament, and especially in the parliamentary army that was soon to turn into Cromwell's New Model, the idea of tolerance of 'tender consciences' was profoundly established in all the fervent revolutionary spirits who were beginning to pant after 'the coming reformation.'

Roger Williams was no writer. He was a storekeeper, an explorer, an organizer, an exhorter, a man of action. Everything he wrote was jotted down like notes for a harangue on scattered bits of paper in the breathless hurry of his life, busy with practical problems to be solved, carried on in a whirl of talk, argument, greeting, sonorous prayer. He was probably a man without many inner processes of thought. To think for him was to speak out, to exhort, to explain, to coax, to inflame. There was always the immediate audience: the large family, the servants and the neighbors, the visiting Indians and trappers, or the travelers and traders from another colony. His letters are scrawled so fast that often whole clauses are left out when his spoken thought gets ahead of his pen. His tracts are full of italics and brackets and strange punctuations with which he tried to set down every inflexion of the voice.

The Bloudy Tenent, written 'in change of rooms and corners, yea, sometimes in variety of strange houses, sometimes in the fields, in the midst of travel; where he hath been forced to gather and scatter his loose thoughts and papers,' is an argument shouted and crooned with all the modulations of pulpit oratory rather than a carefully thoughtout logical treatise. He marshals every weapon of religious feeling behind the impulse for the tolerant attitude toward others' beliefs he finds implicit in Christianity. Reason and logic themselves become suffused with religious feeling instead of being rules for cool chessgames of the mind, as more intellectual writers have pretended.

He gives full justice to the early Baptists as the first to suffer for the idea. He writes in his preface: "The author of these arguments (against persecution) (I have been informed) being committed by some then in power to Newgate for the witness of some truths of Jesus, and having not the use of Pen and Ink, wrote these Arguments in Milke, on sheets of paper, brought to him by the woman his keeper from a friend in London as Stopples in his Milke bottle.

"In such paper written in Milke nothing will appear, but the way of treating it by fire being knowne to this Friende who received the Papers, he transcribed and kept together the papers although the author himself could not correct nor view what himself had written.

"It was in Milke tending to Soule Nourishment even for Babes and Sucklings in Christ.

"It was in Milke, spiritually white, pure and innocent like those white horses of the Word of truth and meeknesse, and the white linen and armour of righteousness in the army of Jesus. Rev. 6 and 19.

"It was in Milke, soft, meeke, peacable and gentle, tending both to the peace of soules and the peace of States and Kingdoms . . . The answer is writ in blood."

He argued that the state had no right to impose religion:

"A national church was not instituted by Christ Jesus . . . That cannot be a true religion which needs carnal weapons to uphold it . . . Evil is always evil, yet permission of it may in case be good . . . Persecutors leave Christ and fly to Moses for the practice and Pattern. The Christian church doth not persecute, no more than a lily doth scratch the thorns, or a lamb pursue and tear the wolves, or a turtledove hunt hawks and eagles, or a chaste and innocent virgin fight and scratch like whores and harlots . . .

"The Civil Power is originally and fundamentally in the People. The civil magistrates are Derivatives or Agents immediately derived and employed as eyes and hands, serving the good of the Whole; hence they have and can have no more power than fundamentally lies in the Bodies and families themselves, which power, might, or authority is not religious, Christian, etc. but natural, humane and civil. Magistrates can have no more power than the common consent of the People shall betrust them with. The spiritual and civil sword cannot be managed by one and the same person. The punishments which civil magistrates inflict upon the church for civil crimes are lawful and necessary. The civil magistrates are bound to preserve the Bodies and Goods of their subjects, and not to destroy them for conscience sake. The civil magistrate owes two things to false worship (1) Permission. (2) Protection.

"Breach of civil peace comes not from the holding forth of doctrines and practices, but from the wrong and preposterous way of suppressing, preventing, or extinguishing such doctrines or practices by weapons of wrath and blood, whips, stocks, imprisonment, banishment and death . . ."

Possibly only those who have lived through one of these periods of revolution and renovation when men's own private desires for greater goodness and order in human life become part of the massmood of the moment, can understand the feelings of joyous intoxication that must have surged up in Roger Williams when from the deck of his broadbeamed Dutchman he sighted the English shore. Thorough was gone and all the old trammeling system. England, in the hands of the Long Parliament, was bubbling and seething with puritan ferment. Men who thought as he did had blown on the ram's horn and the walls of oppression had fallen down. Mankind was rushing forward towards the coming reformation. That Williams felt the full difficulty as well as the immense stimulus of the task is evident from some sentences in *The Bloudy Tenent*: "I confess I have little hopes till those flames kindled in the bloody persecution of Queen Mary are over, that this Discourse against the doctrine of persecution for cause of conscience should pass current . . . even among the sheep of Christ themselves, yet *liberavi animam meam:* I have not hid within my breast my soul's belief."

4. Liberty to Speak to Print

ROGER WILLIAMS was in London by the latter part of the summer of 1642 in lodgings near St. Martin's-in-the-Fields. The London of Civil War times was a far different place from the city of court shows and medieval fairs he had known as a boy. The great crosses in the Strand that had served as pillories had been taken down; the saints had been chipped off the façades of the Gothic churches and the ornamental altars and all Laud's popish trappings had been carted away. Instead of the frilled silks and laces of the days when Buckingham set the fashions, men of substance tended to wear clothes of drab and somber colors and black steeple hats without plumes, and their hair cut in a bowlshape over starched white collars. The theaters on Bankside were closed; old Ben Jonson who had held forth, huge, craggyfaced, jellybellied, and tart of tongue, over his sack in the Apollo room at the Devil Tavern across from St. Dunstan's for so long that people thought of him as perpetual laureate, was dead. Men walking home at night from the drinkingplaces sang jingling psalms instead of the old madrigals. A clatter of hammers came early and late from the armorers' forges, the gunsmiths were busy turning out muskets; in spite of the war there were plenty of buyers in the shopping streets. In every open square and common, trainbands were drilling with fife and drum. There were squads of soldiers in armor on guard at the gates; the citizens hadn't forgotten their great scare the fall before when all at once word had come that the city was wide open to a raiding band of Prince Rupert's longhaired cavalry, and there had been a breathless muster of the militia on Turnham Green, and John Milton, fervent partisan of Parliament and pamphleteer against the bishops, had, half in fun, half in earnest, tacked on the streetdoor of his house on Aldersgate Street the sonnet that begins:

> Captain, or Colonel, or Knight in Arms,
> Whose chance on these defenceless doors may seize,
> If deed of honor did thee ever please,
> Guard them, and him within protect from harms.

The center of London life had moved west towards Westminster where Parliament, sovereign now, amid a storm of hot argument, focused the country's need for a general renovation of church and state.

The Long Parliament, though Hampden and Pym, its two first leaders, soon died, remained a roster of the best brains in England. Government was concentrated in the Commons, sitting in St. Stephen's, and its great administrative committees. As House of Lords, without bishops, without most of the great nobles, a small group of puritan peers carried on a ghost of the old pomp in Westminster Hall. In the Henry Seventh Chapel there sat and gravely wrangled a new assembly, the divines invited from every part of the kingdom to reform the church as Parliament was reforming the state. Although the royal forms were still kept up the republican Commonwealth already existed in fact.

King Charles and the court and the better part of the high nobility and fashionable gentry were at Oxford. In spite of the failure of his two expeditions against the Scotch Presbyterians and the infamy he had incurred by signing away the life of Strafford, his most loyal servant, who had worked so hard to implement Laud's system of Thorough with 'rewards and punishments,' a large part of the country was still with the King. Roughly, the western and northern shires and more than half the county families and most of the nobility were for Charles at any cost, while the trading and manufacturing towns, and Scotland, and the eastern part of England and all the puritan sectaries who had come out of hiding after the fall of old Laud, were for Parliament. Many parliament men were still loyal to the kingship as a principle, but the system of Thorough, the churchstate Laud had so painstakingly tried to build up, had fallen all of a heap, and the 'little low redfaced man,' the archbishop himself, was held a close prisoner in the Tower. A few days before the Long Parliament had met he had written in his diary:

Tuesday; Simon and Jude's Eve; I went into my upper study to see some manuscripts I was sending to Oxford. In that study hung my picture, taken from the life; and coming in I found it had fallen down upon the face, and lying on the floor, the string being broken by which it hanged against the wall. I am almost every day threatened with my ruin in Parliament. God grant this to be no omen.

The Covenanters in Scotland had saved their kirk and had been the immediate lever that brought all this to pass. They were soon to come again to the help of their Presbyterian brothers in England, and to be remarkably well paid in coin of the realm for their trouble. England was a confusion of warring camps, where families and towns and countrysides were split into hating factions; everywhere there was treason and countertreason, and raid and counterraid. Already the parliamentary party was splitting into the two great factions of Presbyterians and Independents. Colonel Cromwell with his Ironsides was becoming known as the right arm of Independency; the day of the Saints was at hand.

Still, when Williams first started picking up the strings of his old connections in England again, Independency, the faction he naturally favored, had only five advocates among the ministers in Westminster Assembly, though possibly more among the lay members. These were mostly Congregationalists who had come back from exile in Holland. The New England ministers, in spite of an invitation that Cromwell and others signed, seem to have been too busy with their own affairs, or perhaps too unsure of the outcome, to send delegates. But with the upsetting of Laud's spy system the lid had blown off controversy. Printing had become virtually free, and pamphlets were coming off the press in stacks, airing every conceivable protestant doctrine with everincreasing boldness. For Williams arriving with his head still whirling from his argument with Cotton over toleration, this moment must have been as full as the moment of his first landing in America twelve years before. The issues already stood out sharp and clear in the glare of the dawn of what he hoped and believed might be a new heaven and a new earth.

His first business was to get his patent for the Providence Plantations. Already Hugh Peters and a minister named Welde, acting as agents for the General Court, were at work with the Earl of Manchester to get the Narragansett section granted to Massachusetts. They had managed to get a document drafted and approved by some members of the Committee for Colonies. But Williams had young Sir Harry Vane working for him, who was every day becoming more indispensable to Parliament as a negotiator, and more powerful through his position as a member of the Committee of the Two Kingdoms. By March they argued Parliament into approving a charter that gave Roger Williams' colony full rights of self-government.

It's very characteristic of Williams that while the business was pending, in addition to bolstering up the Independent cause with personal exhortation and printed tracts, he managed to make himself practically useful. It was an unusually cold winter. The royalists in Newcastle had shut off the supply of coal that ordinarily came by sea from the Tyne to the Thames, so there was great suffering in London for lack of fuel. Roger Williams spent a large part of the winter out with a wagontrain collecting firewood from the country districts and bringing it in to London. He knew how to handle an ax; work in the open was a relief after the learned debates and the crowded

London rooms; already he was developing qualities we like to think of as peculiarly American.

From Robert Baillie's, the agent of the Scotch Kirk's, mention of him in the salty account he sent north to Edinburgh of the proceedings in the Westminster Assembly, which had moved from the drafty chapel to the cozier Jerusalem Chamber for the winter, it is obvious that Roger Williams, though not a member and unable to attend the sessions, had great influence with the more broadminded divines. Baillie speaks of him with personal liking and respect, though, as a hardshelled Presbyterian, he was horrified at his loose teachings, and at the sudden and dreadful growth of libertarian ideas they were inducing. "All this," he wrote, with foreboding, "is from New England."

In January the Independents in the assembly managed to get Parliament to accept their *Apologetical Narration* which was a plea for a modified toleration of 'tender consciences.' Baillie's letters home to Scotland became full of chagrin. He trusted in a rousing victory over the royalists by the Scotch army to show people the virtues of strict church discipline; but the Scots under Leslie did nothing but sit grumbling in their winter quarters, keeping themselves busy with not a little plundering of the northern shires; and the rousing victory, when it came, was won in July by Oliver Cromwell and his hymnsinging Independents at Marston Moor.

At the end of the summer of '44 Williams sailed for home, this time across a summer sea, with the charter in his pocket. Before he left he saw *The Bloudy Tenent* through the press. He took with him Gregory Dexter, who had printed his *Key* and some of Milton's tracts, and his own brother Robert, who, it seems, had so snarled up the family fortunes after their mother's death that it needed a lawsuit to straighten them out, with the result that Roger Williams, having developed a reluctance to swear oaths, was unable to get any of his inheritance from the court.

Toleration was winning in England. On September 13th

Cromwell, now Lieutenant General and already planning the New Model Army, was able to get Parliament to put through an order that tender consciences should not further be molested. In a last flareup the Presbyterians in August had banned *The Bloudy Tenent* and ordered that it be publicly burned. "New Presbyter is old priest writ large," wrote Milton at a later stage of the conflict.

There has been considerable learned controversy about whether it was on this trip to England that Williams first knew Milton, or whether he met him ten years later, or had known him since Cambridge days; what we do know is that while Williams was making his plea for freedom of religion, Milton's mind was busy in the same direction with arguments for freedom of thought in general and specially freedom of printing. As he put it years later in *Defensio Segunda:* "When the Bishops at length had fallen prostrate, aimed at by the shafts of all, and there was no more trouble from them, then I turned my thoughts to other matters,—if I might in anything promote the cause of true and solid liberty; which is chiefliest to be sought for not without, but within, and to be gained not by fighting, but by the right basing and the right administration of life. When, therefore, I perceived that there are in all three sorts of liberty without the presence of which life can hardly anyhow be suitably gone through—Ecclesiastical, Domestic or Private, and Civil— . . . Finally, on the subject of the Liberation of the Press, so that the judgment of the true and the false, what should be published and what suppressed, should not be, in the hands of a few men, and these mostly unlearned and of common capacity, erected into a censorship over books—an agency through which no one, almost, either can or will send into the light anything that is above the vulgar taste—; on this subject, in the form of an express oration, I wrote my Areopagitica."

Areopagitica, one of the completest statements ever made of the case for liberty of printing, came out in November of the same year as *The Bloudy Tenent* in the form of a speech to Parliament, where the Presbyterian party, by now thoroughly alarmed at the swift breaking down of the taboos that centuries had built up to fence in the minds of Englishmen, was trying to put through a licensing act.

John Milton was now a man of thirtysix. He was a Londoner like Williams, the son of a scrivener who lived and kept his shop on Bread Street in the crowded center of the old city near where the Mermaid stood, hangout of Ralegh and the dramatists, and Ben Jonson in his younger days. The father had been a good musician, an amateur composer and poetaster who had encouraged his son's youthful bent for verse and study. Somewhat of a prodigy, young Milton had gone to St. Paul's School and to Cambridge. He had grown up a monastic sort of scholar in the High Renaissance style, full of Latin verse and Hebrew and Greek epigrams and library puns. As a young man he had been possibly more admired for his precocious learning and his slightly girlish good looks than for the early lyric poems, in his very personal development of Jonson's style, which have since been so solidly built into the foundations of the language that we tend to take them for granted. He had studied at Cambridge with the idea of going into the church, but had soaked up the puritan passion for liberty of thought and feeling that was in the air when he was growing up and, as he wrote, was 'churchouted by the prelates.' No man of his massive independence of mind could have stood the life of talebearing and subservience of a clergyman under the system of Thorough. So, after leaving the university, he settled down to a quiet studious existence in the country on a moderate income his father gave him. Where Williams had no other recourse than to emigrate to America, Milton, who had an income, was able to sink himself out of sight in the quiet village life he described in *L'Allegro*.

Several years later young Milton started out on the grand tour so essential to the polishing of the education of a scholar and gentleman. With a servant to wait on him and suitable passports and letters of credit and recommendations to bankers and ambassadors and scholarly continental bigwigs he crossed the Channel and rode across the long bleak hills of the Pas-de-Calais and through the rich rolling farmlands to Paris.

Richelieu, now near the end of his life, had already impressed upon that city the peculiar stamp of his personality. To open up the old reeking rabbitwarren of Valois days, the Luxembourg and its gardens, the middle part of the Louvre, the great arcaded oblongs of the Palais Royal had been built to the Cardinal's taste, in the modified baroque style so admirably adjusted to the scale of the human figure that is the frame of the city to this day; a style a little dry perhaps, but sound and practical, giving life there that scaffolding of graceful order that has made Paris so comfortable for so many generations of men. He had laid out the Jardin des Plantes, and had started the Académie Française on its three centuries of conscious gardening and weeding of the language that was to make French a flavorless, but exact and subtle instrument of thought. It was under the great Cardinal that the actors of the Théâtre Français began the ritual spouting of alexandrines that has often seemed such a strange ceremony to travelers from other nations. Corneille's *Le Cid* had its first night in 1637 and has been running ever since.

Richelieu had put down the last skirmishes of the wars of religion in France and brought both parties to heel. While he crushed political opposition ruthlessly, he reaffirmed Henri Quatre's edict of religious toleration and encouraged lay thought and invention as best he could. He managed to pen up the bigoted court into a pattern of harmless routine at St. Germain, where the great feudal families frittered away their lives in enervating ceremonial and in the unending contest about who should sit on chairs and who on stools, and who should take his hat off to whom, and when. It is not entirely to the Cardinal's credit that René Descartes, the other great Frenchman of the time, thought it wiser to publish his *Discours sur la Méthode,* which laid the foundation of modern mathematical thinking, in exile in Holland; but on the whole Richelieu's influence was against bigotry. He was, it is true, the inventor of the police state, the cruel and spreading cancer under which Europe stifles today, but in general he backed up the protestant cause, which with all its faults was the cause of growth and renovation; and the impact of his sane clear cool intellect, and his skill in organizing men, did much to free Europe from religious persecution. For better or for worse the French mind has shown the qualities of his defects and the defects of his qualities ever since.

The peculiar charms of Paris and the French intelligence were hardly those to appeal to Milton. The chief event of his stay there was, for him, his meeting with the Dutch scholar Grotius, the formulator of the doctrines of international law, against whose *Mare Liberum,* Selden like a good Englishman, already foreseeing the empire upon which the sun never sets, had written his *Mare Clausum.* Grotius had lost out in local politics at home and was an exile from Holland, but had been appointed Swedish ambassador to the court of France by Chancellor Oxenstiern, now regent of Sweden after Gustavus Adolphus' too early death on a German battlefield.

After a spring month in Paris, Milton traveled south by the Rhone, through Nice to Genoa, where he took the Leghorn packet down the coast and landed in a Tuscany that still lived feebly but fairly pleasantly on the fat of former glories. Pisa and Florence were already shrunken cities, but they had academies and poets and antiquarians and mathematicians and villas where, in shady gardens, noble gentlemen sat at marble tables, carved after the antique, writing pedantic verses in an evening Alexandrian haze of fading culture. One great man remained. Seventyfour years old, blind, and still harassed by the familiars of the Holy Office, Galileo was living, the center of a group of disciples, in a villa at Arcetri. Of all the monuments, picturegalleries, libraries, collections of Greek and Roman marbles, gardens and famous stretches of vinewreathed countryside, the sight that remained most vivid in Milton's memory was the blind old man who had dared look into forbidden spaces beyond the churchordained world.

From Florence Milton went on to Rome, where Pope Urban Eighth, a Florentine, was making himself famous by his prodigious industry in enriching his nephews and connections, so that to this day the bees of the coat of arms of the Barbarini family are to be seen on half the palaces of Rome. Milton was taken around the Vatican library and must have seen in the Sistine Chapel Michael Angelo's great frescos of the Creation and the Fall of Man; already they were going out of fashion among the dilettanti, who favored in painting the toothachy sweetness of the school of Bologna, and the new murky style of Salvator Rosa and of the Spaniards in Naples. In Naples he was shown about the city by Manso, a learned and wealthy old nobleman who had been the bosom friend of Tasso, the halfcrazy master of the baroque epic, and of Marini whose ornate and ponderous verses were all the rage with the learned at the time.

It was there that Milton heard the first definite news of the Civil War in England, and decided, instead of going to Greece as he had intended, to go home to play his part. Before he left for the north, after steeping for three winter months in the warm reverie of Augustan Rome that hangs so heavy about the blue bay and the smoking mountain, he sent Manso some pages of complimentary Latin hexameters, to which the old man replied by sending to Milton's inn two silver cups, worked with figures probably as elaborate as those in the verses, and a neat if hackneyed epigram which pointed it out that were it not for his creed Milton would be *non Anglus sed angelus.*

This epigram seems to have echoed the complaint of most of the Italians Milton came into contact with, who felt a little frightened by the blunt frankness with which, under all the bombastic overlay of phrase of the classical scholarship of the period, this young Northerner said what he thought. It was especially shocking at a time when most of the traveling Englishmen came from court circles and affected a fashionable tenderness for the Roman Church. The Inquisition had an ear at every keyhole; the dread of being dragged away into the ugly mystery of its prisons was enough to shut any man's mouth.

"The merchants warned me," Milton wrote later in *Defensio Segunda*, "that they had learnt by letters that snares were being laid for me by the English Jesuits, if I should return to Rome, on the ground that I had spoken too freely concerning religion. For I had made this resolution with myself,—not indeed on my own accord to introduce in those places conversation about religion, but, if interrogated respecting the faith, then, whatsoever I should suffer, to dissemble nothing. To Rome therefore I did return, notwithstanding what I had been told; what I was if anyone asked, I concealed from no one; if anyone in the very city of the Pope, attacked the orthodox religion, I, as before, for a second space of nearly two months, defended it most freely."

He traveled back through Rome to Florence, where of all Italian cities, he felt, like many Americans and Englishmen, most at home; and across the Apennines through Bologna and Ferrara to Venice, without getting into any worse trouble than a completely literary crush he suffered for a blackeyed lady who lived near a ford across the River Reno and to whom he addressed some fairly accomplished Italian verses. In Venice he bought up as much Italian music as he could and shipped it home by sea. Then he rode back through pink marble Verona and over the St. Bernard and along the shore of Lake Leman to Geneva, where he was once more among Protestants and friends.

Among the Italian scholars who had known him, he left, aside from his alarming frankness, a reputation for personal charm of manner and appearance, and considerable surprised admiration for his rockribbed classical scholarship. From Italy he brought away with him more than the sheetmusic of the great composers of the time; he came away with his head ringing with the aftertone of the clanging ardors and of the massive intellectual brilliance of the High Renaissance, all faded now, but still to be heard in the voices of old men like Galileo and Manso, and with the stirring sense of the continuity of humane tastes that is the particular gift of Italy to travelers from the north and west. There clung to him like a remembered smell, after he had forgotten the sound of La Baroni's voice singing Monteverdi, and the hot afternoons under vines, and the slippery eroded Italian oratory and the easy corrupt mornings so full of chance memories of great times and great men and of the stonecut speech of the imperial past, that rotund sense of the pomp and luster of life that was to make him the great baroque poet in English.

Back in London, he settled 'in a pretty gardenhouse he took in Aldersgate Street, at the end of an entry and therefor the fitter for his turn, besides that there are few streets in London more free from noise than that.' (So wrote his nephew.) There he planned to write an epic in English about King Arthur and a tragedy in grand classical style about the Fall of Man. Meanwhile he tried out his theories of education on John and Edward Phillips, his sister's two sons by her first marriage, who went to live with him when she married again, possibly as part of a plan of setting himself up as a schoolmaster and tutor for gentlemen's sons.

The first outlines of several poetic works Milton laid out for himself at this time still exist among his papers; but many years were to go by before he could put his mind to the epic which he planned was to rival Tasso and the ancients. The current of politics ran too fast all round him. The new Reformation had to be accomplished.

He found himself one of the directing intellects of the Root and Branch party, the party that was for utterly clearing the episcopal organization out of the church. All his academic taste for ornate polemics and his inordinate pedant's pride, and the passion for liberty and growth that was hot in every great Englishman's blood in those days, found satisfaction in a ponderous but bitterly effective tract ripping up the bishops. Then he married, unhappily, a fifteenyearold girl of a royalist county family who soon ran away home from his spare scholar's household. Immediately he generalized his hurt feelings into a set of tracts on divorce that caused enormous scandal, so that John Milton, the most ascetic of men, unsuited by his monastic life to deal with a woman in the house or the kitchen, or especially in bed, or in any other way than through complimentary verses or scholarly formal conversation in the library, got the reputation of being a sort of rakish Mormon elder.

The tracts on church organization and on divorce provoked vehement replies. Before he knew it, he was grinding out pamphlet after pamphlet on every important issue of the day, using his classical scholarship as a club to beat his opponents about the head and ears with. His ideas developed fast, as the best minds in England were developing, through Presbyterianism, that soon seemed as cramping as the old bishoprun church under Laud, to Congregationalism and the doctrine that every man had the right to be the judge of his own theology, and that there was no other revelation but personal or private revelation. He became an extreme Independent, virtually a Seeker like Roger Williams.

His horrid opinions had been one reason why Mary Powell ran away from home. It turned out to be his opinions that brought her back. The Independents, because their side had the preponderance of brains and the backing of Cromwell's New Model Army, became the dominant faction in the government of the Commonwealth. Mary Powell's relatives, who needed Milton's help to keep their estate from being sequestered, induced her to go back to him. He seems sincerely to have forgiven her. She lived with him as best she could and bore him four children before she died, still very young, the year he went blind. Perhaps she learned, at least, to respect his enormous industry and his great position as pamphleteer to the Commonwealth. Her bitterness towards what she must have felt was her ruined life was inherited by her daughters, so that Milton's home remained sad and bleak, and all his hot underlying feelings went into his friendships and his work and the backbiting rancor of political and theological controversy.

It was the scandal caused by Milton's pamphlet on divorce that aroused the shocked Presbyterians to push a licensing act for control of the press through Parliament. Prynne was now the great animator of Presbyterian intolerance. He had become the Marat of his party. One of the first acts of the Long Parliament had been to release him from jail and to vote him a handsome compensation for his sufferings at the hands of Laud's executioners and to appoint a delegation which reinstated him in his chambers in Lincoln's Inn amid the cheers of a great crowd of Londoners. He became as violent against toleration as he had been against the drinking of healths and lovelocks and the indecency of stageplays, and, in the time he had to spare from the debates of Parliament and his revengeful hounding of old Laud to his death, kept a continuous stream of written sheets going at top speed from his desk to the printers. Aubrey described him sitting at his desk with a long quilted cap pulled far down on his head to hide the scars where his ears had been hacked away: ". . . about every three hours his man was to bring him a roll and a pot of ale, to refollicate his wasted spirits: so he studied and drank and munched some bread; and this maintained him till night, and then he made a good supper. He was of a strange saturnine complexion. Sir

C. W. [Sir Christopher Wren] said once he had the countenance of a witch."

It never occurred to Prynne's bitter narrow mind that now that his party was on top it should not impose on those he didn't agree with the same restraints against which he had exposed himself so courageously in the days of Thorough. But his endless industry was unavailing to check the spirit of liberty that was spreading through the army.

Then too Presbyterianism in England never lost a certain Scotch flavor. Under James there had been great bitterness against the Scotchmen who infested the court. In the first days of the Solemn League and Covenant enthusiasm for Scotchmen and Scotch ideas had made some headway, but now it was ebbing fast. The levelest heads were for toleration and all its consequences.

Against Independency's three great champions: Cromwell in the army; Sir Harry Vane, subtle political strategist in Parliament, in the Committee of the Two Kingdoms, and in the administration of the Navy; and Milton in his pretty gardenhouse wearing out his eyesight marshaling all his erudition into smashing pamphlets, the Presbyterians, mostly clergymen or smalltown lawyers with only narrow theological training, could do little. The new wave swept over their heads. The aim of the Independents was to unite all godly men to fulfill the immediate needs of the realm. They were gradually finding a common base of discussion and action in the tenet that was implicit in the old Reformation and became explicit in the new: that conscience must be free and inviolable. To these men the heady arguments of *The Bloudy Tenent* and the *Areopagitica* were food and drink. In their mouths Williams' and Milton's phrases became the immediate tools with which to frame, out of the wreckage of the Civil War, an English republic of free men. During a few—too few—years of enormous ebullience of spirit, every link in the social fabric was to be tested and proved by new energetic minds that suddenly found themselves free to think, to talk, to write, and passionately to hope. During these few years Roger Williams and John Milton and hundreds of lesser men like them found themselves swept ahead on a rising tide. England had long been a bubbling spring of energy; suddenly it overflowed all bounds.

5. New England's First Fruits

ROGER WILLIAMS landed in Boston this time in September of 1644, and although along with the charter he showed the magistrates a safeconduct from the Earl of Warwick and a special letter from twelve members of Parliament, it was only grudgingly that they let him go through the Bay Colony. "They were willing," wrote Winthrop, "to maintain a mutual correspondence with him, but as to his dangerous principles of Separation, unless he could be brought to lay them down, they saw no reason why to concede to him or any so persuaded free liberty of ingress and egress, lest any of their people should be drawn away with his erroneous opinions."

The Bay Colony which twenty years before had seemed in the vanguard of change and experiment, was dropping behind the times. It was in England now that the daring inventions of a revolutionary age were in the making, that ideas and habits were being transformed. In New England building houses, clearing land, the control and organization of the great flock of immigrants which had poured into the colony in its first ten years took up all energies. Boston was prosperous; the magistrates were rich. The year before a little pamphlet called *New England's First Fruits* had been published in London to commemorate the founding of Harvard College and to promote colonization. The author listed the blessings direct from the hand of God under which the colony had flourished:

1. In sweeping away great multitudes of the Natives by the small Pox, a little before we went thither, that He might make room for us there.

2. In giving such marvellous safe Passage from first to last, to so many thousands that went thither, the like hath hardly ever been observed in any sea-voyages.

3. In blessing us generally with health and strength, as much as ever, (we might truly say) more than ever in our Native land; many that were tender and sickly here, are stronger and heartier there . . . [i.e. in New England].

4. In giving us such peace and freedom from enemies, when almost all the world is on a fire, that (excepting that short trouble with the Pequots) we never heard of any sound of warres to this day. . . .

5. In subdueing those erroneous opinions carryed over from hence by some of the Passengers, which for a time infested our Churches peace but (through the goodness of God) by conference preaching, a general assembly of learned men, Magistrates timely care, and lastly, by God's own hand from heaven, in most remarkable strokes upon some of the chief fomentors of them; the matter came to such an happie conclusion, that most of the seduced came humbly and confessed their Errors in our publique Assemblies and abide to this day constant in the Truth; the rest (that remained obstinate) finding no fit market there to vent their wares, departed from us to an Iland farre off [Rhode Island] . . . And from that time not any unsound unsavorie and giddie fancie have dared lift up his head, or abide the light amongst us.

6. In settling and bringing civil matters to such a maturity in a short time amongst us having planted 50 Townes and Villages, built 30 or 40 Churches, and more Ministers Houses; a Castle, a College, Prisons, Forts, Cartwaies, Causewaies many, and all these upon our own charge, no publique hand reaching out any helpe: having comfortable Houses, Gardens, Orchards, Grounds fenced, Corne fields, etc. and such form and face of a Commonwealth appearing in all the Plantation, that Strangers from other parts, seeing how much is done in so few years, have wondered at God's blessing on our endeavors.

7. In giving such plenty of all manner of Food in a Wildernesse insomuch that all kinds of Flesh, among the rest, store of venison in its season, Fish from both Sea and Fresh water, Fowle of all kinds, wild and tame; store of Whit-Meale together with all sorts of Eng-

lish Graine, as well as Indian, are plentifull amongst us; also Rootes, Herbs and Fruit, which being better digested by the Sun, are farre more fair pleasant and wholesome than here. . . .

Then the author went on to list the staple products of New England that were already in trade: "Furres, Bever, Otter, etc. Clapboard, Hoops, Pipestaves, Masts . . . Wheat and other graine for Spaine and the West Indies; Fish such as Cod, Haddock, Herrings, Mackerell, Basse, Sturgeon, Seales, Whales, Sea-Horse . . . Oil of sundry sorts, Pitch and Tarre, Rosen and Turpentine . . . Minerals . . . Iron, Blacklead . . . and many others in hopes!" *The First Fruits of New England* is the account of the first North American boom. "(Besides many Boats, Shallops, Hows, Lighters, Pinnaces) we are in a way of building Shippes," he added . . . "of 100, 200, 300, 400 tunne, five of them are already at sea." Already the paths along which New England was to develop for two hundred years were laid out.

However, it is hardly likely that the magistrates gave Roger Williams much time to look around at the improvements that had been made in the nine years since he had been driven out of the Bay. They dreaded his free speaking worse than the smallpox. He set out at once for home past newer and freer towns in the outlying settlements to the westward.

It was along a wellmarked trail rutted and trodden now that he and his friends traveled to Seekonk, where a crowd of settlers from Providence waited to welcome him home with wild enthusiasm. A certain sour backwoodsman named Richard Scott, who evidently didn't like Williams, or anything he stood for, wrote down this account of his arrival: "And there he got a Charter: and coming from Boston to Providence, at Sea-conck the Neighbors of Providence met him with fourteen cannoes, and carried him to Providence. And the Man being hemmed in the middle of the cannoes, was so Elevated and Transported out of himself, that I was condemned in my self, that amongst the rest I had been an Instrument to set him up in his Pride and Folly."

At home in Providence he found his wife and six children well, and plenty of tough knots to untie. His trip to England had cost him money and he had been forced to go into debt. His business was running down. One of the first things he did was to get from old Canonicus, who still doted on him, a tract of land on a deeply indented inlet at Cawcawmsqussik (now Wickford) for a new trading post with the Dutch and Indians. He kept his house in Providence, but for the next seven or eight years he spent most of his time on this isolated cove twenty miles seaward along the bay, where he had a good deep-water harbor for loading vessels, and was within easy reach of his islands with their growing population of goats and swine, and where he could go about his business in peace at a distance from the squabbles of his neighbors. There was more than a touch of the frontiersman in Roger Williams.

He had gotten back to find his friends the Narragansets mourning for their murdered chief Miantonomo and vowing vengeance against the Mohegans and against their allies the Massachusetts English. ". . . for a space of a whole year and a halfe," wrote Samuel Gorton, "they mourned continually, not only by blacking their faces in token thereof; but every day their mourning women, morning and evening upon their knees, with lamentations and many tears a long time together, as ourselves have been eyewitnesses, when we have had occasions among them; and in houses that were more publick, where the wife and the children of the diseased Prince were, there did a man continue a speech (during the time of the womens praying, sighing and lamenting with abundance of tears) declaring what their loss was in being deprived of such a Sachem, and how wrongfully it was done by the enemy, as also how they were all of them engaged to revenge his blood, else it would so lie upon their own heads, as to bring more miseries, and evils upon them."

While Williams was away in England Samuel Gorton, at length out of jail, but a refugee on Rhode Island with the rest of the Shawomet settlers, had induced the Narragansets through Pessicus, Miantonomo's successor as war chief, to make their submission directly to the British Crown, as a measure of protection against the United Colonies and their Indian forces under Uncas. So one of Williams' first jobs when he got home was to fend off the expedition that had been mustered against the Narragansets under Miles Standish at Seekonk. There is no doubt that part of the plan of this expedition was to seize the Providence settlements on the pretext that the Providence people were giving aid and comfort to the Indian enemy, since Williams had made an agreement of neutrality with Canonicus. Williams talked both parties out of the war and so assured the whole region another thirty years of peace.

He had the charter, but even among the four towns he had trouble in getting it accepted. On Rhode Island, William Coddington, who had become the most important settler since the Hutchinsons had moved out, was suspicious of Providence and was carrying on a correspondence with Plymouth and Boston with the aim of joining his island to Plymouth colony and making himself sole proprietor and boss. He was eventually brought around in 1647 and at least accepted the charter in outward form. In May of the same year Samuel Gorton, who had sailed over to England and secured an order from the parliamentary commissioners reinstating his followers in their settlement, was able to shepherd his flock back to the mainland. Since their settlement at Shawomet had been gutted by the Massachusetts troops they had lived on hired land on Rhode Island. They started their town up over again and renamed it Warwick.

Now for the first time the four towns, Providence, Warwick, Newport and Portsmouth, each an independent state in itself in local matters, were formally joined into a chartered colony under the government of a General Court (later known as the

General Assembly). The first Chief Officer was Roger Williams. The fight was not won, but the charter, backed up by the rise to power of the English Independents, gave him a breathing space.

Still, by the summer of 1651 the Narragansett settlers found themselves so much in danger from the continued undermining work of Massachusetts agents in England and of selfseekers like Coddington and the Arnolds at home, that they asked Roger Williams to go back to England to get the charter confirmed by the new government that had taken power after the trial and execution of King Charles. They were specially worried by the patent Coddington had managed to get hold of appointing him governor of Rhode Island for life. The colonists felt that the only man who had enough influence with the new ruling powers to defend their liberties and privileges was Roger Williams. With him they sent John Clark, a physician and preacher, one of the Antinomian heretics who had moved to Rhode Island with the Hutchinsons. Williams sold out his trading post to one Richard Smith for fifty pounds and packed up to go.

The two commissioners sailed from Boston late in the year. Each of them carried in his baggage materials for a pamphlet against the arbitrary doctrines and practices of the Massachusetts magistrates. John Clark's *Ill News from New England* remains one of the best accounts of their long struggle against Boston for what we now consider the commonplaces of civil liberty. Roger Williams' *Bloody Tenent Yet More Bloody by Mr. Cotton's Endeavor to Wash it White in the Blood of the Lamb* was a further installment of his polemic on the subject of toleration of 'tender consciences.'

This time there was no danger that Parliament would order Williams' writings burned. They were headed for a far different England than the warring country dominated by a Presbyterian Parliament, from which Roger Williams had sailed for that happy summer crossing home with his charter seven years before. The Civil Wars were over. The difficulties ahead were the difficulties of victory, not those of defeat or of that stubborn hanging on to an achievement in the face of overwhelming odds which had been Roger Williams' life in the Narragansett country these last years. With the preaching psalmsinging hard veterans of the New Model Army in the lead, the Independents, the party of freedom of conscience, progress, experiment, had swept all England clean of opposition. From every hamlet of the European world eyes were fixed in terrified awe on the men who had dared behead their King.

6. The Form and Face of a Commonwealth

ROGER WILLIAMS reached London around Christmastime. England was still shaking from the news of the decisive battle at Worcester where Cromwell had smashed the royalist cause and driven the young King the Scotch Presbyterian nobles had crowned at Scone into solitary flight. Charles Second was to prove his nerve and his quick wits by making good his escape to the coast and to the Continent, but he still had years of poverty and exile ahead of him before his day came. Since Pride, the foundling drayman who had become a colonel in the parliamentary army, had driven the Presbyterians out of Parliament, the government of England had been in the hands of the Independents, who as result of the purge found themselves in control of what was left of the House of Commons, now known as the Rump. The Rump's executive arm was the Council of State, for which Milton was now Latin Secretary, and where Sir Harry Vane, Roger Williams' old friend, as presiding officer and commissioner for the fleet, was as powerful in civil and naval affairs as Cromwell was in the army. From Worcester on the Presbyterian party was cowed and scattered, but not silenced. As the press was still comparatively free, Prynne, who had shown truly noble courage in rising to defend the King's life, before Pride's troopers shut the doors of the House on him, was still sending sheet after sheet of foolscap to the printers' full of shrill scolding against his opponents. Meanwhile the debris of the Presbyterians, lawyers and divines and country gentlemen mostly, merged with the silent sullen mass of the royalist opposition, and the more active schemers among them joined the underground Cavalier plotters and pamphleteers. Cromwell's secret police under Thurloe was soon to be playing cat and mouse with them.

After Pride's Purge and the fatal frosty day when King Charles had walked with such mild dignity out of the window of Inigo Jones' banqueting hall at Whitehall on to the scaffold, the political situation in England had been hardening fast into a mold that not all Vane's astute diplomacy nor Cromwell's harsh religious fervor or mighty practical generalship were able to break through. The Independents had won, they had the brains and the army, but the people, scared and confused by too rapid changes, were no longer with them. The Roundhead leaders were in the position of the Bolsheviks in Russia after they had seized power in October, 1917. The popular tidalwave had swept away the old order and was already in the swirl of slackwater that preceded the ebb. The revolutionists had the working drawings for a new society ready, but the clay out of which the society was to be molded fell away in their hands. The breakup of old habits and customs was too sudden for the majority of men, and the early hopes of renovation gave way to a sodden mood of inert resistance and longing for the good old times.

In the England of 1649 that mood took the form of the hysterical enthusiasm that greeted the publication of *Eikon Basiliké*, a set of prayers and meditations supposedly written down by Charles while he was waiting for his execution. In spite of anything Parliament or the army could do thousands of copies went from hand to hand throughout the kingdom. Immediately the popular grievances against the Stuarts were forgotten in a welling up of superstitious sympathy for the martyred King. Milton set all the ponderous machinery of his scholarship to work to answer the book by his *Ikonoklastes;* but it was no use. The tide had begun to run against the puritan revolution.

The leaders had gone too far to turn back. From now on every effort they made to make their hopes and plans come true demanded more and more exercise of arbitrary power, until they ended, as the Bolsheviks did, with nothing in their hands but the naked dictatorship of gunpowder and steel.

Of course the analogy can't be pushed too far. The revolution of 1648 was rather one violent stage among many lesser stages in the transfer of supremacy in the state to a new class than the conscious attempt to rebuild society from the foundations that the Bolshevik revolution in Russia was. In seventeenth century England the established property holders never really lost control of events. The estates of malignants, members of the losing party, were sequestered and turned over to supporters of Parliament, most of whom came from the new class of businessmen who were emerging from the ruins of the guilds in the cities. But with that blurring of transitions that has often been remarked on as a happy characteristic of English history, as fast as the businessmen took possession of the estates of the Cavaliers they began to take on the social coloration of the old landowners, so that what happened was merely a heightening of the normal process by which energetic tradesmen were absorbed into the gentry. This country gentry was in time to be the matrix from which sprang that extraordinary phenomenon, the specialized ruling class of the nineteenth century empire.

One violent cleavage did take place in the Civil War years that has left its mark in the English caste system to this day. As small businessmen, freehold farmers, traders and gentry rose in the social scale, the country laborers and artisans and unskilled workers in the towns tended to sink to a position akin to that of the serfs in the Middle Ages. They were forming, at the lowest level of society, that sediment of the disinherited that under the pressure of industrialization was to become the British proletariat.

The disinheriting process had been under way for a hundred years or more, with the growth of enclosures, the taking over of common lands from the villages by powerful landowners, the substitution of sheep grazing and the manufacture and export of wool products for the old beef and grain economy, and all the dislocations that accompanied the transformation of England from a primitive farming into an exporting and trading country. The man who worked with his hands for a living was pushed to the bottom of the heap, and government took it for granted that part of its business was to keep him there. At the end of Elizabeth's regin, the famous Statute of Laborers set a maximum above which wages should not rise. During the seventeenth century and especially during the Civil Wars the cost of living more than doubled and money depreciated in value; so the real wages of the descendants of the old free peasantry and yeomanry of England kept dropping, and consequently their position in the social order. Country magistrates, Cavalier and Roundhead alike, punished severely any demand for betterment that came to their ears. If laborers wanted to improve their lot by moving to another parish they couldn't do so without their local magistrate's permission; as he was often the local employer and landowner too, he very rarely gave it. To move without permission was to incur all the frightful penalties of the laws against vagrants and sturdy beggars. The loss of their estates by the old royalist gentry, who still had in their habits a trace of the feudal tradition of mutual responsibility, made the position of day laborers and tenants considerably worse than it had been, because the place of the cavalier landlords was taken by enterprising tradesmen and businessmen much better trained in that keeping down of the cost of labor on which so much of their profit depended.

It is a proof of how deep and thorough was the stirring up of every class of society under the puritan revolution, and how completely the free press brought complaints and aspirations to the surface, that even the disinherited laborers found spokesmen in the pamphlets of the period. They managed, too, to form the rudiments of a communist political party.

In the early years of the Commonwealth the army and parliamentary leaders were worried by the appearance of a sect of humble people who got the name of Diggers. On moors and commons, and notably on St. George's Hill in Surrey, landless men started to build themselves squatter settlements and to turn over the sod and plant crops. In each case they were dispersed without much trouble by a few troops of horse. They seem to have roused more pity than indignation among the officers of the army who ordered their shacks burned and their plantations rooted up. Jerrard Winstanley, their chief spokesman, has left a wellwritten account of the difficulties of life for poor country people in England in his appeal to Cromwell published in 1652 under the title of *The Law of Freedom in a Platform,* which contained a detailed proposal for a communist England:

If we look into parishes, the burdens there are many.

First, for the power of Lords of Manors remains still over their Bretheren, requiring Fines and Heriots; beating them off the free use of the Common Land, unless their Bretheren will pay them rent; exacting obedience, as much as they did and more, when the King was in power.

Now saith the people, by what Power do these maintain their Title over us? Formerly they held Title from the King, as he was the Conqueror's Successor: But have not the Commoners cast out the King, and broke the band of that Conquest? Therefore in equity they are free from the slavery of that Lordly Power.

Secondly, In Parishes where Commons lie, the rich Norman Freeholders or the new (more covetous) Gentry, overstock the Commons with sheep and cattle, so that inferior Tenants and poor Laborers can hardly keep a Cow, but half starve her; so that the poor are kept poor still and the Common Freedom of the Earth is kept from them, and the poor have no more relief than they had when the King (or Conqueror) was in power.

Thirdly, In many Parishes two or three of the great ones bear all the sway, in making Assessments over awing Constables and other Officers; and what time was to quarter Souldiers, they would have a hand in that, to ease themselves, and over-burden the weaker sort;

and many a time make large sums of money over and above the Justices Warrant in Assessments, and would give no accompt why, neither durst the inferior sort demand an accompt, for he that spake should be sure to be crushed the next opportunity; and if any have complained to Committees or Justices, they have been either wearied out by delays and waiting, or else the Offense hath been by them smothered up; so we see one great man favored another, and the poor oppressed have no relief.

Fourthly, There is another grievance which the people are much troubled at, and that is this: Country people cannot sell any Corn or other fruits of the Earth in Market Town, but they must either pay Toll, or be turned out of Town: Now say they; This is a most shameful thing, that we must part with our estates in Taxes and Free-Quarter beyond the strength of the Land, and the Freedom of the Towns, and yet this Freedom must still be given from us, into the hands of a Covetous Norman Toll-Taker, according to the Kings old burdensome Laws, and contrary to the Liberty of a free Commonwealth.

Now saith the whisperings of the People, The Inferior Tenents and Laborers bears all the burdens, in laboring the Earth, in paying Taxes and Free-Quarter beyond their strength, and in furnishing the Armies with Souldiers, who bear the greatest burden of the War; and yet the Gentry, who oppress them, and that live idle upon their labors, carry away all the comfortable livelyhood of the Earth . . . And is this not a slavery, say the People, That though there be land enough in England, to maintain ten times as many people as are in it, yet some must beg of their brethren, or work in hard drudgery for day wages for them, or starve, or steal, and so be hanged out of the way, as men not fit to live in the earth, before they must be suffered to plant the waste land for their livelyhood, unlesse they will pay Rent to their Brethren for it: wel, this is a burden the Creation groans under; and the subjects (so-called) have not their Birthright Freedomes granted them from their brethren, who hold it from them by Club-Law, but not by righteousness.

The trail of legal reasoning that runs through Winstanley's proposals is characteristic of the period: it was that the normal state of affairs in England had been upset by the Norman conquest and that, now that the monarchy which represented the foreign conqueror was overthrown, the time had come to restore to Englishmen the benefits of common law and common lands. No matter how radical their proposals were, the puritan revolutionists based their demands on their interpretation of the laws and customs of an ideal England before the institution of the authoritarian monarchy and the authoritarian church. These conceptions were often bolstered up by illustrations drawn from the history of the tribes of Israel before the institution of kingship; in this they got their cue from the definite bias against monarchy of the priestly compilers of the Old Testament. This trail of reasoning was used by the whole revolutionary party, from the humble Diggers, through the lower middle class Levellers, and the aristocratic republicans like Milton and Vane, right up to the increasingly powerful 'grandees' round Cromwell, and his huge family connection, whose mouthpiece was Cromwell's son-in-law Ireton.

Infinitely more numerous and more powerful than the Diggers, who were spoken of as their extreme workingclass wing, were the Levellers. In fact the Levellers, in the years between the fall of the Presbyterian majority in Parliament and Cromwell's taking the office of Lord Protector, succeeded in forming the first modern political party in England, with democratically run assemblies, committees of strategy, traveling organizers and a busy press to make available to masses of readers a series of clearly worded platforms for action.

The Levellers represented the embryo of what was to be the lower middle class. The party found its chief supporters among artisans and apprentices in the towns, and lesser officers and private soldiers in the army. The Levellers were at first for government by regularly elected parliaments without king or house of lords, based on proportional manhood suffrage, and a complete separation of church and state, and the reform and codification of the Common Law. Eventually some of them were for a monarchist restoration if it could be arranged so as to leave political power in the hands of a reformed Parliament. The opinions of various spokesmen differed on the details of religious establishment, many going as far as Roger Williams in denying the godliness of a hired clergy; they varied too on the exact basis for suffrage; but on the whole their political ideas tally surprisingly with those of the democratic movement in America and the reform movement in England in the eighteenth and nineteenth centuries. In fact there is hardly a notion of the later political thought and experiment of Englishspeaking peoples that you can't find, couched sometimes, it is true, in the peculiar religious jargon of the day, in the vast literature of the Leveller pamphleteers.

The name Leveller, obviously, was smeared on them by their opponents; the leveling they aimed at, like their successors a hundred and fifty years later, who they so resembled, and who had their roots in the effervescence of the same stratum of society, was equality for all men before the law. Indeed the life of Tom Paine, the pamphleteer of the revolution that succeeded in America, continued, as nearly as one man's life can continue another's, the life of Honest John Lilburne, the pamphleteer of the revolution that failed in puritan England.

John Lilburne's career offers an excellent summary of the changing aspirations and moods of the class he so heroically represented, first in the early hopeful floodtide of the revolution and, afterwards, in the confused ebbing swirl of its failure. He was a younger son of an impoverished country gentleman who had him apprenticed as a boy to a wholesale cloth merchant. His father was evidently a man of legalistic and antiquarian tastes because he is on record as being the last gentleman in England to demand trial by battle in settlement of a lawsuit.

Young Lilburne didn't stick long in the cloth trade. While he was still under age, he got himself associated in illegal agitation with a puritan physician, one Dr. Bastwick, who published a *Letany* that took the hides off the bishops. When Laud got wind of it, the young apprentice had to jump on a boat to Holland with the archbishop's poursuivants on his trail. There he seems to have gone into the business, highly profitable, if dangerous, of distributing puritan books in England.

Back in London, he was caught selling a tract of Prynne's and taken before the Star Chamber about the time of the trials of Prynne and Bastwick. He showed such headstrong obstinacy before the court in refusing to take an oath or to testify against himself, and such gallant courage under the terrific punishment that was inflicted on him of being lashed at a cart's tail from the Fleet prison to Palace Yard, that by the time he was set in the pillory a great crowd of approving Londoners had gathered around. He was so young and harangued the crowd so boldly on his rights as a freeborn Englishman that even the executioners were touched. The only way to keep him quiet and to avert a riot was to gag him. When he was taken from the pillory he was refused a doctor's care and thrown in chains into the filthiest cell in the Fleet. The forces of law and order probably hoped he would quietly die there.

John Lilburne was too tough for them. He not only lived to be released by the Long Parliament at the petition of Oliver Cromwell, but while still in jail managed to smuggle out and get printed a tract inciting the London apprentices to riot against the archbishop. Out of jail he took up brewing, but as soon as the Civil War started he and his brother Robert enlisted in the parliamentary army. The third brother, Henry, was also an army officer and is supposed to have been murdered by his own men on account of a note he sent to the captive King warning him of a plot to assassinate him. John Lilburne fought at Edgehill. As an officer he took part in the desperate defense of Brentford, that saved London from a royalist attack. His troops at Brentford held out long enough to allow the parliamentary artillery train, in danger of being cut off at Hammersmith, to escape. Then they were hacked to pieces by superior forces.

Lilburne was captured and taken to Oxford where the royalists started to try him for treason. They would have hanged him, in spite of the spirited defense he put up in court, if Parliament had not threatened reprisals. After his exchange he was made Lieutenant-Colonel in the Earl of Manchester's dragoons.

He became a warm friend of Cromwell's—in one billet they slept in the same bed—and joined in Cromwell's effort to oust Manchester, whom the extremists thought tepid in the conduct of the war, from his command. Meanwhile, in season and out he kept the presses hot with tracts urging his own claims in the matter of the compensation Parliament had voted him for his sufferings under Laud, and stating and restating the general Independent position in favor of toleration and civil liberties. In connection with the attempt to impeach Manchester he ran afoul not only of the House of Lords, but of the Commons too.

Parliament was the supreme authority in England and touchy about its prerogatives, so Honest John Lilburne was led off to the Tower. There he had leisure to develop his views and, in a stream of tracts, to put the Leveller position before the people of England.

For the rest of his life he was hardly ever out of hot water. Whenever he appeared in court he browbeat his judges with his vigorous interpretation of the civil rights due an Englishman under Magna Carta, the Petition of Right and the Common Law, and defended himself ably with a volume of Coke in his hand. Whenever he got before a jury he won. He became a living embodiment of the rights of the citizen.

During the period of Charles Stuart's captivity after his defeat at Naseby by Cromwell and Fairfax all England seethed with proposals for the peaceful settlement of the kingdom. By far the most closely allied to our constitutional development in America in the following century, was the Levellers' *Agreement of the People,* which outlined a straight republican government to be based on a written constitution. Lilburne was one of its chief inventors and its most fervent proponent in print. The apprentices and younger tradesmen in the towns and a large part of the New Model Army were won over to it, to such a point that the men of substance among the Independents, getting more and more to be known as the 'grandees,' were thoroughly alarmed.

To undercut the Levellers Cromwell's son-in-law Ireton got up his own *Agreement of the People,* put in such form as to secure the rights of property and the power of rural magistrates, and got the Officer's Councils to endorse it. Pride's Purge, the *coup d'état* that established the government of the Rump and the Council of State, put an end to this period of argument and uncertainty. In the excitement of the King's trial the Levellers' proposals were more or less forgotten. All this time the grandees, by typical Cromwellian measures, were trying to win over the popular leaders. John Lilburne himself was awarded an estate at Durham in consideration for his sufferings and services.

Lilburne accepted the estate, but refused to sit on the High Court. In his opinion the King as a freeborn Englishman had the right to a trial by jury in the regular course of law.

After the King's execution, the grandees began to stamp out Leveller agitation in the army by disbanding radical regiments and by stiffening discipline. The mutiny these measures provoked was easily quelled by the enormous personal prestige of Cromwell and Fairfax. One man only, Robert Lockyer, was chosen by lot to be executed out of the group the courtmartial that followed found guilty.

Lockyer's funeral was the occasion of a great political demonstration of the Levellers in London. Lilburne used every argument he could lay to paper and all his skill in agitation to rouse the army against the grandees. More serious mutinies followed, but every one was put down by Cromwell's energy and his power over his men. Old Noll was irresistible to his troops whenever he could come before them himself and talk to them and pray with them and sing hymns with them.

Meanwhile the grandees did their best to conciliate Lilburne. He remained defiant and kept pouring out increasingly violent attacks against the Lord General, like his redhot *Impeachment of High Treason against Oliver Cromwell.* Finally he was indicted for sedition against the House of Commons and the government.

He was tried in Guildhall in a courtroom jammed with his supporters. He defended himself largely on technicalities, but so great was the popular feeling in his favor that there were times when it was doubtful whether it was Lilburne or his judges who were at the bar. As happened so often in seventeenth century state trials in Guildhall the spectators so packed the scaffolding at the back of the room that the benches gave way and legs and backs were broken in the scramble for safety. After being out only an hour the jury brought in a verdict of not guilty.

Lilburne was now at the height of his personal prosperity, but his cause was already lost. After Fairfax retired there was no one left to question Cromwell's control over the army. Gradually there was forming in the minds of the grandees the picture of a Commonwealth of England, which was not very different from the elder John Winthrop's picture of a Commonwealth of Massachusetts. They felt that propertyholders held their privileges by divine law. Godly men of substance were the sacred symbols of the sovereignty of the people and therefore the Elect. As magistrates the Elect directly expressed the will of God. They must be obeyed like the Judges over Israel. In Cromwell's fervent mind the conviction was taking root that he was the ruler ordained by God to lead the Saints and set the English Commonwealth to rights.

When Lilburne was elected Common Councilman in London the Council of State managed to void the election. To support his family he went into the business of soap-boiling. But he was a man who found political implications everywhere. Before he knew it his soap business was a struggle against the guild for the rights of free enterprise.

Meanwhile he continued as the advocate of lost causes. He took up before Parliament cases of tenants wronged by enclosures. He got into a row with the powerful grandee Sir Arthur Haselrig over his, Lilburne's, uncle's claim to some collieries confiscated from royalists at Durham. In the course of this wrangle, the rights and wrongs of which are still unclear, Lilburne published violent attacks on Haselrig and on the Committee sitting at Haberdashers' Hall to settle the interesting matter of the disposal of the properties of the Commonwealth's enemies.

This was Cromwell's chance to pounce; he had long felt that Honest John was too dangerous to the regime to be at large and had been bringing pressure quietly to bear against him from behind the scenes. The Commons suddenly found Lilburne's petition in the matter of his uncle's rights 'false and scandalous' and fined him £3000, with an additional £4000 damages, and banished him from England. It all happened so quickly that before he could put pen to paper he was hustled across the Channel to Holland.

Lilburne had touched the Commonwealth's sore spot; all the new landowners of the winning puritan faction owed their title to the awards of Haberdashers' Hall; to attack that was to attack the foundation of the new order. Parliament rose against him as one man. Like Roger Williams years before in Massachusetts when he came out for respecting the Indians' title to the colonists' land, Lilburne discovered that all heresies are forgivable except those that concern property.

It is probable that the sudden outburst of spite against Honest John was due, too, to the very ticklish condition of affairs for the Independent party. Cromwell, who had reconquered Ireland with measures of such savage repression that his name is used to frighten naughty children there to this day, and had, by a combination of diplomacy and forced marches, occupied Scotland as far north as Edinburgh, had been taken ill in the field of a severe intermittent fever that nearly cost him his life. During the stalemate at the Firth of Forth all the discontented elements in England had started to raise their heads. The winter of 1651 had been a time of conspiracies and savage attacks in print, such as Clement Walker's *History of Independency*, on the Commonwealth, and for a time it looked as if royalists, Levellers and Presbyterians would manage to unite in a concerted rising against the rule of the Saints.

But with the coming of the good spring weather, Cromwell had recovered his health and had started slowly sweeping northward through Fife. The army that had been gathered around young Charles, whom the Scotch, amid such frowning harangues of Presbyterian ministers and such endless knotty sermons urging him to repent of his sins and his father's sins, had so sourly crowned King with only a silvergilt crown the winter before, proved itself unable to stand up to Cromwell's veterans. The young King decided to stake everything on one throw and, while Cromwell was moving north methodically reducing Scotch castles as he went, crossed the border to the west and invaded England. The royalists had been filled with stories of the discontent of the English and expected the march south to be a royal progress.

It turned out very differently. The threat of invasion brought the parliamentary factions together. The dissatisfied gentry sulked in their manors waiting to see which way the wind would set, but gave no help to Charles and his moss-troopers. The Stuart army straggled south unopposed, worn out from the rough country and the hot weather, finding supplies harder and harder to get. Meanwhile Cromwell called out the militia and coolly moved up his troops to shut off every avenue of escape, letting Charles advance deeper and deeper into the trap.

In a desperate effort to get out before the jaws sprung Charles gave up the march on London and shut himself up in Worcester. He had to give his wornout troops time to pick up a little before an engagement. He hoped that Wales and the west country, which was reputed royalist, would send him reinforcements. He waited too long. By the end of August the parliamentary forces had him thoroughly bottled up in the city, and by the night of September 3rd Cromwell was able to write his celebrated letter to Parliament:

For the Right Honorable William Lenthall, Esquire,
Speaker of the Parliament of the
Commonwealth of England;
These haste, haste, post haste for the special service of the state.

SIR,

Being so weary, and scarce able to write, yet I thought it my duty to let you know this much; that upon this day being the 3d of September (remarkable for a mercy vouchsafed to your forces on this day twelvemonth in Scotland), we built a bridge of boats over Severn, between it and Tame, within pistol-shot of our other bridge. Lieutenant-General Fleetwood and Major-General Deane marched from Upton on the southwest side of Severn up to Poyick, a town which was a pass the enemy kept. We passed over some horse and foot and were in conjunction with the Lieutenant-General's forces. We beat the enemy from hedge to hedge till we beat him to Worcester.

The enemy then drew all his forces the other side the town, all but what he lost, and made a very considerable fight with us, for three hours space; but in the end we beat him totally, and pursued him up to his Royal Fort, which we took,—and indeed have beaten his whole army. When we took the fort, we turned his own guns upon him. The enemy hath had great loss, and certainly is scattered, and run several ways. We are in pursuit of him, and have laid forces in several places, that we hope will gather him up.

Indeed this hath been a very glorious mercy, and as stiff a contest, for four or five hours, as ever I have seen. Both your old forces and those new-raised have behaved themselves with very great courage; and He that made them come out, made them willing to fight for you. The Lord God Almighty frame our hearts to real thankfulness for this, which is alone his doing. I hope I shall within a day or two give you a more perfect account.

In the mean time I hope you will pardon, Sir,

Your most humble servant,

Near Worcester, Septemb. 3d, 1651 O. CROMWELL
(10 at night)

After the battle of Worcester, Cromwell was indeed the Cromwell of Milton's sonnet:

> Cromwell our chief of men, who through a cloud
> Not of war only, but detractions rude,
> Guided by faith and matchless fortitude,
> To peace and truth thy glorious way hast ploughed,
> And on the neck of crowned Fortune proud
> Hast reared God's trophies, and his work pursued,
> While Darwen stream, with blood of Scots imbrued,
> And Dunbar field, resounds thy praises loud,
> And Worcester's laureate wreath . . .

He was a man in his early fifties who had made his way with slow smoldering energy from the position of an unsuccessful farmer to the forefront of the nation. He came of a rather humble branch of a Welsh family of Williams that grew suddenly rich from the spoil of the monasteries under Henry Eighth and took the name of Cromwell from a knight who followed Henry Seventh, Prince of Wales, into England. (Whether or not Roger Williams was a relative of Cromwell's is still fairly doubtful, but it is certain that he was looked on as one of them, since the days when he had been the Mashams' favorite chaplain, by the connection.)

After the fall of Thomas Cromwell, Lord Chamberlain and Earl of Essex, the family fortunes had gone gradually downhill, though, when the future Protector was still a small child, his uncle Sir Oliver Cromwell of Hitchinbroke was still rich enough to make himself talked of all over England by his lavish entertaining of James First and his retainers when that Stuart was on his way south to take up the English throne. The Cromwells were connected by blood and marriage with a whole network of puritan landowning families in the eastern counties, the St. Johns, the Mashams, the Barringtons, the Wallers, the Hampdens; all great names under the Commonwealth.

Oliver grew up in Huntington, went to school under a puritan divine named Dr. Beard who had a great influence on him, spent a couple of years at Cambridge without distinguishing himself, somehow got the reputation of being a boisterous roughmannered young man, fonder of fieldsports than booklearning, very much the brawling heavyfisted countryman. He was returned to Parliament from Huntington, where he was burgess and justice of the peace, but seems to have lost out in his home town as a result of the tightening of control of the borough in the hands of men of more property, and moved away in disgust to St. Ives, where he rented some land and went into the business of raising cattle.

It was about this time that he was on the edge of emigrating to New England like so many other puritan gentlemen who found life impossible under Laud's system of Thorough. Things seem to have gone badly for him at St. Ives, but on the death of his wife's uncle he inherited an estate at Ely in the Fens and an income from the cathedral properties that raised him again into the ranks of the gentry. In the Fens he got the reputation for standing up for the rights of the small landowners, and probably through his family connection with Hampden and other puritan leaders, was elected to the Long Parliament from Cambridge. Sir Philip Warwick in his *Memoirs* has left a description of his first appearance in this greatest of parliaments: "The first time I took notice of Mr. Cromwell was in the very beginning of the Parliament held in November 1640, when I vainly thought myself a courtly young gentleman; for we courtiers valued ourselves much upon our good clothes. I came into the house one morning well clad and perceived a gentleman speaking (whom I knew not) very ordinarily apparrelled, for it was a plain cloth-sute, which seemed to have bin made by an ill country taylor: his linen was plain and not very clean; and I remember a speck or two of blood upon his little band, which was not much larger than his collar; his hatt was without a hatband, his stature was of good size, his sword stuck close to his side, his countenance swoln and reddich, his voice sharp and untunable, and his eloquence full of fervor."

It was the release of John Lilburne from jail that Cromwell was urging that day. Whitelock quotes Hampden as telling a man who had asked him scornfully who that fellow was speaking so warmly, 'That slovenly fellow which you see before us, who hath no ornament in his speech; I say that sloven if we should ever come to have a breach with the king (which God forbid) in such case will be one of the greatest men of England.'

In the letter, quoted earlier, written when he was thirtynine years old to Mrs. St. John at Otes, two years before this parliament convened, he speaks of having given up evil courses and having been converted to religion. This conversion and feeling of grace seems to have come to him after a long period of gloom so acute that he went to a doctor to be treated for melancholia. He was a man who found the starting out in life painful and difficult.

It was not until he was over forty and up to his ears in the committee work of the Long Parliament that he overcame a sense of the failure and futility of his life. Even in his years of power, packed with action and organizing of other men's energies in the army and in the government, he was given to morbid moments of doubt followed by gusts of violent self-confidence. His passionately oblique mind was well adapted to impress itself on the questioning believing men of his army who carried the halfcrazy fervor of a revival meeting into everything they thought and did. His speeches never lost their flavor of marketday in a country town. Aside from his skill and generalship in organizing men he had a hick commonsense that made him adored by the countrymen and practical artisans who made up his troops. After Worcester his pre-eminence was absolute over the minds of his party.

While Cromwell was on his way through cheering crowds and illuminated markettowns to London, the lanky young King he had defeated was being smuggled from one loyal country house to another on his long journey to Brighton and the fishingboat that carried him into exile. And troops of prisoners, Scots and Cavaliers, the debris of the ruined royalist hopes, were being escorted across England to jails and places of detention.

Among them was an odd Scotchman, Sir Thomas Urquhart, who liked to style himself Hereditary Sheriff of Cromartie, who was later to make his mark with a magnificent translation into English of Rabelais' first three books. In one of his works, to which he gave the jawtwisting name of *Logopandecteision, or an Introduction to the Universal Language* (which seems to have been an early and fanciful effort towards Esperanto), he describes the loss of his manuscripts in the great defeat:

"No sooner had the total rout of the regal party at Worcestershire given way to the taking of that city, and surrendering up of all the prisoners to the custody of the marshal-general and his deputies; but the liberty, customary at such occasions to be connived at, in favour of a victorious army, imboldened some of the new levied forces of the adjacent counties, to confirm their conquest by the spoil of the captives. For the better achievement of which design, not reckoning those great many others, that in all the other corners of the town were ferreting every room for plunder, a string of exquisite snaps, and clean shavers (if ever there were any) rushing into Mr. Spilsbury's house (who is a very honest man, and hath an exceeding good woman to his wife) broke into an upper chamber, where, finding (besides scarlet cloaks, buff-suits, arms of all sorts, and other such rich chaffer, at such an exigent, escheatable to the prevalent soldier) seven large portmantles full of precious commodity; in three whereof, after a most exact search for gold, silver, apparel, linen, or any whatever adornments of the body, or pocket-implements, as was seized upon in the other four, not hitting upon anything but manuscripts in *folio*, to the quantity of sixscore and eight quires and a half, divided into six hundred forty and two quinternions, and upwards, the quinternions consisting of five sheets and the quire of five and twenty; besides some writings of suits of law, and bonds, in both worth above three thousand pounds English; they, in a trice carried all whatever else was in the room away, save these papers, which they then threw down on the floor, as unfit for their use; yet immediately thereafter, when upon carts the aforesaid baggage was put, to be transported to the country, and that by the example of many hundreds of both horse and foot, whom they had loaded with spoil, they were assaulted with the temptation of a new booty, they apprehending how useful the paper might be unto them, went back for it, and bore it straight away: which done, to every one of those their comerads, whom they met with in the streets, they gave as much thereof, for packeting up of raisins, figs, dates, almonds, caraways, and other such like dry confections, and other ware, as was requisite: who doing the same themselves, did, together with others, kindle pipes of tobacco with a great part thereof, and threw out all the remainder upon the streets, save as much as they deemed necessary for inferior employments, and posterior uses.

"Of these dispersedly rejected bundles of paper, some were gathered up by grocers, druggists, chandlers, pie-makers, or such as stood in need of any cartapaciatory utensil, and put in present service, to the utter undoing of all the writing thereof, both in its matter and order. One quinternion, nevertheless, two days after the fight on Friday morning, together with two other loose sheets more, by virtue of a drizzelling rain, which had made it stick fast to the ground, where there was a heap of seven and twenty dead men, lying upon one another, was, by the command of one Mr. Braughtoun, taken up by a servant of his: who, after he had (in the best manner he could) cleansed it from the mire and mud of the kennel, did forthwith present it to the perusal of his master; in whose hands it no sooner came, but instantly perceiving by the periodical couching of the discourse, marginal figures, and breaks here and there, according to the variety of the subject, that the whole purpose was destinated for the press, and by the author put into a garb befitting either the stationer or printer's acceptance; yet, because it seemed imperfect, and to have relation to subsequent tractates, he made all the enquiry he could, for trial, whether there were any more such quinternions or no: by means whereof, he got full information, that above three thousand sheets of the like paper, written after that fashion, and with the same hand, were utterly lost and imbezzled after the manner aforesaid; and was so fully assured of the misfortune, that to gather up spilt water, comprehend the winds within his fist, and recover those papers again, he thought would be a work of one and the same labour and facility. Therefore, because he dispaired of attaining any more, he the more carefully endeavoured to preserve what he had made purchase of: and this he did very heedfully, in the country for three months together, and afterwards in the city of London; where, at last, I getting notice thereof, thought good, in regard of the great moan made for the loss of Sir Thomas Urquhart's manuscripts, to try at the said Sir Thomas, whether these seven sheets were any of his papers or no. Whereupon, after communication with him, it was found that they were but a parcel of the preface he intended to premise before the Grammar and Lexicon of an Universal Language; the whole preface consisting of two quires of paper, the grammar of three, and a lexicon of seven: the other fivescore and sixteen quires and a half, treating of metaphysical, mathematical, moral, mythological, epigrammatical, dialectical, and chronological matters, in a way never hitherto trod upon by any; being brought by the said Sir Thomas into England for two reasons; first, lest they should have been altogether lost at Stirling, and next to have them printed at London, with the best conveniency that might stand with the indemnity of the author; whom, when I had asked if his fancy could serve him to make up these papers again, especially in so far as concerned the new language? His answer was, That, if he wanted not encouragement, with the favour of a little time, he could do much therein: but unless he were sure to possess his own with freedom, it would be impossible for him to accomplish such a task of so great moment and laboriousness."

The wordy knight seems to have had ample time to run his sentences on and on, in the extraordinarily ornate periods of which he was such a master, during the winter in the Tower of London. When he finally was released on parole it was through the good offices of none other than Roger Williams, as Urquhart testified handsomely in his epilogue to the great work. After thanking various jailers and officers who had been kind to him during his imprisonment he goes on to say:

"The enumeration of these aforesaid courtesies will not permit me to forget my thankfulness to that reverend preacher Mr. Roger Williams of Providence, in New England, for the manifold favors wherein I stood obliged to him above a whole month before either of us had so much as seen other, and that by his frequent and earnest solicitation in my behalf of the most especial members both of the Parliament and Councel of State; in doing whereof he appeared so truly generous, that when it was told him how I, having got notice of his so undeserved respect towards me, was desirous to embrace some sudden opportunity to testifie the affection I did owe him, he purposely delayed the occasion of meeting with me till he had, as he said, performed some acceptable office worthy of my new acquaintance; in all which, both before and after we had conversed with one another, and by those many worthy books set forth by him, to the advancement of piety and good order, with some whereof he was pleased to present me, he did prove himself a man of such discretion and inimitably-sanctified parts, that an Archangel from heaven could not have shown more goodness and less ostentation."

How Williams happened to help out Urquhart we don't know, but the story of his kindness to the eccentric and bailiff-ridden Scotch royalist gives us an inkling of the breadth and variety of his friendships.

As soon as he got settled in the lodgings Vane lent him in Whitehall, Roger Williams found himself in the thick of the Commonwealth leadership at the moment of greatest triumph. London seethed with firstrate minds, bold plans, fresh ideas. At home: law reform, a plan for a really representative parliament instead of one elected by the rotten borough system, disestablishment of the church, the freeing of trade from medieval restrictions, new methods of teaching the young: abroad the great project for a protestant federation to protect liberty of conscience in Europe; and the even bolder plan for outright union with Holland, as with Scotland; for Ireland, a vague intention to resettle with thrifty puritans, if once the popish bogtrotters could be well trodden down into the peat, who would make of the green island another seedbed of godliness like New England. To the men who had overthrown the bishops, cut off the King's head, driven out the peers, anything seemed possible.

Those eighteen months between Cromwell's triumph at Worcester in the fall of 1651 and his seizure of power on April 20, 1653, were the most crucial in English history. The shape of the future was about to be decided. To men living in the fervor and stir of London and Westminster, who were too busy with the immediate needs of day-to-day decisions to feel the sullen popular backwash, it must have seemed as if everything the puritan martyrs had suffered for and the Ironsides had fought for was about to be fulfilled.

The political shifts of the last years had successively thrown into the discard royalists, the uppermiddleclass Presbyterians, and the lowermiddleclass Levellers. Two tendencies remained in uneasy equilibrium: the aristocratic republicans, the party of the Rump led by country gentlemen like Vane and Harry Marten and Algernon Sidney who were for the organization of a republic under a parliament gradually renovated by careful new elections; and the army party under the Lord General Cromwell. No appeal to the nation was possible; for the same reason that democratic procedure even in the soviets was out of the question for the Bolsheviks in Russia once they had broken up the constituent assembly: the masses of the people were balking. The Commonwealth leaders knew in their hearts that no matter how carefully they were rigged, free elections for a new parliament would result in the return of a majority of Presbyterians and brawling reactionary Cavaliers. As in every violent revolution the leaders were up against the hideous paradox of power.

In Roger Williams' too few letters of the period and in the last part of the *Bloody Tenent Yet More Bloody*, I think the reader of today gets the impression that he understood what was going on, but that he didn't much care what form the political government of England took so long as freedom of conscience was assured. By friendship and a certain intellectual affinity, he must have sided with Vane; but he seems to have managed to remain friends with men of all parties, even with Hugh Peters, who at one time had lobbied for the Massachusetts interest against him. In a letter written the younger Winthrop after he got home, telling about his trip, he tells of a visit to Peters: "I was at the Lodgings of Major Winthrop and Mr. Peters, but I missed them. Your brother flourisheth in good Esteem, and is eminent for maintaining the Freedom of the Conscience as to matters of Belief, Religion and Worship. Your father [i.e. father-in-law] Peters preacheth the same Doctrine, though not so zealously as some years since, yet cries out against New-English rigidities and Persecutions, their Civil Injuries and Wrongs to himself, and their unchristian Dealing with him, in excommunicating his Distracted Wife. All this he told me in his Lodgings, at Whitehall, those Lodgings which I was told were Canterbury's; but he himself told me, that that Library wherein we were together, was Canterbury's, [i.e. Laud's], and given him by Parliament: His Wife lives from him not wholly, but much distracted. He tells me he had but two hundred a year, and he allowed her fourscore per annum of it. Surely, Sir, the most holy Lord is most wise in all the Trials he exerciseth his People with. He told me that his Affliction from his Wife stirred him up to Action abroad, and when Success tempted him to Pride, the Bitterness in his Bosom Comforts was a Cooler and a Bridle to him."

It is in this same letter that Williams tells of reading languages with Milton, who was now living in Petty France, in Westminster, very much in the center of everything that went on in the government: "It pleased the Lord to call me for some time, and with some persons, to practise the Hebrew, the Greek, Latin, French and Dutch. The Secretary of the Council (Mr. Milton), for my Dutch I read him, read me many more languages. Grammar rules begin to be esteemed a tyranny. I taught two young gentlemen, a Parliament man's sons, as we teach our children English, by words, phrases and constant talk, etc. I have begun with mine own three boys, who labor besides; others are coming to me."

The latter sentences evidently refer to new theories of teaching that were in the air around Milton, who through all his heavy work as defender of the Commonwealth in Latin and English prose, still felt that his main business in life was teaching. He had written a tract on educational methods, and, under the influence of Comenius and Hartlib, the continental radicals in educational theory of the time, was involved in plans for the founding under Commonwealth auspices of a new university or academy of learning, perhaps an institution based on the classical academies he'd so enjoyed during his year in Italy.

John Milton, now totally blind, was during these years, from the standpoint of Europe, the best-known man in England after Cromwell. His tremendous Latin pamphlets in defense of the Commonwealth had for the time being crushed down his learned opponents by the excellence of their Latinity, their scurrilous violence, and the profoundly English spirit of selfrighteousness that breathed all through them. His diplomatic correspondence as Latin Secretary to the Council of State couched the grand ideas of Cromwell's statesmanship in the best Latin style of the day. For the first time England took its place on the level with the great powers in the opinion of learned and literate Europe.

It was a 'bad eminence' built on regicide and republicanism, but it was an eminence. With a sort of horrified respect European statesmen were beginning to admit that the English spirit was something that would have to be reckoned with in the world.

Outside of his teaching, pamphleteering and routine work with the Council of State, Milton was also the supervisor, if not exactly the editor, of *Mercurius Politicus*, Cromwell's personal newspaper. The actual editor, Marchmount Needham, was a skillful journalist, in the worst sense of the word, whom Cromwell had bought over from the royalist side. In *Mercurius Politicus* under Milton's influence, even the primitive yellow journalism of the day was beginning to show signs of a certain dignity.

With his usual energy, Roger Williams seems to have jumped feet first into local church politics on the side of disestablishment and the abolishing of tithes. Milton was evidently wholeheartedly with him in the attack on 'the hireling ministry' and in the conviction that 'new Presbyter is old Priest writ large.' From London Williams wrote to his and Milton's common friend and occasional printer, Gregory Dexter, now town clerk of Providence, the owner of a limestone quarry and 'a lusty team and lusty sons (being a sanguine cheerful man)' —as Williams described him—wishing that he still had his services as printer and publisher: "It hath pleased God to engage me in divers skirmishes against the Priests, both of old and new England, so that I have occasionally, using the Help of Printer Men unknown to me, to long for my old Friend." The chances are that disestablishment, for which Williams was lobbying and writing with feverish zeal, would have been carried in the Rump if that stump of Parliament had lived long enough to bring it to a vote. But Cromwell had other ideas.

Roger Williams' main business, of course, was confirming the charter for the Narragansett country and blocking the efforts of the Massachusetts people and the various personal intriguers to get their projects through the parliamentary committee which had charge of the colonies. In this he had the help of Vane, who was his host during most of his stay in England, either at Whitehall or at his country seat at Belleau. By the spring of '53 he was able to write to the settlers back home that things were not going too badly for them:

To the Towns of Providence and Warwick

From Sir Henry Vane's, at Belleau in
Lincolnshire, April 1, '53 (so called)

MY DEAR AND LOVING FRIENDS AND NEIGHBORS OF PROVIDENCE AND WARWICK,—Our most noble friend, Sir Henry Vane, having the navy of England most depending on his care, and going down to the navy at Portsmouth, I was invited by them both to accompany his lady to Lincolnshire, where I shall yet stay, as I fear, until the ship is gone. I must, therefore, pray your pardon, that by the post, I send this to London. I hope it may have pleased the Most High Lord of sea and land to bring Captain Christen's ship and dear Mr. Dyre unto you, and with him the council's letters, which answer the petition Sir Henry Vane and myself drew up, and the council, by Sir Henry's mediation, granted us for the confirmation of the charter, until the determination of the controversy. This determination you may please to understand, is hindered by two main obstructions. The first is, the mighty war with the Dutch which makes England and Holland, and the nations tremble. This hath made the parliament set Sir Henry Vane and two or three more as commissioners to manage the war, which they have done, with much engaging the name of God with them, who hath appeared in helping sixty of ours against almost three hundred of their men-of-war and, perchance, to the sinking and taking about one hundred of theirs, and but one of ours, which was sunk by our own men.

Our second obstruction is the opposition of our adversaries, Sir Arthur Haselrig, and Colonel Fenwicke—who hath married his daughter—Mr. Winslow, and Mr. Hopkins, both in great place; and all the friends they can make in parliament and council, and all the priests, both presbyterian and independent; so that we stand as two armies, ready to engage, observing the motions and postures each of the other, and yet shy of each other. Under God, the sheet-anchor of our ship is Sir Henry, who will do as the eye of God leads him; and he faithfully promised me that he would observe the motion of our New England business, while I staid some ten weeks with his lady in Lincolnshire. Besides, here are great thoughts and preparation for a new parliament—some of our friends are apt to think another parliament will more favor us and our cause than this has done. You may please to put my condition into your soul's cases; remember I am a father and a husband. I have longed earnestly to return with the last ship, and with these; yet I have not been willing to withdraw my shoulders from the burthen, lest it pinch others, and may fall heavy upon all; except you are pleased to give me a discharge. If you conceive it necessary for me still to attend this service, pray you to consider if it be not convenient that my poor wife be encouraged to come over to me, and to wait together, on the good pleasure of God, for the end of this matter. You know my many weights hanging on me, how my own place stands, and how many reasons I have to cause me to make haste, yet I would not lose their estates, peace and liberty, by leaving hastily. I write to my dear wife, my great desire of her coming while I stay, yet leave it to the freedom of her spirit, because of the many dangers. Truly, at present the seas are dangerous, but not comparably so much, nor likely to be, because of the late defeat of the Dutch, and their present sending to us offers of peace.

My dear friends, although it pleased God himself, by many favors, to encourage me, yet please you to remember, that no man can stay here as I do, having a present employment there, without much self-denial, which I beseech God for more, and for you also, that no private respects, or gains, or quarrels, may cause you to neglect the public and common safety, peace and liberties. I beseech the blessed God to keep fresh in your thoughts what he hath done for Providence Plantations.

My dear respects to yourselves, wives, and children. I beseech the eternal God to be seen amongst you; so prays your most faithful and affectionate friend and servant,

ROGER WILLIAMS

P.S. My love to all my Indian friends.

The Dutch war that he mentions in this letter had already lasted a year. Most of the Independents felt that it was an unmitigated disaster. Hugh Peters had gone so far as to urge the skippers of British ships not to fight in it.

It was a war that nobody wanted, that was brought on by direct commercial rivalry between the British and Dutch on the sea. With Spain knocked out, and France and Britain engaged in distracting civil wars, the Dutch had managed in a quarter of a century to lay hold of the carrying trade of the world and to establish themselves in colonial trading posts in North and South America and Africa and Japan and the East Indies.

Under Charles the English navy had started new growth, and now, under Vane, it had developed firstrate commanders, Blake and Lawson and the elder Penn. In the end the English managed to sweep the Dutch fleets off the Channel and to get their share of the eastern and American trade, but by the time peace was made the hope of union with Holland as the basis of a protestant United States of Europe was irrevocably ruined.

We know from Williams' letters that he spent a good deal of that spring at Belleau with Lady Vane, while Vane himself was in London engaged on more fateful business even than the care of the fleet and the Dutch war that Williams speaks of. In spite of everything Cromwell, working through his council of officers, could do to hinder it, the republican majority of the Rump was bringing up a bill that had been three years under advisement to establish a new representative system. This bill became the object of Cromwell's deep and smoldering hostility; he was a practical farmer and soldier and could never get over the feeling that the Members of Parliament were a bunch of phrasemakers, bent largely on their own aggrandizement out of confiscated estates. Now these phrasemakers, he felt, were holding up his supplies and endangering the property interest.

The Dutch war had been an expensive business; the pay of the army was in arrears and the soldiers were looking to Old Noll to get them their due. Another result of the war in the Channel was to turn public interest to the navy; Commonwealthsmen were beginning to say that Admiral Blake was as great a man as Cromwell; that the time was coming for the Lord General to step down and retire to his farms in the country as Fairfax had retired. Negotiations for peace between Parliament and some of the Dutch states had started as early as the April 1st on which Williams dated his letter from Belleau. Once peace was signed pressure upon the Lord General to retire would increase.

Cromwell's position was strangely ambiguous. Outwardly he was trying to restrain the army councils from taking action against the Rump. Secretly, the general opinion was that his advice was quite different. At any rate all through the country that spring resentment against the Rump was working itself up into a paroxysm. Whether Cromwell directed this agitation or merely rode to power on the gale of it is still a matter of dispute. Among the evidence is that famous and so Shakespearian conversation about the needs of the Commonwealth that Whitelocke noted down one day in November of the year before when the Lord General put up to him the question: "What if a Man should take upon him to be King?"

The quarrel between the Rump and the Junto of delegates from the officers' councils, meeting at the Cockpit, by this time had settled down to the question of who should superintend the elections for the new representative. A newsletter dated April 1 from London says: "Our souldiers resolve to have speedily a new representative and the Parliament resolve the contrary. The General sticks close to the House, which caused him to be daily railed on by the preaching party, who say they must have both a new parliament and general before the work be done; and that these are not the people that are appointed for perfecting that great worke of God which they have begun. There came a regiment of horse to town this weeke, full-mouth'd against the Parliament, but were not suffered to stay here above 2 days before they, with 3 violent regiments more, were despatcht out of the way towards Scotland."

April 20th was the final date set for consideration of the bill. The night before, Cromwell, and a group of members of Parliament he had invited, held a gusty and inconclusive meeting with delegates of the officers' Junto at the Lord General's lodgings in Whitehall.

In the morning early the group met again to continue the discussion. Messengers kept coming from Westminster with the news that the republican faction had appeared in full force in the house and that they were rushing the bill through to a final reading. At last, hearing that the bill was sure to pass, Cromwell in one of his sudden fits of decision asked some officers present to muster their troops and, calling on a file of musketeers to follow him, hurried to the House.

Leaving his musketeers outside he went in and took his seat in his usual place and for a while listened to the proceedings quietly. He was wearing a plain black suit and his usual gray worsted stockings. Before they could bring the bill to a vote he got up to speak, at first calmly; but finally, lashing himself into a great fit of rage, he started abusing the members in a feverish torrent of words 'like a man distracted.' When a member got up to answer him Cromwell slapped his hat on his head and started walking up and down in the open space between the benches, kicking at the ground with his feet and bawling "Come, come, I will put an end to your prating . . . You are no Parliament . . . I say you are no Parliament . . . I will put an end to your sitting . . . Call them in, I say, call them in." The sergeant threw open the doors and let in five or six files of musketeers who stood in the entranceway with their muskets ready.

The members sat still in their seats. Cromwell turned to the Speaker and pointing at him shouted, "Fetch him down." An officer pulled at the Speaker by his gown and he came down out of the Chair. Algernon Sidney, who was sitting beside the Speaker, was pulled out of his seat by two officers who grabbed him by the shoulders. Meanwhile Sir Harry Vane, who had been, years ago, so warm a friend of Cromwell's that they signed their letters back and forth by the pet names of Brother Heron and Brother Fountain, said from his seat, "This is not honest, this is against morality and common honesty."

Cromwell looked him in the eye and said tauntingly, "Oh Sir Henry Vane . . . Sir Henry Vane . . . The Lord deliver us from Sir Henry Vane." Then he fell to stamping up and down again shouting at the members by name, "Put them out . . . ," and pointing to one man, "There sits a drunkard," and to Henry Marten (of whom, alas, it was quite true), "You sir are a whoremonger." Then he strode to the table in front of the Speaker's chair and snatched up the mace and threw it to a soldier, "What shall we do with this bauble, here take it away." He faced the rest of the members who were cowering in the back of the room, and getting his voice under more control said, "It's you who have forced me to this, for I sought the Lord night and day, that he would rather slay me than put me on the doing of this work."

Then he ordered the soldiers to clear the house and lock it up, and took the Bill of Elections from the clerk and put it under his cloak and carried it home with him. No copy has been found to this day. That night some wit tacked a paper on the door of St. Stephen's: '*This House is to be Lett, now unfurnished.*'

That was the end of the Commonwealth of England and of the great schemes for electoral reform. During the Protectorate Cromwell tried several times to institute something like free parliamentary government, but each time he had to send his Parliament home before it really got started. He wanted to found a representative government but he never got one going that he could trust to continue in the path he had laid down for it.

Vane retired to Belleau. Later he issued the little tract called *A Healing Question* in which he urged to no avail a revival of republican hopes and plans, and of what was already being called 'the good old cause.'

Williams stayed on in England until after the naming of Cromwell Lord Protector amid royal pomp in December of that year, to see that the change in government should not affect the status of the Narragansett country. He probably looked on the dictatorship with some doubt, but at least the Lord Protector was for toleration, and his triumph meant that the priests and presbyters and synods would not rise again to plague the tender consciences of mankind.

When he reached home in the spring of 1654, with the confirmed charter, leaving John Clark as agent to protect the interests of the colony, he wrote his friend Winthrop at Mystic in the letter I have already quoted: "Surely Sir your father [father-in-law, Hugh Peters], and all the people of God in England, formerly called *Puritanus, Anglicanus,* of late *Roundheads,* now the *Sectarians,* (as more or less cut off from the parishes) are now in the saddle and at the helm, so high that *non datur descensus nisi cadendo.* Some cheer up their spirits with the impossibility of another fall or turn, so doth Major Gen. Harrison and Mr. Feake, and Mr. John Simson, now in Windsor Castle for preaching against this last change, and against the Protector, as an usurper, Richard III, etc. So did many think of the last Parliament, who were of the vote of fifty-six against priests and tithes [i.e. against an established church], opposite to the vote of fifty-four who were for them, at least for a while. Major Gen. Harrison was the second in the nation of late, when the loving General and himself joined against the former Long Parliament and dissolved them, but now being the head of the fifty-six party, he was confined by the Protector and Council, within five miles of his father's home, in Staffordshire. That sentence he not obeying, he told me (the day before my leaving London) he was to be sent prisoner into Hartfordshire. Surely, Sir, he is a very gallant, most deserving, heavenly man, but most high flown for the kingdom of the saints, and the fifth monarchy now risen, and their sun never to set again, etc. Others, as to my knowledge, the Protector, Lord President Lawrence, and others at the helm, with Sir Henry Vane (retired into Lincolnshire, yet daily missed and courted for his assistance) are not so full of that faith of miracles, but still imagine changes and persecutions and the very slaughter of the witnesses, before that glorious morning so much desired of a worldly kingdom, if ever such a kingdom (as literally it is by so many expounded) be to arise in this present world and dispensation.

"Sir, I know not how far your judgment hath concurred with the design against the Dutch [the design of fighting the Dutch in America]. I must acknowledge my mourning for it, and when I heard of it, at Portsmouth, I confess I wrote letters to the Protector and President, from thence, as against a most uningenuous and unchristian design, at such a time, when the world stood gazing at the so famous treaty for peace, which was then between the two States and near finished when we set sail. Much I can tell you of the answer I had from Court, and I think of the answers I had from heaven, viz: that the Lord would graciously retard us until the tidings of peace (from England) might quench the fire in the kindling of it.

"Sir, I mourn that any of our parts were so madly injurious to trouble yours. I pity poor Sabando. I yet have hopes in God that we shall be more loving and peacable neighbors. I had word from the Lord President to Portsmouth, that the Council had passed three letters as to our business. First, to encourage us; second, to our neighbor colonies not to molest us; third, in exposition of that word dominion, in the late frame of the government of England, viz: that liberty of conscience should be maintained in all American plantations, etc.

"Sir, a great man in America told me, that he thought New England would not bear it [i.e. toleration]. I hope better, and that not only the necessity, but the equity, piety and Christianity of that freedom will more and more shine forth, not to licentiousness, (as all mercies are apt to be abused) but to the beauty of Christianity and the lustre of true faith in God and love to poor mankind, etc."

Roger Williams never went back to England. As soon as he got home to Providence he was absorbed by the difficulties and excitements of keeping the Narragansett settlement in the right track, and of his trading business and raising and educating his large family, and his preaching to the neighbors and his continual negotiations with the Indians.

The partisan rows of a small frontier community were intense and endless. The joys and pains of the new American life must have somewhat tempered the disappointment he felt when he looked back across the sea to an England getting every day more distant in mood from the puritan settlements. There the ground was caving fast under the order that had seemed instituted of God for all time. From his letters you get the feeling that the old world soon slipped out of his mind and became vague and misty with distance. The day-to-day demands of the rough fresh wilderness life taxed a man's vigor and resourcefulness to the limit. Then too, in spite of his immense practical energy that the frontier so completely satisfied, there was a fierce otherworldliness at the base of all his feelings and thoughts that tended to take possession of him in moments of stress. As he had written in *Experiments of Spiritual Life and Health*, the little devotional book he had published before he left England and dedicated to Lady Vane: "It argues strength of *Grace* that we use this *World* and all the *Comforts* of it with a *weaned eye* and *mind*, as if we used it not: as *English Travellers* that lodge in an *Indian* house use all the wild *Indians* comforts with a strange *affection*, willing and ready to be gone: or as *Passengers* in a *Ship*, willing and ready (when *God* will) to land, and goe ashoar in our ouwn *countrey*, to our owne *House*, and *comforts* in the *Heavens*."

7. The Very Slaughter of the Witnesses

OLIVER CROMWELL died in 1658 on September 3rd, the day of his victories at Dunbar and Worcester. He had managed to make England mighty in Europe, but he had failed in two of his great aims: the building of a league of protestant nations on the Continent, and the setting up of a reformed and stable representative system at home. In spite of the moderation of his repressive measures, the efficiency of his military government and his able steering and handling of men, he had ruled a sullen country.

After his death the organization he had built up kept headway for a while on sheer inertia. Richard, his easygoing son, was proclaimed Lord Protector in his stead and assumed the office at Whitehall amid declarations of approval from the army, the navy, the churches, and the country generally; but London had hardly recovered from the ponderous pageantry of Oliver's lying-in-state and his vast funeral procession and burial in the Henry Seventh chapel in Westminster Abbey before it began to be evident that the Protectorate was slowly running down. The government flopped from tack to tack like a sailboat that's come up into the wind with nobody at the helm.

Government seems to have been something cheerful and ineffectual Richard Cromwell couldn't keep his mind on, so Thurloe, who had been Oliver's political secretary and head of his secret service and was a good strawboss, but no leader, was the real power.

The Protectorate's first need was money. A Parliament was called, not through the partially reformed constituencies that

Oliver had had such trouble with, but by the old uneven system. Among the mass of Thurloe's nominees and Cromwellian rightthinkers a strong minority of republicans appeared at Westminster. Among them were Vane, Neville, Marten, Scot, Ludlow, Haselrig: faces that had not been seen in St. Stephen's for five years.

The political presses started to work again. The pamphleteers came out of their holes. Theoretical discussion revived. The liberal republicanism of ten years before came back for a short bright afterglow.

During the next two years English politics went through one of those dreamlike stages of recapitulation of the past which induced Karl Marx's famous remark that events first come on the stage of history as tragedy and then are repeated as farce. The republicans were not strong enough to do more than form a center of opposition to the Protectorate in Parliament. But discontent began to stir in the army. A new council of officers in permanent session appeared at Wallingford House. If the Good Old Cause were to be revived army magnates like Fleetwood and Desborough felt that the revival should be in their hands. Their first success was in forcing Richard to dissolve his Parliament.

Everybody began to call for the restoration of the Rump as it had been the day Oliver drove the members out of doors. When survivors of that body were called together William Prynne was found sitting in the house like Banquo's ghost and neither threats nor pleading could induce him to leave. Other Presbyterian members of the old Long Parliament gathered round and were only kept out by force when they tried to come back for the next day's sitting.

Meanwhile Richard, finding that nobody was paying any attention to him, resigned. On being assured that the debts of his public office would be attended to, he retired with some relief from Whitehall to a house in the country where he lived on modestly for fiftyodd years, well into the second decade of the eighteenth century, known to the neighbors as 'Tumbledown Dick.'

The Rump was now in the position of trying to force a theoretical republic on a country that didn't want one. The Roundhead religious fervor of Civil War days that had kept the republican theory whitehot with godliness had given way to a mood of cynical lassitude. The men who now burned with religious zeal were Quakers, the followers of Fox and Naylor, Fifth Monarchy men who believed that the second coming of Christ was at hand, evangelists like John Bunyan; they had renounced any effort to deal with the world men live in; that was all the Flesh and the Devil. They dwelt in the world to come. Monarchy and republic were all the same to their extreme nihilism.

In their last gasp of revival, republican hopes had to rely on the purely lay thinking of upperclass intellectuals. For a while the ideas of an amiable curlyhaired gentleman named James Harrington were in the ascendant.

James Harrington came of an old and courtly family. He had traveled a great deal abroad. Like Walter Ralegh, he had been a great reader of Machiavelli and admired above all things the Venetian and Dutch republics. In politics he was of the old Roman school of Harry Marten and Neville. He had been appointed gentleman of the bedchamber to Charles First when that king was shut up on the Isle of Wight and, in spite of his ardent republicanism, had felt towards him a warm personal attachment. A scholar and thinker more than a practical politician, he had, after some difficulty with the censors, managed to publish a scheme of government, dedicated to Oliver Protector, under the name of *Oceana*.

Harrington was a materialist like Hobbes but arrived at the opposite conclusion. Hobbes held substantially that might was right. Harrington held that political power inexorably followed economic power, but that power must be so organized as to avoid its abuse. He planned a republic of landowners, who would vote by secret ballot for a deliberative and executive assembly in which all authorized members of the community should hold office in rotation. He devised the system of balance and division of powers that later so obsessed the framers of the American Constitution.

He spoke, he always claimed, only as a private man, who hoped by the reasonableness of his theories to convince the practical politicians who would put them into effect. He was a man of great personal charm and had the reputation of being a pungent talker, although a wooden writer. He held forth at a club called the 'Rota' that met in the evenings at the Turk's Head in New Palace Yard.

For a while the Rota was the intellectual center of London. Cyriack Skinner, Milton's pupil and the nephew of that Mrs. Sadlier, Coke's daughter, who wrote such tart letters to Roger Williams, was a frequent attendant and often presided. Pepys, as a young man about town on the make, sat in on several meetings without making much out of them. Vane seems to have thought highly of Harrington's ideas and planned to incorporate them in the scheme for the constituent assembly to re-establish the Commonwealth of England on firm simple bases that after all these years was still his dream.

But meanwhile the Government under the restored Rump had come into direct conflict with the army leaders. Major General Lambert was the little Cromwell who drew up his troops at Westminster one fine day and in a second tiny *coup d'état* kept the members from going into the House. He set up a weak sort of compromise government under the name of 'The Committee of Safety,' in which leaders of both parliament and army parties were included. After two months of wrangling and hesitation the army leaders could think of nothing better to do than to set the Rump back on its seat again; so amid cheers of the soldiery and the jeers and derision of the Cromwellian and royalist factions, the doors of the House of Commons were thrown open and the Rumpers and their

Speaker solemnly invited back in to take charge of the country.

All this time General Monk, the man of destiny, the beer-mused beefeater so silent and inarticulate that people never knew whether his words were a result of deep design or plain drunken befuddlement, who commanded the troops in Scotland, was marching gradually into England. He came so slowly and seemed so disarmingly muddled in his own mind that the republicans hardly noticed his advance.

The royalists, who had touched off the summer before an untimely rising that Lambert had easily squelched, now held their breath and waited. Freed from the fear of Cromwell's secret agents, their network of letters, messages, correspondence in code, nods and winks, drinkings of the King's health was spreading fast over England.

With a certain amount of countenance from Fairfax, who came out of his lordly retirement for the purpose, Monk incorporated Lambert's army, which had advanced in martial array to meet him, into his own without a blow being struck and slipped quietly into London. He was offered lodgings at Whitehall and invited to appear before Parliament.

The royalists, both of the old Cavalier and the new Presbyterian and Cromwellian stripe, were playing their game cautiously and well. The fruit was ripening on the tree for them. Soon it would fall into their mouths.

Monk spoke vaguely of a 'settlement' in a speech to the Rump couched in such confused and rambling terms that nobody knew what the devil he meant or whether he meant anything at all. Harry Marten, whose high spirits nothing could dampen, said of Monk that he was like a man who had been sent for to make a suit of clothes and, instead of needles and cloth, had turned up with a bag of carpenter's tools; and when the customer had complained that a hammer and nails wasn't just what was needed had answered: "It matters not; I'll do your work well enough, I warrant you."

But if Monk showed no sign of what he wanted to do,

William Prynne did. Doubt never entered that narrow mind. What he wanted was to get himself and the rest of the members who had been run out by Pride's Purge so many years before back into Parliament. When Prynne had an idea he was not a man to keep quiet about it. For several years now he had been covering the bookstalls with tracts, stating the case for the Secluded Members, until gradually he had produced in the puzzled and jaded popular mind the idea that the first step to the famous Settlement was the restoration of the Long Parliament in its pristine splendor, and with it due constitutional procedure. It was largely Prynne's singlehanded agitation that lashed up the City of London against the Rump and began to make it appear that the Rump was all that stood in the way of that Settlement that all men desired and that every man interpreted according to his own secret hopes.

The London Common Council came to the point of urging the Lord Mayor to stop paying taxes to Parliament, and the Rumpers called on General Monk to subdue the City which they claimed was in a state of insurrection. General Monk obeyed; sullenly, but he obeyed.

He occupied the walls and unhinged the gates and sent patrols through the streets to chase into back alleys the groups of riotous apprentices who were beginning to rag the puritans. But after two days of repression he suddenly announced that he would dine with the Lord Mayor whose citizens his troops had been harrying.

His reception, amid the plate and pompous gravies of a Lord Mayor's feast, was chilly at first, but it improved as course followed course. Warmed at last by the good dinner and the plentiful toasts, he went with the Lord Mayor to Guildhall, where he made a speech to the Council assembled in which he announced that he was going to make common cause with the City against the Rump and to call for a 'full and free' parliament.

Immediately the City went crazy. Bells rang. Cannons were

fired. Windows of puritan shops were broken. Learned divines were hustled and had stones and mud thrown after them as they scuttled to shelter. Bonfires were lit and everybody started roasting pieces of rump in the open. It was the beginning of the twoday brawl known in after years as 'The Roasting of the Rump.'

The smell of roast meat had hardly cleared from the dank wintry air of the foggy streets when the Secluded Members were marched by Monk's soldiery into the House of Commons. To the dismay of the Rumpers they immediately formed a majority and took up the order of the day of the Long Parliament where it had been broken off on December 18, 1648. England was going through all the stages of the Revolution of that year, but this time in reverse.

In the popular mind the Good Old Cause was dead, but only the vague concept of a Settlement had yet taken its place. There was still fervent republicans and separatists in the army, and the best minds in England, Harrington's, Vane's, Milton's were doggedly at work with tracts and appeals to stem the tide before all the new institutions on which so much blood and energy had been spent should be swept away. Milton's last important pamphlet, his *Readie and Easie Way to establish a Free Commonwealth* is addressed, in a sort of desperation, to General Monk himself. Written with the touching earnestness of a man who saw clearly what was happening, it was a last-minute plea to his fellowcitizens not to give up the great hopes of the last years: ". . . After our Liberty and Religion thus prosperously fought for, gain'd, and many Years possess'd, except in those unhappy Interruptions, which God hath remov'd; now that nothing remains, but in all reason the certain hopes of a speedy and immediat Settlement for ever in a firm and free Commonwealth; for this extoll'd and magnifi'd Nation, regardless both of Honour won, or Delivrances vouchsaf't from Heaven, to fall back, or rather to creep back so poorly, as it seems the multitude would, to their once abjur'd and detest'd

Thralldom of Kingship; to be ourselves the Slanderers of our own just and religious Deeds, though done by som to covetous and ambitious Ends, yet not therefore to be stain'd with thir Infamy, or they to asperse the Integrity of others; and yet these now, by revolting from the Conscience of Deeds well done, both in Church and State, to throw away and forsake, or rather to betray a just and noble Cause for the Mixture of bad Men who have ill manag'd and abus'd it, (which had our Fathers done heretofore, and on the same pretense deserted true Religion, what had long ere this become of our Gospel, and all Protestant Reformation so much intermixt with Avarice and Ambition of som Reformers?); and by thus relapsing to verify all the bitter Predictions of our triumphing Enemies, who will now think they wisely discern'd and justly censur'd both us and all our Actions as rash, rebellious, hypocritical and impious, not only argues a strange degenerate Contagion suddenly spread amongst us, fitted and prepar'd for new Slavery, but will render us a Scorn and Derision to all our Neighbors."

The pamphlet came out in late February or early March of 1660. It's quite possible that the last words were dictated by the blind Latin Secretary during the days of the riots against godly men (fanatics, they were now beginning to be called) in that house in Petty France where his second wife (his 'late espous'd Saint') had recently died. They were full of bitter feeling: "What I have spoken is the Language of that which is not call'd amiss *The Good Old Cause:* if it seem strange to any, it will not seem more strange, I hope, than convincing to Backsliders. Thus much I should perhaps have said, though I were sure I should have spoken only to Trees and Stones; and had none to cry to, but with the Prophet, O Earth, Earth, Earth! to tell the very Soil itself, what her perverse Inhabitants are deaf to. Nay, though what I have spoke, should happen (which Thou suffer not, who didst creat Mankind free; not Thou next, who didst redeem us from being Servants of Men!) to be the last words of our expiring Liberty; and may reclaim, though they be now chusing them a Captain back for Egypt, to bethink themselves a little and consider whither they are rushing; to exhort this Torrent also of the People, not to be so impetuous, but to keep thir due Channel; at length recovering and uniting thir better Resolutions, now that they see already how open and unbounded the insolence and rage is of our common Enemies, to stay these ruinous Proceedings, justly and timely fearing to what a Precipice of Destruction the deluge of this epidemic Madness would hurry, through the general defection of a misguided and abus'd Multitude."

The royalist reaction swept through England like a brush fire. Twenty years of the Great Rebellion had not been enough to break up the old habits of feudal subjection and religious ceremonial. People were sick of sermons, of the strain of trying to lift themselves by their own bootstraps into a rational life according to the scriptures. They felt a real need for the pageantry and the bootlicking and the bowing and scraping before nobles and bishops and gentry. They wanted the Christmas puddings and the bearbaitings, and to feel above them the candlelit glittering world of their betters, and the tapping of redlacquered heels on polished floors, and the whoring and the dicing and the skylarking of royalty.

Already a faint sound of revelry could be heard from Charles' court across the Channel. High and low yearned for the old hogwallow.

Quick to sniff the new set of the wind, politicians and clergymen and men of letters were busy in corners quietly changing their coats. Merry England was to have one more carnival, a grim rather hollow carnival, out of the feudal age before it fell again under the subjection of the men of trade and money, this time of a moneyed class that was to substitute a dry formalism in politics and religion for the passion for a better world that had driven men to think and fight and die under the Commonwealth.

On March 16th the Long Parliament put itself to sleep, leaving General Monk as dictator while the elections were going on for the 'free and full' parliament which was called to convene forty days later.

The new House of Commons met, privately overwhelmingly royalist, and with it a timid revival of the House of Lords. After considerable sleight of hand so that everybody should be protected in case of a slip-up, Monk, who had been in secret communication with the Court for months, got a letter from Charles Second at Breda in Holland into the hands of the Speaker.

The Commons went about the Restoration on tiptoes as if they were afraid that the ghost of Oliver Cromwell would suddenly rise from the Abbey and forbid them. The Speaker read the royal letter, treating it gingerly as if it had fallen from the sky. The letter promised amnesty to all young Charles Stuart's loving subjects with the tiny exception of those directly implicated in his father's death. The Commons made a pretty speech in reply in the form of a resolution that 'the Government is, and by right ought to be, by King, Lords and Commons' and England was a monarchy again.

Long before Charles Second and his court landed at Dover amid such universal delirium that Mr. Pepys, invited out for the occasion on Admiral Montague's flagship the *Naseby*, was so anxious to shoot off the first gun in the royal salute that he put his right eye too near the touch hole and almost blew it out, the poets, and particularly those who had been a little overfervent for the past regime, had been getting ready their complimentary verses. Dryden particularly, who was to be the ornament of the reign, had a good deal to unsay. He had been a clerk in Thurloe's office and had turned out stanzas for the Lord Protector. *Astraea Redux* did the trick.

The keynote of the year was struck by Abraham Cowley with his

Come mighty Charles! Desire of Nations, come!
Come you triumphant exile, home.
He's come, he's safe at shore; I hear the noise
Of a whole land which does at once rejoice;
I hear the united people's sacred voice.
The sea which circles us around
Ne'er to land so loud a sound;
The mighty shout sends to the sea a gale
And swells up every sail;
The bells and guns are scarcely heard at all;
The artificial joy's drowned by the natural.

The Ode gives one a feeling of having been written under forced draft; but perhaps a man who feels the hangman's noose around his neck can be forgiven the occasional straining of an anapaest.

If the great majority of English men of letters scuttled to cover with little dignity there were two men whose behavior, each in a different way, was a bloodheating model of civic courage. Blind Milton fought for the Commonwealth to the last with every weapon he had. Andrew Marvell, who had been his assistant in the office of Latin Secretary and had turned out far better verses than Dryden's in Oliver's praise, was elected to the new parliament from his home town of Hull, and went through all the revolutions of the period, quietly attending to the business of his constituents, wittily saying his say to the last, and never eating a republican word.

It was men like Marvell whose lives formed the link between the liberal republicans of the seventeenth century and the liberal Whigs of the eighteenth. His description of Charles' arrival is more to the point and better verse than Cowley's; certainly it's less windy:

Of a tall stature and sable hue,
Much like the son of Kish, that lofty Jew,
Twelve years complete he suffered in exile
And kept his fathers' asses all the while.

At length, by wonderful impulse of fate,
The people call him home to help the State;
And what is more, they send him money too,
And clothe him all from head to foot anew;
Nor did he such small favors then disdain
Who in his thirtieth year began his reign,
In a slashed doublet then he came ashore,
And dubbed poor Palmer's wife his royal whore.

The illuminations had hardly guttered out along the windows of public buildings on the streets that had been graced by the royal progress when the hue and cry began after the great men of the Commonwealth. At first it was only the men who had sat on the High Court and put their names to the first Charles' deathwarrant who were arrested, but gradually, as the courtiers tasted blood, the ban was broadened to include all the powerful personalities of the fallen regime. Although Charles himself seems to have had a certain sense of fair play, it did not apply to men he feared politically or whom he considered his father's murderers. Once the reaction got under way, there was no stopping it until every memory of the English republic had been defaced and uprooted. There's nothing comparable to this hacking of twenty great and generous years out of English history except the extraordinary falsification of Russian history that has gone on in our time under Stalin, who has made the names of a whole generation of Lenin's coworkers as if they had never been. In Parliament, William Prynne led the bloodthirsty pack.

Charles' declaration of general amnesty at Breda had contained the clause: *Excepting only such persons as shall hereafter be excepted by Parliament.* All the Restoration year Parliament was busy broadening and widening that clause, until no man who had held office during the preceding twenty years was safe. First it was decided that only seven of those who had sat on the High Court should be put to death, but once the trials and executions started the intoxication of blood spread and more and more victims were demanded.

Every slaughterhouse detail of the ancient penalty for high treason was meticulously revived. Fashionable London crowded to Charing Cross to see the kingkillers hanged, cut down before they were dead, then disemboweled and the heart torn out and held up by the executioner. Finally the carcase was hacked into four quarters that were trundled in four directions through the city.

To a man the kingkillers met their deaths with courage and made last speeches in the old puritan style defending the Good Old Cause. Major General Harrison, whom Roger Williams had written of as being 'a very gallant, most deserving heavenly man, but most highflown for the Kingdom of the Saints,' was the first man put to death. Hugh Peters, the New England preacher, young Winthrop's father-in-law, had delivered the sermon on the day of Charles' execution, and an absurd story had gotten around that he had been the actual executioner; royalist London saw him die with particular satisfaction.

When they ran out of regicide justices, the courts went on taking the head off any Commonwealthsman who refused to crawl on his belly before the new order. Sir Harry Vane, who had been promised mercy because it was well known that he had been opposed to Charles' execution, ruined himself by his proud and cool defense of his political career at his trial. ". . . And whatever defections did happen by apostates, hypocrites, and time-serving worldlings, there was a party amongst them that continued firm sincere and chaste unto the last, and loved it better than their very lives; of which number I am not ashamed to profess myself to be . . ." he said when all legal arguments failed him. Charles himself wrote Hyde, then at the peak of his power as Lord Chancellor, that as a result of Vane's bearing at his trial he was too dangerous a man to let live, 'if he could be honestly put out of the way.'

In deference to his rank he was beheaded on Tower Hill.

When he had delivered half his dying speech the sheriff snatched the paper on which it was written out of his hand. Like Ralegh's, his last words, when he tried to continue speaking to the crowd round the scaffold, were drowned out by the trumpeters. Sikes, his biographer, quotes him as saying quietly when the sheriff's men went through his pockets to take away the notes he had prepared for the speech, "It is a bad cause which cannot bear the words of a dying man."

Not content with slaughtering the living, the royalists dug up the dead. After ghoulish indignities, the heads of Cromwell, Bradshaw and Ireton were hacked from their carcases and the skulls set up on Westminster Hall, so that no man should ever dare what they had dared.

A few republicans escaped to America and to Switzerland. Algernon Sidney, the brilliant young nobleman who had led the cavalry charge at Marston Moor, was on a diplomatic mission at the time of the Restoration. Friends advised him not to come home. He roamed around Europe for years in exile, finding a vent for his energies in working up his reflections on government that Thomas Jefferson in the next century was so to admire. Harry Marten, the genial wisecracker of the Long Parliament, was condemned to prison for life, and died many years later in an old castle in Wales. James Harrington was kept several years in jail and came out, not altogether mad, but a broken eccentric with the strange delusion that bees and flies were constantly being engendered by his sweat. Where the executioner had left off the great plague finished the business of clearing away the old generation of Englishmen, as the great fire wiped out seventeenth century London. There were great minds in England after the Restoration, but never a generation that had such mighty hopes and walked so fearlessly on the earth as the men of the Commonwealth.

Although his political works were rooted out of the bookstores and turned over to the hangman to be burned, Milton escaped with his life and lived on for fourteen years after the

Restoration. He seems to have been hidden by his friends the day King Charles was proclaimed in London and to have led an underground life, spirited from place to place, for some years. He was committed to jail and then released. In spite of the fact that he was considered a notorious criminal by a large part of the population his name was kept off the proscription lists. His many friends, of whom Masson suggests that Andrew Marvell was possibly one of the most effective, though not the most powerful, managed to get him released and finally to induce the authorities to let him live and publish quietly in London. With the publication of *Paradise Lost* a new reputation sprang up about the blind relic of a dead heroic age, and people began to forget his brimstone republicanism. But he ever after felt himself a Samson among the Philistines:

> Blind among enemies . . .
> . . . I, dark in light, exposed
> To daily fraud, contempt, abuse and wrong,
> Within doors or without, still as a fool
> In power of others, never in my own,—
> Scarce half I seem to live, dead more than half,
> O dark, dark, dark amid the blaze of noon.

With his daily playing of old music and his courteous sarcastic scholarly talk out of another age he managed to show outward equanimity during the long quiet gloaming of his life to those who came to see him. Richardson the painter describes him sitting "in a grey coarse cloth coat, near the door of his house near Bunhill Fields without Moorgate, in warm sunny weather to enjoy the fresh air, and so, as well as in his room, received the visits of people of distinguished parts, as well as quality."

8. The Cup of as Great Liberties

AFTER the Restoration, England and New England, each an extension of the other during the years of the Commonwealth, drew apart as if the Atlantic suddenly had doubled in width. They came to a fork in the road and parted. From now on the Englishmen to the east of the great misty ocean were to develop differently and at different tempo from the Englishmen who were gradually investing the new continent to the westward.

In England the reaction had not meant the hopedfor return of the old order. Feudalism and the Merry England of the Middle Ages had been dead since the first Tudors. After a few stunted years the socalled Glorious Revolution of 1688 swept away the Stuarts and brought into being the imperial England of the eighteenth and nineteenth centuries. But it was not the old puritan union between the lower middleclasses of the towns and the small farmers that brought in William and Mary; it was that new grouping of the landowners and the financial and trading magnates of the cities that was going to express itself politically as the great Whig party. The laboring and tenant classes had long ceased to have any political importance. The lower middleclass of nonconformists and old Puritans had been virtually disfranchised but not destroyed. It remained a rich seedbed of energies encysted by repressive laws within the body of the state, from which were to come all the great movements of humane and religious protest, Quakerism, Evangelism, Methodism, the great inventions and the westward Scotch-Irish migrations that were to keep quick the pulse of American life. The gentry were to produce the specialized ruling class that organized and exploited the money and military empire, while the nonconformist lower middleclass, unable to break through the hard lines of caste stratification at home, spread over the world and founded the republican commonwealths: the United States, Canada, Australia, New Zealand, South Africa, where, though every trace was obliterated at home, there still live and grow societies that have their roots in the first model, the Commonwealth of England.

The last time Cromwell had ridden out at the head of his lifeguards at Richmond, George Fox, his broad hat firm on his head, had seen him go by and noted grimly in his diary that he felt a waft of death go forth against him. In several interviews he had chid the Protector for the repression against his followers, already being scornfully mocked as Quakers, who were carrying the separatist religious ideas of the Levellers, the Seekers, the Diggers and the other extreme sects to their logical end in political nihilism and in the doctrine of the Inner Light. The Quaker answer to the restoration of monarchy and feudal and ecclesiastic privilege was that God was in every man and that all men were equal.

Roger Williams' difficulties with the Quakers, when they started in the late sixteenfifties to make converts in America, tested to the fullest his belief in free speech and civil liberties and his selfcontrol against bitter opponents. Although his Seeker religion had many points in common with George Fox's doctrines, Roger Williams was no quietist. And as an urbane man of the world he was profoundly shocked by the violence and the crazy revivalism of the first enthusiasts; all the same he did everything he could to ward off their persecution in Massachusetts and defended their complete liberty in Rhode Island and Providence, to such a point that he allowed them for a period of years, all the time lashing out at their ideas and behavior in print and in his sermons as violently as was his wont, to take the leadership of the colony away from him.

It is one of the greatest tests of consistency that any political leader has ever had to face.

He got back to Providence from what was to prove his last trip to England in the spring of 1654, leaving John Clark to protect the interest of the Narragansett Settlements. With him he brought letters from people of importance in the new government and assurances from the commissioners that his people's boundaries would be respected. Immediately he found himself up to his neck in a struggle to make the richer colonists accept the charter he had worked so hard to get for them. It was only by continual argument and exhortation that he could keep them at work on his great scheme for freedom, which demanded so much intelligent personal abnegation and such painstaking building of new social habits. That August, when he had hardly been home three months, he was already writing gloomily to the town of Providence:

"WELL-BELOVED FRIENDS AND NEIGHBORS,—I am like a man in a great fog. I know not well how to steer. I fear to run upon the rocks at home, having had trials abroad. I fear to run backwards, as men in a mist do, and undo all that I have been a long time undoing myself to do, viz: to keep up the name of a people a free people, not enslaved to the bondages and iron yokes of the great (both soul and body) oppressions of the English and barbarians about us, nor to the divisions and disorders within ourselves. Since I set the first step of any English foot into these wild parts, and have maintained a chargeable and hazardous correspondence with the barbarians, and spent almost five years' time with the state of England, to keep off the rage of the [Massachusetts] English against us, what have I reaped of the root of being the stepping-stone of so many families and towns about us, but grief, and sorrow, and bitterness? I have been charged with folly for that freedom and liberty which I have always stood for; I say liberty and equality, both in land and government. I have been blamed for parting with Moshassuck, and afterward Pawtuxet, (which were mine own as truly as any man's coat upon his back) without reserving to myself a foot of land, or an inch of voice in any matter, more than to my servants and strangers. It hath been told me that I labored for a licentious and contentious people; that I have foolishly parted with town and colony advantages, by which I might have preserved both town and colony in as good order as any in the country about us. This, and ten times more, I have been censured for, and at this present am called a traitor by one party, against the state of England, for not maintaining the charter and the colony; and it is said I am as good as banished by yourselves, and that both sides wished that I might never have landed, that the fire of contention might have had no stop in burning. Indeed, the words have been so sharp between myself and some lately, that at last I was forced to say, that might well silence all complaints if I once began to complain, who was unfortunately fetched and drawn from my employment, and sent to so vast a distance from my family, to do your work of a high and costly nature, for so many days and weeks and months together, and there left to starve, or beg or borrow. But blessed be God, who gave me favor to borrow one while, and to work another, and thereby to pay your debts there, and to come over with your credit and honor, as an agent from you, who had, in your name, grappled with the agents and friends of all your enemies round about you. I am told that your opposites thought on me, and provided, as I may say, a sponge to wipe off your scores and debts in England, but that it was obstructed by yourselves, who rather meditated on means and new agents to be sent over, to cross what Mr. Clarke and I obtained . . ."

It's only from Roger Williams' own letters that we get an inkling of the extraordinary difficulty of the work he had set himself to do, the cross purposes, the conflicting ambitions he had to keep in check. The slowness of communication with London, to be sure, worked both ways and kept the authorities there from carrying out repressive plans; so that throughout the century, what was done in America, rather than what was ordered in England, won out. But the ambitions and orneriness of the colonists were a continual trial.

Among his other letters backing him up in his enterprise Williams had brought home a letter from Sir Harry Vane calling the colonists down for their endless bickering and backbiting that was putting the whole enterprise in jeopardy. Undoubtedly Williams had a hand in drafting the town's reply that Gregory Dexter signed as Town Clerk. He is explaining the difficulties he faced in getting the people of the four towns to work together and to forget their own imagined interests long enough to pool their efforts for the common good:

First, we have been greatly disturbed and distracted by the ambition and covetousness of some amongst us. Sir, we were in complete order, until Mr. Coddington, wanting that public, self-denying spirit which you commend to us in your letter, procured, by most untrue information, a monopoly of part of the colony, viz: Rhode Island, to himself, and so occasioned our general disturbance and distractions. Secondly, Mr. Dyre, with no less want of a public spirit, being ruined by party contentions with Mr. Coddington, and being betrusted to bring from England the letters from the Council of State for our reunitings, he hoped for a recruit to himself by other men's goods; and, contrary to the State's intentions and expressions, plungeth himself and some others in most unnecessary and unrighteous plundering, both of Dutch and French, and English also, to our great grief, who protested against such abuse of our power from England; and the end of it is to the shame and reproach of himself, and the very English name as all these parts do witness.

Sir, our second answer is, (that we may not lay all the load upon other men's backs,) that possibly a sweet cup hath rendered many of us wanton and too active, for we have long drunk of the cup of as great liberties as any people that we can hear of under the whole heaven. We have not only been long free (together with all New England) from the iron yoke of wolfish bishops, and their popish ceremonies, (against whose cruel oppressions God raised up your noble spirit in Parliament) but we have sitten quiet and dry from the streams of blood spilt by that war in our native country. We have not felt the new chains of the Presbyterian tyrants, nor in this colony have we been consumed with the over-zealous fire of the (so called) godly christian magistrates. Sir, we have not known what an excise means; we have almost forgotten what tithes are, yea, or taxes either, to church or commonwealth. We could name other special privileges, ingredients of our sweet cup, which your great wisdom knows to be very powerful (except more than ordinary watchfulness) to render the best of men wanton and forgetful. But, blessed by your love, and your loving heart and hand, awakening any of our sleepy spirits by your sweet alarm; and blessed by your noble family, root and branch, and all your pious and prudent engagements and retirements. We hope you shall no more complain of the saddening of your loving heart by the men of Providence town or of Providence colony, but that when we are gone and rotten, our posterity and children after us shall read in our town records your pious and favorable letters and loving kindness to us, and this our answer, and real endeavor after peace and righteousness; and to be found, Sir, your most obliged, and most humble servants, the town of Providence, in Providence colony, in New England.

GREGORY DEXTER, *Town Clerk*

The method Roger Williams was always suggesting, since the early days of the settlement when the first officers elected in Providence were called arbitrators, was the mediation of differences by arbitration. His suggestion in this case that the points of dispute be put up to an umpire, foreshadows many of the most useful practices of American business and government procedure of our own day. In the letter to the town of Providence first quoted he went on: ". . . I pray your loving leave to tell you, that if I were in your soul's case, I would send into your opposites such a line as this: 'Neighbors, at the constant request, and upon the constant mediation which our neighbor Roger Williams, since his arrival, hath used to us, both for pacification and accomodation of our sad differences, and also upon the late endeavors in all the other towns for an union, we are persuaded to remove our obstruction, viz: that paper of contention between us, and to deliver it into the hands of our aforesaid neighbor and to obliterate that order, which that paper did occasion. This removed, you may be pleased to meet with and debate freely, and vote in all the matters with us, as if such grievances had not been amongst us. Secondly, if yet aught remain grievous, which we ourselves, by free debate and conference, cannot compose, we offer to be judged and censured by four men, which out of any part of the colony you shall choose two, and we the other . . ."

He had barely gotten Coddington's and Dyer's dispute settled, and had induced the Arnolds and his old friend Richard Smith, to whom he had sold the trading post at Cawcawmsqussik, where he still went to preach once a month, to drop their plans of joining up with Massachusetts or Connecticut and to give the free colony a real trial, when that William Harris who had come with him (then poor and destitute) the first spring to plant at Seekonk, began to get big ideas and to raise himself up a party in town meeting. This Harris turned out to be the Thersites of the enterprise. He had been in turn a Seeker, a Baptist, a Gortonist, a Generalist, and now he suddenly went in for the extreme anarchist doctrine that no type of civil government should bind a godly man. Just as things were settling down to some sort of order Harris raised the cry of 'No lords, no masters' that drew from Williams the matured statement of his opinion on the limits of political liberty:

To the Town of Providence

(Providence, January, 1654-5)

That I should ever speak or write a tittle, that tends to such an infinite liberty of conscience, is a mistake, and which I have ever disclaimed and abhorred. To prevent such mistakes, I shall at present only propose this case: There goes many a ship to sea, with many hundred souls in one ship, whose weal and woe is common, and is a true picture of a commonwealth, or a human combination or society. It hath fallen out sometimes, that both papists and protestants, Jews and Turks, may be embarked in one ship; upon which supposal I affirm, that all the liberty of conscience, that ever I pleaded for, turns upon these two hinges—that none of the papists, protestants, Jews, or Turks, be forced to come to the ship's prayers or worship, nor compelled from their own particular prayers or worship, if they practise any. I further add, that I never denied, that notwithstanding this liberty, the commander of this ship ought to command the ship's course, yea, and also command that justice, peace and sobriety, be kept and practised, both among the seamen and all the passengers. If any of the seamen refuse to perform their services, or passengers to pay their freight; if any refuse to help, in person or purse, towards the common charges or defence; if any refuse to obey the common laws and orders of the ship, concerning their common peace or preservation; if any shall mutiny and rise up against their commanders and officers; if any should preach or write that there ought to be no commanders or officers, no laws nor orders, nor corrections nor punishments;—I say, I never denied, but in such cases, whatever is pretended, the commander or commanders may judge, resist, compel and punish such transgressors, according to their deserts and merits. This if seriously and honestly minded, may, if it so please the Father of lights, let in some light to such as willingly shut not their eyes.

I remain studious of your common peace and liberty.

ROGER WILLIAMS

This time Williams had the best of the argument and in 1657 the four towns firmly united in a workable government, first under his presidency and then under that of Benedict Arnold.

Jails were built, taxes were levied, officers of the law appeared in the records. Rhode Island and Providence Plantations now had all the police machinery that is unavoidable in organized life. But I think it is safe to say that the police machinery was more under the control of the average citizen than it had been on any spot on earth before. The liberties included foreigners as well as citizens. In 1652 the General Court held at Warwick had ruled that Negro as well as white or Indian bondservants should go free after ten years' servitude, or whenever they reached the age of twentyfour, and had slapped a fine of forty pounds on anyone who sold a servant out of the colony to escape the law. Not long after a group of Jews were allowed to open a synagogue at Newport.

The four towns grew and throve off boatbuilding and trade. But Roger Williams was to have no peace in his life. The government was barely organized and functioning before the wave of Quaker revivalism swept along the coast, and, naturally, William Harris was one of the first to take fire and to denounce hypocrites and whited sepulchers in high places, and Roger Williams among them.

Roger Williams' first effort in regard to the new sect was to try to protect them from the Massachusetts magistrates, who as usual lost their heads when they felt that law and order were threatened. The General Court passed a series of savage decrees against the Quakers, finally condemning any of them to death who should set foot within their bounds. Under Williams' influence his General Assembly wrote to Massachusetts, as did towns in Maine, New Hampshire and Williams' friend Winthrop of Connecticut, to try to argue, if not humanity, at least a little commonsense into the heads of the Elect. The statement of the Narragansett people had that combination of worldly wisdom and humane fervor that made Williams so really a statesman: "We have no law among us, whereby to punish any for only declaring by words etc., their minds and understanding concerning the things of God, as to salvation and an eternal condition. And we, moreover, find that those places where these people are only opposed by arguments in discourse, there they least of all desire to come. And we are informed that they begin to loathe this place, for that they are not opposed by civil authority, but with all patience and meekness are suffered to say over their pretended revelations and admonitions; nor are they like or able to gain many here to their way. Surely we find that they delight to be persecuted by civil powers; and when they are so, they are like to gain more adherents by the conceit of their patient suffering than by consent of their pernicious saying."

The Massachusetts magistrates paid no more attention to this piece of simple good sense than did their successors two hundred and fifty years later to the opinion of the world in the case of Sacco and Vanzetti. To the bitter indignation of most of the towns around, they hanged four Quakers on Boston Common, including a certain Mary Dyer, who was the wife of the John Dyer prominent in the affairs of Rhode Island. It was the Restoration government in England, getting ready to put to death old friends and co-workers of the Boston magistrates with even bloodier show, that sent the order that the barbarities against the Quakers must stop.

Once the news of the Restoration came, even before they began to feel its full import, the American colonists were too busy worrying about how it would affect their lives and their various types of social organization to pay much attention to the rantings of fanatics. That winter Williams wrote affectionately to Winthrop about the state of their world in general:

> Loving respects to yourself and Mrs. Winthrop, etc. Your loving lines in this cold, dead season, were as a cup of your Connecticut cider, which we are glad to hear abounds with you, or of that western metheglin, which you and I have drunk at Bristol together, etc. Indeed, it is the wonderful power and goodness of God, that we are preserved in our dispersions among these wild, barbarous wretches. I hear not of their excursions this winter, and should rejoice if, as you hint, Uncas and his brother were removed to Long Island, or any where, or else, as I have sometimes motioned, a truce for some good term of years might be obtained amongst them. But how should we expect that the streams of blood should stop among the dregs of mankind when the bloody issues flow so fresh and fearfully among the finest and most refined sons of men and sons of God. We have not only heard of the four northern nations, Dania, Swedia, Anglia, and Belgia, all Protestants, (heretics and dogs, with the Pope, etc.) last year tearing and devouring one another, in the narrow straits and eminent passages and turns of the sea and the world; but we also

have a sound of the Presbyterians' rage new burst out into flames of war from Scotland, and the independent and sectarian army provoked again to new appeals to God, and engagements against them. Thus, while this last Pope hath plied with sails and oars, and brought all his popish sons to peace, except Portugal, and brought in his grand engineers, the Jesuits, again to Venice, after their long just banishment, we Protestants are woefully disposed to row backwards, and bring our sails aback-stays, and provoke the holy, jealous Lord, who is a consuming fire, to kindle again those fires from Rome and hell, which formerly consumed (in Protestant countries) so many precious servants of God. The late renowned Oliver, confessed to me, in close discourse about the Protestants' affairs, etc., that he yet feared great persecutions to the Protestants from the Romanists, before the downfall of the Papacy. The histories of our fathers before us, tell us what huge bowls of the blood of the saints that great whore had been drunk with, in (now) Protestant dominions. Sure her judgment will ring through the world, and it is hoped it is not far from the door. Sir, you were, not long since, the son of two noble fathers, Mr. John Winthrop and Mr. H. Peters. It is said they are both extinguished. Surely, I did ever, from my soul, honor and love them even when their judgments led them to afflict me. Yet the Father of Spirits spares us breath, and I rejoice, Sir, that your name (amongst the New England magistrates printed, to the Parliament and army, by H. Nort. Rous, etc.,) is not blurred, but rather honored, for your prudent and moderate hand in the late Quakers' trials amongst us. And it is said, that in the late Parliament, yourself were one of the three in nomination for General Governor over New England, which however that design ripened not, yet your name keeps up a high esteem, etc. I have seen your hand to a letter to this colony, as to your late purchase of some land at Narragansett. The sight of your hand hath quieted some jealousies amongst us, that the Bay, by this purchase, designed some prejudice to the liberty of conscience amongst us. We are in consultations how to answer that letter, and my endeavor shall be, with God's help, to welcome, with both our hands and arms, your interest in these parts, though we have no hope to enjoy your personal residence amongst us. I rejoice to hear that you gain, by new plantations, upon this wilderness. I fear that many precious souls will be glad to hide their heads, shortly, in these parts. Your candle and mine draws towards its end. The Lord graciously help us to shine in light and love universally, to all that fear his name, without that monopoly of the affection to such of our own persuasion only; for the common enemy, the Romish wolf, is very high in resolution, and hope, and advantage, to make a prey on all, of all sorts that desire to fear God. Divers of our neighbors thankfully re-salute you. We have buried, this winter, Mr. Olney's son, whom, formerly, you heard to be afflicted with a lethargy. He lay two or three days wholly senseless, until his last groans. My youngest son, Joseph, was troubled with a spice of epilepsy. We used some remedies, but it hath pleased God, by his taking of tobacco, perfectly, as we hope, to cure him. Good Mr. Parker, of Boston, passing from Prudence Island, at his coming on shore, on Seekonk land, trod awry upon a stone or stick, and fell down, and broke the small bone of his leg. He hath lain by of it all this winter, and the last week was carried to Boston in a horse litter. Some fears there was of a gangrene. But, Sir, I use too much boldness and prolixity. I shall now only subscribe myself,

Your unworthy friend,

ROGER WILLIAMS

Sir, my loving respects to Mr. Stone, Mr. Lord, Mr. Allen, Mr. Webster, and other loving friends.

John Clark managed to get the royal regime to confirm the Rhode Island and Providence charter and to appoint Roger Williams one of the assistants in charge of the new government until elections should be held. Indeed Charles Second himself seems to have had a certain interest in protecting the experiments in America, although he never scrupled to slice the continent up on paper into enormous grants whenever he wanted to make a favorite or a creditor happy. Anyway confirmation of the charter gave Williams a new breathing space.

During these years of reaction and repression, there was a definite slackening of the rate of growth of the colonies in America. The first wave of migration from England had spent itself fifteen years back. The wars with Holland cut trade with the West Indies. The richer part of the fur trade was now channeled through the St. Lawrence and in French hands. Although the Navigation Acts, forbidding the colonies to trade anywhere except with the mother country, were not yet very strictly enforced, the pace of development was slowing down.

The first boom period was over. A new generation of farmers and stockraisers and shipbuilders was taking the place of the first generation of fishermen, traders and explorers. The settlements were tightening, consolidating, throwing down roots into the rocky New England earth. People, wrote Williams with apprehension, were beginning to itch with 'a depraved Appetite after the great Vanities, Dreams and Shadows of this vanishing Life—great Portions of Land—Land in this Wilderness, as if Men were in great necessity and danger for want of great Portions of Land . . .' Again in a letter to Winthrop he wrote: "SIR;—Meeting (this instant before Sunrise, as I went to my field, etc.) an Indian running back for a Glasse, bound for your parts, I thought (since *nihil sine Providentia*) that an Higher Spirit than his own, might purposely (like Jonathan's Boy) send him back for this hasty salutation to your kind self and your dear Companion.

"Sir, I waited for a gale to return you many cordial thanks for your many Cordial expressions of ancient kindness to myself, and the publike peace and Wellfare: I have since been occasioned and drawn (being nominated in the Charter to appear again upon the Deck,) from my beloved Privacie; my humble desires are to contribute my poor mite (as I have ever, and I hope ever shall) to preserve plantation and publike interest of the whole, and not interest of this or that town, colony, opinion, etc.

"Sir, when we that have been the eldest, etc., are rotting, (to-morrow or next day) a Generation will act, I fear, far unlike the first Winthrops and their Modells of Love; I fear that the common Trinitie of the world (Profit, Preferment, Pleasure) will here be the tria omnia, as in all the world beside: that

Prelacy and Papacy too will in this wilderness predominate, that God Land will be (as now it is) as great a God with us English as God Gold was with the Spaniards, etc. While we are here, noble Sir, let us *viriliter hoc agere, rem agere humanum, divinam, Christianam,* which I believe is all of a most publike Genius . . ."

It was about land that Williams' next contest developed with William Harris, who besides becoming a Quaker seems to have become a man of property full of legalistic quirks. The row was about the interpretation of the original deeds from the Narraganset Indians to the Providence and Pawtuxet grants. Williams, an old man now, and set in his ways, defended bitterly what he considered the rights of his Indian friends. He seems also to have resented the application of English legal chicanery to matters concerning the colony. He wanted all disputes settled by reasonable and friendly arbitration. At one time the argument got so hot that the Williams party lodged Harris in the new town jail. Eventually Harris won his suit against the Town of Providence, but Williams, who among his other avocations was the chief surveyor for the region, seems to have cannily defeated him by his own peculiar method of surveying the grants. The dispute was the beginning of the long wrangle between the proprietors and the voters that was to keep the New England towns stirred up for the next hundred years.

William Harris took ship to England to put his case before the Privy Council, but he had the bad luck to be captured by Algerine pirates, who with the laying up of the great fleet that had ruled the seas under Cromwell, and the reduction of England to a puny vassal of Louis Fourteenth under Charles Second's reckless rule, had been picking up British ships with impunity. He was carried off to Africa and sold as a slave. His friends ransomed him and got him back to London, but his health was ruined and he died there. According to the already fastfading convictions of the puritan generation, that saw the hand of God in every item of the news of the day, that probably meant that poor William Harris was in the wrong.

Meanwhile George Fox, after a record of imprisonments and quiet defiance of authority that surpassed Honest John Lilburne's (who himself had died a Quaker), had traveled, making converts at every meeting, to the West Indies and up the Chesapeake and across the Delaware and through the wilds of West Jersey and up the Sound to Narragansett Town, where he spoke in a great barn. He seems to have left the country without meeting Williams, whom he probably scorned as a rival and outmoded apostle, but his followers, puffed up with the pride of their humility, seem to have taunted Williams and declared that the old man had been afraid to meet and dispute with their great George Fox. One Quaker came to the old man to discourse on heavenly things while he was gathering apples, helped by an Indian servant, on the townlot next his house in Providence. The adjoining house had burned and the fence had been broken down and Williams was afraid that the crop would be stolen. So when the Quaker addressed him he said, "Come let us gather apples," intending to argue as he picked.

The Quaker considered this a great show of worldliness and proclaimed far and wide that Roger Williams was afraid to meet the Friends. That got the old man's dander up, so he challenged three Quakers to argue the whole question of religion with him on three successive days. When they took him up, Williams (he was possibly seventyone at the time) shoved off in his heavy boat, 'rowing all day with my old bones so that I got to Newport towards midnight before the morning appointed.' The arguments on both sides were longwinded and abusive and don't seem to have clarified the points at issue, though they were the occasion for the parade of a vast amount of theological lore and prejudice. When Williams published his side of the story under the name of *George Fox digg'd out of his Burrows* the book at least, for the first time in his life, earned him the approbation of the Boston hierarchy of ministers, who began to announce that, in spite of his youthful follies, he had 'the root of the matter in him.' Too bad John Cotton and old John Winthrop didn't live to read it.

However much Williams pleased the Massachusetts synod, the Quakers seem to have convinced the folks back home. The Williams party lost control of the Assembly and the Quakers elected most of the town and provincial officers. Though they differed on doctrinal points, on the main question of toleration and civil liberties they were in agreement, so the Quaker regime changed things very little. It did intensify the already strong pacifism of the settlers.

This pacifism had a rude interruption in 1676 with the rising of the Wampanoags and of most of the great Narraganset tribe among whose chiefs Williams had so many lifelong friends, and whose interests, as well as those of the small holders, he had been trying to protect in the litigation with Harris. The leader of the Indians was a son of that Massasoit (also known as Ousamaquin) who had put Williams up in his lodge at Sowams the snowy winter the magistrates had driven him out of Salem.

The young chief had been much with the whites as a boy and they had given him the nickname of Philip of Macedon. He was a man of intelligence and energy and as he grew up watched with bitter feelings the progressive weakening and disinheritance of his people, their loss of lands and hunting-grounds and their sinking to a helot position, in spite of the generous friendliness with which, ever since the days of old Canonicus, many of the tribes had kept the peace with the whites.

The war was long and bloody. No quarter was given on either side. Williams led the Providence trainbands as captain and organized the building of the fort that saved the lives of most of the settlers when the town was attacked by an overwhelming force of Indians. The women and children had been sent to the islands. Though few lives were lost, the settlers were not able to save the town. Twenty houses were burned before their eyes.

There's a story that old Williams sallied out from the fort with only a cudgel in his hand to meet the attacking braves to try to talk them out of the attack as he had talked them out of so many bloody projects in the past. This time it was no use. On both sides they knew it was a war to the death. It ended with the complete destruction of the tribes of the Narragansett region and of all the system of mutual fair play between white man and native that Williams had worked so hard all his life to establish.

In the town records of Providence for 1676 there's an entry that gives us one of those views of the past as bright and sharp and close as something going on in a brightly lit adjoining room seen through a crack in the wall:

> Memorand: that on the 25 of August (so-called) there came into this Towne One Chuff an Indian, so-called in time of peace, because of his Surliness against the English. He could Scarce come in being wounded Some dayes before by Providence Men. His wounds were corrupted and stanck and because he had bene a Ring leader all the War to most of the Mischiefs to our Howses and Cattell and what English he could: the Inhabitants of the Towne cried out for Justice against him, threatning themselves to kill him if the Authoritie did not. For which Reason the Cap. Roger Williams caused the Drum to be beat, the Toun Councell and Councell of War called, all cried for Justice and Execution: the Councell of War gave sentence and he was shot to Death, to the great satisfaction of the Towne.

Roger Williams, if no one else, must have remembered the old days when he had 'thirsted after the native's souls.' He was an old man and the world he had wanted, that he had always been willing to risk his life in building, was crumbling to pieces at the edge of fulfillment. In his letter of about this time to Captain John Mason, still in defense of his colony against Massachusetts encroachment, he wrote, falling into one of those momentary moods when a man feels too acutely the narrow limits of any one man's effort in the world: "Alas, Sir, in calm midnight Thoughts, what are these Leaves and Flowers, and Smoke and Shadows, and Dreams of Earthly Nothings, about which we poor fools and children, as David saith, disquiet ourselves in Vain? Alas what is all the scuffling of this World for but *Come will you smoke it?*"

There's another oldtime New England story about King Philip's War that used to be told every schoolchild. When the Indians attacked the town of Hadley a graybearded man wearing the armor of the roundhead troopers of the New Model, suddenly came out of some hiding place and stepped up to lead the defense. It was his coolness and soldierly training that beat off the attack and saved the town. After the battle the Hadley people looked for him to thank him, but he had gone. According to the legend this man was Goffe, one of the signers of King Charles' deathwarrant who had come to America with another of them, his father-in-law, Major General Whalley, the brother of the Jane Whalley whom Roger Williams had so burned to marry when he had been the young chaplain at the Mashams' house at Otes. They had managed to leave England on the ship *Prudent Mary* the day Charles Second was proclaimed king. They had both been great men under Cromwell. With a third member of the High Court, Dixwell, who lived happily for many years in New Haven under an assumed name, they had managed to keep out of sight during all the hue and cry after them and had lived hidden in Connecticut valley towns ever since the Restoration.

A number of their letters were found among Increase Mather's papers. For years, that canny brahmin seems to have managed to forward their letters to their wives and families in England, in the care of that same Jane Whalley, now an old widowed woman fallen on evil days. Eventually it became too difficult or too dangerous. Goffe's last letter from somewhere in the backwoods west of the rich riverlands gives you the feeling of how utterly, even in America where men cherished the memory of the Commonwealth as much as they dared, the puritan generation was rooted out of English life. The letter is dated April 2, 1679, and ends with this paragraph: ". . . I am also greatly longing to hear from my poor Desolat Relations; and whether my last summer's letters gott safe to them. It was a trouble to me that I was forced to send them to yourself so badly directed, and hoped to have received a few lines from you concerning it, and how you would have me direct them for the future. I beseech you, Sir, to pardon my giving you this long and great trouble, and let me receive a word or two by this Bearer. If I have missed it in anything, upon the least intimation, I shall endeavor to rectify it, or reform for the future. Dear Sir I earnestly beg the continuance of your fervent prayers to the Lord for me and mine . . ."

While in England all that was left of the great blaze of the Commonwealth generation were a few paltry embers being trodden out by the courts under the lead of 'hanging judge' Jeffreys, in America the republicans had taken root. In Providence Roger Williams lived on a lively old patriarch almost to the end of the century. Changing generations of young men, who were American and not English, grew up under the influence of his personality, yet as alien to it as a new growth of scrub pine growing up under the shade of an old oak. That doesn't mean that he left no influence behind him. But it was much later that the seeds of his convictions started to sprout vigorously again in the minds of the descendants of the settlers. The year of the quiet fading out of Roger Williams' life in the retirement of his prosperous and loving colony was also the year that Judge Jeffreys did to death the last of the other mighty minds of the Commonwealth generation. After a trial that was one of the most shocking to any sense of justice or fairplay in the long history of Anglo-Saxon frameups, Algernon Sidney was beheaded on Tower Hill on December 7, 1683.

As he belonged to one of the great families of England, the

King had allowed him to be beheaded instead of suffering the usual fate for treason in the reaction years, the fate that Jeffreys, lolling in his seat with his wig askew, is said to have read out to him with peculiar drawling pleasure letting his lips curl luxuriously over every word: "That you be carried hence to the place from whence you came and from thence you shall be drawn upon a hurdle to the place of execution where you shall be hanged by the neck, and, being alive, cut down. Your privy members shall be cut off and burned before your face, your head severed from your body, and your body divided into four quarters and then be disposed at the pleasure of the King."

Sidney called on God to witness that he had not had a fair trial and that his blood was not on England's head, but on the heads of his prosecutors. Jeffreys roared at him that he had better stop complaining and start getting ready for the next world as obviously he was not fit for this. Sidney held out his arm and told Jeffreys to try his pulse to see if it beat one whit the faster. The jailers hurried him out of the courtroom and Jeffreys went back to his drinking with the strange carrion birds that were his familiars.

For years they had been out to get Sidney, and at last managed to snarl him in one of the plots that kept being discovered by a gang around the King that was making a very good thing out of the repression during the hysterical period of the bill against a Catholic succession. He had come back to England, after assurances that he would not be molested that had come through his friend Henry Savile, the ambassador to France, to see his old father, the Earl of Leicester and to straighten out a tangle of lawsuits through which his brothers were trying to get his inheritance away from him. Since the Restoration he had been roaming round the Continent from Germany to France to Italy and back again, everywhere finding any employment to which he could put his abilities as a soldier and a diplomat blocked by letters and agents from King Charles. Oddly enough, it was in Rome where he was best treated. In spite of the fact that he was known as a republican and an extreme Protestant, the cardinals treated him kindly and Pamphili put him up for months at Frascati at his famously beautiful Villa Belvedere. There he found 'health, quiet, solitude' and managed to settle down for the first time in his life to a course of consistent study . . . "I am with some eagerness fallen to reading," he wrote his father, "and find so much satisfaction in it, that, though I every morning see the sunrise, I never go abroad till six or seven of the clock at night; yet cannot be so sure of my temper as to know certainly how long this manner of life will please me. I cannot but rejoice a little to find, that when I wander as a vagabond through the world, forsaken of my friends, poor and known only to be a broken limb of a shipwrecked faction; I yet find humanity and civility from those who are at the height of fortune and reputation. But I do also know well I am in a strange land, how far those civilities do extend, and that they are too airy to feed and clothe a man . . ." It was these periods of quiet leisure that gave him the opportunity to set down the ideas he had been slowly maturing concerning the relationship between the citizen and the state, in those *Discourses Concerning Government* that did so much to keep the spirit of liberty alive in successive generations of Englishmen and Americans.

The Restoration had caught Algernon Sidney at Elsinore on a diplomatic mission for the Protector to mediate a senseless war between Sweden and Denmark, in accord with the Commonwealth policy of working for a union of protestant Europe. While there was still hope that if he behaved like a repentant sinner the royalist party would take him in, he cut off all chance of compromise by scrawling out, when he was asked to sign in a visitors' book at the University of Copenhagen, the libertarian motto

> '. . . manus haec inimica tyrannis
> Ense petit placidum, sub libertate quietum.'

In England various friends and relations had tried to arrange a sure amnesty for him. He was doubtful, with some reason, as he wrote the old earl: "I confess we are naturally inclined to delight in our own country and I have a particular love of mine. I hope I have given some testimony of it. I think that being exiled from it is a great evil and would redeem myself from it with the loss of a great deal of my blood. But when that country of mine, which used to be esteemed a paradise, is now like to be made a stage of injury; the liberty which we hoped to establish oppressed; luxury and lewdness set up in its height, instead of the piety, virtue, sobriety and modesty, which we hoped God by our hands would have introduced; the best of our nation made a prey to the worst; the parliament court and army corrupted; the people enslaved; all things vendible; no man safe but by such evil and infamous means as flattery and bribery; what joy can I have in my own country in this condition? Is it a pleasure to see, that all I love in the world is sold and destroyed? Shall I renounce all my old principles and learn the vile court-arts, and make my peace by bribing some of them? Shall their corruption and vice buy my safety? . . . I have ever had it in my mind, that when God should cast me into such a condition as that I cannot save my life but by doing an indecent thing; he shows me the time is come wherein I should resign it; and when I cannot live in my own country, but by such means as are worse than dying in it, I think he shows me I ought to keep myself out of it . . . In short where Vane, Lambert, Haselrigge cannot live in safety, I cannot live at all. If I had been in England, I must have expected a lodging with them . . . I must expect to follow their example in suffering as I have been their companion in acting . . ."

Sidney had found his political education, like so many other English noblemen's sons, in Parliament. An irrepressible brawling young officer who had seen service in Ireland, it had been almost by accident that he had taken the parliament side in the Civil War, and found himself, after being badly wounded in the famous cavalry charge at Marston Moor, one of the popular heroes of the House of Commons. He had taken his position as a good Commonwealthsman seriously from the first and had done his best to oppose Cromwell's rise to supreme power. Even after he was forced to retire to Penhurst, the family estate, he caused great scandal among the Cromwellians and greatly upset the timid earl, and his elder brother Lord Lisle, who was of that great majority who wanted to stand in right with whatever authority there was, by playing, so the story goes, Brutus in a performance of Shakespeare's *Julius Caesar* he put on for the entertainment of his friends. With his long horseface and haughty look and his curly hair and mustache, he looks more like a Cavalier than a Roundhead in the portraits of him that have come down. In his life and in his writings he was the type and embodiment of the aristocratic republican tradition that sprang from the rustic independence of the English country gentleman. Bishop Burnet, who knew him after his return from exile under the assurances of safety that proved so illusory, wrote of him: "That he was a man of extraordinary courage; a steady man even to obstinacy; sincere but of a rough and boisterous temper that could not bear contradiction. He was a christian, but in a peculiar form of his own; he thought it was to be like a divine philosophy in the mind: but he was against all public worship and everything that looked like a church. He was stiff to republican principles, and such an enemy to everything that looked like a monarchy that he felt himself in high opposition against Cromwell, when he was made Protector. He had studied the history of government in all its branches beyond any man I ever knew."

The brutal hurry and disregard of legal forms with which Jeffreys conducted Sidney's trial was too much even for many monarchists. There'd been so many frameups Jeffreys wasn't taking much trouble with them any more. He'd always been able to get his man; he was getting careless about appearances. But his course hadn't long to run. One of the first acts of the new Parliament that followed the crowning of William of Orange and the establishment of constitutional monarchy in 1688 was to reverse the sentence upon Algernon Sidney and to return his property to his heirs.

If in England it seemed as if the Commonwealth generation had lived in vain, in America it was different. Here, on the rocky coast that bounded the wilderness to the westward, the Commonwealth had taken root. The very soil of the New England towns was impregnated with the concept of the duties and liberties of every man alone.

To the last in the Providence records, there are glimpses of Roger Williams as a hale old man. Almost continually he holds office in the small slowly growing community. He is busy reconstituting the town records that the Indians defaced and threw into a pond during the war, he serves as town clerk, as moderator at townmeetings, as captain of the trainband, as arbitrator in the business of disposing of the broken remnants of the Narragansets, some of them being allowed to remain as indentured servants (according to the Rhode Island system) and some of them shipped away as slaves. The last notations in the town record are in connection with a certain Sarah Neile, a poor woman with a child whose father's name, if it had one, does not appear; she has been accused of slandering and vilifying the town and its citizens, and of residing there without consent of the town or 'color of law.' Townmeeting has ordered her to leave. Roger Williams and two other citizens give bond that they will be responsible for her if she should become a public charge to the amount of thirteen pounds, six shillings and four pence, each. By January 27, 1683, something has evidently been done to settle the fate of Sarah Neile, because the bond is remitted by the town clerk. Some time in the spring of that year Roger Williams died and was buried in his own orchard, near his house the Indians had burned and that he had never rebuilt. At the end of a page of the town record somebody has written:

The Venerable Remaines of Mr. Roger Williams, the Father of Providence, the Founder of the Colony, and of Liberty of Conscience

III

ON THE WHITE PORCH OF THE REPUBLIC

Objects for the attention of an American:—Agriculture. *Everything belonging to this art, and whatever has a near relation to it. Useful or agreeable animals which might be transported to America. Species of plants for the farmer's garden.* . . . Gardens *particularly worth the attention of an American because it is the country of all others where the noblest gardens may be made without expense. We have only to cut out the superabundant plants.* . . . Architecture *worth great attention. As we double our numbers every twenty years, we must double our houses. Besides we build of such perishable materials, that one half of our houses must be rebuilt in every space of twenty years, so that in that time, houses are to be built for three-fourths of our inhabitants. It is, then, among the most important arts; and it is desireable to introduce taste into an art which shows so much.* . . . Politics *of each country, well worth studying so far as respects internal affairs. Examine their influence on the happiness of the people. Take every possible occasion of entering into the houses of the laborers, and especially at the moments of their repast; see what they eat, how they are clothed, whether they are obliged to work too hard; whether the government or their landlord takes from them an unjust proportion of their labor; on what footing stands the property they call their own, their personal liberty, &c, &c.* . . . Courts. *To be seen as you would see the tower of London or Menagerie of Versailles, with their lions, tigers, hyenas and other beast of prey.* . . .

CLIPPED FROM THE TRAVEL NOTES THOMAS JEFFERSON JOTTED DOWN FOR TWO YOUNG AMERICANS LEAVING FOR A GRAND TOUR OF EUROPE, JUNE, 1788

1. Preferment and Place

BENJAMIN FRANKLIN, an immensely precocious, immensely industrious, immensely curious young man, not quite turned nineteen, arrived in London for the first time the day before Christmas, 1724, after a rough passage on the ship *London Hope.* Young as he was he had already acquired an uncanny knack for landing with his nose in the butter. With him went James Ralph, a friend with poetic aspirations who was walking out on a wife and child and on the colonial small-town life of Philadelphia to make a career among the theaters and coffeehouses and the fullbottomed literary wigs of Augustan London. They had gone on board as steerage passengers, but young Franklin's engaging manner had won them an invitation up to the cabin. There they occupied the berths and ate the choice stores that had been put on board for a famous admiralty lawyer who at the last minute was prevented from sailing. During the long chilly days of rolling and pitching over the wintry sea Franklin made the acquaintance and won the esteem of a Mr. Denham, a Quaker merchant who had made his pile in America and was on his way back to pay off the creditors he had left behind him in England. Ralph was setting out full of highflown hopes of climbing into preferment and place on an endless ladder of heroic couplets, but Franklin was bound on less exalted business: he was going to London to buy types and presses for Sir William Keith, Governor of Pennsylvania, with which to set up a publishing house. As he supposed, and as the Governor had assured him, letters of recommendation to literary men and friends of that somewhat crackbrained functionary's were in the ship's mailbag when she sailed. They were to establish young Ben's credit, and to put him on the smooth road to fortune.

As it turned out both the young men's hopes of London went up in smoke the first winter. Franklin didn't make his fortune, but in the eighteen months he spent there, in the capital of the growing commercial empire working for his living as a printer and learning the methods and styles of the best shops, he soaked up a surprising amount of the intellectual spirit of the Augustan age.

The London the two young Americans saw and smelt and heard about them when they first stretched their legs, that still felt light from the straining and heaving of the ship, on the muddy cobbles, was already the great capital, the *urbs et orbis* of eighteenth century England. It was a foggy crowded city of clattering lanes and narrow streets, opening here and there into smoothpaved courts and pumpyards and into the new great squares flanked by façades in the very personal style which Sir Christopher Wren had a generation before worked up out of memories of Palladio and Vitruvius for the rebuilding after the great fire of 1666. The greenbrown Thames, cut across by the difficult barrier of London Bridge that divided the barges and wherries of the upcountry river traffic from the seagoing fleets of the crowded tidal estuary, was still the main artery of the city. Like taxidrivers today the sharptongued watermen who ferried passengers from bank to bank and up and down the stream were the carriers of the gossip and wisecracks of the town. But hackney coaches were already multiplying, and passable thoroughfares were opening up to link the wharves and exchanges of the City with the shops and promenades and royal residences and the new town houses of the rich and powerful that were building beyond Westminster and Hyde Park. Seaward and landward along the Thames and on the heights of Hampstead the very special life of the London suburbs had begun.

Although the population of England was only something like eight millions, nearly one tenth of it was crowded into the great seaport city. Franklin already knew three towns: the huddles of tiny brick buildings along wharves that were Boston and New York and the amply spreadout squares of Philadelphia, where the houses opened their back doors on quiet orchards and kitchengardens; but London, where the close-packed houses stretched for miles hemming in grimy docks and ships packed with spars and spiderweb tackle, must have seemed marvelous to him. The streets were full of racket of hugewheeled carts and coaches, and clattered with horses' hoofs and rang with the cries of hucksters, fishwives, oysterwomen, applesellers, boys yelling papers and almanacs and running after gentlemen to shine their shoes. There were few sidewalks as yet, but in the better streets big stone posts protected those on foot from the wheels that squdged through mud and streaming gutters, and from the jostling of porters bowed under heavy loads or of strapping fellows in livery carrying people of means around in sedan chairs. Fops and elegants when they walked carried long canes with silver pommels to help them over the uneven pavements. Women covered their dresses with hoods and cloaks to protect them from the spattering mud and clattered along on wooden pattens. The crowds were full of streetwalkers and pickpockets. At night respectable people went out with misgivings after leaving their valuables at home. Holdups were frequent as few streets were lighted. A vast criminal network was much more actively organized than the police under gangleaders like the famous Jonathan Wild. The days of the mohawks, nickers, and scourers were not quite over. The only protection for the citizen who went out without his own band of chairmen and linkboys was the watch. The watchmen with their pikes and long cloaks went through the streets gingerly in groups and shook their lanterns from corner to corner to call for help when they needed it. Around the waterfront dives, pressgangs were often busy kidnapping seamen for the royal navy. It was a raw tough city where dog eat dog was the law.

The young hopefuls took lodgings at three and sixpence a

week in the anthill's very center, in Little Britain, and began to look about them. When it dawned on Ben that Governor Keith's backing had been all talk and that he had sent him no letters of recommendation at all, he promptly went around to Palmer's famous shop in Bartholemew Close and got himself a job as a compositor. Poor Ralph, stagestruck and full of confidence in his talents, first managed to obtain an interview with Mr. Wilks, the famous actor at Drury Lane, but was advised by that worthy to keep off the boards at all costs. Then he tried to get a publisher to set him up as editor of a weekly that would outdo the *Spectator* and, failing that, to get work as a hack writer or copying documents at the Temple, but it was no use. In the course of his pursuit of the muses, however, he contrived to get himself an attractive mistress, a girl who kept a millinery shop in the Cloisters. Between them they helped Ben spend the money he was saving up for his passage home making the rounds evenings of amusementplaces and coffeehouses and chocolatehouses and theaters. In the first months the free life of the great city so appealed to Ben that he wrote Deborah Read (the girl he was engaged to and whom a few years later he married) warning her that it might be a long time before he was back in Philadelphia. The implication was that he might not come home at all. As the young Americans had been brought up in a land where the stage was considered the very anteroom of hell, it was natural that their main pleasure was in going to the play.

The theater of the reign of wheezy George First of Hanover and his two fat mistresses was the theater of the Restoration in its waning. The middleclass conscience of England, dormant since the death of Prynne, had already risen up in the censorious form of Jeremy Collier, and in the powerful societies for the reformation of manners sponsored as much by nonjurying Tories of the High Church stripe as by Puritans of the dissenting sects, but the Licensing Act that was so to inhibit the growth of the English stage had not yet passed Parliament.

The great masters of the comedy of manners had long since disappeared. Etherege and Wycherley and Farqhar were dead. The versatile architect Vanbrugh's last works were on the boards. Congreve had given up writing and retired to the country.

The comedy of manners had depended on the willingness of brash court wits to laugh at their own vices. But in the court of George First the King didn't understand either the English language or an English joke. The theater, more and more dependent on middleclass patronage, was slowly running down under the suave rule of Colley Cibber and his family. It was becoming largely a theater of revivals, adaptations, translations. A great deal of it stemmed from Molière. After seventyfive years Shakespeare had come back to life, rewritten to the modern taste by Dryden and by the great Cibber himself. As the playhouse broadened its scope to appeal to the City rather than to the court, the plays lost energy and freshness, but the theater was still the living bridge between the working and trading population of London and the closed circles of authority and government. Looking up from the pit or down from among the gods of the gallery, young Franklin and his poetical friend could see face to face the world of power and rank. It was somewhat later that veils of middleclass decorum were to be draped over England until no man's right hand knew what his left hand was doing.

To a curious young man from the colonies, avid for discussion, information and discovery, the coffeehouses and taverns of London were the next great attraction. There men of wit and reputation, indeed all kinds of men, went to meet their friends and to talk. The clubs of the London coffeehouses were like the *tertulias* that survived up into our own time in the cafés of Madrid. Men went there to show themselves and to be seen and to expound and to listen. While they waited for their friends they read the daily papers and the reviews and the newsletters.

A great deal of an Englishman's life was still spent in public places. Englishmen of that day were not yet sealed up into their castes and categories; the Englishman's home had not become the tight shell he scuttled back to after work as nervously avid for privacy as a hermit crab. Even though the brilliant days of Will's Coffee House and the Kit-Cat were over, strangers were taken first thing to the coffeehouses to look at and, if they were lucky, to listen to the Augustan great.

The great they saw, it is true, were the great of a second generation. Addison had obtained preferment and place and the Countess of Warwick and had died. Steele was coming to the end of his gay career paralyzed and broke in a Welsh farmhouse. Swift was living in bitter exile in his Dublin deanery. Pope, the little sickly spidershaped man whose sting was always ready for friend or foe, still lurked in his garden at Twickenham, undisputed master of the realms of gold, but was rarely seen in London.

The piping times had passed when a wellbalanced set of verses, nicely dedicated to a cabinet minister or a royal mistress, could make a young man's fortune. The tone of talk in the coffeehouses was more metaphysical than purely literary or political. A generation that stemmed from Hobbes and Locke was trying to estimate human conduct on a purely material basis. The deists were at work taking Christianity away from the clergy and turning religion into a simple reverence for a First Cause. The notion of the existence of natural laws, like Newton's Law of Gravitation, that a man could try out for himself, was superseding the intense otherworldly imperatives of the last century. The Church of England, re-established on Laud's model, had weathered the High Church reaction, but it had become rather the worldly instrument of government than a supernatural institution. The divine authority that Laud had dreamed of vesting in the King had become diffused through the whole class of landowning gentry. As long as people paid their tithes and occasionally set up the parson to a glass of port, the Church cared less and less about what they thought. A flat and rather sordid but thoroughly sound commonsense was the keynote of the time. Only gradually, as the century grew older, some of the upper layers of thought were to soak up the hot passion for justice of the humanitarian reformers.

Franklin went often to Batson's Coffeehouse in the hope of someday seeing Sir Isaac Newton, who was spending his last years in the quiet post of Master of the Mint, but never got a glimpse of him. He did meet Dr. Mandeville, a Dutch physician who was the Mencken of the day and whose *The Fable of the Bees* was immensely popular at the time, and Sir Hans Sloane, the explorer and botanist and popularizer of quinine. He sold Sir Hans a purse made of asbestos he'd brought with him from America, and went to his house in Bloomsbury Square to see his collection of curios.

But mostly young Ben, who remained, as an American, all his life free from the sense of social classification, associated with printers, mechanics, old ladies in lodginghouses, chance acquaintances of the street and tavern. Ready as a sponge to soak up everything essential he touched, he didn't need to sit across the table from the great masters themselves. The style they had invented was everywhere; the neat jocular verse, the cool prose based on the cadences of conversation, rather than on the boom and bluster of pulpit oratory, pervaded the smoky air of the city. The streets Ben walked in were the streets of Gay's *Trivia*. The groups in the coffeehouses were the *Club* out of *The Spectator*. Events in the world of power were flavored with the sharp partisan bitterness of Swift's pamphlets. The Augustan pomposities of the classical past that Dryden had set up like stage scenery at the end of every vista were focused sharp and clear and small by the diminishing lens of Pope's precise and narrow mind. It is not surprising that in these eighteen months Franklin's writing lost the routine provincial sound of his boyish journalism and that he went home to Philadelphia with one of the simplest and most direct-from-the-lips English styles ever written.

His school of writing was the playhouse and the reviews and the bookstalls where he found secondhand the works of the generation just drawing to a close. From the Augustans he caught the habit of taking for granted a republic of letters, universal brotherhood of brains, curiosity, discovery, which had been implicit in the best works of the age, and which remained the framework of his thought and behavior all his life. The attitude gave scope to that unfenced openness of mind which he was to transmit, in his long career of influencing all classes and types of men, to generations of Americans.

During his eighteen months in London Ben made considerable impression among the printers he worked with by his mechanical skill, his physical strength, his frugal habits and hard work, but they shook their heads at the pert freedom of his conversation on matters human and divine. In his spare time he printed up a number of copies of a small pamphlet, which he was rather ashamed of in later life, called *A Dissertation on Liberty and Necessity, Pleasure and Pain,* embodying in a set of paradoxes the materialistic ideas which, sprouting from Hobbes and Locke and the disillusioned writers of the Restoration, were the commonplaces of the bolder coffeehouse wits of the day. London under the first George was in a debunking state of mind. This kind of backtalk at the droning authority of the pulpit had already been part of the atmosphere of his brother James' newspaper in Boston, daily in revolt against the voice of God as interpreted by the Mathers. In the comparative freedom of London Ben was able to meet this train of thought at the source and to get over the greensickness of the provincial rebel. In its place appeared a broad tolerance of the views and opinions of others and that active and passionate curiosity to examine the world at first hand and to prove whatever can be proved about it by direct and personal experiment that is the basis of the scientific method.

During the latter part of Franklin's eighteen months on the loose, there was another young foreigner in and out of London, moving in more brilliant and fashionable circles, to be sure, but also deriving immense stimulus from the English scene. A brilliant and erratic young Frenchman, who had recently changed his name from Arouet to Voltaire, had managed by his sharp tongue and active pen and by the fantastic impudence of his career to make totalitarian France too hot for him, and was taking refuge for a while in the freedom and hospitality of the Whig country houses of England. The two men who were in their respective ways most to influence the century and to personify it in their own lives never met, but each went home steeped with something that was in the air in London in the seventeen twenties.

When he gave up hope of getting work in the capital James Ralph lit off for the country and got himself a miserably paid job teaching school in a village in Berkshire, leaving the pretty milliner more or less dependent on Ben. From his village, where he went under Franklin's name so as not to demean his own, instead of remittances he sent Franklin by every mail sections of an epic poem he was writing. It was this same poem that later rated Ralph a flick of one of Pope's couplets in the *Dunciad*. Ben, who was rearranging his life on the theory that man was the measure of all things and who very much needed a woman, started to make love to the pretty milliner: after all he was supporting her and he was a thrifty fellow. The milliner wrote Ralph about it and Ralph, stung because Ben appreciated his verses too little and his girlfriend too much, broke off their friendship and said that furthermore Ben's behavior had canceled the debt between them, which by that time amounted to twentyseven pounds sterling.

Ben changed his lodgings and got a job in a different printinghouse, but after his row with Ralph he began to feel homesick for the fresh air of Philadelphia. In England all he had to look forward to was the slummy life of London and hard work for low wages in somebody else's shop. Among his other attainments he had made quite a stir among the young men about town by his skill as a swimmer, so that a friend suggested that the two of them go abroad and bum their way around the Continent teaching swimming to noblemen's sons. Ben was about to take him up, when Mr. Denham, the Quaker merchant he had met on the *London Hope*, offered him a job clerking in a new store he was going to set up in Philadelphia. Ben jumped at the chance and sailed with Mr. Denham for home.

This is how he sums up his gains during that period in London in the first part of his autobiography, which he wrote again in England, years later, a rich and famous man and diplomatic agent of his colony, during a vacation at the country house of the liberal Bishop of St. Asaph: "Thus I spent about eighteen months in London: most part of the time I worked hard at my business, and spent but little upon myself except in seeing plays and in books . . . I had by no means improved my fortune; but I had picked up some very ingenious acquaintance, whose conversation was of great advantage to me; and I had read considerably."

The all too brief journal Franklin kept of his trip home on the *Berkshire* is the first example we have of the clear cool selfless faintly amused style of writing that is the making of the *Autobiography* and of his letters. Instead of the raw youth who had wangled his way into the cabin on the *London Hope*, the Ben Franklin who came back from London on the *Berkshire* was the Franklin the world was gradually to get to know: Mr. Franklin, the sharp man of business so canny in the ways of the world, who understood so well the uses of money and respectability, without ever being quite won by them; Dr. Franklin the philosopher and mechanic, the ingenious amateur who loved to tinker with scientific appliances and with metaphysical notions and droll rhymes and sayings, who out of his keen inspection, quite uncolored by egoism, of the men and women around him, of the weather, of the ocean and its currents, of thunder clouds and of a great series of ingenious contraptions, managed slowly through his long life to build himself up into one of the epic figures of his time, the *bourgeois gentilhomme* who was to set his stamp on the whole American nation.

During the period of young Franklin's stay in London in the seventeen twenties Daniel Defoe, another master of English popular writing, was living in retirement at Stoke Newington. Defoe's *Essay on Projects* had been Franklin's favorite reading when he was a boy in Boston, but he has left no record of having seen or heard of Defoe while he was in London. We don't even know whether Franklin read any of the editions of *Robinson Crusoe* that were coming off the press in rapid succession while he was there. Probably the romantic story of the shipwrecked sailor wouldn't have seemed sufficiently instructive to the ambitious young American: after all desert isles and prints of savage feet were common enough where he came from. But in energy, in diversity of interests and a certain indomitable cheerfulness of outlook there was much in common between the two men. The difference was that Defoe's career was a series of failures while Franklin's was one of the most successful in history.

It is tempting to speculate on how the men would have turned out if their positions had been reversed: if Franklin had stayed on in England, and if, in the course of one of his many difficulties with the police, Defoe had been transported, like so many of the characters in his novels, to America. In spite of the fortyodd years' difference in their ages there is considerable similarity between the characters and backgrounds of the two men. Between them they pretty well sum up the practical aspirations of English men of business rising up on both sides of the Atlantic at the time. Both of them foreshadowed in the cast of their minds the century of invention and industrial growth that was to come.

Defoe, like Franklin, came from the class of dissenting small shopkeepers and artisans. He was the son of a Baptist tallow-chandler named Foe who rose in due time to the more respectable occupation of butcher. Daniel Foe was born in the heart of London in the parish of St. Giles, Cripplegate, about the year of the restoration of Charles Second. He grew up during the period of greatest repression of nonconformists, learned to read on the Bible, as a child piously copied out large sections of it in shorthand, when a rumor went around that the High Churchmen were going to confiscate the dissenters' scriptures, and being deemed a likely youngster by his family, was sent to the academy at Newington Green, under a divine named Morton (who moved to America later and became a vicepresident of Harvard College), to study for the ministry. Young Daniel's bent turned out rather for this world than for the next, so he was taken out of the academy and apprenticed to a wine-merchant. In connection with the business he traveled in Spain and Portugal and probably in the Low Countries, rose rapidly in the world, got caught in the speculative fever of the time, and became such a successful man of business that he had failed before he was thirty for the sum of £17,000. Meanwhile his non-conformism had taken political form. He had written Whig pamphlets and 'ridden out' with Monmouth's premature and shortlived rebellion against the last Stuart, and on the great day of William of Orange's entry into London, had been seen, wearing a new wig and the gaudiest outfit money could buy, riding a fine horse in the protestant monarch's train.

But the England that emerged from under the courtly brilliance and the bloodshed of eighteen years of Stuart reaction was no longer the rapidly evolving fluid society of Elizabeth and the Commonwealth. It was the 'tight little island' of highly stratified castes that continued almost to our own day. At the bottom was the great mass of laborers and tenants, disfranchised, illiterate and helpless, a prey to pressgangs and recruiting sergeants and laws against change of residence or association, under the direct, often paternal, but always absolute rule of the magistrates and country squires. In the early years of the eighteenth century, a period of rising prosperity, wages tended, it is true, to rise in relation to the price of wheat, so that the working class was possibly in better shape economically than in the century before, but opportunity for a working man to improve his station in the world was almost nil.

Immediately above the working class came the stratum that Defoe and Franklin came from, the dissenting tradesmen and artisans, the undestroyed remnant of the defeated Commonwealth. They were barred by law from holding office, and separated from the rest of the community by differences in social and religious habits. Above them came the landowning gentry, who governed the country districts through the assizes as justices of the peace, whose sons went to the universities and made up the personnel of the great institutions of the Law and the Established Church. These county families were already allying themselves with the rich bankers and merchants and shipowners of the towns, with the commercial interest that gradually grew in importance until eventually it swallowed everything else.

At the very top there remained in ermine and coronets the remnants of the old nobility, a class that had lost its feudal and military prerogatives but kept its power through its great entailed estates and through the prestige of the House of Lords. But the House of Lords itself was coming, through the influence of the bishops and the creation of new peers for political purposes by whatever party happened to be in power, to represent the great institutions as such, rather than hereditary power. Feudalism in the continental sense had been broken up under the Tudors. The ladders of ascent to the upper levels of society, as the eighteenth century opened, were already pretty much established as the universities, the church, the acquisition of land: for a dissenting tradesman like Daniel Foe there was little hope of reaching even the foot of any of these ladders.

After his bankruptcy Defoe had to hide out for a while, first in the sanctuary round the Mint and later in Bristol, where, as bailiffs and process servers only operated on weekdays, he was able to come out for a walk on Sundays and, noticeable on account of his elegant dress and fashionable manner, was known to the townspeople as the 'Sunday Gentleman.' Eventually he managed to satisfy his creditors and to get back to London.

He already had taken up the habit of picking up a little money by writing when business got bad. He caught the attention of his adored King William by the satirical poem *The True Born Englishman* taking off the perennial prejudice against foreigners, and was rewarded for his faithfulness to the constitutional monarchy by a couple of small positions, that of director of a lottery and collector of a tax on glass works, and, so he tells us, by the personal friendship of the subtle Hollander himself. It is possibly under William that he started the sort of backstairs information bureau for the Government which he conducted during several subsequent reigns. In spite of his bankruptcy, he was very much the prosperous merchant at this time, with a mistress and a country house at Tilbury and a small yacht of his own on the Thames Estuary.

Defoe was forging boldly ahead as one of the leaders of the King's party, when the King's horse stumbled and threw him while he was riding in the park. All over England Tories and Jacobites drank the health of the horse; only the dissenters were really devoted to the House of Orange. William was already in bad health and never recovered from his injuries. After the death of his royal idol, nothing ever went completely well with Daniel *De Foe*. Somewhere during his rise in fortune he had managed to get the French particle into his name. He clung to it through good times and bad. It was the only respectable acquisition he never lost.

The reign of Queen Anne came in like a lion. The Queen was a sickly rather querulous creature very much under the thumb of her women friends and of the highflying tory divines. Her one passion was for the Church, for Laud's High Church of

England that taught passive obedience to the monarchy and touching for the king's evil. The Jacobite reactionaries felt that her reign was a chance to restore the Stuart line and the good old times. The Roman Catholics encouraged by her high-churchiness were raising their heads hopefully. The country gentlemen of the tory Parliament felt that the time had come to squelch the nonconformists who had been getting too uppety under the last reign.

Defoe jumped flatfootedly into the row by publishing a pamphlet called *A Short Way With Dissenters* which anticipated the ironic method of Swift's *Modest Proposal* for solving the Irish question by selling steaks off Irish babies, by proposing a series of measures against dissenters so tough that Defoe thought they'd seem funny. The highflying divines fell into the trap and took the recommendations of the pamphlet seriously. The dissenters themselves were too scared by the fire and brimstone being breathed out against them to appreciate the joke and Defoe found himself in hot water indeed. In spite of abject apologies and his very characteristic offer to raise a regiment of horse and go fight for the Queen in the Low Countries, he was arrested and sentenced to the pillory and to imprisonment at the Queen's pleasure.

There followed one of those explosions of popular feeling that have made and kept England a free country throughout the centuries in spite of despotic laws, a rigid caste system and the dominance of the property interest. Defoe's exposure in the pillory turned into an ovation. Instead of emptying chamberpots on his head and throwing rotten vegetables at him, the townspeople of London drank his health in mugs of ale, and brought him nosegays. Hawkers did a landoffice business selling copies of his *Hymn to Pillory* and, the last day he was brought out, the pillory itself was wreathed in greenery and flowers. The joke was turned back on the highflyers and the tory divines around the Queen.

In the excitement there was a cabinet shakeup and a moderately whiggish country gentleman from Devonshire named Robert Harley got into the saddle. Harley came from a puritan family. He had been Speaker of the House of Commons when Defoe was riding to prominence at the head of the friends of good King William at the time of the Kentish petition. While Defoe was in jail, strings were being pulled in his behalf by William Penn and other highly placed friends of toleration, and Harley, who understood the power of the press, got the idea that Defoe's writing might be useful to him. After much devious negotiation, Defoe emerged from prison the editor of *The Review* and Harley's backstairs confidant.

Meanwhile Defoe's latest commercial venture, a tile factory, had gone to smash and with it his hopes of a really respectable business career. Swift, too, was to work for Harley, but he went in to see the minister by the front door, as befitted a learned churchman, while Defoe had to use the tradesman's entrance. Swift wrote for the court and the universities and the literate gentry. Defoe wrote for the business men and artisans and apprentices of London. In the end Swift pulled a deanery out of his work: all Defoe got for infinitely greater service was a wavering subsidy and a furtive career under continual threat from bailiffs and magistrates.

During the years of Harley's administration it was Defoe's job to explain his policies to the commercial interest in *The Review.* He traveled continually about the country looking into the state of public opinion and feeling out the electoral inclinations of the dissenters in the small towns. While Harley was engineering the Act of Union he transferred his activities to Scotland. When Harley turned his coat from moderate Whig to moderate Tory, Defoe and his publications turned with him. Meanwhile he went in for endless speculations on the side, each time sure that this time he'd be in the money, and published, for small change, occasional narratives of current happenings like *Some Account of the Late Storm* and the magnificently written *Apparition of Mrs. Veal.* Defoe was the first writer to understand and to appreciate the possibilities of that great goldmine of journalism, the middleclass public, just as Robert Harley was the first statesman to appreciate its political importance. The fortunes of the two men became inseparable. When Harley went into eclipse Defoe's income suffered, though he managed haltingly to carry on his various and devious activities under Harley's associate, Godolphin. When Queen Anne died and Harley was sent to the Tower, Defoe immediately found himself haled into court.

The wind of the new dynasty filled the sails of the Whigs. Like his patron Defoe had managed to get in wrong with both parties, but especially with the Whigs who felt he had ratted on them. The long administration of Robert Walpole initiated the rule of the whig squirarchy and Defoe's journalistic and political career came to a close. His business speculations had been pretty generally failures. To support his family in the suburban retirement of Stoke Newington, he turned altogether to writing and published volume after volume of educational and improving reading for the middle class. His *Family Instructor*, as well as being used by every butcher, baker, and candlestickmaker in the country, was used by the House of Hanover for the edification of the royal children. The period of the great leveling of the mind through journalism had begun.

Defoe was already a man in his late fifties when he started on the series of the sturdy narratives, which, starting with *Robinson Crusoe* in 1720, expressed so perfectly the ethics, the aspirations, and the daily realities of the life of the rising commercial class. The books were enormously read, but Defoe himself remained the not quite respectable speculator, the flybynight journalist, the backstairs intelligence agent. He never gave up the gambler's hope for the golden throw that would make him rich and respected and raise his family into a higher sphere. But his ship never came in. He lived on far into the century, a miserable peevish old man continually rowing about money matters with his relatives, full of sure secret schemes and combinations for moneymaking that grew more and more fantastic as his mind weakened; and finally in the last year of his life, he ran away from home, frightened by some fancied or real threat of blackmail or of seizure for debt, and died hiding out alone in a London lodginghouse.

Meanwhile Franklin in America, a man of fairly similar background and makeup, was swept up into financial ease by the booming growth of Philadelphia, and found ample room to develop his rich and diverse interests, becoming, as an old man, one of the great and rounded and dominant characters of the century. Dr. Franklin, the philosopher, could meet on a basis of moral and intellectual equality all the great and powerful of the period, without feeling the cramping restrictions of caste or station. In situations where Defoe had to stand cringing with his hat in his hand, Franklin could go forward with a backwoodsman's beaver cap on his wise old noodle instead of the wig that etiquette required.

It is hard to overestimate the advantage Americans in the eighteenth century had in growing up with only the sky over their heads. The slumlife of London cramped and warped the great men of the rising business class in England like a ghetto. When they rose above their station it was only by conforming to all the preconceived deformations of the ruling squirarchy. The defeat of the Commonwealth in the last century had been the defeat of a whole nation. The rise to empire of the gentry through prosperous years of successful trade and booming manufactures and lucky wars and conquests left the small tradesmen and artisans where they were, and depressed the workingclass into the situation Marx was to describe in the middle of the nineteenth century. Only in America were Englishmen able to make real the hopes and possibilities that had been latent in the fervently personal religion of individual conscience and in the discussions and searchings of the men of the Commonwealth. At the end of the century the thirteen colonies were to win their independence and lay the foundation of a new nation because Americans had man for man more opportunity for growth and development than their blood relations in the crowded British Isles where every man's life was hedged into established paths by deeprooted privileges and interests. It was as if the air the Americans breathed were fresher and more lifegiving.

2. Spawn of the Old Cromwellians

IN his entry for January 15, 1766, John Adams noted in his diary that he had ". . . spent the evening with the sons of Liberty, at their own apartment in Hannover Square, near the tree of Liberty. It is a counting room in Chase and Speakman's distillery; a very small room it is.

"John Avery, distiller and merchant, of a liberal education, John Smith the brazier, Thomas Crafts the painter, Edes the printer [of the whig *Boston Gazette*] Stephen Cleverly the brazier, Chase the distiller, Joseph Field master of a vessel, Henry Bass, George Trott the jeweller were present . . . I was invited by Crafts and Trott to go spend an evening with them and some others—Avery was mentioned as one. I went and was very civilly and respectfully treated by all present. We had punch, wine, pipes and tobacco, biscuit and cheeze &c. I heard nothing but such conversation as passes at all clubs, among gentlemen, about the times. No plots, no machinations. They chose a committee to make preparations for grand rejoicings upon the arrival of the news of the repeal of the Stamp Act, and I heard afterwards they are to have such illuminations, bonfires, pyramids, obelisks, such grand exhibitions and such fireworks as were never before seen in America. I wish they may not be disappointed."

The stumpy young lawyer from Braintree had evidently gone somewhat gingerly to call on the leaders of the 'mobility,' as the Tories called the partisans of Sam Adams and James Otis, and was relieved to find them not wearing horns and a tail. When he went to see them the organization of this 'spawn of the old Cromwellians,'—so one of the British functionaries bitterly wrote of them in a letter home,—had reached the final and complete form that was to produce such satisfactory results ten years later when the colonies rose against the Crown.

John Adams, a moody young countryman of philosophic and literary tastes, was just beginning to make a name for himself by his wellpondered arguments before the Circuit Court of Massachusetts. He had recently married a girl as stubborn-minded as himself, Abigail Smith, the daughter of the Congregational minister at Weymouth, and was just beginning to feel that maybe he had a career ahead of him. Ever since the great day he had sat in the hushed council room listening to James Otis' flaming argument against the Writs of Assistance, he had felt himself drawn to the popular side of the controversies that had left the province breathless with an impending sense of events. As he was an ambitious young man with more brains than worldly goods, it was fairly natural that he should discover himself to be a Whig.

An intense local feud had been going on for half a century in Massachusetts between the small group of wealthy families, led by the Hutchinsons, who believed in hard money because they had plenty of it in their strongboxes, and who controlled most of the high offices of the province, and the general mass of merchants, artisans and small farmers who wanted some kind of flexible paper currency. This upper crust had mostly returned to the Church of England, while the colonists generally continued Congregationalists.

The French and Indian War had brought a great boom to New England shipping and its successful conclusion had lifted the menace that barred expansion to the west. The colonists began to feel their oats. At the same time exciting new ideas seeped in from England where all classes were stirred up by the agitation for parliamentary reform that centered around John Wilkes' expulsion from Parliament and prosecution for his articles in *The North Briton.* This, so the reformers claimed, called the right of every freeborn Briton to have voice in his government into question.

Ever since George Third had come to the throne and had tried to act on his German mother's admonition, "George, be a king," the dissenting classes had been uneasy. Now the old fight for a really representative parliament was on again. George, who had the mentality of an English country squire of the Walpole type, and who had been coached in authoritarian ideas by his dour Scotch tutor Lord Bute, was learning all too well how to manipulate the rotten borough system. The echoes of this contest between the Crown and the voters of London set off all the smoldering jealousy for their liberties of the New England towns. As George's government had to exploit every possible source of revenue after the great expense of waging the Seven Years' War abroad and felt the need to buy ever more parliamentary seats at home, the ministry was working around to the idea of really enforcing the revenue laws, which would mean heavy taxes on American shipping. Hence the row about the Writs of Assistance, by which the customs officers were supposed to get the help of colonial functionaries in searching for and seizing smuggled goods. This measure was particularly painful at a time when the trade in rum, sugar and molasses with the West Indies, the best business the merchants had, was all technically smuggling. So it was inevitable that the fight against the few leading families at home and against George's actively authoritarian government in England should merge into one in people's minds. When the colonists began to take up English party labels, the Hutchinsons and their friends became Tories and the citizens who opposed them, Whigs.

This situation Thomas Hutchinson never could get through his head. A direct descendant of Anne Hutchinson, the Nonsuch, and a painstaking historian and collector of colonial records, he felt he was more a Massachusetts man than any of them. Then, after a long career of successfully imposing himself as head man of the colony he took it for granted that all the important offices should be in his hands or in those of his friends and relatives. He had come to feel that Boston was as much his estate as his country house at Milton. He couldn't understand how anybody could object to this happy situation, as he knew how much he had the welfare of his fellowcitizens at heart. He even agreed with them, up to a certain point, on the Writs of Assistance and the Stamp Duties. He was doing his best to argue the home government into a more yielding attitude towards the prejudice in favor of selfgovernment that he had not yet been able to coax out of their heads; but he felt, naturally, that any protest must be made in such form as not to disturb privilege and prerogative. He was a goodhearted coolminded man who had absolutely no idea how other people, and particularly people less fortunately situated, felt about anything. So long as his own position in the world was not involved he was able to argue both sides of any of these questions of the day without losing his temper. When his opponents went so far as to attack him personally, he was very much hurt and considered them ruffians and dangerous people. It was this basic lack of imagination that was behind his genius for making himself unpopular.

When young John Adams began to be noticed by his fellow members of the bar it was natural that he should mix with the rising whig contingent rather than with Hutchinson's small exclusive coterie that surrounded Governor Bernard. These opposition forces were grouped at first behind the Otises, father and son. Although the younger Otis was the orator of the whig party, a quiet strange kindly man who was a distant cousin of John Adams' was already becoming very influential behind the scenes. No public speaker, his powers lay in talk man to man and in the discussions of private groups and in the stirring up of bright young men to the good cause. Especially he was a pillar of Boston townmeeting.

As John Adams, taking sides more and more with the

Whigs, got to know Samuel Adams better, he was so struck by him that he made enthusiastic entries about him in his diary: "S. Adams is zealous, ardent and keen in the cause, is always for softness and delicacy and prudence, where they will do, but is staunch and stiff and inflexible and rigid in the cause . . . Adams I believe has the most thorough understanding of liberty and her resources in the temper and character of the people, though not in the law and constitution: as well as the most habitual radical love of it, of any of them. As well as the most correct, genteel and artful pen. He is a man of refined policy, steadfast integrity, exquisite humanity, genteel erudition, gentle engaging manners, real as well as professed piety, and a universal good character, unless it should be admitted that he is too attentive to the public, and not enough to himself and his family . . ."

Samuel Adams was at that time a man in his early forties whose tremulous voice and strangely shaky hands belied a vigorous constitution and gave him a deceptive air of timidity and irresolution. His hair and scraggly eyebrows, which with a rather sharp chin made him look, some people said, exactly like their idea of Satan, were prematurely white. People who met him for the first time wondered where this odd man's great influence came from. As they began to know him they felt the extraordinary force of a somewhat narrow mind intently directed towards one aim.

He came of the Boston Adamses, a family so highly respected that he was fifth in his class when he graduated from Harvard College, where in those days people were frankly listed according to their rank in the Massachusetts social hierarchy, while his distant cousin John Adams, who came from the farmer Adamses, only rated fourteenth. His father, Samuel Adams, Sr., had been a prosperous brewer and along with Elisha Cooke, a leader of the popular party in the contest over the currency that divided Boston into two bitter factions all through the middle years of the eighteenth century.

Young Sam Adams inherited a feud with the Hutchinson connection from the day of his birth.

He was born and brought up at his father's house on Purchase Street in the North End, that adjoined his wharf and malthouse. His father, as an advocate of paper money, became a director in the Land Bank, chartered by the General Court, that the popular party set up to furnish the colony with a currency based on land values. The hard money faction, which Thomas Hutchinson led, as men of means and Episcopalians had the ear of official circles in London. They opposed the paper money scheme and managed to get a bill through Parliament outlawing the Land Bank. The act aimed to force the directors to take up, at its hard money value, the paper they had issued. The currency was so confused that the colonists still used everything from wampum to tenpenny nails as a means of exchange. So, as the Land Bank paper had followed all other types of Massachusetts money into depreciation, the act meant bankruptcy for the popular leaders. Commissioners were appointed to liquidate the affairs of their bank. For the next twenty years the Adamses father and son were hanging on by their eyelashes fighting off efforts of the commissioners to seize the malthouse and their home on Purchase Street. The blow fell while young Sam was at Harvard. Its immediate effect on him was that his allowance was cut off and he had to work the rest of his way through college by waiting on table at commons.

This happened at about the time that the Great Awakening hit Cambridge. George Whitefield, the revivalist who rivaled Wesley, preached at meetings and stirred the undergraduates to their depths. Young Sam was swept away with the rest. Ever afterwards Sam Adams' religion had a strong Methodist tinge. Whitefield, with his denunciation of the pomps and vanities of the world, appealed particularly to poor men who found themselves cut off from those pomps and vanities, and furnished an emotional outlet to the underdog classes. Participation in the abounding Grace of God gave them the feeling of power and glory that they were denied by their position in the political framework of society.

Though Sam Adams thought of himself as a reincarnation of the old puritan founders of the City of God in the wilderness his fear and hatred of the frivolities and vanities from which his sudden poverty was cutting him off had a good deal of the outlook of modern Methodism. It was logical that this state of mind should form an amalgam with the intense republicanism he imbibed from his reading of John Locke, the theorist of 'the Glorious Revolution' in England, and from the Commonwealth writers James Harrington and Algernon Sidney, whose works were just being resurrected by liberal London scholars and printers in new editions, and from the intensive study of Cicero and the Roman republican writers that had been his pabulum at the Boston Latin school. When he took his Master's degree in 1743, he presented a dissertation in which he took the affirmative side of the thesis: *Whether it be lawful to resist the Supreme Magistrate if the Commonwealth cannot otherwise be preserved.*

Once he was out of college what to do with young Sam became very much a problem to his father and mother. He hadn't wanted to study for the ministry. His mother didn't want him to study law. That he had no head for business became obvious when he was placed as a clerk in Thomas Cushing's counting-house. Too much interest in local politics kept his mind straying off his columns of figures. His father put up a thousand pounds for him to go into business for himself with, but Sam lent it to a friend who promptly lost it in speculation. His father got him a political appointment from the town as one of the clerks in Boston Market and tried to interest him in the business of the malthouse. As soon as his father died he showed his real bent by starting a secret political club of young patriots who wrote the articles for a paper called *The Independent Advertizer* that weekly dusted the jackets of the Hutchinson connection and of the royal Governor.

The Independent Advertizer kept on until the Governor's Council placed the printer in jail one day and started a hue and cry against the anonymous journalists who wrote the leading articles. That was the end of Sam Adams' first venture in political agitation. Meanwhile, although the brewing business his father had left him was going to pot, he married and started raising a family.

He neglected his own business, to be sure, but his interest in the town's increased all the time. His father had been admired and respected as their champion by artisans, apprentices, and the smaller merchants generally, and Sam stepped into his shoes. He was a good churchmember at Jonathan Mayhew's West Church, he was a good mixer at the Caucus Club, and was tireless in attendance on townmeetings. His name began to appear on committees for the visitation of schools, or to look into the danger of smoky chimneys; he served as fireward, as town scavenger, as moderator, and finally as collector of taxes.

His fellowtownsmen must have known that he was hopelessly improvident in money matters, but by this time the political struggle between the factions—the Whigs, whose citadel was Boston townmeeting, and the Tories entrenched in the Governor's Council, from which the Governor's veto kept out popularly elected councilors—was so acute that the people of Boston were electing officers more for their party regularity than for their efficiency in business. It turned out that a worse choice could hardly have been made. It wasn't that Sam Adams wasted his money in high living, since even his enemies had to admit that, although a great talker of politics in the backrooms of taverns, he led a life of rigid abstention from sensual pleasures and follies. But he never could press anybody for payment, if a man came to him with a hard luck story he let him off his taxes; money just naturally slipped through his fingers. When he finally gave up the job of taxcollector in despair, he owed the town around seven thousand pounds. The Tories shouted that it was defalcation and breach of trust on the part of 'Sam the Publican,' as they called him, but the court gave him six months to make up the amount. Friends pitched in to help him scrape up the money. To show their confidence the voters in townmeeting re-elected him to the office, but he very wisely refused to serve again.

When his first wife died, Sam Adams was left just about penniless, with two small children to support, and nothing but a rundown house and a Negro slave girl, whom he promptly freed, to do it on. His only further asset was a large Newfoundland dog. But his importance in Boston grew as his worldly goods diminished. Sam Adams was no public speaker as James Otis was, nor was he a political pamphleteer like Tom Paine; his extraordinary influence was due to his unwavering adherence to a few simple convictions and to a knack he had developed of being able to induce all kinds of men to pool their efforts in a common cause.

As a boy he had gone with his father to meetings of the Caucus Club which had become a sort of executive committee of townmeeting. In the seventeen sixties Boston counted eighteen thousand people, and as the town grew in size, townmeeting even in the fine roomy hall built for it above the new market, had become unwieldy. On crowded days the voters had to overflow into the South Meeting House. To buck the preponderant influence of the rich Episcopalian families, the leaders of the popular party had taken to getting together to decide measures to be proposed in advance of meetings so as to be able to get out the vote for their side. The shipwrights and ropewalk hands and sailmakers and stevedores of the North End had had for years the habit of gathering evenings in a group that at one time was called the Caulkers' Club. Whether by misspelling or by confusion with the name of one of those mythical chiefs so dear to early American folklore, it became known in the papers as the 'Caucus Club.'

In John Adams' diary there's a good description of this gathering in the period just before the Stamp Act agitation:

". . . the Caucus Club meets, at certain times, in the garret of Tom Dawes, the Adjutant of the Boston Regiment. He has a large house and he has a moveable partition in his garret which he takes down, and the whole club meets in one room. There they smoke tobacco until you cannot see from one end of the garret to the other. There they drink flip, I suppose, and there they chose a moderator who puts questions to the vote regularly; and selectmen, assessors, collectors, wardens, firewards and representatives are regularly chosen before they are chosen in the town . . . They send committees to wait on the merchants' club, and to propose and join in choice of men and measures . . ."

Elisha Cooke seems to have first gotten the idea of taking politics into these meetings to make friends for his own particular brand of populist ideas in the early days of his Country Party. The elder Adams, who as an openhanded sociable brewer, was at home with all sorts of people, had, after Elisha Cooke's death, made the Caucus Club his personal political machine. Young Sam inherited a great deal of his father's influence there. The common people who made up most of the membership felt the old man had fought their fight, and loved the son for a chip off the old block. As he grew older, he developed the fairly casual organization into exactly what the name implies today, a caucus of the popular party in town-meeting. As the club grew in size during the Stamp Act agitation, and was frequented by young merchants and professional people, its quarters were moved to a large room in the back of Samuel Shed's grocery on Milk Street.

Through his long experience in practical politics, Sam Adams had learned to generalize his own personal hatreds and all the petty animosities of provincial factions into a broad and simple political program. Its basic principle was simply that the American colonies had been inherently free and independent since their first settlement, and that any authority the Crown or Parliament exercised without their consent was usurpation of the rights of the colonists as freeborn Englishmen as laid down in Magna Carta and, in the case of Massachusetts, in the charter of 1691. At first he was willing for the colonies to remain selfgoverning members of a British empire under the Crown, but gradually he shifted his ground until he held that, as men had a natural right to govern themselves as best suited their convenience, nothing but complete independence would do.

When early in 1765, the news that the threatened Stamp Act had actually passed reached Boston, it found the merchants and artisans struggling with a business slump that had followed the great boom of the West Indies trade during the war. Business houses were failing; people were out of work; tempers were short. The Wilkes agitation in England had given new circulation to the word Liberty. Soon mobs of men and boys were charging up and down King Street yelling, 'Liberty and Wilkes.'

Boston was accustomed to a certain amount of popular uproar as was any seaport town in those days, but this time the Tories looking out disapprovingly through the expensive glass windows of their fine houses, noticed more method in the rowdy madness of the streets than usual. To the great surprise of the administration in England, which had picked the Stamp Tax because Grenville claimed that the colonists would accept it with a minimum of grumbling, it was arousing everywhere the most determined and organized opposition.

Among the speeches in Parliament for and against the bill the words of a certain Colonel Isaac Barré, as reported in *The Gazette*, caught the popular fancy. Colonel Barré had been with Wolfe at the taking of Quebec and was reputed to be a friend of the great Pitt, whom nothing but the malice of George and his toadies was keeping out of the ministry; he had risen to defend the right of the colonists to tax themselves and had spoken of them as 'sons of Liberty.' All at once all the livelier young men of the Caucus Club and the Merchants' Club and among the Masons and the Trueborn Whigs took to strutting around calling themselves the Sons of Liberty. Their headquarters was the little room in Chase and Speakman's distillery that John Adams wrote of visiting during the following winter, where sat a sort of executive committee which came to be known as the 'Loyall Nine.'

It was early in August before the names of the collectors for the infamous tax were made public. When news got round the streets that the collector for Boston was Andrew Oliver, Thomas Hutchinson's brother-in-law, the town boiled over. Already James Otis had been declaring in his reckless way that he knew the very room in the Governor's mansion where the whole business had been planned. Now it seemed proved that the government in England and the Tories at home were putting their heads together to subvert American liberties and ruin business.

During the hot August days that followed the taverns and the meetings of the clubs were full of citizens indignantly declaiming. At Wednesday lecture and in their Sunday sermons the Congregational ministers preached on the defense of liberty as a religious duty. The words of the Reverend Jonathan Mayhew, Sam Adams' pastor, were particularly sizzling, so that the congregation poured out of the West Church hot for a holy war of resistance.

The morning of the fourteenth some strange objects were found hanging from the boughs of the Liberty Tree. There was a stuffed rag effigy marked Andrew Oliver and a big bootjack with a devil's head sticking out of it, to stand for the King's tutor, Lord Bute, and other symbolic objects. A Tory claimed to have seen Sam Adams standing under the tree, peering up through the leafy branches with a look of satisfaction on his face. When Governor Bernard went to the statehouse for a meeting of the General Court, he ordered the sheriff to have the unseemly objects removed. The sheriff answered that the townspeople would take them down in due time.

That afternoon crowds began to gather round the tree marshaled by the Sons of Liberty, and through the waterfront streets were heard the whistle and horn the mobleaders used to call their mobs of journeymen and apprentices together. First they took down the frame of a wooden building Oliver was putting up, it was claimed, for a tax office, and then, led by the effigy of Oliver on a bier, they paraded through the passage under the statehouse shouting, 'Pitt and Liberty, Liberty Property and No Stamps,' and roaring and whistling at the dignitaries in session above. Governor Bernard called for the ranking militia officer in sight to order his drummers to beat to quarters and was told that the drummers were in the mob, the militiamen were in the mob, the sheriffs were in the mob. Following the bier were carried in triumph the lumber and uprights for Oliver's new building.

They passed under the statehouse and poured out through the streets to Oliver's own house on Fort Hill. There they built a bonfire and to the accompaniment of yells and whoops first beheaded the effigy and then burned it. By this time the more respectable Sons of Liberty had tired of the sport and had begun to trickle off home to get some sleep for work tomorrow, leaving a sprinkling of tough characters still roaring out songs and drinking rum round the bonfire. The day had been tame for the tougher elements in the South End and North End mobs, so when somebody suggested they go get old Oliver himself, there was a general rush towards his house. They broke down the doors and ransacked the place looking for him, destroying a certain amount of furniture in the process. Fortunately for him he was not to be found, so they amused themselves throwing cobblestones and brickbats through the windows of his empty house until they got sleepy and straggled off home.

Andrew Oliver, who was an old man and a timid man, had gotten together his family earlier in the day and slipped out of town. Governor Bernard went with him, in a great stew at discovering that he had absolutely no way of upholding the royal authority. They went over in a boat from Quincy to Castle William, on an island in the bay, where they felt fairly safe under the protection of the cannons of the small artillery company that defended the port. There they settled down to spend the summer.

Hutchinson, the Lieutenant Governor, who was a man of courage and who couldn't imagine, knowing his own good intentions, that any of his fellowcitizens should want to do him harm, held his ground. He was going to show that crackbrained Otis, and Adams, and their ruffianly rabble that he knew how to uphold the dignity of his offices and prerogatives. He stayed on in his fine town house. He didn't yet understand that he had become for the citizens of Boston the symbol of all the forces they felt were working against them. During the days that followed there was an uneasy brooding feeling about the town. At the Caucus Club and at the Merchants' Club and at the Green Dragon on Union Street and the Bunch of Grapes on King Street, people talked of Patrick Henry's great speech on the Virginia resolutions and of riots in New York and Charleston. The more levelheaded patriots were busy organizing a boycott of British goods. But in the streets the tougher element felt that it was up to the people of Boston to show that they were as much men as the colonists to the southward.

A cobbler named Alexander Mackintosh, who was a great brawler and cudgelman and leader of what was known as the 'North End mob' in its occasional rows with the inhabitants of the South End, made up his mind one night towards the end of August when he'd been drinking and roaring around the streets with his rowdies that now was the time to do his bit for Liberty. He started by getting his men together round a bonfire on King Street. After many a noggin of rum had been passed round, a few hardy spirits, deciding that the bonfire was burning down, broke into the office of the Admiralty Court that was the center of the proceedings against smugglers, and hauled out the records and fed the flames with them. When that building was thoroughly wrecked they went on to the house of the Collector of Customs and gutted it. It was late at night by that time. The men and boys of the mob were drunk and crazy and singed and sooty from their fires. Word went from mouth to mouth that this was the night to get the traitor Hutchinson and raze his house to the ground.

Hutchinson was warned only a few minutes before they came pouring round the house from all sides, yelling and whooping and carrying torches and axes and staves. He got his sister and his small children out in their nightclothes to a neighbor's. He wanted to stay to face the crowd but his daughter dragged him across the garden wall and through the alleys in back just as the leaders of the mob started splitting in the front door with their axes, or he might very well never have lived to write the account of his misfortunes.

They poured into the house tearing and ruining everything they laid their hands on. They raided the cellar and distributed his fine French wines and madeiras. They broke into his strongbox and gutted his library, throwing his books and papers out through the windows. They broke up his fine walnut and mahogany furniture and smashed his mirrors and wrecked his sister's spinet. Even the baby's cradle was smashed to pieces. They dragged out his fine clothes, and carried off his scarlet judicial robes, and his plate and his china and his microscope and his new telescope razors and his silverhilted sword. It was only because the house was one of the best built in Boston that they weren't able to pull it down about their ears. "Not contented with tearing off all the wainscott and hangings, and splitting the doors to pieces, they beat down the partition walls; and although that alone cost them two hours, they cut down the cupola or lanthorn, and they began to take the slate and boards from the roof and were prevented only by the approaching daylight from a total demolition of the building. The garden house was laid flat and all my trees etc. broken to the ground."

So he wrote in one of the many accounts of his misfortunes he poured out to friends and to the authorities in England. Eventually the Crown made him handsome compensation for his losses, although the Massachusetts Assembly never would. The greatest loss in the sack of his house was his collection of provincial records stretching back to the earliest days of the Bay Colony. The first volume of his history had been published the year before, and as his bad luck would have it, had furnished a great deal of ammunition to the opponents of his authority out of the old documents. The completed manuscript of the second volume was found the next morning by a neighbor trampled into the muddy gutter and returned to him, along with a mashed silver coffeepot and some tattered fragments of damask and silk.

Poor Thomas Hutchinson was never quite the same after the outbreak against him. It must have puzzled and worried him immensely. During his easy agreeable painstaking life, while he had been collecting the honors and offices that had seemed to him merely his due, a change had come over his little provincial town of Boston. He had done his best to combat it. He had kept two generations of popular leaders at bay, with their silly ideas about a paper currency and popular rights. With God's help he had won the fight for hard money and been very much praised by all parties for it. His careful scheme for stabilizing the currency had served business. He had always done what kindnesses he could to the poor and destitute and there was not a man in the colony outside of the agitators and rabbleraisers who could honestly say he had been wronged. He loved his town and his province and had done the best he could to put his laborious colorless but keen mind to work to preserve the memorials of their great past in his history. But he had never noticed that through these years, of what according to his lights was service to the community, he and his friends and relatives, holders of all honors and places, had little by little cut themselves off from their fellowtownsmen so that, when the test came, not a man, not a provincial officer, not a sheriff, constable or militiaman could be found to protect him against an unwarranted attack from a drunken mob.

The next morning, whitefaced shaking and sleepless, wearing some old clothes he had borrowed from the neighbors, he walked down to the statehouse to go about his duties.

Josiah Quincy, another young country lawyer and a cousin of John Adams, was in the Superior Court the next morning and describes in his diary the strange appearance the Chief Justice made: "He came in . . . his look big with the greatest anxiety, clothed in a manner which would have excited compassion from the hardest heart, though his dress had not been striking contrasted with the other judges and bar, who appeared in their robes. Such a man in such a station, thus habited, with tears starting from his eyes and a countenance which strongly told the inward anguish of his soul—what must his audience have felt, whose compassion had before been moved by what they knew he had suffered, when they heard him pronounce the following words, in the manner which the agitation of his mind dictated:

" '—Gentlemen, there not being a quorum in the Court without me, I am obliged to appear. Some apology is necessary for my dress: indeed I had no other. Destitute of everything,—no other shirt, no other garment but what I have on; and not one in my family in a better situation than myself. The distress of a whole family around me, young and tender infants hanging around me, are infinitely more insupportable than what I feel for myself, though I am obliged to borrow part of *this* clothing.

" 'Sensible that I am innocent, that all the charges against me are false, I cannot help feeling: and though I am not obliged to give an answer to all the questions that may be put to me by every lawless person, yet I call God to witness,—and I would not for a thousand worlds call on my Maker to witness to a falsehood—I say I call my Maker to witness that

I never, in New England or Old, in Great Britain or America, neither directly nor indirectly, was aiding, assisting or supporting—in the least promoting or encouraging what is commonly called the Stamp Act; but on the contrary did all in my power, and strove as much as in me lay to prevent it . . .

" 'I hope the eyes of the people will be opened, that they will see how easy it is for some designing, wicked man to spread false reports, to raise suspicions and jealousies in the minds of the populace, and enrage them against the innocent: but if guilty this is not the way to proceed. The laws of our country are open to punish those who have offended. This destroying all peace and order of the community,—all will feel its effects; and I hope all will see how easily the people may be deluded, inflamed and carried away with madness against an innocent man.

" 'I pray God give us better hearts.' "

In the gray light of the next morning it was obvious to every citizen of Boston that this was not the way to proceed. While Hutchinson was making his heartbroken speech to the Superior Court, the citizens in townmeeting were passing a somewhat crestfallen resolution disclaiming all responsibility for the outrage. While people in general went around clucking their tongues and shaking their heads, Sam Adams was at work in his own peculiar way.

If the royal Governor couldn't uphold law and order in the town, it was up to the Sons of Liberty to assure it by their own methods. Sam Adams after half a lifetime of small municipal offices knew everybody in town by his first name, as the modern saying goes. There was hardly a man, outside of the uppercrust families, who was not beholden to him for some small favor or kindness. Especially he'd let many poor people off their taxes. The first thing he did was to get hold of the leaders of the two organized mobs and to inculcate in them, as he would have said, the principles of Liberty. The leader of the North End mob was a man named Swift. Adams got hold of him and talked him around. In the reaction to the sacking of Hutchinson's house, Mackintosh and a few others had been placed in jail. After they'd cooled off there a few days the Sons of Liberty went to the jail and quietly released them. A banquet that was later known as the 'Union Feast' was arranged. The leaders of the two mobs met and pledged themselves, amid toasts and patriotic songs, to eternal friendship in the cause of the colonies and of Liberty.

Up to that year the South End and North End mobs had kept up a quaint custom of rioting on Guy Fawkes Day, November 5, to commemorate the discovery of the Gunpowder Plot of the Papists against Parliament in King James First's reign. In Boston it was known as 'Pope's Day.' A parade would start out with a rag effigy stuffed to represent the Pope and the two mobs would fly at each other with clubs and brickbats until one or the other carried it off. Often a few stores were looted in the excitement. There was boundless drinking and cracking of heads, gouging out of eyes, tearing off of ears, stamping in faces, mayhem and occasionally murder. Respectable citizens left town or shivered in their shuttered houses. The first sign of the new order in Boston was that instead of a riot the Sons of Liberty put on a military parade, instead of cudgelplay patriotic speeches, toasts and songs. Swift and Mackintosh appeared in the uniform of the militia with small canes resting on their left arms and music at front and flank. To the amazement of the Tories, Pope's Day, 1765, passed without a single cracked skull.

Sam Adams had a good voice and ear and for some years had been coaxing the waterfront huskies into singing societies, where they could get their high spirits off their chests in unison; his gleeclubs tamed the savage breasts of the Boston mob. As part of his program of bringing patriots of all walks of life together, he had Swift and his hearties around to his house. To his mind there wasn't a man in town who couldn't be useful to the cause if inculcated with the proper principles. There's an entry in the diary of John Adams, respectable young man that he was, that speaks of spending 'an evening at Mr. Adams' with him and Brother Swift, very sociably' that almost certainly refers to this same gangleader from the South End.

During that summer that Sam Adams was organizing the ragtag and bobtail of Boston through the Sons of Liberty, as he had previously organized townmeeting through the Caucus Club, the colonists up and down the coast were getting in touch with each other to plan for mutual aid and defense. In November the first Continental Congress of delegates from all the colonies came together in New York to see what measures could be taken in common. At the same time, letters and messengers were linking up the various groups of Sons of Liberty in Connecticut, New York, Massachusetts and South Carolina to prepare a system of military defense in case King George should send troops to enforce the Stamp Act.

The act had gone into effect on November 1st but was everywhere completely nullified. After a sort of general strike that lasted a couple of weeks, lawcourts and customhouses and mercantile houses started going quietly about their business, handing down decisions, signing contracts, clearing ships without stamping the documents. When news came that the Stamp Act was repealed and that there was a hope of a new ministry under Chatham, the elder Pitt, the colonists felt that America had come of age in the world. Everywhere the Sons of Liberty rang churchbells, got up patriotic banquets where subscriptions were opened to set up statues and to unveil paintings in honor of the great and popular empirebuilder, to whose influence the change was credited. The groundwork had been laid for the astonishing organization that through the Committees of Safety and Committees of Correspondence was to be the backbone of a new nation when the apparatus of the Crown authority in America collapsed ten years later.

In Massachusetts it was the experience of the Stamp Act agitation that enabled Sam Adams to hold so many strings in his hands during the occupation of Boston and just by writing letters to keep the New England states together during the desperate trial of seven years of war. During this time too, he was pulling his own life together, to boot. The day before Christmas in '64 he had married Betsy Wells, a sensible strong-minded woman, as convinced a patriot as Sam himself, who happened, for good measure, to be one of the best housekeepers in Boston. Although they continued poor she managed her household and such of Sam's affairs as could be salvaged so well that instead of sinking from one failure to another he was able to conduct the gregarious business of his life more sanely from the now restored and tidiedup house on Purchase Street. Before the Stamp Act and his marriage to Betsy, Sam Adams had walked through Boston a well liked and wellintentioned crank, making a mess of one town office after another. Now the voters in townmeeting recognized the new Sam Adams by electing him to fill the Boston Seat in the Assembly.

As James Otis grew more and more erratic, especially after being cracked on the head by a Tory in a tavern brawl, and took to drinking harder than ever and finally lost his mind altogether, Sam Adams became the man to whom the patriots looked for advice and support. From his position as clerk of the Assembly and as virtual editor of Edes' and Gill's *Gazette* he was to direct the Massachusetts end of the campaign that culminated in Independence.

During the two years between the repeal of the Stamp Act and the occupation of Boston by royal troops the Tories fretted helplessly. The province was getting along without them. There were no more mobs after a highly organized group had led poor old Oliver once more to the Liberty Tree one rainy December day, and forced him to stand bareheaded and write his resignation as the Stamp Act distributor. Townmeeting, sheriffs, juries, the Assembly, all the engines of government were now in the hands of the Liberty Boys. The Hutchinson faction was a fifth wheel. There was nothing to it but to bring in the military if authority was to be preserved.

Sam Adams was a thorough and entire hater. He never ceased to consider Hutchinson the source of all ills, responsible for the troops as he had been for the stamps. He was soon to see his adversary, humbled and ruined, slink away into exile. He never pretended not to enjoy his victory. As he wrote in his famous letter to James Warren: "Recollect the time when he was oblig'd to abandon his Troops, by which he had hoped to awe the People. It was then, if Fancy deceived me not, I observ'd his Knees to tremble, I thought I saw his face grow pale (and I enjoyed the Sight) at the Appearance of the determin'd Citizens peremptorily demanding redress of Grievances."

3. A Portico Facing the Wilderness

AT eight o'clock a fine April morning in 1782, one of the general officers of Lafayette's staff, who was taking advantage of the unaccustomed peacefulness of the spring after Yorktown to make a little tour on horseback of the hilly country of Virginia, set out from the inn where he had passed not too comfortably the night, to follow the wagonruts up the forested valley to Monticello. He was the Chevalier de Chastellux, a military gentleman of philosophic tastes, with an enthusiasm for landscape and travel and the habit of jotting down what he saw and heard in his notebook every evening.

As he rode he was surprised by the sharp heat of the morning sun and the backwardness of the season. The trees were barely coming into leaf. He pulled up his horse from time to time to admire the abundant singing and the pert behavior of the mockingbirds. When the trail came out on a clearing he began to see blue mountains ahead of him through the light haze of green of the budding twigs. He rode on and on without seeing a house. The trail got more and more tangled in dense thickets that cut off the view of the mountains, and was made confusing by crisscrossing paths. The Chevalier had just about lost his bearings when he caught sight of a man on horseback ahead of him. The rider turned out to be an Irishman who had settled in the western part of North Carolina.

Full of lively curiosity about things American, the Chevalier, so he put down in his notes, had his way made short by the Irishman's conversation, and furthermore was reassured about the road to Mr. Jefferson's house. The Irishman had been wounded in the war and still carried a British musket ball in his hip, which, the Chevalier noted, in no way affected his high spirits. He had settled on the extreme frontier beyond Catawba. Farming there was subsistence farming. The settlers had to raise or shoot their own meat, to weave their own cloth and to cobble their own shoes. Until their appletrees grew up enough to bear, or they could afford to import a still, their only drink was water or milk. Their tools were the broadax and the saw. The main thing they lacked, the Chevalier was surprised to hear, was nails: everything else they made for themselves. They built fences and shingled their houses without a single nail. Of course whittling wooden pegs took time, and labor was scarce and high in those parts, as one could imagine. The only cash crop was horses. It didn't cost anything to drive their horses to market because they grazed them as they went. On this present trip alone, the Irishman said, he had covered a good four hundred miles in the saddle.

"While the conversation," so the Chevalier wrote down in his notes, "went on briskly, we were reaching the foot of the mountains. We recognized without difficulty the house of Mr. Jefferson on one of the summits: because it can truly be said to shine alone in its retreat. He built the house and chose the site himself; to tell the truth, although he was already the owner of considerable lands in the vicinity, in such a desert there would have been nothing to hinder him from setting himself up wherever he chose. But nature owed it to a Sage and to a man of taste to furnish him on his own inheritance with the spot where he could best study her ways and enjoy her beauties. He named this house Monticello, surely a very modest name, for it is placed on a really high mountain, but a name that announces the attraction the Italian tongue holds for the proprietor, and especially the Fine Arts of which that country was the cradle and of which she is still the asylum. From now on I needed no guide; I said goodby to my Irishman; and after having climbed more than a half an hour up a fairly convenient path, I arrived at Monticello. This house, of which

Mr. Jefferson was the architect and on which he did much of the work with his own hands, is built with considerable elegance in the Italian style, not however without some defects; it consists of a large square pavilion, into which one enters by two porticos ornamented with columns. The ground floor is principally occupied by a great highceilinged drawingroom which will be decorated in absolutely antique style: above the drawingroom is a library of the same shape; two little wings that have only a ground floor and an attic flank this pavilion and probably communicate with the kitchens, servants' quarters, etc., which will form on each side a sort of subbasement surmounted by a terrace. It's not to enter into a description of the house that I subscribe these details but merely to prove that it is far different from those one usually sees in these parts; so that one may truly say that Mr. Jefferson is the first American who has consulted the Fine Arts in the matter of putting a roof over his head. But I want to put my time in on the man himself: I should paint a man not yet forty years of age, tall of stature, with a refined and friendly countenance, in which the evidence of wit and learning could take the place of any possible external charms; an American who, without having ever left his country, is a Musician, a Draftsman, a Geometer, an Astronomer, a Physicist, a Jurisconsult and a Statesman: an American Senator who sat two years in the famous Congress, author of the revolution of which they never speak here without respect unfortunately mixed with too many regrets; a Governor of Virginia who filled this position of difficulty during the invasions of Arnold, of Phillips and of Cornwallis; finally a Philosopher retired from the world and its business, because he loves the world only so far as he can flatter himself that he is being useful, and because the education of his fellowcitizens has not yet developed to the point where they will stand for enlightenment or brook contradiction. A gentle and amiable wife, some pretty children he brings up with great care, a house to beautify and great possessions to improve, science and art to cultivate; this is what is left of Mr. Jefferson, after having played a distinguished role on the theatre of the New World, and this is what he prefers to the situation of Minister-Plenipotentiary in Europe. The visit I was making him was not unexpected; long since he had invited me to come to spend several days in the bosom of his society, that is to say of his mountains. All the same I found his first greeting unsmiling and even cold; but I hadn't spent two hours with him before I felt as if I had lived with him all my life; walks, the library, and especially conversation;—always varied, always interesting, always sustained by the satisfaction two people feel, who in communicating one to another their feelings and their opinions, find themselves always in accord, and able to understand each other with half a word,—made four days pass like four minutes. This conformity of sentiments and opinions on which I insist because it's something for me to be proud of, (and we sometimes have to let our egoism show itself) this conformity I say, was so perfect, that not only were our tastes similar, but also our predilections: those predilections that dry and methodical spirits make fun of as *fad* and which men of sensibility and animation glory in as *feeling*. I can remember with pleasure that one evening when we were chatting over a bowl of punch after Mrs. Jefferson had gone to bed, we fell to talking of the poems of Ossian. It was an electric spark that passed rapidly from one to the other: we reminded each other of the passages in these sublime poems that had most struck us and entertained with recitations of them my travelling companions, who fortunately knew English well and were capable of appreciating them but who had never read them. Before long we got the idea that the book itself ought to take part in the toast, we went to fetch it and it was placed beside the punchbowl. One thing and another had already led us pretty far into the night, without our noticing how late it was. Other times it was Physics or Politics or Art that was the subject of our conversations; for there is nothing of the sort that has escaped Mr. Jefferson, and from his youth up he seems to have set his mind, like his house, on an elevated place from which he could contemplate all the universe."

From accounts of members of the family and of later visitors we can form a pretty fair picture of how the amiable Chevalier passed his time at Monticello. The first meal of the day, served around nine, was an eighteenth century breakfast, with broiled meats and the cold joints from the day before, washed down with cider and beer and plenty of hot coffee. Jefferson, who had been up writing and reading since daybreak, would meet his guests at the table. After breakfast the company couldn't help stepping out on the terrace to look for a moment at the great view of the valley of the Rivanna and the blue ridges beyond the gap above the little village of Charlottesville. Jefferson sometimes would say that the only thing he regretted was that there was not a body of water in the foreground or perhaps a volcano in the distance. Then he would take his guests around to the other end of the house to point out the little conical hill which was the only thing that broke the flatness of the leafy plain sweeping to the horizon to the south. He used to tell them this little hill was just about the size and shape of the pyramid of Cheops and describe the peculiar forms the mirage sometimes made it take on.

Landscape was one of the great pleasures of Jefferson's life. In planning his gardens and planting his hilltop he had put much thought into how best to open out and emphasize the features he liked best in the view. The type of landscape that appealed to him was the landscape of the first burst of English romanticism. Oaks were 'venerable and antient,' evergreens were 'gloomy,' vales were 'solitary and unfrequented,' walks were winding, gardens naturalistic. His garden was the park-like English garden of the romantic school where all the planting was supposed to look as if it had grown there of its own accord. It was a taste that went with grottoes, and the sudden reversal of the color of the word Gothic, and with the enthusiasm for the imaginary Celtic epics of Macpherson's Ossian, which Jefferson as a young man had shared with the fashionable reading public of the time to such a point that he wrote a friend in Scotland to get him, no matter at what cost, a copy of the original manuscript and a grammar so that he could study the poems in Gaelic. No wonder the fashionable Chevalier de Chastellux was surprised and pleased to find his host so versed in the *dernier cri* of cosmopolitan sensibility. It was like coming on a reader of James Joyce in an African rubber plantation.

After the view had been admired there were the gardens and the park to visit, possibly astride one of the blooded horses that Jefferson raised and cared for with the passionate pride in a good horse and an easy seat in the saddle that he shared with his Virginia neighbors. Undoubtedly the Chevalier was again surprised by the number of European fruits and vegetables and by his host's knowledge of their names in French and Italian as well as in botanical Latin. Some years before a young Italian named Mazzei had come to a neighboring plantation with a number of Italian gardeners and vineyard hands, and immediately Jefferson's little garden notebook had filled up with the names of Italian vegetables. From then on zucche, broccoli, savoy cabbage, sorrel, peppers and Italian squashes and marrows of all kinds were part of the yearly sowings in the kitchengardens that were terraced into the south slope of the hill. From Mazzei too Jefferson had learned the newest technique for grafting and budding fruittrees. Besides strawberries and currants, and asparagus for which Monticello was famous, he planted a great variety of fruits in orchards on the slopes of the hill and in rows instead of hedges between the wheat and cornfields in the valley. Even before his marriage, when as a young man he was laying out his countryseat on the scale of a Roman emperor's villa, he had planted appletrees, pears, peaches, nectarines, apricots, quinces, medlars, pomegranates, figs, plums, cherries and walnuts. To all these he had added rows of vines planted out in the Italian style, put in according to Mazzei's instructions, and olivetrees and bitter oranges as an experiment. His neverending and daily task was to induce the listless darky slaves, whom he treated with fatherly and indulgent patience, and the overseers who could keep their minds only on cash crops, to keep all these trees properly pruned and weeded. Possibly some of the fruit-trees were still in bloom the April day of cloudflecked blue skies, full of the endless chirruping of songbirds in a variety so amazing to Europeans, when Chastellux was shown around.

After the gardens came the park. There the morning sun-light, hot even in April, was cooled a little, if not yet quite cut off, by the various greens and the pink and bronze fuzz of buds just coming into tiny leaf on the great forest trees Jeffer-son had left where he found them. Perhaps on the way he had silently pointed out to his visitor the enormous oak on top of the hill under which Dabney Carr, his brother-in-law and the great friend of his boyhood, the father of the little nephews and nieces he was raising in his own family, lay buried, and where the family burying ground, so indispensable a part of a Virginia plantation, had already sprouted a few small fresh stones. In the park was an enclosure where some red deer lived, as well as peacocks, guineafowl, rabbits, squirrels, pheasants, partridges and pigeons. Jefferson would point out that he was hoping to get hold of a buck elk or a buffalo to give the place more interest and to prove to European visitors that Buffon was wrong in his theory that animals tended to run smaller in the Western than in the Eastern Hemisphere.

Back at the house, they went upstairs to the library, where Jefferson brought out his favorite edition of Palladio, printed with magnificent plates by Leoni in London in 1715, or the poems of Collins or Shenstone, or volumes of Shaftes-bury and Bolingbroke and Locke and Algernon Sidney. If the talk turned to novels he would point to *Don Quixote* and to

Sterne's *Sentimental Journey* as his favorites. Among the classics it was Homer he never tired of. By that time the colored butler was tapping on the door to announce with a flourish that the ladies were in the drawingroom waiting to be taken in to dinner. Mr. Jefferson would have to put off till later the explanation of his meteorological instruments and of the records he was keeping of the weather and of his theory of how the prevailing winds were affected by the progressive clearing of the forests as the settlers hewed their way west.

After four days of this typical Monticello entertainment, after having ridden one afternoon into Charlottesville with Mr. Jefferson to dine with a French colonel who was drilling a newly recruited regiment there and who had a young black wolf for a pet, Chastellux and his retinue rode off across Rockfish Gap to visit the famous natural bridge up in the Valley. It had turned out that the bridge and the canyon below it was the property of his host, who considered it one of the most beautiful spots on earth; Mr. Jefferson had explained that he would have to deny himself the pleasure of accompanying the amiable Chevalier on the excursion on account of the delicate health of his wife.

Although Chastellux was never allowed to know it, he visited Jefferson during one of the unhappiest periods of his life. From the moment of Cornwallis' surrender at Yorktown early in the previous autumn the Revolutionary War was won; but Jefferson looked back on his own public career with a stinging sense of failure. Negotiations for peace were under way. The existence of the new nation he had done so much to launch was assured. But he had retired, he honestly believed forever, from public life under circumstances infinitely distressing to a man so touchily sensitive to the opinion of his neighbors as he was in those days.

In spite of his many warm friendships he had always been a solitary man, somewhat haughty and retiring in his relations with the world. After the backbiting of the legislature and the rough lessons of his governorship he had come home to the retreat he had picked for himself as a boy, that he had planned and built every inch of, and to his wife Patty he so tenderly loved, and to his little girls, and to the compact home group so tightly knit by the extraordinary ardor of family feeling that characterized the isolated households of the Virginia landowners of the time. He had come back to projects for building and farming and to the doglike flattery of his houseservants, and to his books and his music and his draftingboard and the delightful work of planning and completing his halffinished mansion according to his own adaptation of classical architectural style into what he felt a free man's house should be. In Virginia it was the letdown period after a great accomplishment when everybody starts to show his worst side. Jefferson had come home seeking a refuge and that refuge he had found made bitter by the most painful daily anxiety any man can feel. His children had never been very strong. His little son was dead. And now Patty whose health was so frail was going to have another baby. The fear that she would not live through another birth was always in the background of his mind.

He had come to that period in his life, which seems to come to most men around their fortieth year, when all the blank checks of youth have been cashed and a man has to face himself as an adult, the way he's going to be until he dies; that is the point from which a man of ability either goes on to mature and to take his place for better or worse in the world, or else drops back into the great army of might-have-beens.

Up to those years of the governorship Jefferson's career had been brilliant and easy. The eldest son of an energetic farmer, who had risen from what the Virginians in those days spoke of as the 'overseer class,' to marry a Randolph and to become a great landowner, he had had every advantage the colony could offer a young man growing up. Shadwell where he was born had only been settled a few years before, so the country he was raised in still had the freshness and freedom of the frontier, and as has so often happened on the American frontier, contained a high proportion of vigorous and welleducated men and women.

His father was a surveyor and mapmaker; he had finished Byrd's survey of the North Carolina line; through him must have come that taste for exact figuring and laborsaving inventions. His mother's people, the highfalutin' Randolphs, were almost a caricature of the British county family transplanted to Virginia. As a child he grew up in the cozy hotbed of flattery and indulgence from Negro servants that so often brought out the worst in white people, but at least inculcated into their very bones the assurance that a white man was the paragon of animals. In Jefferson, as in not a few similar men of aristocratic upbringing, selfrespect was so strong it became a feeling of respect for all mankind. His family and friends in early life were people who felt they were equal to, if not a little better than, any man on earth. They were willing to do other men the courtesy of considering them as highly as they considered themselves. It was the type of leveling that comes from a sense of complete personal security. In young Jefferson's case there was, besides the spur to ambition that lay in the need to prove to the world that a Jefferson was as good a man as any nameproud Randolph of the lot, perhaps an underlying suspicion that he was as much kin to the people who weren't Randolphs as to those who were.

His father's death when he was fourteen threw him on his own early. As eldest son he immediately was sole arbiter of all the daily decisions of the life of a series of estates, of his mother's household affairs and of those of his small brothers and sisters. It's characteristic of him that in the first letter of his we have handed down, written when he was about seventeen, he's politely but firmly suggesting to his guardian, Colonel Harvey, that the time has come for him to go to college at Williamsburg. Bossing a farm and a lot of household servants under the isolated conditions of pioneer life trained those Virginians early in making their own decisions. Their daily horseback riding, alone, was an education in applying their will to their environment.

At Williamsburg Jefferson had the great good luck to fall in with a little group of remarkable men. Dr. Small the Scotch professor of mathematics at William and Mary was the bosom friend of George Wythe, a Virginian of wealth and broad classical culture, who was the great liberal lawyer of the time. The pair of them were the special cronies of Governor Fauquier, a courtly beau of the Augustan school, a man of good education and sound taste in the fads and fashions of St. James' Park and the pumproom at Bath and the Whig country houses of England, who spread round him in the provinces some of the religious skepticism, the harsh commonsense, the predilection for the fine arts, and the craze for gambling of the London wits of Queen Anne's day. Governor Fauquier was very fond of music; so, as young Jefferson had scraped a fiddle from boyhood, and Dr. Small had taken an immediate fancy to him as a favorite pupil, he soon found himself part of Fauquier's amateur orchestra and a frequent diner at the 'Governor's Palace,' as the brick mansion that represented the House of Hanover at Williamsburg was called. The lanky redheaded lad from the foothills became, while still in his teens, the habitual fourth at the Governor's little exquisite dinners. There he imbibed, instead of the taste for three bottles of port and cards and foppish behavior that might have been expected, the enthusiasm that possessed him all his life for music and architecture, for light wines, good conversation and for getting to the bottom of a subject.

The first subject he tried to get to the bottom of was the English law. He studied Common Law under George Wythe, who saw it, as the long line of English liberal lawyers back through Coke and Littleton had seen it, as a charter of liberties, rather than as a rule for protecting privilege. He worked so hard at it that he even gave up his horses. Not that he lacked any of the passion for horseflesh and hard riding of his contemporaries, or their taste for foxhunting and cockfighting and brawling and drinking and dancing, and other entertainments in which the young men at Williamsburg sowed their wild oats; but he found he couldn't spare the time. To get his reading done he had to cut down his exercise to an hour's run each evening. Before long he was studying Anglo-Saxon in order really to understand the origins of the Common Law. Like the men of Commonwealth days he caught early the bias for their imagined free previous England of the Teuton tribes as against the Latinized authoritarian England of the Norman conquest.

Meanwhile he remained good friends with a wild young man of Irish extraction he'd met in his foxhunting days, a great drinker, fiddler and hunter, who managed to give a slender body of legal learning expression in an amazing flow of natural eloquence. Later Jefferson wrote of him with a kind of awe that he spoke as Homer wrote. Although Jefferson's studies began early to interfere with his pleasures Patrick Henry stayed with him whenever he came to Williamsburg. At twentyfour, Henry had managed to go bankrupt as a storekeeper and had gotten himself admitted to the bar after a few weeks' study. Although he was older than Jefferson, it was probably from Jefferson's talkative friendship that he picked up what little education he had. The young men had in common the good nature that comes from physical strength and health and an enthusiasm they could hardly have explained even to themselves for the word Liberty.

Jefferson was just twentytwo when he stood in the doorway of the House of Burgesses to which Henry had only recently been elected, and heard him read his resolutions against the Stamp Act and defend them with the speech that brought the smoldering opposition of the colonies to George Third's imperial schemes to a blaze in the proposition: no taxation without representation. "Caesar," Henry roared in his summing up, "had his Brutus, Charles the First his Cromwell and George the Third . . ." Young Jefferson's breath must have caught in his throat. There were shouts of 'Treason' from the speaker and the more conservative burgesses . . . "may profit by their example." As the uproar continued he finished boldly, "If this be treason make the most of it."

Jefferson himself was no orator, but his learning and methodical habits seem to have made him much respected and even to have brought him in some cash when he began to practice law before the Virginia bar. Looking over his notebooks tends to raise the suspicion that perhaps he didn't collect many of his fees. A lawyer at that time spent a good deal of time jogging around on his nag to the county courts with his briefs in his saddlebags. Clients were scattered far and wide and nobody had much hard money. Most of Jefferson's cases, however, were in Augusta and Albemarle counties, so much of his work must have been done at home. This gave him time to superintend the farming at Shadwell. His courage in saying what he thought and his intoxication with free institutions soon made him a leader among the 'associators' who met in the Apollo room of the Raleigh Tavern at Williamsburg to implement their defiance of the British cabinet with a boycott on British goods.

As a youngster he'd been popular with the girls on account of his lively dancing and fiddling and the breakneck riding he was already famous for; he'd courted a number of young ladies but had never quite come to the point of popping the question because he was obsessed with the notion that he wanted to take a great trip around the world, to England and Italy and Greece, before settling down. As it turned out the most travel he managed to get was a tour of Annapolis, Philadelphia and New York the summer before he was admitted to the bar. A Virginia landowner was lord of all he surveyed, but he was dependent on his agent in England for cash; and if his tastes were as expensive and his interests as varied as young Jefferson's, he was usually in the red on his tobacco account. Besides, Thomas Jefferson had the responsibility of his mother's estates and the care of his younger brothers and sisters to tie him down further.

He was established as a rising lawyer and had served a term in the House of Burgesses (where one of his first acts had been to introduce a bill, which was promptly defeated, to make it possible for planters to free their slaves) when, in June 1770, he wrote to his agent in London to ship him a Forte-piano 'in a case of fine mahogany, solid not veneered, the compass from Double G to F in alt, and plenty of spare strings; and the workmanship of the whole very handsome and worthy of the acceptance of a lady for whom I intend it' . . . 'By this change (in the goods drawn against consigned tobacco) I shall be brought into debt' . . . and to discharge it he would ship to Mr. Adams, the agent, the first tobacco he got to warehouse in the fall. The lady for whom the piano was intended was a musical young widow with whom Jefferson had often played duets, daughter of a popular lawyer who was master of The Forest on the James River. Her name was Martha Skelton.

When they were married on New Year's Day 1772 they drove away from The Forest in a light snow that turned into a blizzard as they advanced, headed for the hill which had been his favorite lookout and place of rumination from boyhood and which he already called Monticello. Since his mother's house at Shadwell had burned Jefferson had been living up there alone in the little brick building that accents one of the ends of the flat U that the terraced wings of the mansion cut out on top of the hill. The bride and bridegroom had to leave their chaise with friends at Blenheim in the valley because the snow was too deep. They rode up through the silent forest on horseback. When they got to Monticello they found that the Negroes had all turned in. Their little house had only one room. Jefferson put the horses in the stable below and made up a fire in the brick fireplace. On a shelf behind his books he found a bottle of wine, and he and Patty drank it together in the solitude and the snow before going to bed.

His wife's father was well off and she was expecting that a considerable portion would come to her when he died. Jefferson's own part of his father's estate seemed ample and he was making money as a lawyer. Even if his account stood in the red with his agent in England, he was a rich man; he had determined to build himself a seat as fine as any Roman villa of his classical reading. Beside his passion for the Common Law, there had been growing up in Jefferson a strong practical interest in architecture. For years the most prized book in his library had been the magnificent 1715 London edition of Leoni's translation of Palladio's *Four Books*. That and Gibbs' handbook seem to have been his only school, along with the occasional houses of some pretensions to style he had seen in Williamsburg or Annapolis or on such Virginia estates as Mount Airy. Out of a few plates and plans, and some basic idea of a dignified order for the life of man in his head, and probably some discouraging advice from a few practical masons and bricklayers, he invented his own peculiar version of the Palladian style. Thus he became the originator of the colonnaded type of brick building which for some reason we describe as 'colonial,' although these houses were all built under the republic.

In a letter written later in his life Jefferson said that architecture was the most important art to study in a young country because 'it shows so much.' He might have gone on to say that it showed everything. The manner of building and decorating buildings in any particular country or at any particular time shows you more directly than anything else the truths and shams of the society involved. Architecture is the one art that cannot be faked. The arts that use words, sounds, colors are infinitely deceitful, but a building is there. You can look at it from all angles, you can walk around in it, you can use it. Inevitably it will tell you what kind of life the people who built it lived, and hoped to live, and whether their claims to such and such a standard of civilization were false or sound.

Jefferson was a man who felt and expressed one branch of the English culture of his time with peculiar intensity. It was a culture of the gentry. The peculiar circumstances of landowning in Virginia made each gentleman a little monarch on his estate and built up every latent tendency to selfreliance and independence he had in him. In England the gentry had already been institutionalized by the sycophancy of the life of the court and of fashionable London. The Virginians were too far away to get to court and lived more like the English landowners of the early seventeenth than of the eighteenth century. Along with the somewhat perfunctory religiosity of their Anglican church (the Virginia church was the Low Church of the early English reformation; the churches had no steeples and used communion tables instead of altars), their first schooling was in the classics and especially in that selection of the classics that expressed the stoical philosophy of the country gentlemen of the late republic and early empire of Rome. In England the leading men of the republican cast of mind had been wiped out in one of the most successful bloodpurges in history: whatever energies their descendants possessed found expression in building themselves careers in the institutions that were the basis of the maritime empire. In America the great estates kept out of bankruptcy just long enough to give a group of men of brains whose bent had been formed by them the leeway they needed to put all their energies into public service: the establishing of the republic that was heir to the whole line of English libertarian thought. When Jefferson turned his mind, reinforced by the innate mechanical skill necessary for the work, on building, it was immediately the Greco-Roman tradition that appealed to him. It was the natural style for an English republican to turn to. Typical of Jefferson's thoroughness and eagerness to get to the bottom of things was his working his way through Gibbs' more or less perfunctory builder's handbook, to the sources in Palladio and Vitruvius.

Palladio was an architect who worked in Vicenza and in the Venetian hinterland during the late sixteenth century. With less taste and originality, perhaps, he revived the aims of Brunelleschi and Bramante, builders of the earliest Florentine renaissance, which were to get back to architecture as it had been actually practiced by the Romans of the time of Augustus. Palladio went around measuring the Roman remains, studied the Roman textbook that had come down under the name of Vitruvius and embodied what he considered the Vitruvian laws of proportion and precedure in his own manual, his famous *Four Books*. These influenced all the architects of Europe during the period of reaction to the rhetorical style that developed from Michael Angelo's intensely personal use of the antique elements, the style we now call 'the baroque.' Palladio's measurements of the ancient buildings were all a little off, and indeed researchers tell us that Vitruvius's were too, but the *Four Books* contained an excellent set of plates and a very clear exposition of the classical rules for using the Greek orders as applied to Roman domed, vaulted and arched buildings of brick and rubblework. The palaces he built for the small nobles of Vicenza, who must have been a race of fourflushers too big for their boots, bristle with theatrical effects and archaeological bombast. That part was not of much use to Jefferson. But Palladio had also built and illustrated in his work a set of country villas for the practical businessmen of Venice who had estates along the Brenta, in which he tackled exactly the problem a Virginia landowner had to face, the problem of giving unified style and elegance to the complicated buildings of a farm.

Basic in Palladio's theory was the idea of the module. The module was the unit of measurement; say, the diameter of a column. If the diameter of the columns were so much, then they must be so many modules high, so many modules apart, and the unit must be embodied, according to a mathematical scheme, in every detail of the building. Here was a rule that appealed immediately to a man with a mathematical turn of mind and some training in music. An amateur needed a short-cut of this kind that allowed him to figure out his effects according to rule, because he had no practical apprentice's experience in building to start on. Jefferson didn't stick to his measurements any more than Palladio or Vitruvius had, but the system gave him a sense of a building as a whole and gave his work that proportion and musical order that is his personal stamp on a house. In my own opinion, no architect has ever done better in the Palladian style than Jefferson did in his houses at Monticello, Bremo, Poplar Forest or the big front room at Farmington.

His design for the state capitol at Richmond (in its original form that can still be seen in the plaster model) is in a slightly different class, as are the designs he made at the end of his life for the buildings of the University of Virginia. As soon as he got to Europe he went right to the bottom of the classical revival by going to look at the ancient buildings themselves. For the Virginia state capitol he adapted the actual Maison Carrée at Nîmes just as it had come down from the time of Augustus. In making the model he had the help of the meticulous drawings and of the advice of the antiquarian painter Clérisseaux and of the technical skill of his draftsmen and stucco workers. But the idea and the invention were Jefferson's, who thus produced the first of a long line of designs, developed later by Latrobe in this country, that went deliberately back to classical originals (in Latrobe's case to the Greek) and set the course of American architecture for fifty years.

We know what kind of buildings Jefferson built; they are still standing; but nothing in his writing tells us in so many words why he wanted to build that way. At Bremo on the James, not far from the house Jefferson designed for his younger friend, the eccentric and philanthropic General Cocke, are the general's own previous efforts in the 'picturesque' style of Queen Anne, so we know it was not inevitable that a Virginia gentleman in the late eighteenth century should turn to the antique when, as Chastellux quaintly put it, 'he consulted the fine arts in the matter of putting a roof over his head.' The current type of building of the houses Jefferson saw as a boy, the true 'colonial,' was a much less emphatic style that had sifted into England from the Italian renaissance originals through Inigo Jones and Sir Christopher Wren and into America through practical builders' handbooks. Jefferson was in personal matters the least articulate of men, it is probable that he never expressed his deepest feelings even to himself in other than legal and political phraseology, but it becomes fairly obvious as you read through his letters, and become familiar with the sort of thing he left unsaid in them, that his architecture was the most direct and personal expression we have of the turn of his mind, the frame for the sort of life he wanted to live and wanted his fellowcitizens to live. Monticello and the Declaration of Independence are two key achievements of the same man and they are not incompatible.

In the first place the buildings Jefferson designed are admirably contrived to give full scale to the human figure. His country houses are manorial mansions in the sense the English country houses were, but with the feudal factor left out. Jefferson hated flunkeys and personal service, and spent a great deal of his time working out contraptions that would let him live at ease without them. No footmen threw open the glass doors of his drawingroom, they were arranged so that they both opened simultaneously at a touch. To run a big place like Monticello, to clean, to keep the fires going, to fetch water, to make the beds and empty the slops, he had to have a mass of servants, but every effort was taken in planning the house to keep them at least out of sight. In his dumbwaiter and his little elevator for bottles of wine and the rotary servingdoor between kitchen and diningroom he planned for General Cocke at Bremo he was heading towards the modern mechanized house where the householder and his family can do all the work themselves. He wanted a house where a free man could live in a society of equals. Already he had seen the possibility, which is even more teasing and tantalizingly near today, that, with the growth of mechanical invention, the productive work of the world can be made so light that the men who do it can be free and equal to those who organize and exploit production. It was for the free men of the future republic, when Negro slavery would have been done away with, when every citizen's son should have as good a chance for an education as any other and as much of an opportunity to show what he had in him, when every man could have his farm and his garden and his house, it was for the free men of the vast westward continent of the future that Jefferson planned the white porches with their careful modulation of columns and windows and pediments and their severely simplified ornaments 'from the antique.' Even today, with all the certainty under our skins of a world so heartbreakingly different, it is hard to stand on one of those porches, looking out at the sweep of landscape rich in great trees which the columns frame, without feeling a lift of the spirits.

In the years since he had sat a somewhat stiff fourth at Governor Fauquier's little dinners Jefferson's architecture and his gardening had been, with some music thrown in, the main pleasure and occupation of his life at home. He managed to turn a hobby into a career of invention and accomplishment that would have made him important in early America as an architect, if he'd never done anything else. But all the while he was carrying on a difficult and wearing public life of negotiation, committee meetings and close work on the law books. With a few friends who thought as he did he was trying to turn the Old Dominion into something like a modern democracy.

In the fall of 1776 he had refused re-election to the Continental Congress and accepted a seat in the Virginia legislature instead, because he wanted to be home with his family and because he felt his first allegiance was to his own state. Immediately he set to work, using all his prestige as signer of the Declaration of Independence and leader of the new national government, to liberalize the laws and administration. Virginia was still organized like an English county under the Walpole squirarchy; dissenting ministers could not preach without running the risk of being put in jail, Unitarians could not testify in court, a Quaker stepped across the state line at his peril, property went to the eldest son under entail, every man had to pay his tithe to the established church: all the bloody laws under which great British landowners had kept tenants and daylaborers and, in Virginia, slaves and bondservants in subjection for centuries were on the statutebooks. With George Wythe and the conservative leader John Pendleton he sat on a committee to humanize the code of law. It meant months of close detail but in the end the delegates accepted their work.

Then Jefferson's troubles began. He introduced a bill for complete religious toleration and church disestablishment. It was only passed years later after a strenuous fight by Jefferson's friends led by his young neighbor James Madison. He did manage to get through a bill repealing the laws of entail, a measure he hoped would break up the big estates and keep landholdings small, but the landowners were already getting balky. In the matter of slavery he had been so completely unsuccessful before that he and his friends thought it better to wait; his plan was to tack on some conservative bill an amendment to regulate slavery to the effect that all Negroes born after a certain date should be free. He did induce the delegates to prohibit further importation of slaves.

His greatest disappointment was that he could not argue

the legislature into passing three bills for public education he had prepared. This scheme was the key to his whole plan for democratic selfgovernment and its failure did more than any other single factor to ruin his hope of turning Virginia into a democratic agrarian commonwealth. The plan was that the counties should be divided into wards and that each ward should support a free school for all children, to be paid for by local taxation and superintended by a local school board. Over these was to be established a set of regional colleges or high schools for the further education of the brightest students, and William and Mary was to be turned into a state university to which the star students in the colleges should have their way paid. People of means were to be allowed to send their children to the public schools too by paying for them, but the system would make it sure that no child of ability should lack the best education the state could offer. Associated with it was a plan for a state library.

The Virginians had none of that enthusiasm for education the New Englanders had inherited from their puritan forebears, who had been truly people of the Book. The delegates would not be convinced, so the one measure failed that could have given a selfgoverning base to Virginia and the whole South and could possibly have saved those states the lost years of ruined plantation economics and guttering gentility and ended in the smashup of their whole system in the Civil War. At the end of his life Jefferson did manage to embody part of his great plan in the University of Virginia, but he himself knew and always said, that the lack of primary selfgovernment in the counties and of primary education would be the ruin of Virginia democracy. Up to his death he dinned it into the ears of his followers that without the wards as a popular unit to correspond to townmeeting in New England, selfgovernment would fail in Virginia.

Patrick Henry, rapidly degenerating into a selfsatisfied conservative, had been a fizzle as the commonwealth's first

Governor. As the second Governor, Jefferson managed to do an immense amount of useful work, but he retired from the office with even less credit than his old friend.

He had been chosen Governor on the first of June 1779. It was the blackest time in the whole war. In Europe the surrender of Burgoyne at Saratoga and the subtle diplomatic webs that Franklin sat weaving like a genial gray-worsted spider in Paris were stacking the cards against England; but in America French help had not yet taken effect.

The economic situation was desperate. Continental paper and the paper of the various states had been inflated to the vanishing point. Hard cash couldn't be laid hold of. Farming and commerce had been ruined by the blockade.

Washington was sitting in his camp up the Hudson watching the British force in New York. He was already committed to the Fabian policy, temporarily at least so disastrous, of not scattering his troops even if it meant leaving his native state open to the enemy. The British had command of the sea, and on land their armies ravaged wherever they pleased.

In the South things were bad indeed. Charleston had fallen. General Gates, the hero of Saratoga, had let himself be whipped at Camden.

From the minute Jefferson was sworn in as Governor he was busy helping the Continental forces by stripping his own state of levies and military supplies to send them north to Washington and Lafayette and south to Nathanael Greene in the Carolinas, where that longfaced Rhode Islander was sourly pulling together strings Gates had left untied. Jefferson had confidence in Washington's master plan, but it took time. Farmers laughed at Virginia currency, so supplies and horseflesh had to be impressed. Governor Jefferson had gotten in wrong with the clergy by advocating disestablishment, with the conservative landowners by the repeal of the laws of entail and by all this talk about educating the poor and freeing the slaves; now he had to superintend the forcible seizure of the goods of his own constituents. He worked doggedly supplying the armies and seconding Washington's grand strategy in every way he could. It didn't make him popular with the farmers.

Things were already quite bad enough when, in the winter of his second term, a British force under Benedict Arnold, whose treason had been one of the worst blows the Continental cause had suffered, sailed up the James and made a sudden landing at Westover, just seven miles below Richmond. The capital had been recently moved to the mill village of Richmond above the falls for security from just such raids. Jefferson rode around until his horse fell dead under him directing the removal of stores. He was not a military man and strictly left the military command to the professionals, but he had to do what he could. Some munitions he managed to save, but Arnold entered Richmond unopposed and destroyed a foundry for cannons and an arms depot, and did a great deal of damage before he sailed off down the river again with a fair wind.

British raids continued. Towards spring, Cornwallis, who had shaken off Greene's army that was supposed to keep him in the Carolinas, marched up the coast to Petersburg. The Virginia legislature fled to Charlottesville. The delegates had barely gotten settled in the Charlottesville taverns when they had to run again with Tarleton's dragoons right on their coattails. The seat of government was moved breathlessly to Staunton in the Valley, but Jefferson and the speakers of the two houses were almost nabbed at Monticello by a British detachment. Meanwhile Colonel Lynch had handled a near insurrection in Montgomery County so roughly that his name became a proverb; the Virginians were penniless, their farms were ruined, they had seen their cattle driven off by the British and by their own elected officials and all they had in return was saddlebags full of paper money that wouldn't buy anything, and they were sore. The legislators were still in a funk from their narrow escape at Charlottesville. Grumbling and recrimination increased every day. Jefferson had already refused a third term and suggested the appointment in his stead of the man he had put at the head of the militia, General Nelson.

There was a painful irony in the fact that, after Jefferson had been the scapegoat for all the worst of it, the tide turned in that same summer of '81. The Virginia campaign of Washington and Rochambeau, backed by the blockade of the Chesapeake by De Grasse's fleet, brought about the surrender of Cornwallis' army in Yorktown by October. Suddenly it was all over. The states were free and independent.

During the dark days young George Nicholas had jumped to his feet in the legislature to demand an enquiry into Governor Jefferson's conduct during the British raids. By the time the enquiry came off things were sunny again, animosities had faded and Nicholas made such handsome amends that he and Jefferson continued fast friends all their lives. The legislature tendered Mr. Jefferson a vote of thanks. But it did not make up for the slights he had undergone nor for the sense of failure he felt at not having been able to accomplish the reforms he had felt most important.

Things were not made any better by the fact that he was in a bad way for money. He had had heavy expenses during the war. His salary as Governor had been in almost worthless paper and Cornwallis had amused himself by destroying the house and the crops and carrying off the slaves at Elk Hill, one of the best farms that had come to him through his wife. At Monticello the British had done no damage, though they had given his butler a bad scare, so it was to Monticello he retired, with that sense of relief that every Virginian felt in getting back to his own acres after an excursion into the world.

He had left the field and gone to skulk in his tent, but he was no man to skulk in idleness. While he was Governor he had found time to draft a plan for modernizing the government buildings at Williamsburg. A century and a half later the architects of the recent reconstruction used his drawings as the basis of their work. While he was laid up after a nasty fall from a horse, he wrote his *Notes on Virginia* in answer to some enquiries of the Marquis de Marbois, an attaché of the French Legation in Philadelphia, who was collecting information about the geography, economic social and political, of the new states. Jefferson had been so much impressed by the set of the public mind against him and his ideas that he did his best to keep the book from being published in America; for fear, as he said, that his remarks on slavery would do more harm than good; that they would tend to deepen the prejudices of his fellowcitizens rather than argue them away.

Jefferson had reached that barrier that every original mind eventually encounters in dealing with the generality of men. In the end he was to take the Boyg's advice to Peer Gynt: 'Go roundabout,' but for a while he was stopped dead.

It is part of the nature of consciousness, of how the mental apparatus works, that free reason is only a very occasional function of people's 'thinking' and that much of the process is made of reactions as standardized as those of the keys on a typewriter. Some sets of words, in any given situation, are positively charged and give sensations of pleasure and approval, while others are negatively charged with sensations of disgust and disapproval. The verbal apparatus through which people keep in touch with the social and political organization under which they live is particularly full of inhibiting machinery. The process of getting people to accept political changes or novelties, even those from which they will immediately benefit, has broken the hearts of innovators since history began. "I have found," Fred Taylor, the management engineer who first methodically rationalized factory work, wrote in 1909, "that any improvement is not only opposed but bitterly and aggressively opposed by the majority of men."

Socrates tried tricking people out of prejudice by asking

them questions. Somewhere in *Mein Kampf* Hitler exclaims with naïve surprise on how much it is constantly necessary to deceive people for their own good. Habit, selfinterest, fear of change, and purely automatic reflexes of negation are hurdles every reformer (be his work good or bad) has to reckon with.

It is the discovery of this barrier that breeds the hasty cynicism and low estimate of mankind that is at the inner core of the average successful politician. If he manages to get past it at all, he ends up too often with the state of mind of a confidence man who has found it's as easy to pass bad checks as good ones. The surprising thing, I suppose, is that men are bred at all who are able to climb that barrier in their fellowmen where so much that is fresh honest inventive hopeful stops dead, and who having climbed it keep some of their first honesty of purpose. Perhaps the survival of the race itself demands the handing down from generation to generation and the occasional emergence of the type of mind that can't shake off a feeling of responsibility for other men, the type of mind in which the qualities grouped under the tag 'the parental bent' are dominant.

Anyway it is plain that among Virginians who took the side of Independence during the Revolutionary War, this parental bent was very strong. There was something about the secure family life, the daily work of keeping a plantation going, even perhaps their patriarchal relations with their Negroes, that produced a race of men who were skillful enough in the art of inducing their fellows to take action to be effective and who still were unwilling to use their ascendancy for their own selfish ends. Washington, who was certainly not a brilliant man in other ways, owed his pre-eminence to the dominance of that quality in his makeup. It wasn't only the Virginians; because the small town printer and merchant Franklin had it to an immense degree. It was strong in the Adamses for all their crotchets and vanities. Even Hamilton had it. But it was particularly compelling in Monroe, Madison and Jefferson. In reading the letters and documents of the period you get the feeling that it was particularly from the Virginians that emanated the intellectual and moral tone that gave such stature to the men who governed the United States during our first twentyfive or thirty years of being a nation.

When Jefferson came home sore and smarting from his exoneration by the legislature, he had not yet found how to dodge the automatic veto of prejudice and habit. He was bitterly disillusioned. He was determined to fill his life entirely with the routine of his farm and his home, with raising his children and his nephews and nieces, and his crops and his fruit-trees and his horses and his gristmill, and his projects for building and the endlessly diverting daily meticulous study of the climate and the plants and the animals of his own Albemarle County. But it was not on the books that Jefferson should be a private man. The center of all that rich family world was his wife, whose health was never off his mind when he was forced to be away from her. In September 1782 she died.

4. Citizen Barlow of the Republic of the World

JOEL BARLOW was the youngest son of a Connecticut farmer. He was born in March 1754 in a house on the ridge in Redding, then part of the township of Fairfield. His father, Samuel Barlow, had raised two families and some pretty fair crops off his hundred and seventyodd acres of stony land; when he died he left about a thousand pounds, Connecticut money, some stock and a slave girl named Dinah to be distributed between his widow and the six sons and two daughters who outlived him.

Young Joel seems to have been the pet of the family. When as a small boy he'd begun to make up rhymes and to show a taste for books he'd been put in the care of the Reverend Nathaniel Bartlett, the Congregational minister at Redding Center, who had added a smattering of the humanities to the drilling in the three R's the local farmboys underwent at the nearest schoolhouse. Probably his mother hoped he was headed for the ministry, although already by the mid-eighteenth-century ambitious New England farmers' sons were taking up the law instead of preaching as a path to eminence in the community. One of the last acts of Samuel Barlow's life was to take young Joel, a strapping chubbyfaced hobbledehoy of nineteen, out into the wilderness to Hanover in New Hampshire, where the Reverend Eleazer Wheelock had recently founded Dartmouth College as a seminary to prepare young Indians and whites for carrying the gospel among the heathen to the northward. For those who were not far enough along in their studies to enter the college he also conducted a preparatory school known as Moor's School. It was in Moor's School that his father placed young Joel.

The Reverend Eleazer Wheelock believed in the dignity of labor as well as of study. Manual work on the farm and in the gristmill was part of his curriculum. Samuel Barlow made the arrangement that Joel would work his way waiting on table and running errands, and that besides his own services, the efforts of a certain Miss Elizabeth Burr, whom the Barlows were to pay for 'overseeing, superintending, and directing the affair of cooking for the college and school and managing the prudentials thereof' were to help balance the price of the boy's schooling. In return for his own and Miss Burr's work Joel was to be provided with 'eating, drinking, washing, firewood, candles, study room and tuition.' It looks as if the Reverend Eleazer Wheelock had driven a hard bargain. But Samuel Barlow wanted the boy educated at all costs. Indeed in his will, made on the day of his death three months later, he directed specifically that, as it was his intention that his son Joel should have a liberal education, Joel's portion of the estate should be paid him in installments for that purpose without waiting for him to come of age.

Joel's mother was appointed his guardian and executor of the will. He continued on at Hanover all that winter and the following summer, studying Virgil and Cicero and the Greek Testament in preparation for Dartmouth College.

But in spite of all Eleazer Wheelock's labor in the vineyard of the Lord the young men of Joel's generation don't seem to have been able to keep their minds on carrying the gospel to the heathen. The students at Hanover were restless and troublesome; they complained a great deal about the food and showed a worldly spirit and a lack of enthusiasm for manual labor. The year before Joel went to Hanover, John Ledyard, another promising young Connecticut Yankee, had set the institution into an uproar by his worldshaking restlessness. He had fomented the putting on of a stage play, Addison's *Cato*, had induced the boys to climb mountains in the dead of winter, and had taken the study of Indian affairs so literally that he'd been absent without leave three months in the lodges of the Iroquois to the northward. His final exploit had been to build himself a dugout canoe and to paddle off in it down the Connecticut River with nothing but a Greek Testament, a volume of Ovid and an old bearskin for baggage, so beginning the travels that were to take him round the world with Captain Cook and on foot round the Gulf of Bothnia in winter and across Siberia and to his death in Cairo far from the cozily cultivated landscape of his native state.

The following autumn, after he had won his admission to Dartmouth College, young Barlow, who doesn't seem to have had much flair either for spreading the gospel, suggested with characteristic tact to President Wheelock that, the circumstances of his family having been straitened by his father's death, it would probably be better for him to attend college nearer home; so he was sent off to New Haven with a letter recommending him to President Daggett of Yale as 'a good genius and a middling scholar.'

At New Haven he got along very well. He wasn't a very good student and he was backward for his age, but he was friendly and cheerful, a young man whom people found it very hard to dislike, and he had a sense of humor and a knack for composing plausible verses in the fashionable manner of the day. He studied under Ezra Stiles and the learned Timothy Dwight, then a recent graduate and a tutor, and was admitted into a literary society known as 'Brothers in Unity,' where he became the friend of Oliver and Alexander Wolcott and of that pernickety grammarian, Noah Webster.

Among the tutors who struggled to hammer some learning into the undergraduates' heads was Abraham Baldwin, an ambitious young man about Joel's age. With him and his brother

Dudley, Joel formed one of the close associations that were a part of his easy gregarious way of living.

It was a time in Connecticut when a general equality of wealth and education made people's relationships and contacts simple, and gave life in the small neat towns, joined up only by the worst of rutted wagon roads, a pleasant tone of frank conviviality. There wasn't much cash around but want was unknown in the wellbuilt farmhouses so cleverly located beside their barns in wellwatered valleys and on the sheltered slopes of rolling stony hills. Since Jonathan Edwards' great defeat enough of the skepticism of the century had seeped into the churches to lighten the load of calvinist theology without disturbing the close community life or the cheerful imperatives of family ethics. Connecticut farmers lived easy. Sermons and Wednesday lecture were taken for granted, but townmeeting and the gazettes and roadside talk and huskingbees and roofingparties were the real training grounds for young people's minds.

Joel's formal education, in spite of his father's tender care for it, turned out scrappy. He'd hardly gotten settled at New Haven when the news came of the fighting at Lexington and Concord. College was suspended and the undergraduates set to drilling. When college opened again after Bunker Hill, the students were already formed into a trainband sufficiently exercised to escort General Washington across town with fife and drum when he went through New Haven on his way to take command of the Continental forces at Cambridge. Noah Webster was the sergeant and snapped out the commands. The smart appearance of the students was noticed in the gazettes.

That summer Joel's mother, Esther Barlow, died. In her will she left him all the livestock on the farm and appointed him sole executor of her estate. After settling up her affairs at Redding he went back for the fall term already a man on his own. His cozy relationship with the Baldwins filled the gap in his life caused by the closing up of his own home. He went to live at their house in New Haven.

All their lives Abraham and Dudley were like his own brothers. He was all kinds of good friends with their sister Ruth too; only gradually it was coming over them all that there was something warmer growing up between Joel and Ruth. 'The Old Gentleman,' as they called him, Michael Baldwin, the father, was uneasy about it from the first, though his only objection to Joel as a son-in-law was his complete lack of worldly prospects; but he doesn't seem to have had much influence with his children.

During the winter of '76 the fact that war with Great Britain was on in deadly earnest was brought home to Joel by the news that his favorite brother Sam had died at Poughkeepsie from some sickness he'd caught on Montgomery's unhappy expedition against Quebec. During the summer vacation Joel and a number of college friends got their baptism of fire themselves. With some local levies of militia they joined the Continental Army on Long Island in time to see a disastrous defeat. Some time before the bloody battle at White Plains, however, Joel took sick himself and was invalided home.

The college kept its sessions going fitfully throughout the war, occasionally suspended on account of an epidemic of 'camp distemper' or by the shortage of victuals for commons. At length in March 1777 President Daggett announced with chagrin in chapel one morning that college would have to be dismissed again on account of the impossibility of procuring provisions and that furthermore he was going to resign. The next summer the corporation managed to pull some of the classes together under Joseph Buckminster up in the country at Farmington and Glastonbury where they were out of the way of British raids. The students and the corporation got into a row about how and where the studying was to be done. A number of students, Barlow among them, settled down to teaching school to pick up a little money. The trustees disapproved of this practice and ordered the students back to New Haven. In the spring of 1778 Ezra Stiles accepted the presidency of the college and thereafter there was better order in the academic groves. The senior class was graduated, after some hurried cramming under the learned president, in July. Barlow read the class poem, *The Prospect of Peace,* which began:

> The closing scenes of Tyrants' fruitless rage,
> The opening prospects of a golden age,
> The dread events that crown th' important year
> Wake the glad song and claim th' attentive ear.

After graduation, like so many bright young men before him and after him who have made a name for themselves in college, Barlow went through a painful period of doldrums. *The Prospect of Peace* had been universally admired. Right away he set to work on another patriotic poem to be called *The Vision of Columbus,* which he hoped and his friends hoped would be the epic of the young American republic, as the *Aeneid* had been the epic of the new empire of Augustus. The trouble was how to make a living meanwhile.

He applied for the job of tutor at Yale, but the trustees evidently didn't feel that a knack for tossing off heroic couplets was enough qualification, or that patriotic ardor was a sufficient substitute for that profound devotion to calvinist theology and 'solid learning' they demanded in their instructors. Barlow scraped up a little cash teaching school at New Haven and borrowing from his older brothers, who seem to have felt, as his father and mother had felt, that they should make any sacrifice they could to further the young poet's career. In ordinary times it would have sufficed for his board while he studied for a Master's degree, but the price of living was rising and the value of money was falling.

He lived on as best he could in New Haven, boarding with the Baldwins and very much the center and pet of a group of bright young people. Elizabeth Whitman and Betsy Stiles, the president's daughter, and other girls set their caps for him, but there was now no doubt in anybody's mind that he was in love with Ruth Baldwin, so little indeed that old Michael blew up and ordered Joel out of the house and sent his daughter away to Guilford.

But Joel had warm friends, in college and out. Timothy Dwight invited him to Northampton, where he could pay for his keep by helping out with the school Dwight kept there. Buckminster revised his couplets for him and wrote him encouraging letters. Noah Webster and the Wolcotts were busy trying to find him a position tutoring in some wealthy family. David Humphreys, whom he'd recently met, was writing letters to his friends trying to find a patron for the great poem. He'd written Colonel Wadsworth soon after meeting Barlow that he considered him 'one of the most considerable geniuses in poetry which we have ever had rise up amongst us.'

Meanwhile Joel rode around Connecticut from one hospitable friend's house to another, having a good time wherever he went, but gnawed within by the knowledge that his small stock of money was running out and that there was no more where that came from. The price of living kept rising. Nobody had any hard money. The whole economic life of the thirteen states had been thrown out of kilter by the war. What with the British raids, and the difficulty of getting farm products to market, and with continental paper and the emissions of the states swirling into hopeless inflation, he couldn't very well ask his brothers to help him any more.

Another thing worried him night and day. He and Ruth Baldwin were crazy in love with each other. Since her father and stepmother had set themselves against the match she was no longer happy at home. It was time they got married. He had to find some way of making a living.

Brother Abraham, 'Prom' as they called him, had gotten himself an appointment to the army as a chaplain. In spite of Joel's distaste for preaching a doctrine he only vaguely believed and in spite of the suspicions of the Connecticut Association of Ministers, who felt that his views were far from orthodox, an appointment as chaplain to the Fourth Massachusetts Brigade was managed for him. He hurriedly boned up on his theology and was licensed as a candidate for the ministry in New Haven in August 1780. Barlow's friendly innocence of manner and his patriotic couplets won the day even with the Connecticut clergy.

With considerable misgivings, the Reverend Cleremont, as in his letters to Ruthy he called himself in his clerical form, in contradistinction to Quamminy the poetic sprite who polished up the couplets, set off to join his regiment at Hackensack. After the horrors of preaching his first sermon were over he found he enjoyed the life of an army chaplain. Prom was stationed near him and they found themselves a billet together in a Dutchman's neat stone house. At the funeral of General Poor he met Nathanaël Greene, to whom he had already been recommended by Humphreys, and a number of other high ranking officers. His pleasant country manners and the humorous straightforwardness of his talk immediately won him friends. As a preacher he wasn't much of a success, because theology was a subject he couldn't put his mind on, but his songs were sung around the army and increased his reputation as patriot and poet.

One day he sat down to write Ruth regretting that he'd drunk too much at dinner at General Greene's the night before. ". . . there were a number of gentlemen &c. You know what I mean. I wish I was not so foolish . . ." Even while he was writing friends came in to get him to go with them to André's execution. When he went back to his table to finish the letter he wrote ". . . A politer Gentleman or a greater character of his age perhaps is not alive, he was 28 years old, he was dressed completly and suffused with calmness and cheerfulness. With the Appearance of Philosophy & heroism he observed that he was buoyed above the fear of Death by a consciousness, that every action of his life had been honorable, that in a few minutes he should be out of all pleasure or pain. Whether he has altered his mind or whether he has any mind is now best known to himself . . ." and added that his heart was in a flutter from the sight. Arnold's treason, however, gave him a chance to preach a sermon about something he really believed, his passionate enthusiasm for his country and the cause of liberty. It went over very well and made up, in the opinion of the army, for the lukewarmness they couldn't help noticing in his religious outpourings. A few days later he received an invitation to dine at headquarters with General Washington. "How do you think," he wrote Ruth, "I felt when the greatest man on earth placed me at his right hand with Lord Stirling on his left?"

When he went on leave he was very much the lion at Redding and preached a sermon from the pulpit of his old schoolteacher, the Reverend Bartlett. His brothers felt that young Joel was indeed a credit to the family. By this time he'd probably discovered that patriotism was a good substitute for religion in a sermon and no longer had that hollow feeling of sham when he got up to call on the name of the Lord. At least, for the first time in his life he had a regular salary.

On the strength of it he and Ruth were married in Farmington by the Reverend Benoni Upson of Kensington Parish. On account of old Baldwin's opposition they had decided to keep their marriage secret for a while. Ruth stayed in Kensington and Joel ostensibly lived in Hartford nearby, working on his poem and writing her copious letters whenever he was away from her. When his leave was over he rode back to his regiment, now quartered at West Point, going around by New Haven to visit his friends there. President Stiles invited him to read a poem at the next commencement. He set to work on it as soon as he got back to camp. During the summer he was sent up to Vermont on some army business and came back with a violent fever. Prom Baldwin and another friend, Sammy

Cogswell, nursed him back to health. While he was recovering at Mandeville's house on the Hudson he made up a song for Ruth:

> Soon my charmer soon returning
> That impatient hour shall come
> When, my soul with rapture burning,
> Peace and Love shall call me home.

He was up and about in time to attend the Yale Commencement in September 1781. It was the first public commencement in seven years. Relief and jubilation were beginning to run through the thirteen states. Although the war wasn't over yet, there was a feeling abroad that it was won. A friend shepherded Ruth round the ceremonies while Barlow delivered a sermon in chapel and at the exercises recited a poem entitled *The Genius of Literature* which he pieced together out of couplets collected for the preliminary sketch of *The Vision of Columbus*. Such sentiments as

> . . . New arts ascend
> New manners rise, new wealth and power extend,
> Allure the hero, feed th' enquiring sage,
> Enlarge the genius, dignify the age,
> Till laws and empires swell the rising reign
> And their own navies whiten on the main

went big with people who felt a premonition of Yorktown in the air. It was announced that the verses were a sample of *The Vision of Columbus*. To crown his successes the corporation elected him tutor. But he was already making better money as an army chaplain. He declined the honor with thanks.

When the army went into winter quarters he got leave again and settled down for several months in his brother Aaron's house at West Redding. There Quamminy worked like a beaver piling couplet on couplet, counting out the invariable pentameters on his fingers, and in the end produced an edifice that has about as much relation to poetry as a Mississippi steamboat has to architecture, but that manages to create a similar effect of provincial pomp. With all its faults it was a thoroughly national production, and, from that viewpoint, it is possible even now to understand the endearing qualities that Barlow's friends and contemporaries felt in the work.

While Quamminy was picking out adjectives and burnishing his heroic epithets, gossip was running from farmhouse to farmhouse along with the sleighbells of the Connecticut winter to the effect that the patriot poet and Ruth Baldwin were secretly married. Dudley went to break the news to the Old Gentleman lest he hear it from a third party and go off into a tantrum. Eventually Dudley and Prom talked their father into a better humor with his new son-in-law, but the Old Gentleman never was sufficiently mollified to shell out any cash to help the young people set up housekeeping.

By the following fall *The Vision of Columbus* was far enough along to justify Barlow's starting to find a publisher. The only way possible to publish such a poem in America at the time was to collect the cost of printing ahead by subscription. In the company of General Lincoln and the Paymaster General, Mr. Pierce, Barlow left camp, where his wife had been visiting him staying at the Mandevilles' house, to ride across the Jerseys through the brilliant October countryside to Philadelphia. It had been suggested that the poem should be dedicated to Louis Sixteenth, the birth of whose son and heir had lately been celebrated at West Point by an elaborate ball for the French officers. General Lincoln was going to introduce Barlow to the French ambassador, through whom he was to secure His Most Christian Majesty's permission for the dedication; and friends were writing Dr. Franklin in Paris to interest him in the book. The treaty with England was being negotiated, the thirteen confederated states of North America were free and independent and everybody felt it was fitting that their victory and the peace should be celebrated by a poem in the heroic style.

After seven years of war it was not without emotion that

army officers in buff and blue and periwigged members of Congress read Barlow's *Hymn to Peace:*

> . . . From scenes of blood, these beauteous shores that stain
> From gasping friends that press the sanguine plain,
> From fields, long taught in vain thy flight to mourn,
> I rise, delightful Power, and greet thy glad return.
> Too long the groans of death, and battle's bray
> Have rung discordant through th' unpleasing lay;
> Let pity's tear its balmy fragrance shed,
> O'er heroes' wounds and patriot warriors dead;
> Accept, departed shades, these grateful sighs
> Your fond attendants to th' approving skies . . .

When they met him and found him a modest and unassuming young man, a comical talker and tablecompanion over the wine after dinner in spite of a good deal of homespun shyness in his makeup, naturally they took him to their hearts and vowed that along with the greatest commander and the wisest statesmen of all time, America had produced a poet.

Full of hopes for the future Joel went back to Hartford to give his poem its last scrubbing up and to start housekeeping with his adored Ruth. In his riding round Connecticut from friend's house to friend's house in search of good company and encouragement he had found himself spending more and more time in Hartford.

He had gradually gotten to be good friends with John Trumbull who lived there and practiced law there. John Trumbull came of a leading family of Connecticut and, since publishing the first cantos of *M'Fingal,* had been considered the main literary light of the state if not of all America. He was a crony of Dwight's and Humphreys' and had the distinction of having studied law in the office of John Adams in Boston in the days when Boston was in the van of the fight against the tyranny of the British Crown. He was thick with a local physician named Lemuel Hopkins, a gentleman of literary tastes who had a great enthusiasm for satiric and mock heroic verse. As

Hartford was the state capital, his college friend, Oliver Wolcott, Jr., son of the Governor, who was already making his way in politics in his own right, was often there. Noah Webster, too, busy with his *Grammatical Institute*, came in and out of town and was invited to the first meeting of the club that was planned as a center for what was rapidly becoming a flourishing literary community. The Barlows settled down in Hartford in the society of this warm and cozy group of highly diverse friends lumped together by literary gossip under the name of 'The Hartford Wits.'

The first thing Joel had to do was to find some way of making a living. His army pay wouldn't last forever and no patron had appeared for the heroic poem. As a beginning he started a printing, stationery and bookselling business in partnership with a certain Elisha Babcock. Between them they published a weekly paper called *The American Mercury*, which proposed 'to furnish a useful and elegant entertainment for the different classes of customers,' as well as to print in installments the London account of Captain Cook's last voyage. As publishers Barlow and Babcock brought out Timothy Dwight's *The Conquest of Canaan* and a new edition of the Psalms of the famous Dr. Watts, revised by Barlow, and Part III of Noah Webster's *Grammatical Institute*, in which were cited, as examples of stylistic felicity, a number of passages from the not yet published *Vision of Columbus*, as well as quotations from *The Conquest of Canaan* and *M'Fingal*. They also plagiarized an almanac and almost got themselves into a lawsuit over it.

Plagiarism was something that was beginning to hit home to Barlow and Trumbull. One of the first things the Hartford Wits needed, if independent writing were to be possible at all, was the passage of a copyright law. Barlow wrote to various influential friends urging them to put such a law through the state legislature and the federal Congress. No such thing as literary property existed in America. Poor Trumbull whose *M'Fingal* had sold enormously was never able to make a cent out of the book, and what was worse he saw all sorts of scurrilous doggerel published under his name without being able to do anything about it.

As a publisher Barlow wasn't much of a success, or it may have merely been that there wasn't enough business in Hartford at the time to furnish a living for two families; anyway, after a year his partnership with Babcock was dissolved, on a friendly basis to be sure, by the publication of the following notice in *The American Mercury* for December 5, 1785:

JOEL BARLOW & ELISHA BABCOCK

HAVING by mutual consent dissolved their partnership, request all those who have accounts open with the late firm of BARLOW & BABCOCK to forward them for settlement as soon as convenient. Those who are indebted to them may depend on having their payment made easy provided it is made soon.

Said BABCOCK will carry on the printing business and attempt to please every body.

Said BARLOW has opened a store of BOOKS and other Goods at the house of the late Doctor Jepson near the South Meeting House; where may be had the new Edition of Psalms and hymns,

LIKEWISE,

RUM, Molasses, Hyson and Bohea Teas, Alspice, Ginger, Broad Cloths, Coatings, Camblets, Chintzes, Callicoes, Gauzes, Ribons, & ** Any kind of Public Securities or Country Produce taken in Payment.

It looks as if Ruth must have been taking a hand in the business of making a living for a poet.

Perhaps on John Trumbull's advice, he had decided to study law. Even before the Revolution the thirteen colonies had swarmed with lawyers and the Yankees in particular had been famous for their contentiousness; now more and more, the law was getting to be the avenue up which bright young men could climb into politics and into the dominant position in the community that had been previously held, in New England at least, by the clergy. Barlow had many friends in official positions, he was popular with the local Cincinnati and had been asked to speak before their state association. He had served a term as town councilor of Hartford. His friends decided he had the makings of a lawyer.

The dissertation he prepared to read at Fairfield (his home town) for his bar examination dealt with the need to weed out the out-of-date and feudal rubbish from the sound body of English Common Law. His ideas on the subject were in tune with the reforms Jefferson had managed to put through in Virginia a few years before. He had the same attitude towards English law that his friend Noah Webster had towards English grammar and vocabulary, that it was up to the citizens of the new nation to make over the fundamentals for their own use.

The law, however, didn't take with him any more than the ministry or publishing or teaching or storekeeping had. Barlow was a man who developed slowly and found it hard to discover just where he belonged in the world.

It was a restless time. The honeymoon period of the North American confederacy was over, if indeed it had ever existed. Up to Yorktown all sections and classes had been to some extent united by the exigencies of battle. A man was a patriot or he was a Tory, and the Tories had been pushed off the map. But now that the war was over, as happens after every war, the problems that had been left unsolved for duration came flocking home to roost. All the latent local antagonisms, the sectional jealousies, the class divergences that had been anaesthetized by the need to unite against the redcoats, began to make themselves felt. Business was paralyzed by a flood of worthless paper money and almost worthless certificates of debt issued by the Continental Congress. In rural sections of New England farmers were going back to barter for the exchange of goods. In the cities speculators were buying up every conceivable commodity from 'indents' to potatoes. Producers of goods felt everywhere at a disadvantage. Farmers couldn't sell their produce for any money that was worth anything and felt that the men of the counting house were to blame. As the Continental Army disbanded and Washington went back to his own agricultural problems at Mount Vernon men felt the union was falling apart. 'A hoop for the barrel' began to be the toast in the taverns. The state legislatures wouldn't pay their assessments for the upkeep of the national government. The grand old Continental Congress was losing ground every day; in fact that body never recovered the loss of honor and dignity it suffered when it let itself be chased out of Philadelphia to Princeton by a few drunken recruits whose pay was in arrears brawling under the windows of the State House. A strong federal government just had to be.

It was inevitable that people of wealth and position should blame the rabble and that people without wealth and position should blame the rich for this state of affairs. Joel Barlow didn't have wealth or position but his Hartford friends did, so, as he was a man who had not yet thought very deeply about political or social questions, he was to some extent carried away by their side of the story. In that confused struggle between the advocates of hard and paper money, and between the rank and file Revolutionary veterans and the retired officers of means grouped round the Society of the Cincinnati which came to a head in Shays' 'rebellion' in Massachusetts, Barlow took the side of law and order.

David Humphreys had just come back to his native state after a brilliant official career. He had been one of Washington's aides-de-camp along with Hamilton. He had been voted a sword by Congress for gallantry at Yorktown. He had gone abroad as secretary to the legation in Paris and London and had learned to dress and strut according to the style of high society and had come back, not exactly full of Toryism, but full of fashionable English Whiggery on the model of Brookes' gambling club and the Prince of Wales' set in London. He lashed up Dr. Hopkins and Trumbull and their crowd to enter the fray with a series of mock heroic verses taking off the popular party which they published in *The New Haven Gazette and Connecticut Magazine* under the title of *The Anarchiad.*

The twelve installments of *The Anarchiad* were of very uneven merit, ranging from Humphreys' tasteless song, *The Genius of America*, through some effective lampoons on a certain Mr. William Williams who was a leader of the Connecticut antifederalists, to the fairly high level of campaign verse of the *Speech of Hesper*, an invocation to the Constitutional Convention, that ends

> But know ye favored race one potent head
> Must rule your States and strike your foes with dread,
> The finance regulate, the trade control,
> Live through the empire and accord the whole.
>
> Ere death invades, and night's deep curtain falls,
> Through ruined realms the voice of UNION calls
> Loud as the trump of heaven through darkness roars,
> When gyral gusts entomb Caribbean towers—
> When nature trembles, through the deeps convuls'd,
> And ocean foams from craggy cliffs repuls'd
> On you she calls! Attend the warning cry:
> YE LIVE UNITED OR DIVIDED DIE!

For the taste of the ages these verses are pretty heavily meteorological, but at the time they went through the *Gazettes* and *Posts* and *Advertizers* of the whole country like wildfire and possibly did as much as the close reasoning of the *Federalist* papers to convince authoritarians and antiauthoritarians alike that a federal constitution was needed and that any constitution was better than no constitution.

The label 'Federalist' didn't have the meaning in 1787 it was to have in 1797, and Barlow's Hartford was a quite different place from the later Hartford of the Hartford Convention. The 'Wits' were young and full of high spirits and even managed to see the humor of their own bombast. One number of the *Echo* series which followed *The Anarchiad* was a tremendous piece of mockheroic spoofing describing the burning of a barn; and Trumbull was heard to remark about his friend Timothy Dwight's *The Conquest of Canaan* that the poem had so many thunderstorms in it the printer ought to furnish a lightning rod with every copy.

Meanwhile the great wish of Joel Barlow's life was coming to pass. The subscriptions had come in, the proofsheets had been corrected. On May 14, 1787, just in time to get some copies to Philadelphia for the use of the delegates to the Constitutional Convention that was about to be called to order, Hudson and Goodwin, printers of Hartford, got *The Vision of Columbus* off the press.

For America the book went pretty well. The first printing was followed by a second, and in the fall of the same year an English edition came out; even the English reviewers spoke of it on the whole with respect, but it was the sentiments and the philosophical reasoning that they praised rather than the poetic style. The ninth book with its suggestion of a parliament of nations that would establish universal peace was stimulating to liberals everywhere.

Europe as well as America was feeling the disastrous effects of the century's series of dynastic wars. Thoughtful men on both sides of the Atlantic were allowing themselves to hope that in a new enlightened age courts and kings would give way to parliaments of reasonable men, men whose business was the peaceful pursuit of commerce and industry, under the influence of philosophers who would know how to put an end to the senseless bloodletting and waste. Politically America had led the way. English was the language of liberty. It was logical that an American poet should be the first to challenge the old order in the name of that 'Republic of the World' that was to be the driving political aspiration of the next quarter of a century.

Joel Barlow was a famous man now, but still he hadn't found any way of making a living. He had only his wife to support:

they loved each other dearly and hadn't yet given up hope of raising a family; even if they didn't have children they had to eat and to keep up a decent appearance in the world.

Perhaps it was through Prom Baldwin, who had solved his own economic problem by going to Georgia, where educated Yankees were still scarce, to practice law and there had gotten himself elected to Congress, that Joel met Colonel William Duer, a New York businessman, at one time Secretary of the Board of the Treasury of the Continental Congress, a friend of Alexander Hamilton's and a contributor of several papers to the *Federalist* series.

Colonel Duer had been appealed to for help by Dr. Manassah Cutler, preacher, botanist, lawyer and speculator in public lands, who had been sent down to New York as their lobbyist by a company of Massachusetts men who were looking for big profits in the settlement of Ohio lands. Most everybody was in favor of selling off the western lands, recently deeded by the states to the confederacy, as a way of paying the national debt. Dr. Cutler's scheme was open and aboveboard. A survey had been made. Suitably hardy colonists of Yankee strain were waiting to set off. The capital was on hand to pay for the land. But a strange sluggishness pervaded Congress. Cutler was packing his bags and threatening to leave New York and to buy his land direct off the states, when Duer thought up a scheme to enliven the jaded legislators and to stimulate the interest of what he vaguely described as 'many of the principal characters of America.'

Duer's scheme had such an electric effect that the day after it was broached Cutler found several congressmen waiting on him at his lodgings before he was up, to beg him to stay over a few more days in New York. The scheme was, briefly: to form, alongside of the public Ohio Company, a private company to be called the Scioto Company which would also sell lands, and in which these legislators and 'principal characters' would presumably be interested. Congress would make the grant to the

Ohio Company, but the Ohio Company would execute a deed for the western section of the land to the private and secret Scioto Company.

The West was endless. In all the warworn seaboard cities people dreamed of getting rich off western lands.

A hundred and twenty years before, old Roger Williams, in agony at the land craze that had come over his Providence settlers, had written to his friend the younger Winthrop that he feared a generation was rising up 'to which the God Land would be as great a God with us English as the God Gold was with the Spaniards . . . as if Men were in great necessity and danger for want of Great Portions of Land.' The Revolutionary War had barely come to an end before a similar craze for land burgeoned in every one of the thirteen states.

Half of it was colonization and half of it pure speculation. The gambler's itch so natural to Americans had had little to feed on with the cutting off of commerce during the war. Now the sale of western lands and the buying up of continental paper offered two unparalleled opportunities for getting rich quick. There was hardly a public or private man who wasn't bitten at one time or another. It was the ruin of Robert Morris, the financial genius of the war. Now Colonel Duer, musing on how to get Cutler's bill through Congress, had thought up this very ingenious scheme. It was the kind of scheme that in the language of the time was known as a 'job': Congress would sell five million acres of Ohio land at a little more than a dollar an acre. Of this a million and a half acres would be sold publicly in Massachusetts through the Ohio Company. The rest would be divided privately among the 'principal characters' and would be sold abroad. The European buyers would pay half, or around sixty cents an acre, in cash: with that cash the 'principal characters' would buy 'indents,' continental promises to pay, at ten cents on the dollar and therewith would pay Congress for the land. It would mean, if all went well, the cutting of one of the juiciest melons in the whole history of inside financial operations in America.

From then on everything was smooth as silk. Dr. Cutler got his land and started his emigrants off down the Ohio in flatboats with the spring freshet. At the mouth of the Muskingum they founded a town which they named Marietta after His Most Christian Majesty's Queen, Marie Antoinette. Meanwhile Daniel Parker, Duer's agent in London, and a Major Rochefontaine in France were supposed to be selling the land, assisted by the glowing reports Brissot took home with him from his travels in the Western Country, but for some reason sales in Europe proceeded slowly. Something had to be done, and that quickly, because as state after state ratified the new Constitution, confidence in the United States rose. Belgian and Dutch bankers started buying up the 'indents' and caused their price to rise. Poor Colonel Duer helped in the work of his own destruction by writing papers for the *Federalist.* It began to be noised abroad that the new government was going to pay one hundred cents on the dollar on the old government's debts. Duer, an ardent Federalist and hard money man, was in danger of being hoist on his own petard. Before it was too late, an agent had to be sent to Europe to hurry up the land sales.

In the winter of 1787-88 somebody sold Colonel Duer the idea that the man to send was Joel Barlow, the patriotic poet, whose *The Vision of Columbus* was already inflaming the enthusiasm of lettered Europe for the New World. Joel was all his life a man who never turned down a trip if he could help it. Besides, he was probably swept off his feet like the rest of them by the idea of combining the patriotic duty of paying off the national debt and colonizing the West with a little quick easy money. I don't know whether he was let in on the inside finagling of the job or not. On the face of it the Scioto Company looked just as much on the level as the Ohio Company. In Paris it seemed all right to Jefferson, who indorsed it. So, having left Ruth with her brother Dudley at Greenfield Hill in his home town of Fairfield, being furnished with letters from all the bigwigs of young America to all the liberal bigwigs of Europe, with a power of attorney from Colonel Duer and a certificate of ownership of some shares of the Scioto stock, he set out from New York on the French packet in the latter part of May 1788.

Joel had never been to sea before. The packet was an English sixteengun frigate which had been captured by the French during the war. A few crude partitions had been slapped up for the mail and passenger service. She had hardly poked her nose outside the Narrows before Joel began to feel qualms. When he crawled into his bunk he found it a miserable little pen lined with dirty calico, the home of an active group of fleas and a regiment of bedbugs. The boat stank abominably of bilge and garlicky grease from the galley. He didn't know enough French to get any service. The food was brought on swimming in fat; the bread was made of moldy flour; for the last two weeks he couldn't keep anything but boiled rice on his stomach. The captain didn't seem to care whether the passengers lived or died; for the whole month of the crossing the unhappy poet lay retching in his bunk.

He was so sick that it was days after the ship made port before he could get his innards working properly for him again. Writing in his diary from his refuge in what he describes as the fourth loft of the Hôtel de l'Aigle d'Or in Havre where he lay in bed waiting to get his land legs back, he was drearily jocose about an argument he'd had with a fellow passenger concerning that absurd notion of Buffon's, which had so annoyed Jefferson, about the respective sizes of European and American animals. Buffon, Barlow argued, undoubtedly based his theory on the greater size and ferocity of the European flea, which he claimed was heavier by a grain than his American cousin. The population of his lodgings in Havre, he went on, bore him out only too well in this contention.

As he walked about the cobbled streets of his first French

seaport he could still feel the hideous heave and lurch of the packet. Everything was gray and strange and ancient. He was very much taken with the Hôtel de Ville which he found much handsomer than the City Hall in New York. Little complicated odds and ends of Gothic interested him because they were so different from any architecture he had ever seen or imagined. He was hospitably dined by the Swedish consul and, in company of two Swedes he met at the consulate and a young son of General Greene's who was going to Paris to be educated, whom he'd been asked to keep an eye on, he set out in a carriage for Paris.

The drive through Normandy, incredibly green with early summer, was delightful. They spent half a day in Rouen. Barlow was carried away with the vast bristling cathedral steaming with incense, the humpbacked bridge over the Seine, the canalboats, the old gates, the daintily laidout promenade, the narrow stone streets of halftimbered houses that smelt of cider, the faces of nuns demure and yellow under their white coifs. The lower classes, he noted, looked less poor and miserable than he'd been led to expect. When they reached Paris he was so busy he forgot to make any entries in his diary. A few days later he was off again for London via Boulogne in a postchaise in the company of Duer's European correspondent Mr. Parker.

Daniel Parker was a Massachusetts man who had been a merchant in New York but had gotten in too deep in furnishing supplies to the Continental Army. Possibly for no fault of his own he had been threatened with jail and had had to skip out for Europe, leaving his partners holding the bag. These were tricky times for merchants. Before the passing of the Bankrupt Act, bankruptcy meant jail. Be that as it may the general impression was that Parker was a rather slippery character. He had hung around Jefferson and Adams during their negotiation with the bankers in the Low Countries about the American debt. He seems to have had some sort of "in" with the Van Staphorsts of Brussels and was involved in Robert

Morris' international speculations that ended in that financial genius' dying flat broke in jail.

Money turned out to be tight in London. While waiting there for Parker to get ready to go back across to Brussels to try out the Van Staphorsts, Joel roamed around seeing the sights. He went, as did all Americans, to St. Paul's Cathedral and to the Tower to look with curiosity and scorn at the wax-works of the kings. He admired the illuminations and the brazen faces of the tarts at Vauxhall. He went to Richmond and Hampton Court and got out of his carraige to look at the little island of Runnymede, where, so he'd learned in school, the foundation of British and so of American liberties had been laid. He was struck with the charming planting, all by the poet's own hand he was told, of Pope's garden at Twickenham. American affairs and Yankee ingenuity were still somewhat the style in London; fashionable crowds were inspecting at a shilling a head the wooden project for Mr. Paine's iron bridge and the model of Mr. Rumsey's steamboat. Joel was enough of a New Englander to be interested too in a newly invented harpoongun that was to improve the whaler's chances.

John Trumbull, the painter, a cousin of Joel's Hartford friend, took him out to Windsor to see the castle and the forest and the tame deer; and in the royal chapel, a Monday morning, he saw the reigning King and the royal family in the flesh. Probably because he was a stranger, he thought, George Third turned his head and stared at him; Barlow, like a good republican from America, tried to stare the King down. He didn't know, nor did anybody else till his collapse two months later, that poor George was in the process of losing his mind. "Well, thought I, 'a cat may look at a king,'" he wrote in his diary, "and by the same ascending scale a king may look upon me,—and so, stare away."

He was taken to call on the Marquis of Landsdowne in Berkeley Square, and on Sir Joseph Banks, President of the Royal Society. Americans in England fell at the time into two social groups: the Tories gathered round Ben Franklin's illegitimate son, ex-Governor Franklin of the Jerseys, reactionaries more royalist than the King, who were to form a little later a sort of matrix for the highflying Federalist social set that turned John Jay's head at the time of the infamous treaty; and the Whig and patriot groups that moved in the stratum of the English liberal reformers, like Dr. Price and Horne Tooke and the Marquis of Landsdowne and the great parliamentarians of the buff and blue. Towards the end of Barlow's first stay in London, he noted that (on August 27th) he had dined with Mr. Paine in the company of Horne Tooke.

"I dine abroad at least six days in the week; this, to a man of business would be a bad economy of time," he wrote somewhat apologetically in his diary; "but for me it is the best way of collecting information, and does not interfere with other business." There was no better way at this moment of being informed about European politics than by dining with Paine.

Tom Paine was living one of the few really happy periods of his life. Walker's Ironworks at Rotherham in Yorkshire was preparing to build an iron bridge according to the design he'd worked over for so long. He was fairly well off for money. He found himself accepted as an equal by the London society that had seemed so immeasurably far above him during his early days as a poor exciseman and shopkeeper. Although out of power since the fizzle of the Fox-North ministry, the party of the buff and blue was still fashionable. As the author of *Common Sense* and one of the prime movers of the successful Revolution in America, Paine was toasted at the meetings and dinners where the enthusiastic reformers of the Revolution Society and the Society for Constitutional Information gathered to plan a renovation for the government of England: elimination of rotten boroughs, annual parliaments, suffrage conducted on a rational basis; in short: liberty American-style. Reform was showing its power by the impeachment proceedings against Warren Hastings that had been the great show of that spring's

London season, where as managers for the Commons before the peers Fox and Burke and Sheridan had poured out eloquence like so many Ciceros indicting Cataline. It was a period of pamphlets and toasts and harangues. As one of the greatest pamphleteers in the language Paine was in his element. He felt again all round him the effervescence of ideas and hopes that had been meat and drink for him in Philadelphia in 1776.

Horne Tooke, the vicar of Brentford, had left the Church of England to give his whole time to agitation for parliamentary reform years before during the great struggle with George Third's political machine to prove Wilkes' right to represent the people of London in Parliament. He was an aggressive liberal and a man of great scholarship. His interest in grammar and philology must have made Barlow think of his old Connecticut friend Noah Webster. The probabilities are, though, that in August 1788 it was politics rather than Anglo-Saxon roots that they talked about.

The rumblings of change underground were as strong in London as in Paris. The Lord George Gordon riots ten years before had shown thoughtful men what a volcano underlay the green parks and gardens and the ivycovered ruins and the slums swarming with the disfranchised poor that made up the established English order. Some sort of reorganization had to come. Freedom seemed to be working out in America. Freedom was not yet unrespectable in England. There was still a chance that reform might capture the government. That very summer Pitt had gone to considerable personal trouble and had kept members of Parliament away from their country seats long after the usual season, in order to force a bill regulating the slave trade through the House of Lords. It was still possible to think of him as the young reformer merely biding his time. England, and all Europe, were certainly on the edge of some sort of transformation. Amid the excited talk of London dinner-tables, Barlow must have felt, in one of those flashes of understanding of your own country that often come from the impact of a foreign country, that the simple life of the Connecticut villages he knew so well and the drama of the Revolutionary War he'd been raised in was taking on in the world a new and broader meaning than he'd ever imagined.

Barlow was already thirtyfour, but he came from a country where men matured slowly. He was just beginning to learn to use his head. He was discovering that he'd inherited a nose for business from his Yankee forebears. He was finding out where he stood in relation to the cleavages that were appearing in society as a forecast of the civil war to come. He was already beginning to see clear through the confusing quaintness of the Old World and its odd costumes and hierarchies. The fun of travel quickened his pulse. He was beginning to understand that he'd landed plumb in the center of events at a very important moment in history.

Before he left London he witnessed one of the strangest and most typical sights of that great capital, a Westminster election. From his point of view, the right man won, Lord John Townsend, Charles James Fox's intimate friend, over Lord Hood, the candidate of Pitt and the government, but the process was somewhat shocking to a Connecticut Yankee accustomed to a certain solemnity at the polls: "This day ended the long contested Westminster election . . . It was really no less than a contest between Charles Fox and George the Third, and, to the satisfaction of every disinterested beholder the former has won the day and Townsend is elected. On this occasion the Treasury is opened, and orders are drawn directly on it for the expense on the royal side. It is computed that the money spent on the king's side was 30,000 pounds; that on the opposition actually 20,000. Of this latter sum the Whig Club subscribed 10,000 beforehand, and on the tenth day of the election, finding there would be a lack of money, the Duke of Bedford drew on his banker for 5000, and sent word that 50,000 more would be at the service of the opposition if needed. The other 5000 is supposed to have come from the Prince of Wales, and others less open in the cause of the opposition. This extraordinary expense will not appear strange when it is known that the simple article of ribbons for the cockades of the Townsend party cost 4000 pounds; and that about 100 'bludgeon-men,' as they are called, were hired at five shillings per day to outmob the mob upon the other side, and that two-thirds of the voters (the whole of which in this poll were 12,000) were actually paid for their votes. Add to this that for 15 days, 200,000 people are constantly kept in an uproar. Not a tradesman, if he is disposed, can carry on business, for he is every day haunted by both parties, and his journeymen every day drunk for the honor of the candidates. Several persons have been killed on the spot, and many more languish under broken heads and legs, and it was as much as a man's pocket were worth to come within 200 yards of the hustings. The way of conducting the business is for the canvass to begin some time before the election begins and to continue till it is closed. The first nobility of both sexes employ themselves in canvassing: they go to every house, stall, shop, and dockyard and solicit the vote and interest of every person in favor of their candidate. Then comes a card in the newspapers requesting the voters in such a street or parish to breakfast with such a duke or lord and to proceed with him to the polls. Thus he puts himself upon a level with the most ragged, vile and worthless of creation, who move in a tumultuous procession through the streets, reeling and huzzaing, with His Grace or the candidate at their head."

Early in September Barlow and Parker crossed back to Calais, where Barlow, like Jefferson, the year before, could think of nothing but *The Sentimental Journey*. He put up, too, at the hotel Sterne wrote about, 'an old, large, magnificent, but not over cleanly establishment.' From Calais they drove in a chaise to Brussels to see the Van Staphorsts. The bankers wouldn't fall in with Duer's proposition. Already it must have been becoming apparent to Barlow that the Scioto scheme was a shaky business. The only hope left was to get the French to buy land. The French were in a daze with the dream of liberty and abundance in the New World, and distrusting the finances of His Most Christian Majesty, were shipping, as is their wont, their capital abroad.

By the end of the month, Barlow was back in Paris. He called on Jefferson the twentysixth and dined with him the next night in the company of Lafayette, the ubiquitous Mr. Parker and an Italian gentleman whose name Barlow couldn't catch.

Jefferson was completing his fifth and last year as American minister to the French court. His house on the Route des Champs Elysées, then a country road leading out to the Bois and the suburban villages of Boulogne and Neuilly, had taken the place of Dr. Franklin's house at Passy as the center of the American vogue.

Jefferson was a dryer man than Franklin. He hated to waste his time with the parties and the sexy repartee and the hand-kissing and the breathing down the powdered necks of fine ladies, and all the chatter over teacups of the silkyrustling rather stuffy highlife that the old philosopher in his coonskin-cap had, for all his intellectual interests, been so much the center of. Jefferson was a man who liked to feel when he went to bed at night that he'd learned something and had accomplished something during the day. He just couldn't be bothered with the incessant triangles, the little notes tucked under chocolate-pots, the scuttling behind screens, the bribing of chambermaids on back staircases, and the complicated depravities of Parisian social life. He never forgot that he was in Paris to do a job for his country. But what little spare time that left him every day was too short for his own manifold interests, his music (for the first time in his life he was in a city where he could pick and choose among concerts), his studies in architecture, his curiosity about mechanical contraptions, and the need he felt to increase his knowledge of practical agriculture. He was not the fashionable rage so much as the philosophical doctor, but he lived in the full current of ideas, political, philosophical and scientific, at one of those moments, not infrequent in the history of Europe, when Paris, for better or worse, has been the hub round which original thought revolved.

In Jefferson's peculiarly American combination of good intentions towards his fellowman, tempered by a fairly harsh horsesense in dealing with him, French thinkers of all the various schools found, as they had in the great doctor, a needed corrective to their tendency to live on a floating island of theory. When Buffon was making himself and his real achievements ridiculous with his pronouncement that the climate of the Western Hemisphere was moister than that of Europe and that therefore animals there were smaller and weaker than in Europe, Jefferson didn't refute it by launching a counter theory. He wrote over to his friend General Sullivan in New Hampshire to shoot and stuff a goodsized bull moose for him. The moose finally arrived somewhat the worse for wear at the cost to Jefferson of sixtythree guineas, but he settled the discussion for all time.

In politics, too, he kept trying to put his practical experience in working with men at the disposal of the enthusiastic and generousminded ladies and gentlemen of Lafayette's drawing-room. He tried continually to insinuate to them that the mere enunciation of a principle wasn't enough to make it come true.

He had had the luck to get to know France in one of the most interesting moments in its great career as the brains of Europe. But he did not forget that ever since Richelieu France had been a totalitarian monarchy and that the French mind had been trained in hierarchical ways of thinking.

For fifty years the complicated edifice that Louis Fourteenth had completed had held together only by the inertia of its past progress, corroded in every shaft and cog by all the social diseases tyranny induces. By some miracle of national energy Frenchmen had managed to keep their heads clear. Voltaire had been the incarnation of the paradox of intelligent despotism. His peculiar humor, the backstairs humor of the court, had filled the mind of the century. Very much the authoritarian in politics himself, he had never thought it inconsistent to follow the example of Henri Quatre who said Paris was well worth a mass, by letting himself be reconciled to the Church just long enough to be elected to the French Academy. He was all for the political system of hierarchy if it would let the humane mind of a decent man play on it and temper its bloodier aspects.

The trouble was that nothing in the system had stood up under the bright light of Voltaire's reason. Belief in authority crumbled away, leaving a vacuum which the halfpeasant Swiss schoolteacher Rousseau immediately filled with that belief in and enthusiasm for the uncorruptible spirit of man, of any and every man, that has been such a nuisance to governors and organizers of hierarchies since the day when Pontius Pilate passed the buck back to the High Priest. Where Voltaire had tittered and scolded, Rousseau solemnly intoned a creed out of the protestant ethics of Geneva. These two great personalities had generated in a host of lesser men, who mostly went to England for their political models, the theoretical basis of the French Revolution.

England, Jefferson told them, was no model for anything. By that he meant the England of George Third and the squirarchy, the source of all the evils he had fought in America. The England of the Common Law was a different matter. Common Law procedure was the real school of politics by which the theoretical statements that read so well in the manifestoes could be implemented. There existed a curious almost blind sixth sense by which the English had managed through the centuries to balance abuse against abuse into the weird patchwork of their Constitution. He explained how, by attending always to practice instead of theory, the English people had managed, under the worst possible conditions of class rule, always to keep some glimmer of human liberty going in some part or other of the body politic. Jefferson had written manifestoes himself and he knew how easily men could be induced to cheer and to die for them, but how difficult it was to get men doggedly to work and to live for them through the confusions of everyday life.

While he stayed in Paris he acted as a sort of gyroscope to the plunging revolutionary enthusiasms of Lafayette and his friends. Particularly on Lafayette, who was already dreaming of becoming the Washington of his country, he had great influence. But while Jefferson was teaching he was learning. Even after he came home to America he never ceased to understand what the European Revolution was about, and to remain in touch with the progressive core of theory and speculation, that through all the political extremes of the Terror and the Empire, kept growing and branching until it had renovated the life of all Europe and become the basis of nineteenth century thought.

That afternoon in the fall of 1788 when Joel Barlow first went to dinner at Jefferson's, and for the first time put his fork into the light and tasty dishes, served with an abundance of green vegetables, for which the American minister's table was famous; and then sat, after the cloth had been taken away, Virginia style, drinking the light Beaujolais and listening to his tall redheaded host's explanation of the political situation in France; glancing from time to time across the table at Lafayette's narrow face, that had an intent lean blooded racehorse look above his frilled neckband, he must have felt, behind the amenities of polite conversation, in the background of every word, the roar of the floodwaters of history like the roar of a distant waterfall. Again, as when last month he'd dined with Tom Paine in London, the provincial poet from Connecticut found himself on the main thoroughfare.

In the months that followed the stream began to move too fast for ruminative thought; the Revolution was entering the phase of action and slogan. Meanwhile Barlow was learning

French and making friends and his sensibilities were spreading and expanding under those minute pleasures of the daily life of Paris gardens and cafés and restaurants and streets that have always cast such a spell over Americans. He had managed to float a French company to buy Scioto lands. Under some officers who had served with Rochambeau a batch of five hundred settlers and their families started to get ready to sail for the banks of the Ohio. Men who had had a taste of America were finding it hard to settle down again into the narrow life of Europe.

In France things were bad. The government was just about bankrupt. The winter of 1788-89 was exceptionally cold; grain supplies gave out. Prices rose. In the cities and on the vast estates of the nobles, mortgaged and neglected, the poor were starving as they had starved so often before. The difference was that this time they didn't starve quietly. A race of glib young men had risen up in every manor and village to whisper that Liberty was the cure for starving. Liberty was bread, land, schools. Poor people didn't need to starve, they needed to act.

On October 3 Barlow complained in his diary that it had rained every day since he'd been in Paris. He had just been dining at Lafayette's where there was 'much company chiefly American.' He noted the enthusiasm of the French for a free constitution, but he was doubtful, as Jefferson sometimes was, of their ability to establish such a constitution: "I presume there are not to be found five men in Europe who understand the nature of liberty and the theory of government as well as they are understood by five hundred men in America. The friends to America in London and Paris are astonished at our conduct in establishing the New Constitution. They say we have given up all we contended for. They are as intemperate in their idea of liberty as we were in the year 'seventyfive."

The next morning he was off for Dunkirk. "This way of travelling," he noted at Peronne, on the road, "is very amusing and not in the least fatiguing, provided your carriage is strong and good. We have our own courier who rides on horseback and rides forward to get the horses ready at every stage. On all the great roads they give us good horses and good postillions, and in this way a man may travel eight miles an hour, day and night, for a week together if he choses."

During that winter and the next summer Barlow was very much on the move, mostly oscillating between Paris and London. These were times when it was hard to keep still. Englishmen and Americans who lived in London kept running over to Paris to see what was going on. In political excitement, effervescence of speech, multitude of pamphlets daily off the press, the two capitals were neck and neck. For a while it looked to the more sanguine as if the radicals of England and the reformers of France would perform the revolution by mutual aid. Barlow was working hard to sell his lands and to collect the money for them, to get the business into shape so that he could settle up and go home to Ruth in the fall. The rest of the time he ate drank and slept politics.

In Paris he lived at the Hôtel d'Angleterre on the rue St. Honoré, the artery of all the fever of that year. At the end of May, Gouverneur Morris, Washington's particular friend, who had arrived in Europe that winter to represent Robert Morris in a landselling scheme rival to Barlow's, and to lend a hand in the negotiations about the American debt, wrote spitefully in his diary that he'd met Barlow at dinner at Jefferson's and had put him out of humor by paying attention to a certain Mrs. Blackden, 'a lady of fading charms' whom the poet seemed rather taken with. This was the wife of a Colonel Blackden who'd been with Montgomery in the Quebec expedition that had caused Joel's brother Sam's death. Barlow had become friends with him and he was helping sell Ohio lands. They lived at the same hotel. Colonel Blackden was in the shipping business and it may have been through him that Barlow got into the speculations that finally put him on his feet financially and enabled him to get out from under the incubus the Scioto scheme turned out to be. The Blackdens and the Barlows were friends for years, so Morris, whose head was a little turned by his success with the ladies of title since he had arrived in Paris, and saw *intrigue galante* in every batting of an eyelash, was probably mistaken about Barlow's feeling for the lady.

That day particularly Morris was mazed in the *pais du tendre*. The noble ladies of France had bewitched him. After dinner he left Jefferson and the company and rode alone round the Bois de Boulogne, making up verses in honor of the Duchess of Orléans, whose rank or whose beauty had much impressed him when he'd met her some time before, and noted rhapsodically the charm of the forest and the deer skipping about and the belles and beaux making delicious groups in the long summer gloaming. Meanwhile Jefferson's house, though Morris was already beginning to dislike his politics too much to admit it, was the center for levelheaded information about what was really going on at Versailles.

From the moment the States General had met in the early spring the government of France had been jibing wildly from one tack to another. The King let himself be talked into one thing by the liberal nobles like the Rochefoucaulds and Lafayette one day and into another by the reactionaries who had the ear of the Queen the next. With each racking change of course the complicated doweling of interests into privileges that held together the structure of the ancient regime loosened and strained. The vessel wallowed waterlogged in the trough of the sea.

"The Assembly," wrote Jefferson, referring to the delegates of the Third Estate, the commons whose members had sworn a few days before in the tennis court at Versailles to let no force on earth dissolve them until they had accomplished their purpose of giving France a free constitution, "now entered on the business of their mission, and first proceeded to arrange the order in which they would take up the heads of their constitution, as follows:

"First, and as Preliminary to the whole, a general Declaration of the Rights of Man. Then, specifically, the Principles of the Monarchy; Rights of the Nation; Rights of the King; Rights of the Citizens; Organization and Rights of the National Assembly; Forms necessary for the enactment of Laws; Organization and Functions of the Provincial and Municipal Assemblies; Duties and Limits of the Judiciary power; Functions and Duties of the Military power.

"A Declaration of the Rights of Man, as the preliminary of their work, was accordingly prepared and proposed by the Marquis de La Fayette. [Jefferson had himself made a draft of it for Lafayette.]

"But the quiet of their march was soon disturbed by information that troops, and particularly the foreign troops, were advancing on Paris from various quarters. The King had probably been advised to this, on pretext of preserving peace in Paris. But his advisers were believed to have other things in contemplation. The Marshal de Broglio was appointed to their command, a high-flying aristocrat, cool and capable of anything. Some of the French guards were soon arrested, under other pretexts, but really, on account of their dispositions in favor of the National cause. The people of Paris forced their prison, liberated them, and sent a deputation to the Assembly to solicit a pardon. The Assembly recommended peace and order to the people of Paris, the prisoners to the King, and asked from him the removal of the troops. His answer was negative and dry, saying they might remove themselves, if they pleased, to Noyons or Soissons. In the meantime, these troops, to the number of twenty or thirty thousand, had arrived, and were posted in, and between Paris and Versailles. The bridges and passes were guarded. At three o'clock in the afternoon of the 11th of July, the Count de La Luzerne was sent to notify M. Necker of his dismission, and to enjoin him to retire instantly, without saying a word of it to anybody. He went home, dined, and proposed to his wife a visit to a friend, but went in fact to his country house at St. Ouen, and at midnight set out for Brussels. This was not known until the next day (the 12th,) when the whole Ministry was changed, except Villedeuil, of the domestic department, and Barenton, Garde des Sceaux . . . The King was now completely in the hands of men, the principal among whom had been noted, through their lives, for the Turkish despotism of their characters, and who were associated around the King, as proper instruments for what was to be executed. The news of this change began to be known at Paris, about one or two o'clock. In the afternoon, a body of about one hundred German cavalry were advanced and drawn up in the Place Louis XV, and about two hundred Swiss posted at a little distance in their rear. This drew people to the spot, who thus accidentally found themselves in front of the troops, merely at first as spectators; but, as their numbers increased, their indignation rose. They retired a few steps, and posted themselves on and behind large piles of stones, large and small, collected in that place for a bridge, which was to be built adjacent to it. In this position, happening to be in my carriage on a visit, I passed through the lane they had formed, without interruption. But the moment after I had passed, the people attacked the cavalry with stones. They charged, but the advantageous position of the people, and the showers of stones, obliged the horse to retire, and quit the field altogether, leaving one of their number on the ground, and the Swiss in the rear not moving to their aid. This was the signal for universal insurrection, and this body of cavalry, to avoid being massacred, retired towards Versailles. The people now armed themselves with such weapons as they could find in armorer's shops, and private houses, and with bludgeons; and were roaming all night, through all parts of the city, without any decided object."

The popular reaction was violent and immediate. "In effect," wrote Gouverneur Morris in his diary on July 13th, "the little City of Paris is in as fine a Tumult as anyone could wish. They are getting Arms wherever they can find any. Seize sixty Barrils of Powder in a Boat on the Seine. Break into the Monastery of St. Lazar and find a Store of Grain which the holy Brotherhood had laid in. Immediately it is put into carts and sent to the Market and on every Cart a Friar. The Gardemeuble du Roi is attacked and the Arms are delivered up, to prevent worse Consequences. These however are more curious than useful. But the Detail of the Variety of this Day's Deeds would be endless . . . After dinner dress and walk to the Louvre after having previously ornamented my Hat with a green Bow in Honor of the Tier, for this is the Fashion of the Day which every Body is obliged to comply with who means to march in Peace. It is somewhat whimsical that this Day of Violence and Tumult is the only one in which I have dared to walk the streets [on account of his peg leg], but as no Carriages are abroad but the fiacres I do not hazard being crushed and I apprehend nothing from the Populace."

The next day the people of Paris rushed the Bastille. The King took fright and decided he'd be a good boy. Three days later somebody picked Gouverneur Morris's pocket, and got away with a favorite handkerchief that had romantic associations, while he was escorting the lady who was on the way to being his best ladyfriend, the charming and literary Madame de Flahaut (whose titular lover already was none other than a certain Bishop of Autun soon to become somewhat known to the world under his own name of Talleyrand), up a crowded stairway to a window in a house on the rue St. Honoré to get a view of the procession that brought the King, led by Lafayette on the whitest of white horses, into Paris to show himself to his loving subjects.

"The King came to Paris," wrote Jefferson, "leaving the Queen in consternation for his return. Omitting the less important figures of the procession, the King's carriage was in the centre; on each side of it the Assembly, in two ranks a foot; at their head the Marquis de La Fayette, as Commander-in-chief, on horseback, and Bourgeois guards before and behind. About sixty thousand citizens, of all forms and conditions, armed with the conquests of the Bastile and Invalids, as far as they would go, the rest with pistols, swords, pikes, pruninghooks, scythes, &c., lined all the streets through which the procession passed, and with the crowds of people in the streets, doors and windows, saluted them everywhere with the cries of 'vive la nation,' but not a single 'vive le roi' was heard. The King stopped at the Hôtel de Ville. There M. Bailly presented, and put into his hat, the popular cockade, and addressed him. The King being unprepared, and unable to answer, Bailly went to him, gathered from him some scraps of sentences, and made out an answer, which he delivered to the audience, as from the King. On their return, the popular cries were 'vive le Roi et la nation.' He was conducted by a garde Bourgeoise to his palace at Versailles, and thus concluded an 'amende honorable,' as no sovereign ever made, and no people ever received."

Meanwhile the Americans in Paris were having a fine time going around telling all and sundry how to run their revolution. They conducted themselves with more or less tact according to their characters, but no one of them could help feeling a certain elation over their position as godfathers of the new age.

On Sunday July 19th, Morris called on Mr. Jefferson to ask for a passport for a servant he was sending away with some letters, then he dined at Madame de Flahaut's at the Louvre with a very agreeable party, consisting of the Bishop of Autun, the Duc de Biron and the Abbé Bertrand. After dinner they went around to a painter's studio, probably David's, which was then in the ground floor of the Louvre, and saw some pictures. ". . . in one of which the actual Execution of Perspective goes beyond my Power of Imagination, particularly in the right Hand of the principal Figure which stands out so completely from the Canvass that one absolutely sees all round it, a Thing scarce credible but which is none the less true. The subject is Love escaped from his Cage and leaving by his Flight the

Ladies in Anguish and Despair . . . I tell him he had better paint the Storm of the Bastile, it will be a more fashionable Picture, & that one Trait will admit of a fine Effect. It is of one of the Garde Française who, having got hold of the Gate and unable to bring it down, cries to his Comrades of the Populace to pull by his Legs, and the Man has the Force and Courage to hold while a dozen of them pull him like a Rope and bring down the Gate, so that he actually sustains the Rack. To represent him drawn out of Joint with his Head turned round, encouraging them to draw still harder, must I think have a fine Effect. L'Evêque d'Autun agrees with me entirely in this sentiment . . ."

Mr. Morris was in fine form that afternoon. In fact he enjoyed the whole fine summer's day. That night he had a pint of claret with his supper and noted before going to bed that it had done him much good.

The next morning he went down to the Hôtel de Ville to call on Lafayette and found him 'much exhausted by a variety of attentions.' The marquis invited him to dinner and he accepted, with the proviso that he should bring his own wine, as he was somewhat indisposed. At dinner he told Lafayette about his plan for turning the *Garde Française* into a wellpaid and welldisciplined militia that would keep order while the difficult transformation of the government was taking place. He suggested too, possibly in an effort to make himself agreeable, that the King ought to make Lafayette governor of the Isle de France: "He tells me that he would prefer that of Paris simply. That he has had the utmost Power his Heart could wish and has grown tired of it. That he has commanded absolutely an hundred thousand Men, has marched his Sovereign about the Streets as he pleased, prescribed the degree of Applause which he should receive, and could have detained him Prisoner had he thought it proper. He wishes therefore as soon as possible to return to private Life . . . In this last Expression he deceives himself or wishes to deceive me; a little of both perhaps. But in Fact he is the Lover of Freedom from Ambition, of which there are two Kinds, one born of Pride, the other of Vanity and his partakes most of the latter."

Morris was a shrewd observer, and one of the great diarists of all time, but he often let the political cynicism of a Hudson River landowner carry him too far. He was right about Lafayette's vanity, which his best friends admitted, but wrong, as Lafayette's whole life proved, about his lack of principle. Meanwhile Morris went stumping about his business in Paris, noting everything he saw with a cold sharp eye. Two days later, when he was walking under the arcade of the Palais Royale to take a little air after dinner while waiting for his carriage, he saw a sight that shocked him profoundly: "In this Period the Head and Body of Mr. de Foulon are introduced in Triumph. The Head on a Pike, the Body dragged naked on the Earth. Afterwards this horrible exhibition is carried through the different Streets. His Crime is to have accepted a Place in the Ministry. This mutilated Form of an Old Man of seventy five is shown to Bertier, his Son in Law, the Intendant of Paris, and afterwards he also is put to Death and cut to Pieces, the Populace carrying about the mangled Fragments with Savage Joy. Gracious God what a People."

Already there are whole days in Paris when the mob is out of control. The prisons have been opened and strange things have come out in the light of day. Hatreds and resentments that have been distilled through bitter centuries blow up in the faces of the reformers who are trying to harness them to the machine of progress.

Feverishly in the Palais Royale the orators are talking, in the Assembly, in committees, in the clubs, men of reason are trying with a multitude of words to direct the great popular mass on the move. One day late in the summer when Jefferson was waiting, with his books and his instruments and his pictures and his drawings all packed, expecting every day to get permission to go home to America on leave, Lafayette and a group of the prime movers of the National Assembly, at their wits' end from the lack of progress made, invited themselves to dinner with him at the American Legation.

"In this uneasy state of things, I received one day a note from the Marquis de La Fayette, informing me that he should bring a party of six or eight friends to ask a dinner of me the next day. I assured him of their welcome. When they arrived, they were La Fayette himself, Duport, Barnave, Alexander la Meth, Blacon, Mounier, Maubourg, and Dagout. These were leading Patriots, of honest but differing opinions, sensible of the necessity of effecting a coalition by mutual sacrifices, knowing each other, and not afraid, therefor, to unbosom themselves mutually. This last was a material principle in the selection. With this view, the Marquis had invited the conference and had fixed the time and place inadverently as to the embarrassment under which it might place me. The cloth being removed, and wine set on the table, after the American manner, the Marquis introduced the objects of the conference, by summarily reminding them of the state of things in the Assembly, the course which the principles of the Constitution were taking, and the inevitable result, unless checked by more concord among the Patriots themselves. He observed, that although he also had his opinion, he was ready to sacrifice it to that of his brethren of the same cause; but that a common opinion must now be formed, or the Aristocracy would carry everything, and that, whatever they should now agree on, he, at the head of the National force, would maintain. The discussions began at the hour of four, and were continued till ten o'clock in the evening; during which time, I was a silent witness to a coolness and candor of argument, unusual in the conflicts of political opinion; to a logical reasoning, and chaste eloquence, disfigured by no gaudy tinsel of rhetoric or declamation, and truly worthy of being placed in parallel with the finest dialogues of antiquity, as handed to us by Xenophon, by Plato and Cicero. The result was, that the King should have a suspensive veto on the laws, that the legislature should be composed of a single body only, and that to be chosen by the people. This Concordate decided the fate of the constitution. The Patriots all rallied to the principles thus settled, carried every question agreeably to them, and reduced the Aristocracy to insignificance and impotence. But duties of exculpation were now incumbent on me. I waited on Count Montmorin the next morning, and explained to him, with truth and candor, how it had happened that my house had been made the scene of conferences of such a character. He told me, he already knew everything which had passed, that so far from taking umbrage at the use made of my house on that occasion, he earnestly wished I would habitually assist at such conferences, being sure I should be useful in moderating the warmer spirits, and promoting a wholesome and practical reformation only. I told him I knew too well the duties I owed to the King, to the nation, and to my own country, to take any part in councils concerning their internal government, and that I should persevere, with care, in the character of a neutral and passive spectator, with wishes only, and very sincere ones, that those measures might prevail which would be for the greatest good of the nation. I have no doubts, indeed, that this conference was previously known and approved by this honest Minister, who was in confidence and communication with the Patriots, and wished for a reasonable reform of the Constitution."

In August Gouverneur Morris had gone over to London, having written Washington from Dieppe a letter full of foreboding for the future, and of an acute sense of personal disappointment in the breakdown of a regime he had barely gotten to know, and that he found, particularly on the female side, so thoroughly delightful. At the end of September Jefferson started home, carrying away a love for France and French people and the French intellect that never left him. The liberal Revolution of which he was in some ways the center had nearly run its course. Those early summer days of hot eloquence, those adolescent enthusiasms for the rights of every man, so brilliantly put into words round dinner tables, those nights of generous argument were never to be repeated. Events began to come too fast. There was a fleeting chill of premonition even in the exaltation of the enthusiastic letter Joel wrote Ruth from Paris: "All the true things which you see published, however horrible, however cruel, however just, however noble memorable and important in their consequences, have passed under my eye, and it is really no small gratification to me to have seen two revolutions in favor of liberty. Everything is now quiet in Paris. I look upon the affairs of this nation as on the point of being settled on the most rational and lasting foundation . . . Nothing but the contemplation of the infinite happiness that I am sure will result to millions of human beings from these commotions could enable me to tolerate the observance of them."

A fissure was beginning to split the world. Every day the men who were for going on to the future were further apart from the men who were for bolstering up the past. Joel Barlow found himself with a political creed at last fully formulated, among those who believed that a better future was building out of the breakdown of institutions of that year 1789 in Paris.

He'd been fairly successful in selling the Scioto land. In the middle of the winter the first shipload of French immigrants arrived in Alexandria. In desperate earnest Barlow had written Duer to impress on him 'the immense undertaking' this colonization was 'to the poor creatures who adventure in it, a situation in which all the passions are alive to the slightest impressions. They who lead the way trust their lives and fortunes to the representations that I make to them.' He begged Duer to send a suitable agent to Alexandria to meet them and make the trip out to the Ohio easy. He didn't know that by the time the unlucky Frenchmen landed in the little busy brick town on the Potomac, the whole scheme would have blown up sky high. Duer had failed to raise enough money to take up his option with Congress. All the politicians and 'principal characters' of America hurriedly went to work and burned any papers they had in their lockboxes that mentioned the business, a fact which has made it a hard nut for historians to crack. Duer, like poor Robert Morris, went bankrupt and died in the precincts of the jail. For Barlow the whole thing was epitomized in a draft Duer in desperate straits had drawn on him for a hundred thousand livres. Wherever he went in Europe it turned up to make life miserable for him. In London the bankers were threatening to put him in jail if he didn't pay.

Barlow protested the draft, explaining that he had no means of honoring it; eventually the trustees of the company sent over a man named Walker to check on his behavior. According to Barlow's biographer, Todd, this Colonel Walker gave him a clean bill of health in the matter. Be that as it may, the collapse of the Scioto business left Barlow on his own in Europe with no visible means of support.

Meanwhile he'd been writing Ruth passionate loveletters to get her to make up her mind to follow him. The idea scared her. She wrote him that she was too much the simple country girl to do him credit in the capitals of Europe. He answered that he was more afraid she'd be more 'disgusted with the folly than awed at the splendor of this decrepit old world.' Finally she consented and, with her heart in her mouth, sailed from New York for England on the vessel of a Captain Wolsey. When she got to London she went to the address he'd indicated at Mrs. Roger's house on King Street, Cheapside. There she found some very loving letters but no Joel.

Ruth was a girl of spirit. She flared up and vowed she'd sail right home again. Meanwhile pathetic notes poured in from Joel on the Continent begging her to be patient and to enjoy herself seeing the sights while he disentangled himself from business difficulties enough to come for her. The truth of the matter was he didn't dare go to London.

It was a tough moment for a Connecticut girl with a conservative background to land in Europe. The Connecticut society she knew had been hardening and stratifying faster than she, being part of it, could have been aware of since Joel had left two years before. With the establishment of the federal Constitution Americans were giving up political and intellectual speculation and settling down to the business of getting rich. The loose comradeship of wartime had given way to a more rigid society, in which people of means felt it was up to them to put on style, and to keep the lower orders in their place. The more restless spirits, like Ruth's brother Prom, had moved south or west to find quick careers in other states or were emigrating to Ohio valley farms, or speculating in the public funds in New York, or going to sea aboard the rapidly increasing Yankee merchant fleet, or merely roaming about the world in search of information like that incorrigible Yankee traveler, John Ledyard. The people left at home were putting money in the bank and feeling themselves superior to the illiterate trash of Irish immigrants that had begun to trickle through the country from every seaport. They were determined that the better element should keep its hands on the reins.

Once landed in London, instead of a member of one of the best families in Connecticut, Ruth suddenly found herself a mere colonial (and a rebel one at that) in the middle of the corrupt and gaudy hierarchies of the world's greatest city. In Fairfield she'd been the wife of Mr. Barlow the poet, the local boy who'd made good and was abroad on business representing 'some of the principal characters of the republic,' she'd been the sister of Dudley Baldwin, a flourishing businessman, and of Abraham Baldwin, Senator from Georgia in the Federal Congress. In London she was nobody, and from all accounts, her husband she loved so much was skipping around Europe dodging protested notes and liable any minute to be sued and jailed for debt. Everybody she met talked politics, Joel's American friends who came to call on her and evidently loved and respected him, didn't look very respectable themselves.

To cap everything, Europe seemed about to turn topsy-turvy with war and revolution. Naturally she didn't like it.

At last after several weeks alone in London, Joel, who couldn't go to England on account of the protested note that was still howling like a wolf after him down every London street, prevailed on Ruth to push farther into the unknown, in the company of his friends the Blackdens, and to come across to France. He met her in Calais and took her with him to Paris. In spite of all he could do she hated it there at first. She broke out about Paris in a letter to Mrs. Dwight: "O it is altogether disagreeable to me. It is only existing. I have not an hour to call my own except when I sleep. Must at all times be dressed to see company, which you know my dear madam, is not to my taste. We are pent up in a narrow dirty street surrounded with high brick walls, and scarcely see the light of the sun. We have no Sabbath: it is looked upon as a day of amusement entirely. O how ardently I do wish to return to America, and to Greenfield, that dear delightful village."

During the next three years Joel had to be all the time wooing her like a lover to keep her from going back home in a huff. Only gradually he got her to put her mind on learning the French and Italian languages he'd fallen in love with and to enjoy meeting the odd and illassorted people that the restless life of the time churned up about them, and to feel the savor he felt in the crack of the postilion's whip and the merry grind of the postchaise's wheels over the gravel and the accidents of the road and the ancient walls and spires of the villages, the *sole frite* eaten in seaside inns waiting for the packet, the sleety wind and the huddling in the lurching cabin during Channel crossings, and the newspapers and the pamphlets and the neverending dinnertable talk; talk about wars breaking out, ministries falling, speeches in Parliament and in the National Assembly. Perhaps she even began to feel a little sometimes, as Joel now felt it tingling in his blood to his fingertips, the excitement of hope that the world might shake off the groveling and the subservience of fearsoaked centuries and become suddenly all open and free like America, the hope that was soon to begin to be expressed in the toast to which Joel's political friends lifted their wineglasses after dinner: 'To the Revolution of the World.'

Through it all Joel and Ruth remained coolheaded Connecticut Yankees, not forgetting that no matter what kind of a world it was going to be, commerce and industry would have their innings and the cool eye of a good gambler would be respected, and that they owed themselves a niche in the world.

Joel didn't want to get rich for the sake of riches. He wanted to make enough money to settle down to his writing. Already he was revamping his Columbus poem on a more grandiose scale; he was collecting materials for a history of the French Revolution; he was putting his political ideas into form.

Still he was enough of a Yankee to enjoy the business of making money. He had no intention of letting the collapse of the Scioto business, which after all he didn't feel had been his fault, lick him. He'd managed to pull out of the wreck a few shares in Ohio lands to which he had perfectly good title. In the crash of currencies and the fluctuation of government debts and of the price of grain and of every other conceivable commodity, opportunities kept turning up for a man who knew the ins and outs. It was the golden age for the private entrepreneur. In spite of wars and embargoes American ships were beating into all the ports of Europe, landing and loading cargoes. The mere fact of being an American who knew the languages and the bankers' addresses and how to talk to the custom officers and who could be trusted not to decamp with funds entrusted to him gave a man an opportunity for all sorts of agency operations. While the new world of Europe was building amid speechifying and bloodshed and bankruptcy, there was money to be made. Without Ruth he possibly wouldn't have taken the trouble. But here she had given up the security of her quiet country life to come over to him. He wanted to prove to her that he was the sort of man her father would have considered substantial, a man who could make his way wherever he landed in the world. The least he owed her was a decent living.

Meanwhile Mirabeau holding forth in the Assembly and Lafayette riding around on his white horse at the head of the National Guard were the leaders of a France that seemed on the point of crystallizing into the sort of liberal constitutional monarchy, with the fat stupid genial King as a figurehead, most of the Americans in Europe at the time would have approved of.

During the summer of 1790 there was more travel than ever between London and Paris. The warlike barriers of antique differences seemed to be melting away. In Parliament Pitt was offering France a commercial treaty. Fox and Sheridan and their many upperclass followers were enthusiastic for French liberties and were getting ready to drive an opening wedge for the same sort of thing in England with a bill repealing the Test and Corporation Acts and so throwing open political life to dissenters. The liberal clergymen Priestley and Price were pouring out muchapplauded sermons in praise of the National Assembly. Amid fanfares of oratory Lafayette in Paris presented the key of the Bastille to Tom Paine to transmit to President Washington in America. Lafayette had reason to feel at last, and all his flatterers told him so, that he was playing the role Washington had played in America, the role of Cincinnatus the liberator of his country. Deputations went back and forth from constitutional and learned societies exchanging mutual compliments. The free presses on both sides of the Channel clanked night and day turning out books and pamphlets written from every conceivable libertarian angle.

In Paris the center of the whirlpool was the Palais Royale, with its gardens and its restaurants and its shops and its bookstores where people elbowed their way among the stalls to snatch up the pamphlets as fast as the printers' devils brought them from the press, and its gambling houses and its strutting dandies and processions of painted streetwalkers under the arcades and its gaudily decorated cafés where orators endlessly discoursed to the packed tables and to underfed groups of ragged people outside on the pavements who pushed close to the long open windows. It was in the Palais Royale, up four flights of stairs over one of the big gambling establishments, that Joel had found lodgings. He had a knack for getting into the middle of things; but what a strange world this world of Manon Lescaut and Camille Desmoulins must have seemed to Ruth, fresh from her prim Connecticut villages.

All summer the tension increased. Lafayette torn by conflicting loyalties, crazy to do the right thing, trotted anxiously on his white horse from the army, where nothing seemed to get organized, to the Assembly that was bogged deep in theoretical arguments over Abbé Sieyès' constitution, to Versailles where Marie Antoinette, amid dances and costumeparties, never ceased her intrigue for the restoration of privilege, and back to the army again. George Washington's boots were proving too big for him.

The voices of orators that echoed under the arcades of the Palais Royale in Paris were reverberating across France and across Europe. Everywhere ragged and hungry groups were listening. Congenital conservatives like Gouverneur Morris felt it in their bones the way rheumatics feel a coming change in the weather.

In London Edmund Burke, with that faithfulness to British institutions that has often characterized brilliant Irishmen who have made their careers in England, was beginning to sniff danger in the air and suddenly like a good watchdog, gave tongue. This nonsense had gone far enough. Privilege, protocol, parliamentary procedure, the green lawns and ivyclad oaks of the gentry: everything Burke had come to live by was in danger. The first of November he published his *Reflections on the French Revolution.* He gave words to the uneasy feelings of the uppercrust everywhere. This nonsense must stop.

Paine had got wind of the book and of Burke's state of mind through his bookseller before it came out. Intensely disappointed in the man he considered his friend, whom he admired devotedly for his defense years ago of American rights, he set to work to answer it. The result was the first part of *The Rights of Man.*

Argument rose so loud in England it quite took people's minds off events in France. All that winter the friends of liberty and reform were organizing. Paine at his lodgings at the Angel Inn in Islington and Burke in Parliament headed the rival G.H.Q.'s. King George had somewhat recovered his wits and, being a man of great political acumen, immediately made Burke a present of a fat pension from the civil list; the King saw a chance to win back all the ground authority had lost. In all walks of life Englishmen took sides. In May Burke's violence in defense of the aristocrats came to a head in a public quarrel in Parliament with Fox. With Fox in tears they broke off their friendship of years' standing. Meanwhile Pitt kept his counsel, but let it be known that the flirtation with liberal France was off. Burke became the idol of all the emigré nobles now prowling penniless through the courts of Europe in search of a champion.

When the fat King, goaded by Marie Antoinette, who was desperate for some action, ran off to try to join the reactionary coalition that was forming in Germany, the Commune of Paris took the lead in the pursuit. Louis didn't run fast enough and was caught at Varennes and brought back to Paris. People were beginning to call him Monsieur Capet, and to feel that the monarchy was a costly and dangerous toy.

The day of the republicans had come. The Americans felt that now was the time to tell what they knew. That summer the Barlows were in London living on Great Litchfield Street. Joel was at work on an argument for republicanism, another answer to Burke's *Reflections. Advice to the Privileged Orders,* as well as being a carefully reasoned argument for popular selfgovernment, gives an excellent picture of the state of 'the decrepit old world' seen through the eyes of an American liberal. It is still interesting today because Barlow went much further than Paine in looking into the relation between human rights and property rights. So far as I know it contains the first treatment in modern terms of the theory that, if the aim of a state is the free development of every individual man so far as he can go without infringing on the development of his fellows, then it follows that when property rights conflict with human rights, human rights must be regarded first. This predilection has been basic in the thinking of liberal democrats in the United States from the beginning. At the time the book had great influence in Europe, and later in America became valuable campaign material in the building up of the movement for democratic selfgovernment that elected Jefferson to the presidency in 1801.

After the publication of *Advice to the Privileged Orders* in London in February '92, Joel Barlow was a labeled man. Fox spoke praising his work in Parliament, and Burke, every day more irritable personally and more obsessed with the sufferings of the aristocrats, made sarcastic remarks about the prophet Joel, and called for his arrest.

Pitt had become convinced that, for the time being at least, the British people had all the liberty that was good for them. He began to plan the same sort of *cordon sanitaire* against the spread of French ideas that another Tory British administration organized against the Bolsheviks in Russia in 1917. He produced proclamations against seditious writings and began to intimidate booksellers and printers. Spies and intelligence men began to infest meetings of radicals. English mobs broke up meetings, burned Tom Paine in effigy; the summer before they had burned Priestley's house at Birmingham and with it his library, his scientific instruments and half a lifetime's valuable notes on Bastille Day; they were proving, if it needed to be proved, that there could be violence from the Right as well as from the Left. The substantial people of England, like cattle in a field when they scent an unfamiliar animal, began to toss horns and back into a hollow square. Pitt was their man. Sympathizing with the French there remained only a rabble of tradespeople, dissenters, artisans, and the highlife set round Fox, toffs who the British felt were rich enough to afford the luxury of ideas, as of champagne suppers to balletgirls and the ruinous betting at Brookes'. But that rabble was half of England. It took all Pitt's skill to sit on the lid.

In the spring of '92 Barlow, who had just blown off his feelings against the Coalition that was brewing a war on France in a lively political tract in verse called *The Conspiracy of Kings,* went off to the Continent on a sudden urgent mission to Lafayette, who, disgusted with the King and politics, was at Metz trying to pull the French army together in time to meet the threatened invasion. It seems probable that this mission was somehow connected with the Society for Constitutional Information, to which Barlow had just been elected. *Advice to the Privileged Orders,* although it did not have the enormous distribution of Paine's *Rights of Man,* had immediately put him at the forefront of liberal agitation in England. This agitation centered in a series of societies that were sometimes merely dinnerclubs, but that at the height of the reform wave just before Pitt's repression and the popular revulsion against the bloodshed in Paris, were the outlet and bond of union for hundreds of thousands of middleclass people. The first of these societies to come to life had been the Revolution Society that dated from Defoe's time, when a group of liberals and dissenters started meeting for dinner on the anniversary of what they toasted as 'the Glorious Revolution' that had brought Defoe's great idol William of Orange to the English throne. During the agitation for electoral reform and the long contest between George Third and the people of London over the seating of Wilkes in Parliament that had run parallel to the Stamp Act agitation in America, Horne Tooke had founded the Society for Constitutional Information to spread sound ideas on equal representation and annual parliaments through the masses of tradespeople and artisans, who through the Test and Corporation Acts against dissenters and the strange workings of the rotten borough system, had remained disfranchised ever since the great reaction that blotted out the Commonwealth. With the breakdown of the ancient regime in France, all the immensely vigorous progressive and dissenting forces in England and Scotland, bottled up for a century with only emigration to America as a remedy, felt that the time had come to put their shoulders to the wheels of that decrepit squireruled England that had met such signal defeat at Saratoga and Yorktown. One more shove and, with equal representation, Parliament would be out of the mire and equality of opportunity would be established in England as it had been in America.

Barlow in London had met most of the prime movers of the literary wing of this movement. He knew William Godwin, who was writing the first history of the Commonwealth told from the republican side. He was a friend of Hayley and Tooke and Mackintosh and the eager reformers of the Corresponding Society. *Advice to the Privileged Orders* was a luminous statement of their political aims and hopes. Added to his personal prestige as an American, was the friendly conviviality of his manners and his enthusiasm for what he thought was right that still had a reckless boyish drive to it. As a friend of Lafayette's and a man who spoke French, it was natural that he should be chosen as an envoy of the British liberals to the French liberals. The reform party in those years was not the mere sect of middleclass intellectuals it has been described by most historians. Its adherents included groups of illiterate weavers who huddled about a reader who spelled out *The Rights of Man* to them under a candle in a fried fish shop, and the solid tradesmen of the dissenting religious groups who were chafing against the restrictions that disfranchised them and made them live a sort of ghetto life, and the fashionable philosophic gentry of Fox's set that had the somewhat alcoholic sympathy of the rounder Prince of Wales. When Barlow set out he must have felt that at last he was on the way to playing a part on the great stage of the world. From then on the agents of Pitt and Dundas had him on their lists as a fellow to be watched.

Joel Barlow was a man who never turned down a trip if he could help it. He set off full of zest by the packet to Ostend and by chaise across Belgium. But luck was against him. All sorts of heartbreaking accidents delayed him on the road. By the time he arrived at the lines fighting had begun. He was arrested by the Austrians and turned back. It was too late for mediation. He had to go back around through Belgium to get to Lafayette's headquarters. He wrote Ruth from Dunkirk: "Ever since I wrote you from Aix last month it has been out of my power to write you, that is, to say anything that I wished to say, as I expected my letters would be opened; then I expected every day to have got into France, when I should be free to tell you all. But the cursed tyrannies of men and the more supportable ones of the elements, have fought against me ever since. I thank God I have escaped them all, though our new philosophers in London have not taught me to subdue them. I left that seat of the 'Forsaken Villains' Coblentz on the 3rd of May, after having concocted a good plan with my friend to render an essential service to France. I was to make the best of my way to France to communicate my scheme to Lafayette, who was then near Metz—(cast your eye upon the map). The 4th day I had got within a mile of the parties, when I was taken up by the Austrians and sent back to Luxembourg . . ."

He tried to go by sea from Ostend and spent three days on a 'dullsailing Dutchman' baffled by head winds, fuming and seasick in front of Dunkirk before he could land. He posted to Paris and out to Lafayette's headquarters. Whatever the mission was it failed. It was not on the books that Lafayette should be the Washington of his country. All he could do was entrust Barlow with enthusiastic messages to mutual friends in Paris. But there was no more magic in the liberal phrases. Barlow found the constitutional monarchy swimming vaguely in circles before it sank.

By midsummer he was back with Ruth in London. The fat was in the fire for fair. The Commune of Paris, backed by the rabbleraisers at the Jacobin Club, had seized power. The sodden King and the defiant Austrian Queen were helpless prisoners. The call went out for a national convention to frame a new constitution. On the frontiers the Duke of Brunswick had rallied the aristocrats and monarchists with a proclamation at Coblenz that outlawed the Revolution. In Paris, Danton became Minister of Justice. It was to be war without quarter.

In spite of Mr. Pitt's uneasiness about French ideas, the current of republicanism was still flowing east rather than west. Early in the autumn Paine had made a rapid trip over to Paris to help Brissot, still full of enthusiasm from his travels in America, draft a manifesto calling for a republic. From London, Barlow wrote a letter to the assembling National Convention suggesting the groundwork for the new constitution, in which he laid down the premises on which American self-government rests:

". . . I am confident that any people, whether virtuous or vitious, wise or ignorant, numerous or few, rich or poor, are the best judges of their own wants relative to the restraint of laws, and would always supply those wants better than they could be supplied by others . . .

". . . After laying down the great fundamental principle that all men are equal in their rights, it ought to be the invariable object of the social compact to insure the exercise of that equality, by rendering them as equal in all forms of enjoyments as can possibly be consistent with good order, industry and the reward of merit. Every individual ought to be rendered as independent of every other individual as possible; and at the same time as dependent as possible on the whole community . . .

". . . But of all individuals, those who are selected to be the organs of the people, in making and in executing the laws, should feel this dependence in the strongest degree. The easiest and most natural method of effecting this purpose is, to oblige them to recur frequently to the authors of their official existence, to deposit their powers, mingle with their fellows, and await the decision of the same sovereign will which created them at first, to know whether they are again to be trusted . . .

". . . It is essential to the character of a free republic, that every thing should be reduced to the standard of reason; that men and laws should depend on their own intrinsic merit, and that no shadow of deception should ever be offered to the people; as it cannot fail to corrupt them and to pave the way to oppression."

The whole *Letter to the National Convention* is worth reading as one of the simplest statements, and one of the most coolly and freshly worded, of what was in the minds of the majority of Americans when they accepted their new government, and of what sort of order Americans living in Europe during those tremendous years hoped would come out of the collapse of the ancient regimes.

The first thing the Convention did, bankrupt for lack of a reliable king, was abolish the monarchy. The Commune of Paris, dominated by the Jacobins, who were violent unitarian patriots, rather than republicans in the American sense, was the seat of power. The Convention was the sounding board. The threat on the eastern frontier brought out all the latent energy of the French people freed from feudal bonds. Volunteers from the provinces started pouring into Paris. A group from Marseilles sang as they marched a new song that Rouget de Lisle had made up in Strasbourg: '*Allons enfans de la patrie . . .*'

Lafayette, who had found he no longer had any influence with his army or with anybody, suddenly dropped the whole business in disgust and, with a large group of moderates, fled on horseback towards Brussels. He hoped to meet his wife in Holland to sail for America and to leave Europe and its bloody problems behind him forever. He was captured by the Prussians and held in prison in the best medieval style. To the surprise of all Europe and especially of the recently appointed American minister, Mr. Gouverneur Morris, who had been announcing to all and sundry that the Duke of Brunswick could walk into Paris when he pleased, the French armies began to stiffen.

In a fit of republican enthusiasm the National Assembly, during the last weeks of its career, had conferred French citizenship on Washington, Madison, Hamilton, Paine and on a group of members of the British Society for Constitutional Information. On this second list appeared the name of the American poet, Joel Barlow, so he was now doubly on the dangerous list for Pitt's police. Paine, who was already under indictment for sedition in connection with the second part of *The Rights of Man*, had been elected to the Convention by four French departments. England was no place for a citizen of the French Republic. In September he left England just one jump ahead of the officers and crossed to Calais where he was received with all sorts of tricolor delirium. Joel followed him in November, leaving Ruth worried and dismayed at their comfortable lodgings on Great Litchfield Street.

The night he got to Paris there was a big dinner at White's Hotel on the passage des Petits Pères to celebrate the victories of the French armies over the Coalition. Paine was undoubtedly there, among deputies to the convention, a delegation of the military and visiting English and Irish reformers. Speeches were made, toasts were drunk to Priestley, Fox, Sheridan,

Tooke and to the patriotic societies of England and Ireland and to Barlow himself. Ten days later, Barlow accompanied John Frost, an English radical lawyer who had traveled to France with him, to the Tuileries to read from the bar of the Convention a message of congratulation from the Society for Constitutional Information of England, and to express the hopeful conviction that soon the French would have an opportunity to send a message in return to a similar constitutional convention in England. Adding deeds to words like practical Anglo-Saxons, they informed the Convention that their society was presenting the French nation with six thousand pairs of shoes.

Barlow and Frost sent back a report to London:

CITIZENS AND ASSOCIATES:—

We have executed your commission to the National Convention of France, in a manner which we hope will meet your approbation. A translation of the papers herewith enclosed was yesterday presented at the bar of the convention and received with universal applause. After which the president gave us the kiss of fraternity in behalf of the French nation, which we returned in behalf of our society. The scene was truly interesting to every feeling of humanity, and drew tears from a crowded assembly. It gave rise to reflections, which can scarcely be conceived by men in any other circumstance of life; it was the reconciliation of brothers, who had long been excited to a mutual enmity by misunderstanding and mutual imposition. The wounds which had bled for ages were closed and forgot, while the voice of nature declared they should never more be opened. The president pronounced a discourse in answer to our address, which we likewise enclose.

JOEL BARLOW
JOHN FROST

Paris November 29 1792.

About that time somebody suggested that Joel, like Paine, ought to be a member of the Convention and that as Savoy, recently liberated by the armies of the Republic, was being organized into a new department, that was the place for him to get elected. Joel Barlow was a man who never turned down a trip if he could help it. Delighted at the prospect of seeing some new country, he immediately set off for Savoy; there he took up his quarters at an inn in Chambery.

He was mad about the Savoyards; he enjoyed the mountains; he liked the inn. He settled down to write a letter urging the inhabitants of Piedmont to the eastward to throw off the yoke of the oppressor. Savoy made him think of Connecticut. He was snug as a bug in a rug there. But instead of getting himself elected to the Convention, what he did was to write a poem, *Hasty-Pudding*, the best poem he ever wrote in his life, and, so far as I know, some of Philip Freneau's lyrics possibly excepted, the first really decent piece of verse to be written by an American.

In London poor Ruth was worried sick. Joel had seemed just about to take his place again as a respectable member of society after the clearing up of the Scioto business; now everything was spoiled: "Here you cannot return at present," she wrote him in January. "Everything evil is said of you and I am obliged to avoid company not to hear you abused . . . Our friends the P's have quite withdrawn their attentions, I have not seen nor heard from them in more than a month on account of your politics I suppose, but am not sorry . . . You are very obnoxious here, and it is thought you cannot return with safety: the Alien Bill could prevent you, if nothing else . . . I fear, my love, you did wrong in going to Paris with Mr. F—t: his character here is so bad it has injured yours, hitherto spotless . . . Your affairs here are all a wreck . . . My feelings have been much wounded as you may suppose, to see and hear my beloved, my best friend, thus scandalized as he has been here, when I know so well the goodness, the rectitude of his heart and intentions." Whether he came or not she had made up her mind to go home in the spring. "This you will undoubtedly advise, hard as it is for us both. My heart revolts at the idea, but it must be." He answered her not to worry; things weren't so bad as they seemed, if they had to go home they'd both sail home from France together.

The Savoy election was in February. Luckily for him on the whole, he wasn't elected to the Convention. He got back to Paris in March to find the political stage again transformed. It was the sixth month of the Year One of the Republic, One and Indivisible. In spite of Gouverneur Morris's undercover work to get poor Louis spirited out of the country and Tom Paine's courageous efforts from the floor of the Convention to save his life, he was tried and found guilty and his addled head hacked off after two tries by the guillotine that wasn't working so cleanly that day. The Mountain was winning over the Gironde. The Convention was still too busy exterminating aristocrats and traitors to get around to the new constitution. The French people, their armies fighting on every frontier, treason and stealing and the tussle for command making every office shaky, were to toss in a nightmare of power and butchery until suddenly the fever would end with the death of Robespierre. With Marat denouncing strangers every day in *L'Ami du Peuple* it was hopeless for foreigners to try to influence the course of events.

Joel, who had induced Ruth to come back trembling across the Channel to bloody France, philosophically took a pleasant little house at Meudon. Instead of sailing home he had gone into some sort of shipbrokerage business with a Massachusetts colonel. Since he believed the Republic had come to stay, he invested his makings in the national debt and in Paris real estate, as a good republican should. Among other military men of brains a sawedoff Corsican who spoke French with a dreadful Italian accent, a certain Buonaparte had begun to rise in the service of the Convention. Eventually it was the Little Corporal's victories that sent French consols up on the exchanges and made Joel Barlow a rich man.

Joel believed in the Republic, but he couldn't stomach the Terror. As he didn't have Paine's acute sense of personal responsibility, he didn't risk his life as Paine did by trying to stem the tide. He merely sat back and went about his business of making two dollars grow where one grew before. Among all the executions, probably the only one he approved was that of the King, who was certainly guilty of treasonable intelligence with the enemy if any man ever was. To sing at one of the dinners of international enthusiasts frequent at White's Hotel in those days, he made up a parody of *God Save the King* that greatly scandalized the godly:

Fame let thy trumpet sound,
Tell all the world around
How Capet fell.
And when great George's poll
Shall in the basket roll
Let mercy then control
The Guillotine.

When all the sceptered crew
Have paid their homage to
The Guillotine,
Let Freedom's flag advance
Till all the world, like France,
O'er tyrants' graves shall dance,
And peace begin.

Under the Terror, Americans in Paris lived like people in a stormcellar during a tornado. Since the treason of General Dumouriez, who after winning at Valmy and Jemappes the first victories for the Revolutionary Army, had gone over to the enemy in a pet, Robespierre had become the moving force. He terrified and fascinated the Convention and the Committee of Public Safety like a snake in a rabbit hutch. His mission was to purify the country of treason. Robespierre's pure Republic, One and Indivisible, was another form of the monolithic despotism of the Grand Monarch. It was *l'Etat C'est Moi* inside out. The life of every patriot must be focused into the will to conquer of the nation as a whole. To deviations and doubts the only answer was the guillotine.

It was a state of mind that left no room for wellintentioned foreigners, Anglo-Saxon liberals like Paine and Barlow, or vagueminded German humanitarians like Clootz. Practical Americans and English people couldn't get what Robespierre was after through their heads. He seemed to them merely a bloodthirsty monster. Establishing a republic was to them a day-to-day business of adjustment of men's rights; the means were allimportant. For the French who followed Robespierre the means didn't matter: the Republic was a mystic and bloody ritual; the end was unity.

Like so many Americans after him, who have tried to become citizens of Europe, Barlow had suddenly found himself at a point where he could go no further. From all accounts, in our own time, some revulsion of the same sort went over another American political agitator and enthusiastic traveler in foreign lands and languages and thoughts, who in some ways rather resembled him. People who talked to Jack Reed in his last days in Russia say that he too had come to feel that he couldn't go through with the foreign insanity of that later terror. Jack Reed caught typhus and died before he could get home to the commonplace sanities of his own people. Barlow lived on to continue his genial wellmeaning blundering interested progress through life.

Already Barlow's political exploits in France had been somewhat exaggerated at home in Connecticut. It must have been with a bitter laugh that he read a letter brought to him in the summer of '93 by a young man from New Haven. President Stiles of Yale, his old friend, wrote Joel in his ornate strangely illegible cuneiform handwriting, which was the result perhaps of too much study of oriental tongues:

> I congratulate you upon the celebrity and fame which your poetical and political writings have justly merited and acquired to you, partly

in procuring your conspicuous elevation and seat in the National Convention in France, one of the most important and illustrious assemblies that ever sat on this terraqueous globe; an assembly charged with the highest bestowments, and coming up from the people with the express power and authority for the accomplishment of three great works: the form of a Constitution, the taking into their hands the public administration and national government in the interim, and sitting as the judiciary tribunal on the life of a king—works great and arduous, momentous and of great consequence to the cause of public liberty, the rights of sovereignty and the indefeasible rights of man. May you, may the whole National Assembly, the authoritative and empowered representatives of 25 millions of people, be inspired with light and wisdom by the Supreme Arbiter of Public Right.

Old Ezra Stiles had, as his New Haven predecessors of a century before might have said, 'the root of the matter' in him. In spite of the mannerisms of the provincial pedant he had remained a good republican and a Congregational minister of the broad conciliatory school. He had even shocked the godly by learning French late in his life out of enthusiasm for the overthrow of royalty, feudalism and popery in France. For years his little book about the three regicide justices, Whalley, Goffe and Dixwell, who were hidden by the good Roundheads of Connecticut, was, along with Parson Weems' *Washington*, considered patriotic fodder suitable for the minds of small boys in all the schools in New England. If he didn't write the inscription which used to be seen in the cave on West Rock, where the legend had it the New Haven people had hidden the kingkillers: '*Rebellion to tyrants is obedience to God,*' it was thoroughly in the style of his theology. It wasn't until after his death that Yale College solidified into the lump of Federalism and reaction it remained for so many years.

When the young man delivered President Stiles' letter, Barlow had already given up any hope or expectation of taking part in French politics, and was probably thanking his stars that the good Savoyards he'd liked so much hadn't elected him as their deputy. If they had he would probably have gone to jail in the Luxembourg along with his friend Tom Paine, instead of pleasantly dividing his time between Meudon and Paris, occupied with the, for him, still fairly novel business of making money.

Paris that summer was full of American seacaptains. Pitt, largely to save the old order at home, had finally shoved England into the war on the side of the Coalition. The Convention in totalitarian mood had declared an embargo on all shipping and the French fleet had captured ninetytwo American ships and had brought them into Havre, Brest and Bordeaux. White's Hotel was the center of negotiations of the American captains to get their cargoes freed of the embargo. From there they joggled packed angrily into cabs between Gouverneur Morris's house at Sainport, where Mr. Minister had retired to be away from the smell of blood, and Paine's lodgings in a house that had once belonged to La Pompadour way out on the rue du Faubourg St. Denis.

For a while it looked as if the United States had two ministers. The split between Federalists and anti-Federalists at home was reflected in Paris by the strained relations between Morris, who like Burke was every day more burned up by the woes of the aristocracy in emigration, and Paine, who still represented the spirit of '76 to the ordinary run-of-the-mill American. Paine and Morris were both men with a tendency to a chip on the shoulder. They had entertained a sort of an acquaintance for years on account of Paine's friendship with Gouverneur's elder brother Lewis, but as politics got more and more bitter mutual tolerance broke down into spiteful enmity. Morris thought that Paine was intriguing to get his job as minister away from him, and Paine believed to his dying day that Morris had tried to cause his death by not claiming him as an American citizen when he was arrested by Robespierre's direct order and sent to the Luxembourg.

Paine was arrested the night of December 27th. He had

been expecting it. He and that strange ambiguous Abbé Sieyès, who survived everything, were the only members of the Convention's committee for drafting the Constitution to remain alive. He had been a friend of the Gironde, and he knew he had made powerful enemies by his frank arguments for saving the King's life. Then too he had taken advantage of his official position to spirit out of France all sorts of Englishmen and Americans who thought themselves in danger. When the gendarmes came for him at White's where he was dining he asked, on the pretext that he spoke no French, to be taken to Barlow's house. Barlow by this time wrote and spoke French fluently. He and his wife had moved into town for the winter to the *Hôtel de la Grande Bretagne* on the rue Jacob. All his life Barlow had a peculiar quality of being able to get along with the most varied people. It was known that he was a republican, a man of letters, and now quite outside politics, so he was the most useful man in Paris to an American in a jam.

Barlow went with Paine and the gendarmes to Paine's lodgings to interpret for him while they searched his papers. The search took all night and most of the next day. Barlow seems to have convinced the agents that there was nothing suspicious to be found in Paine's writings. They let him take to the printers the first part of *The Age of Reason,* which Paine had been working on feverishly in the hope of setting up a reasonable belief in God, the First Cause, against the hysterical atheism that was part of the popular creed of revolutionary Paris. He had just finished it that morning. Paine remained during the rest of the Terror in the Luxembourg, and almost died there of prison fever.

Barlow and a group of seafaring Americans in Paris got up a petition to the National Convention asking for his release as a fellow citizen and offering to take him back to America with them, but arguing with the Convention that winter was about as useful as arguing with a Bengal tiger. Things seemed so bad that Barlow, who hadn't yet gotten his speculations in such shape that he could go home, thought it wise to move Ruth to Amsterdam.

He was on business up in Altona, across the river from Hamburg where he had made himself quite a nest of friends, including hale old Klopstock and some German professors, when he heard of Robespierre's last desperate speech before the Convention that was at last freezing up against even him, and of his arrest and execution. The sun seemed to shine again.

The Paris the Barlows went back to was more like the old pleasant city of the early days of the National Assembly. The nobility had gone. The clergy had gone. The revolutionists had gone. Outside of the army the businessman was supreme. The American colony was much pleasanter since Morris had packed off to Switzerland to follow his odd destiny among the Bourbons and the noble ladies of the emigration. Monroe, Jefferson's neighbor and devoted friend and follower, had arrived as American minister. One of his first acts had been to get Paine out of jail. He and his wife were nursing him back to health at the legation. While waiting for the French funds to rise enough to make it worth while to sell out and go home, the Barlows settled down in a pleasant apartment on the rue du Bac.

Instead of going home Joel went to Algiers. He was a man who never turned down a trip if he could help it. Now, through his old crony David Humphreys, who had become a hangeron of Washington's and for several years had held the post of minister to Portugal, the State Department asked him to represent the United States in its negotiation with the pirate state that was holding a hundred and thirty Americans as slaves in Algiers. Before he knew what he was doing he'd said he'd go. It would be an interesting trip, he pointed out to Ruth who'd hoped he'd reformed, and besides it was a chance to be useful to his countrymen in deeds instead of words. He'd talked a lot about Liberty, hadn't he? Well, freeing Americans from slavery was a practical way of working for Liberty.

The survival in the year of enlightenment 1796 of Barbary pirates was a tribute to the sublime ineptitude of that old order in Europe which American Federalists and Pitt's conservative Tories and Whigs and all the ragtag and bobtail of ruined feudalism in the Coalition were so anxious to restore. For over a century the great empire of the Ottoman Turks had been shrinking up in disease and confusion, only held together by the fact that the courts of Europe were too busy fighting among themselves to put an end to it. The most prosperous dependencies of the Sublime Porte were the ports of North Africa, which were run by groups of Turkish soldiers, who had gone west to make their fortunes, each town under the leadership of whatever Pasha by skill of swordplay and poisoning had managed to hack his way to the top. This gentleman, in return for a certain amount of specie and slaves, was recognized as regent by the Grand Signor in Constantinople. As they had long ago exhausted the resources of the country and the wealth of the local Moors and Berbers, the only way these soldierstates could live was by piracy. This piracy they organized with considerable skill. The system was to pick on the ships of one particular country at a time and then extort tribute in the guise of a treaty of peace. They were a little scared of the English and French, so they didn't bother them much, but they pillaged the smaller nations unmercifully. The Spaniards bought the freedom of the sea round their own coasts with an enormous tribute. The British felt that the Barbary pirates were useful to cut down competition in the carrying trade. It was rumored that the Admiralty was not at all displeased when in 1785 the Dey of Algiers, having discovered that a new nation of unbelievers had sprung up across the western ocean, gave orders to his merry men to bring in American ships. The Algerines cruised far to sea and captured several American vessels off Portugal; their cargoes were seized and their crews made slaves by the Dey.

In the ten years that followed, the United States government paid protection and ransom money through the religious order of the Mathurins, and sent all kinds of agents to negotiate with the Algerines without accomplishing more than the occasional release of an individual. At last Humphreys hit on Barlow and got the State Department to appoint him to go to Algiers to talk to the leading ruffians and to make a treaty with them no matter what it cost. It wasn't the sort of appointment the Department felt like offering to a respectable Federalist, but Barlow was a poet and almost a Jacobin and a man who never turned down a chance for a trip, so he might do. The assignment was made somewhat tougher by the fact that Algiers was a leading focus of bubonic plague. The lives of the Americans held there, already made hideous by the slavery of the Turks, were in danger from the plague every day that negotiations dragged.

So before dawn one raw January morning Joel Barlow found himself giving Ruth, still warm and intimate in her frilled dressinggown, a last hug and kiss, and leaving his comfortable apartment on the rue du Bac with its high rooms hung with lace curtains and damask portieres that smelt of Paris must and furniture polish, and its intricate chairs and tables and the comfortable stuffiness of the little coal stoves and the reek on the heavy damp frosty air of stables and drains from the cobbled court, and saying good-by to the bonne and to his little dog named Mignon, and setting off for the *midi*. Strapped to the caved creaking roof of his traveling carriage, and a great strain on the axle and on the springs and on Joel's nerves, was a huge portmanteau known in France at that time as a *vache*, stuffed with jewelry and gewgaws to the value of almost two hundred thousand livres as presents to the Dey of Algiers and his mamelukes.

The drive to Lyons was unpleasant. It was a jittery time in the French countryside. The peasants, citizens now, were settling uneasily on the patches of confiscated land they had bought from the nation, but the woods and hills were haunted by bandits, bloody ghosts of the old regime, *les chauffeurs* they called them, guerrilla bands that specialized in cutting the throats of republicans. In spite of all the Directors (members of the fiveheaded executive board established by the new constitution) could do to swathe themselves in pomp of embroidered cloaks and silk sashes, in spite of elaborate fêtes in Paris squares and of the victories of the republican armies that were sweeping Europe, the mass of the people had begun to sigh for the good old times.

All the way Barlow heard the same story. He found postilions quarrelsome and extortionate, postmasters rude and obstructive with that peculiar enthusiasm for obstruction of the small French functionary throughout the ages. The roads too were in bad repair. The *vache* was never off his mind. At Lyons he hired a barge and with his carriage on board floated pleasantly and swiftly on it down the Rhone to Avignon.

On account of the bad roads and the insecurity of the country and the incubus of the accursed *vache* stuffed with jewels he had to give up going to see Petrarch's Fountain of Vaucluse and to content himself with roaming around the lightcolored streets of Avignon and looking up at the square Romanlooking walls of the fortress of the popes. He drove on more pleasantly through Aix to Marseille across the pale landscape of Provence, where from white bluffs and blue olivetrees and low farmhouses among vines, gray pasturelands flattened out towards the sea and the still lagoons, in the honeycolored sunlight and the sharp dark shadows, under the high Mediterranean sky blown clean and clear by the northwind.

In Marseille he saw with some interest his first Moors at the house of Mr. Cathalan, the American consul. The usual delays in getting a ship cleared held him up some weeks in Marseille. He spent much of his time writing Ruth, urging her not to waste too many evenings playing cards, to get plenty of air and exercise and take care of her health, to read Plutarch and Voltaire's *Siècle de Louis XIV*, *Charles XII of Sweden* and *Candide* and the *Confessions* and *Emile* of Rousseau, and above all not to worry and to have a good time and to think of him when she gave Mignon his dinner. He asked her to buy him poor decapitated Madame Roland's *Memoires* and not to forget to keep an eye out for books and documents on the French Revolution. She wrote back that she was desperate without him; that if he did find he had to pick up a Moorish sweetheart to tell her the truth about it. The mails were irregular. Their letters are full of anxieties about each other, little complaints and references, the afterglow of the close life together of a man and woman who have for years been happily hopelessly in love. They took it for granted Joel would be back in three or four months.

He sailed from Marseille just in time to be driven, after several days tossing seasick and miserable in the Gulf of Lyons, into the shelter of the Bay of Rosas. At Rosas, after a day of arguments in the stuffy customshouse, impediments, documents spelled out word by word for illiterate officials, he went ashore and hired a little twowheeled muledrawn chaise to carry him to Alicante. He was all for taking any possible leg of a journey by land to avoid the horrible seasickness that never left him at sea.

He enjoyed the drive. The mule jingled along slowly and cheerfully over the bad roads. The Spanish drivers, who walked on ahead urging on the mule with shouts of '*arré!*' were honest selfrespecting and polite. Spring was beginning. Almond trees in bloom stood out against the dry blue distant mountains. He went through the crumbling fortress towns of Figueras and Gerona, admired the prosperity of the shops along the well-laid stone streets of Barcelona, where there was an air of neatness and industry that contrasted with the priestinfested misery of the countryside. To his relief the Spanish inns weren't so bad as he'd been told; it was true that you slept over the stables and that little pigs and all the barnyard poultry ran in and out of the kitchen, but the beds were fairly clean and although fleas were numerous and active there were no bedbugs. Valencia was poor and dirty and encumbered with strutting nobles, but he found magnificent the five stone bridges across the river and the great boulevard on the opposite bank where the population promenaded in the afternoon. The countryside was richly green and there were oranges on the smoothstemmed trees round the houses. Barlow reached Alicante in time to be taken by Mr. Montgomery, the American consul's brother, to the theater to see in a dingy kind of wooden barracks a play very stiffly acted and enlivened between the acts by some remarkably bad dancing.

In Alicante he got news that Donaldson, the previous American agent on the Barbary Coast, had already signed a treaty with the Dey. All that Barlow needed to do, so they said, was to pay over the tribute and ransom money and to confirm the arrangement. He'd be back home in no time. Humphreys was sending the money by sea from Lisbon. While waiting for letters from Humphreys he drove down to Cartagena to take a look at the great harbor and naval base there. As the mail seemed to take forever getting back from Lisbon, Barlow, anxious to get to work, set off without waiting further, and reached Algiers four days later in a howling March gale.

Before leaving Alicante, he wrote Monroe in Paris a concise account of the whole business: "It appears that in the treaty made by Mr. Donaldson no precise time was fixed upon for the payment of the money stipulated to be paid by the United States, but it was understood that it would be within about three months. The treaty I believe, was signed in the early part of September. After the expiration of the above term the Dey began to be impatient and to manifest his uneasiness that the money did not appear, and that there was no sign of its appearance, saying that he was sorry he'd made the treaty, as under present conditions it was against the interest of the Regency [the Dey was theoretically Regent for the Grand Signor], but as he had signed the treaty it should be faithfully executed on his part, provided the money was paid in a reasonable time. Mr. Donaldson, being somewhat alarmed at these appearances, and hearing nothing from the money procured a Moorish barque and sent Mr. Sloan his interpreter, to Alicante with despatches for Mr. Humphreys [in Lisbon] . . . He being obliged to perform quarantine, Mr. Montgomery, our consul here, took the despatches and proceeded himself to Lisbon, supposing the affair too pressing to admit delay and the despatches too important to be entrusted to the post. Sloan was one of the American prisoners, and had been employed as a domestic servant by the Dey. He is now here awaiting an answer from Lisbon. [Diplomacy was at the mercy of wind, tide and mud in those days.]

"We will now look to Lisbon and the causes of delay in that quarter. You know the credit on which the money was to be raised was lodged in London. You know too, that Mr. Humphreys, who left Havre some time in October, had a passage of more than 40 days to Lisbon. Mr. Donaldson had despatched Captain O'Brien from Algiers to Lisbon by sea early in September. He probably arrived within that month. Mr. Humphreys did not arrive until towards the end of November; everything must have remained inactive during that interval. I am informed that Mr. Humphreys, after his arrival, could not negociate bills on London for more than one fourth of that sum, and it appears on this account he did not negociate any. Of this however I am not sure. But in consequence of his not being able to raise money in that place sufficient to fulfil the contract with the Dey, he sent Captain O'Brien to London to bring the specie from thence . . . in a brig . . ."

Later in the same letter Barlow gave Monroe the key to the sudden interest the Barbary pirates were taking in American shipping. The British had had trouble with the Dey and had just been to considerable inconvenience to get a new treaty out of him: "In consequence of this new treaty with England he has refused to accept the same consul who was there before the rupture, but has desired that the old one may be sent, a Mr. Logie, who was there in 1793, and who persuaded him to the truce with Portugal at that time by holding up the advantages of going out of the Straits [of Gibraltar] after the Americans. Sloan says he was present at some of these conversations, and that he saw Logie, in the presence of the Dey, instructing the captains by the charts where to cruise for the American ships, saying he would forfeit his head if they did not catch a dozen of them in a month, provided they would follow his directions. It is certain the most inveterate enemies we have in that place, as well as in all others under heaven, are the English."

When Barlow's vessel dropped anchor in the roadstead of Algiers the sea was so rough that it was twentyfour hours before a boat could get him into the inner harbor behind the mole to set him ashore. Algiers in those days consisted of what's now called the Kasbah, a maze of narrow whitewashed streets zigzagging in steps up a steep hill. There was no street wide enough for a cart or carriage. Baggage was transported on the backs of porters or burros. Women were veiled to the eyes. The streets were full of filth and beggary. The common language was the bastard *lingua franca* of the Mediterranean; Moorish and Berber dialects were jabbered in the markets by the country-people; Arabic was spoken among the desert traders and merchants in the covered bazaars, and Turkish was the language of the ruling soldiery. Hassan Pasha the Dey lorded it over the enslaved multitudes with scimitar and bastinado. For part of every season the plague was the town's real ruler. The Dey's bankers, whose fingers were in every pie, were the members of the Jewish family house of Bacry.

Barlow was entertained at Donaldson's house, introduced to the Jews and to his colleagues, the other European consuls, and taken to pay his respects to the Dey. The dim light of the Dey's palace, the carpeted rooms without furniture, the salaamliks and the taking off of shoes and the squatting and the insolence of the Turks and the crouching affability of the Jews and the silence and grumpiness of the big bearded brute who was absolute master of this strange world made a deep impression on Barlow. He couldn't help thinking that behind every dark ferocious face, in every veiled mealbag of a woman, in the ulcerous filth of every beggar, and in every porter's glistening sweat, the plague waited silent and allpowerful, and wondering whether he was going to leave his carcase there in Algiers like poor Ledyard in Cairo. One hopeful sign he noted. For some reasons, slaves as they were, the Americans in Algiers had managed to make themselves more respected by the Turks than the other Europeans.

A few days after he'd arrived he wrote Ruth, almost with relief, that there was nothing he could do in Algiers, the money hadn't come, the Dey wouldn't wait, the treaty was off. There was nothing to it but to go home. In eight days the Dey would send the American agents away and in thirty days more the Algerines would start raiding American commerce again. The captives who'd been crazy with joy when Barlow arrived, had sunk back into despair. It seemed that nothing was left to them but to wear out their lives there till the plague reached out for them or till some day some Turkish owner would happen to feel peevish and would have their heads hacked off. This business of American citizens held as slaves had been bad enough in the abstract; but now that Barlow knew them himself, personally, for a fine bunch of young men, New Englanders mostly, he couldn't stand it. He had to do something for them.

Gradually he began to make out how Algiers worked and to set his wits to getting round the Dey, and to appreciate that at that moment the real power in the regency was in the hands of the Jews. The Bacry had complete ascendancy over the Dey and when he was in a good humor could talk him into anything. Although a peevish and bloody despot the Dey was at bottom a fairly simpleminded fellow and anxious to do right by his lights. Some day, Barlow wrote home, the Turks would rise and slaughter the lot, but for the present the Jews pulled all the strings.

The first people who had to be pleased were the Jews. The Dey had picked up as his personal interpreter a man named Cathcart whom the Jews hated because he somewhat stood in the way of their own manipulating of that flightly potentate. Especially Brobar, the most active of the Bacry house, wanted to get rid of Cathcart. So Barlow got the notion of having it suggested to the Dey, that as he was a sovereign whose arm stretched far across the western ocean, it was befitting his dignity to send his personal envoy to the Pashas of the Americans, to see what those dogs of unbelievers were up to, and why they were so slow in sending the specie to pay for their treaty. Obviously Mr. Cathcart was the man to go. Mr. Cathcart went.

That pleased the Jews. Now something had to be done to hop up the Dey. As the Barbary pirates were pretty good seamen and so admired the trim American vessels and the snappy seamanship of their crews, Barlow got the idea of offering the Dey, through the Bacry of course, a present as a consolation for having to wait so long for his money. Gradually he got him interested in the idea of having for his own a new American fullrigged ship of twentyfour guns. If he'd wait patiently for another six months for his money Barlow pledged that the United States would send such a ship as a gift to his daughter. The Dey grouchily raised the ante to thirtysix guns, but Barlow could see that the idea appealed to him. He made more promises. He offered the Bacry ten thousand sequins to spread round the town where it would do the most good, with the understanding that a good deal of it would remain with the house of Bacry, where much good had been done already. Meanwhile Donaldson had gone to Leghorn to try to raise money on American credit, and Barlow was alone in Algiers with his worries and his Jews and an endless amount of paperwork. In his letters to Ruth he took to cursing out his old friend Humphreys whose dumbness had caused all this mess . . . 'If we had a good bankers' clerk in a certain place for a minister . . .' But the Dey was letting himself be thawed. He presented Consul Barlow with a horse.

Joel borrowed a saddle and bridle and took to riding out in the country around the town. He made pleasant acquaintances among the French and Swedes. Everything was delightful: the landscape, the fruit, the gardens. Except for the plague and the general state of barbarism only man was vile. On May 8th he wrote Ruth: ". . . I remain alone and I work like a slave. I sent today a large packet for Lisbon and for Philadelphia. If Donaldson comes with the money to finish here, he will go to Tunis and I can fly to your arms. If he does not come I shall be driven from here, so I shall be free soon in any case. I shall have now very little to do after the departure of the ship which carries this. Then I shall try to amuse myself in my garden—for I have taken a country house here for the sake of appearances, as they believe me a fixed consul, and will think when I go, it is to bring my wife and other necessities for a long residence. Ah well! I shall bring her whenever she and I consent to bury ourselves in Barbary."

He's kidding Ruth along a little in this letter. The real use of a country house was to keep away from the city when the plague had its annual flareup. But by this time Joel was so popular with the Dey he didn't dare tell him he was planning to leave as soon as his business was completed. That year the plague was delayed for some reason. It was three months later than usual before the tale of deaths began to run through the city. It began with the slaves living in filth in the bagnios.

The last day of May Barlow wrote Monroe: "I have now to add the frightful news that the plague has broken out at Algiers . . . It usually commences in February and begins to go off in June. The hot dry weather kills it in this country, so we hope it will not be severe nor last long. One of our poor fellows is attacked and will probably die."

All summer he tried to get the Dey to let him take the

American slaves awaiting ransom out to his house in the country. For some who were so sick as to be useless to their masters he seems to have wangled it. But in June he wrote Humphreys in despair: "Two of our finest young fellows, Nicholas Hartford of Portsmouth and Abraham Simmonds of Cape Anne, have already fallen . . . Since my last Joseph Keith, a native of Newfoundland, one of our mates, has died of the plague. Lunt is still in the hospital and John Thomas, a black man from Massachusetts. The contagion rages with greater severity than was expected."

The night of July 8th, at his wit's end he sat down in his airy sweetsmelling gardenhouse to write a long farewell letter to his wife. He'd made up his mind that he wouldn't get out of this business alive. Tomorrow he was going back to Algiers to work on a little scheme he'd thought up as the last chance of ransoming the Americans before they all died. He wrote:

"My dearest Life and only Love: I run no risk in alarming your extreme sensibility by writing this letter, since it is not my intention that it shall come into your hands unless and until, through some other channel, you shall have been informed of the event which it anticipates as possible . . . A pressing duty of humanity requires me to expose myself more than other considerations would justify, in endeavoring to save as many of our unhappy citizens as possible . . . and to embark them at this cruel moment for their country . . .

"Since I write this as if it were the last poor demonstration of my affection to my lovely friend, I have much to say, and it is with difficulty that I can steal an hour from the fatigue of business to devote to the grateful, painful task. But tell me (you cannot tell me), where shall I begin? where shall I end? how shall I put an eternal period to a correspondence which has given me so much comfort? with what expression of regret shall I take leave of my happiness? with what words of tenderness, of gratitude, of counsel, of consolation, shall I pay you for what

I am robbing you of,—the husband whom you cherish, the friend who is all your own?

"But I am giving vent to more weakness than I intended. This, my dear, is a letter of business, not of love, and I wonder I cannot enter upon it, and keep to my subject . . .

"I have often told you since the year 1791, the period of our deepest difficulties (and even during that period) that I had never been so easy and contented before. And I have certainly been happier with you during the latter years of our union than I was in the former years:—not that I have loved you more ardently, or more exclusively, for that was impossible; but I have loved you better; my heart has been more full of your excellence, and less agitated with objects of ambition, which used to devour me before . . ."

He explained that his will and a schedule of his business interests was enclosed and that everything would be in her hands. He suggested that she take an annuity of around $7000 a year for herself and with the rest (the amount would depend on the condition of the French funds) she should help his relatives and hers, their dear friends the Blackdens, if they should ever come to need it, and also Mary Wollstonecraft, with whom they had become very intimate in Paris. ". . . Poor girl, you know her worth, her virtues, and her talents; and I am sure you will not fail to keep yourself informed of her circumstances. She has friends, or at least *had* them, more able than you will be to yield her assistance in case of need. But they may forsake her for reasons which, to your enlightened and benevolent mind, would rather be an additional inducement to contribute to her happiness . . ."

Then he went on to suggest ways in which she could spend money usefully, lending money to poor debtors stuck in jail, by making herself an example of charity which richer friends might emulate, and advising and helping young people in ways of starting on industrious careers at that point that comes in every poor man's life where a small sum of money properly used means a start in the world. ". . . I certainly hope to escape from this place, and return to your beloved arms. No man has stronger inducements to wish to live than I have. I have no quarrel with the world; it has used me as well as could be expected. I have valuable friends in every country where I have put my foot, not excepting this abominable sink of wickedness, pestilence, and folly,—the city of Algiers. I have a pretty extensive and dear-bought knowledge of mankind; a most valuable collection of books; a pure and undivided taste for domestic tranquility; the social intercourse of friends; study; and the exercise of charity. I have a moderate but sufficient income; perfect health; an unimpaired constitution; and to give relish to all enjoyments and smooth away the asperities that might arise from unforeseen calamities, I have the wife that my youth chose . . .

". . . I will use every precaution for my safety, as well for your sake as mine. But if you should see me no more, my dearest friend, you will not forget that I loved you . . ."

The little scheme he had thought up to pay the ransom of the slaves, in the course of which he had to expose himself to contagion by moving back into the city from the comparative security of his garden walls, was a pure Yankee trick that would have done credit to any son of the Nutmeg State. It worked.

He explained it in a letter to Jefferson, to whom he wrote thinking he was still Secretary of State, which he sent with the captives when he shipped them home. The scheme was so simple it was silly, but if Barlow hadn't secured a certain personal ascendancy over the Dey and the bankers, he never could have pulled it off. Here's how he explained it: "I have the pleasure at last to announce the liberation of our citizens from slavery at this place . . . My being able to secure the liberation of the captives at this time has been owing to an accident. Money has been extremely scarce here for some months back. The Jew house who serve as our brokers and who do the greater part of the business here, have had their funds for some time in the hands of the French government to the amount of half a million dollars. The operations of some other houses for a year past had centred nearly in the same point, so that there was no money left in the public treasury. Though I had so far gained the confidence of the Jews that they declared to me that they would advance the money to the amount of the redemption if it could be raised, I had little faith in these professions because I believed they said so under the idea that the money could not be had in the town. The plague broke out in the latter end of May, & very much increased my anxiety for the fate of our people. Some time in June a new French Consul arrived, & by some brilliant presents revived the influence of the Republic with the Dey, so as to borrow from the public treasury about $200,000, which he paid into their Jew house. I immediately insisted that they should prove the sincerity of their friendship by lending me this sum, & as much more as the redemption would amount to, for which I would give them my bills on Mr. Donaldson at Leghorn."

The Bacrys, stimulated by esteem for Joel, vague philanthropy, a desire to continue to do business as honorary consuls with the new nation in the west, and by the fact that discounts on bills drawn on Leghorn were unusually high, came across. The Dey, whose mind was not built to follow these financial intricacies, saw the cash counted out in front of him and accepted the ransom. Barlow immediately packed such of the American seafaring men as had survived the plague on board the ship *Fortune* which belonged to the house of Bacry and to which Barlow gave American registry for the trip and which was put in charge of an American skipper, Captain Calder. They set sail for home. Barlow himself had to stay on until cash came in, a sort of living promissory note of the United States government.

Barlow wrote Ruth in September that he was the only American slave left in Algiers. Letters had come from Humphreys announcing that the gold had been shipped from Lisbon early in July on the brig with Captain O'Brien. But where the devil was the brig? Even with the worst of winds a vessel couldn't take three months between Lisbon and Algiers. Day followed day. Barlow was in despair at the thought that she'd been lost.

The Dey made up his mind that he'd been had. He got into such a pet that not even the Bacry could put in a word for the American. The Dey's pets tended to be dangerous to the bystanders. What made him sorest was that ransom money for slaves went into the treasury of the regency to be divided among all the Turks, while the peace money would most of it go to him personally. The slaves had been a security. Here he'd let this unbelieving dog trick him into letting them slip through his fingers. Nobody dared utter any word that sounded like American in earshot of the Dey. It was now a year since he'd signed the treaty, and he'd kept it, and he'd been promised cash in three months. There was no answering him. He began muttering that he'd have that smooth Americano's head. To make matters worse the British blockaded the Mediterranean, thus cutting off Donaldson who was trying to get bills of exchange through the Leghorn bankers. Barlow was at the end of his tether. There was nothing to do but keep out of sight. He let his mustaches grow long and interested himself in getting ready for the vintage at his gardenhouse in the country.

All the while American ships, since Humphreys was announcing to all and sundry that he had settled the treaty with the Barbary states a year ago, were pouring into the Mediterranean. During the early days of September Barlow was busy writing to American consuls at Gibraltar and Marseille and Alicante and Lisbon to do everything in their power to stop them. But the skippers were keen for business and fretted at consular formalities. Barlow heard that the American flag had been seen as far east as Smyrna. What was worse, the supercargo of a vessel from Ragusa told of having spoken a Tripolitan pirate on her way into Tripoli with two prizes that had a Yankee rake to them. One was a twomaster and one a three-master. They'd been captured in the Atlantic off the Portuguese coast by an unusually enterprising pirate that was captained by a British renegado. Gradually news seeped into Algiers that one of the American boats that had been taken into Tripoli was Captain O'Brien's brig with the tribute on board.

October 1st, when everything seemed blackest, an American brig come unexpectedly to anchor off the port of Algiers. The skipper was rowed ashore in the longboat. It was O'Brien.

Immediately Barlow's luck changed. Now he was the father of all the consuls. The Dey's ill temper blew off in the direction of Tripoli. He'd have that Bey's head off for molesting a ship that had his passport. On board the brig were two ambassadors from Tripoli to beg the Dey's pardon. Now that that potentate had somebody else to pick on Barlow Effendi, father of all the consuls, was in highest favor. The Dey even broached the idea that the Americans were hardly unbelievers or Christian dogs at all. They didn't bow down to graven images, and they worshiped one God, like the Moslems, and they kept their word like good Turks. This is the account Barlow wrote the State Department: "As soon as O'Brien came on shore, I perceived that his having been taken by Tripoli was to be considered and improved as a fortunate event. We went together to the Dey, presented the President's letter & that from Mr. Humphreys. O'Brien went through the story, confirming what I had lately said of the Frigate, stores, &c., & what I had always said of the various disasters that had happened to the funds; every tittle of which was now as true as though it had been found in the Koran, for the proof was in the Brig. He then recounted the affair of the capture, presented the passport which the Dey had given him a year before, laid a proper emphasis on the insult offered to it by the English Renegad, & the neglect with which it had been treated by the Bey of Tripoli in the detention of the Brig for so many days.

" 'Well,' replied the Dey, 'I shall take care of that business.' Then turning to me—'my friend,' said he, 'I have long admired your constancy & courage. I now find you are true to me as well as to your country. I have treated you with great severity, but you must allow that I have had uncommon patience; for I have always felt something at the bottom of my heart which told me, that man cannot lie. God has rewarded you for all your suffering. We shall be friends forever.' "

The upshot of his speech was that the Dey would lend the Americans the extra money needed to make their peace with Tunis and would insist on the Tripolitans coming to an agreement too. If necessary he'd go to war with Tripoli to teach those lowlives to respect his allies the Americans. At the end of it the Dey seized Barlow's right hand, put his left to his heart and swore eternal friendship. Barlow was so relieved he couldn't keep back his tears. It was a very touching scene.

Negotiating the treaty with Tripoli took up only two months but the business with Tunis dragged on and on. The Bey of Tunis was slippery as an eel. The Dey of Algiers blustered and threatened and even declared war on him, though he never got around to bringing Barlow his enemy's head as he'd promised. In the end after an endless haggle about the price the Tunisian Bey settled. Assured that the signed treaty actually was on the way, Barlow got a new American agent installed in Algiers, and at last he was ready to go home to Ruth. Instead of four months he'd been away sixteen.

During the latter part of his stay he'd had time to make the wine from the grapes at his gardenhouse, to see the country a little, to attend a boar hunt, and also to do a little business. In partnership with Herculais, the French envoy, he had bought the American brig *Friendship*, sold as a prize in Tripoli, and the *Rachel*, whose captain had gotten into complications in Oran. He wrote Ruthy with considerable triumph that she was the halfowner of a fine brig that was even now roaming the seas in search of a cargo. One of the happiest days of his life was the day he sailed for Marseille on another fine new American vessel.

July 30th he was writing Ruthy in the highest spirits from the lazaret at Marseille rhapsodizing about the beauty of the very letters of the name of Marseille. The weather was delicious. He was feeling thoroughly fit. In front of him, when he stepped out of his door, was the steely blue bay that stretched sparkling between the ashwhite hills and steep islands with their white forts that hemmed in the crowded town and the landlocked harbor bristling with masts and tackle and sails drying. He had to spend forty days in the quarantine station, but it was such a relief to be out of Algiers that he actually enjoyed it; besides, it was a chance for a good rest, the quarters were comfortable, the food was excellent, there was clear water for swimming: anywhere was a delight after Algiers.

He wrote daily letters to Ruthy, mostly in lively and affectionate French. For years now, since the tough times of '91, they had been writing their loveletters in French which they had decided was a more affectionate language than English. Joel had tried Italian a little but hadn't kept it up. One day he enquired whether he should cut off the rich and flowing mustaches he'd grown in Barbary before or after he met her. ". . . I wear long mustaches—long beautiful and black—(a little gray, however). Do you wish to cut them here, or do you wish to see them & cut them yourself? It is necessary to say why I let them grow. There is a proverb which is only too true, although very humiliating for humanity. *Who makes himself mutton, the wolf eats;* nowhere is this so useful as in Barbary. I discovered that on arriving there, and as I am a lamb at heart, it was necessary for me to conceal this character beneath the exterior of some other animal, & my mustaches give me very nearly the air of a tiger, a beast which the wolf does not eat. They have been very useful in my business: I attach to them no value, except as a souvenir of the services they have rendered me. I place them on your altar: pronounce their fate . . ."

Ruth was never a girl who cared much for adventure; she

wrote begging him to cut them off right away. He made them a sacrifice, so he put it in another letter, on the altar of the Cyprian. ". . . Je suis gros comme un cochon—je me beigne dans la mer—je plonge—je nage fort loin—je m'en trouve à merveille," he added.

He was back in Paris by the middle of September, feeling fine as silk, and ready to pose as a 'barbaresque' figure for his friend John Trumbull the painter. He found Ruth in better health than usual. Ruth was a smart girl. She'd been taking good care of herself and of his affairs while he was fretting in Algiers so that his business losses turned out much less than he had expected. Soon it seemed to them they could sell out and go home to America.

As it turned out, it was to be years before he disentangled himself from the series of shipping partnerships, speculations in wines and brandies and other varied importing and exporting ventures he'd gotten involved in as an indirect result of the African trip, all rendered lucrative but enormously precarious by the terrific state of Europe and the world.

The wheel of fortune had made several spins while he'd been gone. This time it seemed to be England instead of France that was in eclipse. The mutiny in the British fleet the spring before had given the British rulers their greatest scare of all time. Frenchmen were hoping that the busy worms of revolt were already eating through the tough conservative oak of *Perfide Albion*. In spite of all the putting of crowned heads together of the Coalition and all the money Pitt had spent to keep treason and reaction alive, the Directory, that had seemed so shaky when Barlow had left for Africa, was still on its feet. Cochon and Carnot had crushed the conspiracies on the left, for which Babeuf and his friends had lost their heads under the guillotine, and now Hoche and the battalions of Sambre et Meuse, by merely putting on a parade through the streets of Paris, had driven the curés and monarchists of Pitt's reaction to cover, and put the quietus on Cochon and Carnot themselves. Lareveillière-Lépeau, the philosophic botanist, the Jeffersonian republican who really believed the slogans his colleagues used for bunting, was the man of the hour. The key word in the talk of Paris was *Fructidor*.

There was even a temporary lull in the great war. After beating the Austrians at Rivoli, Bonaparte, for reasons that were not yet evident to the general public, had made peace with them at Campo Formio. Already he was behaving with strange moderation towards the papacy and the empire. But with Carnot, the organizer of the armies since the days of the Convention, out, the Bonaparte family interest seemed for a while to have lost its tunnel into the government. The Little Corporal was still merely one of the Directory's great generals. It was only after Hoche died that it became evident that under all these webs that Josephine and the Bonapartes and all their busy friends were spinning, a chrysalis of real power was stirring and swelling. Out of the tangle of cross purposes and interests and every man's struggle for a career and money and women and power from day to day, some kind of living organization had to emerge; but nobody knew yet what sort of beast it would be.

It was in that winter of '97-'98 that the plans were laid for switching to Egypt the expedition against England that had been so much talked about. Bonaparte had begun to dream of hacking out new colonies for France by a dash for the East, where empire was stored among the heapedup diamonds of India. There Cornwallis, a patient hardworking functionary of the British Crown, was busy wiping out the memories of his misfortune at Yorktown by laying the foundations of the greatest source of proconsular wealth for a ruling class the world had ever seen. Bonaparte made up his mind that the place to strike was India before the British Raj was thoroughly rooted there. Bonaparte with his sensitive nose for power could smell it on the east wind. There like Alexander he'd center his empire.

What Bonaparte didn't know and never knew, what was to wreck all his calculations, was that right under the green English sod was a source of more riches than all the treasuries of the moguls put together. Coal and iron worked by the so easily exploited labor of the disfranchised poor would build a new kind of empire that would ruin him and make his whole stagey conception as obsolete as a group of knights in waxwork.

In Paris where *incroyables* and *merveilleuses* strutting in newly fanciful costumes were beginning to set the stage for the imperial show to come, the Barlows settled down into their cozy life together. Among their American friends they missed the Monroes. Since Jefferson had resigned as Secretary of State the contest between the American wings of the great worldwide battle between popular action and authoritarian reaction had become increasingly bitter. Old friends no longer bowed on the street. Congress and the nation were dividing into Federalist Anglomen and Gallophile Republicans. The scurrilous violence of the press whooped up party feeling out of all proportion to the issues involved, until Republicans really believed that Washington and Hamilton and John Adams were plotting to turn the United States into a monarchy on the English model, while New England preachers and shipowners and bankers and bondholders were dead certain that Jefferson was preparing to lead his rabble in their atheistic Jacobin libertycaps to the assault of the homes and the countinghouses of the wealthy, and that if popular selfgovernment won, it would mean that honest men and ladies and gentlemen of substance would be hustled into the tumbrils, like the poor aristocrats of France, upon whose fate Burke had taught the owners of the world to weep such warm sweet tears.

Washington had appointed General Pinckney to succeed Monroe in Paris, but the Directory in a fit of highmightyness, suspecting him of being attached to the British interest (Pitt's agents were their daily nightmare), refused to receive him. When John Adams became President he haughtily sent Pinckney back, and associated with him Elbridge Gerry and John Marshall as envoys extraordinary to settle all the points at issue between the two countries. They arrived in Paris soon after Barlow got home.

The main trouble with these gentlemen was that they knew absolutely nothing about the affairs of France or of Europe and that, such was the suspicion that had sprung up between Americans of differing opinions, they had no way of finding out by talking to their fellowcountrymen like Paine and Barlow who understood French politics. Through the intermediaries they designated in their dispatches by the famous letters W X Y and Z, they let themselves be tricked into a long intrigue by Talleyrand who, back in Paris after his prudent world tour during the height of the Terror, was just beginning to feel his oats as Foreign Minister. Probably he did think he'd be able to get some money out of them. Diplomacy, he was discovering, could be made immensely profitable. It was a moment when the French government, in spite of the moralistic rigor of speech of the Directors, who claimed to be reestablishing the eternal ethical verities, was at a stage of corruption not surpassed even during the last years of the Third Republic. Money and women decided everything. Or it may be that Talleyrand just found it useful and entertaining to make monkeys of the American envoys as part of his campaign of subtly undermining the republican idea. Talleyrand had come back from his travels a convinced authoritarian of the old Grand Monarch school. Certain it was that our three zanies were no match for him. All sorts of strange fish came to the surface of the muddied waters of the American treaty. They all wanted their palms greased. There was the inevitable mysterious lady who came to show a leg to the envoys and even the aged wit, Beaumarchais, popped up out of the ancient regime with a demand for money he claimed the United States had owed him since the brave old days when he and Franklin and Vergennes had formed the firm of Hortalez et Cie.

John Adams huffed and puffed and recalled his envoys. The nation as a whole fully joined in the President's fit of temper and for a while France and the United States were virtually at war. Congress and the President lost their heads with spy and sedition jitters. Frigates were launched in a hurry. Washington again unsheathed his sword.

All the while it was evident that nobody in the government of either republic really wanted war. Under the pompous huffiness of the small town celebrity, Adams had a core of honest good sense. Dr. Logan, a Philadelphia Quaker of means, took it upon himself to go to France to talk to the Directors personally to explain that the people of the United States didn't want to go to war with the people of France. In Paris he found that Barlow was quietly working to the same ends, although, so he always claimed, he had had no personal contact with the French government since all his friends had lost their heads in '93 and he himself had felt such an itching of the neck that he had picked up his wife and dashed off on a sudden business trip to Amsterdam.

The efforts of the Republicans to avert war caused the Federalist press to go off into a yelling fit. Instead of thanks for his pains the good Quaker had a bill passed against him in Congress and was only saved from being prosecuted by the clause in the Constitution that prevented ex-post-facto laws.

Barlow got his share of ignominy. He joined with other Americans in Paris in an address to the Directory, and wrote a public letter to Washington asking that much-revered old gentleman to keep a cool head on his shoulders. These he followed up with two printed letters to the citizens of the United States that were prime ammunition for friends of liberty in the campaign of 1800 when they finally crumpled up that last resurrection of before the war Toryism, the Federalist Party. In spite of his recent services at Algiers, Barlow's efforts for peace won him the undying hate of all the besotted authoritarians who were making a last stand for theocracy in the pulpits of his home state. Many old friends turned on him so spitefully they were never friends again. Like Jefferson's letter to Mazzei, a letter Barlow wrote his brother-in-law Senator Baldwin got into the press in a very garbled form and started a landslide of filthy abuse in his direction. So far as I know this is the first time it has been printed entire:

TO AB. BALDWIN
IN CONGRESS
Paris 4 March
1798

My dear friend,

It is now a long time, even many years, since I have indulged myself in communicating to you my political opinions, because I have generally thought, it is useless, and at some moments dangerous, to trust them to the ordinary modes of conveyance. But the oppertunity of sending by my friend Mr. Lee, who will probably put this letter into your own hands, and the very serious aspect that our affairs have assumed in this place, induce me to throw off restraint, & to speak to you with freedom; though I am far from indulging the hope that any material public benefit can arise from the communication.

The misunderstanding between the two governments has become extremely alarming. Confidence is so completely destroyed,—mistrust, jealousy and a disposition to a wrong attribution of motives are so apparent, as to require the utmost caution in every word & action that are to come from your executive; I mean, if your object is to avoid hostilities. Had this truth been understood with you before the recall of Monroe, before the coming and the second coming of Pinckney,—had it guided the pens that wrote the speech of your president and the answer of your Senate at the opening of Congress in November last, I should probably have had no occasion to address you this letter.

To point out the remedy for the evil at its present height, if indeed a remedy can be found, it is necessary to call to mind the causes that have produced it; for these causes are many, and some of the most operative ones are generally overlooked by the most attentive observers on your side the water. That act of submitting to the British Government commonly called Jay's treaty, is usually considered both by its friends & enemies as the sole cause, or at least the great cause, of the present hostile dispositions of the French Republic towards the United States. This opinion is erroneous. Other causes & those of less public discussion, have had a much more decided effect. It is true that, considering the circumstances under which that treaty was made, when England was flying & the coalition was crumbling before the armies of France, it served to humble us in the eyes of all Europe,—it is true that the manner in which it was thrust down the throats of the people of America by the man whose monstrous influence formed an inconceivable contrast with the weakness of his political talents has effectually humbled us in our own eyes, and has taught our citizens to pride themselves on a renunciation of national dignity;—it is likewise true that as this treaty affected France it was a serious and undignified attack upon her interests; it was giving the lie to all our professions of friendship & sympathy with her in her distressed situation; it was narrowing the freedom of commerce, multiplying the articles of contraband, and throwing every advantage that we could throw into the hands of her enemies. In all these & many other respects the treaty with England has not yet been & probably never will be, censured so much as it deserves. It was a measure substantially hostile and ostentatiously irritating to our best friends.

But it often happens in public as well as private affairs, that the gravest injuries are forgiven or excused, while slighter ones, especially such as border on contempt, excite the most ungovernable resentment & lead to the greatest acts of vengeance. A striking example of this has fallen under my observation in the conduct of these two republics.

At the moment when the old government of France was shaken to its foundation, the new government of the United States was consolidated and was beginning its operation under the most promising auspices. A great revolution in America had completed its work; it convinced the world of the solidity of its principles, and held up to view an unexampled prospect of public happiness. A much greater revolution in France was opening its career. Its authors & conductors, though frightened at the immensity of the undertaking, were animated by our success and instead of shrinking from the task of solving the frightful problem of representative democracy they contemplated that problem as already solved by us. Our energy was praised, our wisdom exaggerated & our example quoted by them on all occasions. George Washington, a name at that time dear to Liberty, was placed at the head of our administration, and his election was known to be unanimous. The French therefore saw in Washington the people of the United States. They counted upon his friendship, they drew consolation from his supposed sympathy. While their principles were calumniated & the nation threatened with war by all the cabinets of Europe, they grew strong from a sense of danger; & they were proud of the reproach of princes because they were confident of the approbation of the American people, the elder sons of Liberty. It is difficult for you to conceive to what degree their sensibility was carried on this subject at the beginning of the revolution. It was clear that a sensibility of such force must be the foundation of the most extravagant affections. If properly nourished it would beget a confidence without bounds; if slighted or answered with indifference it must end in a jealousy uncontrolled by the rules of justice & blind to the light of truth.

And what was the conduct of your president on this occasion? Thomas Jefferson was then your ambassador in France, where his superior talents & republican principles had rendered him exceedingly dear to all the friends of liberty. It was well known here that his intention was to retain this place during the revolution; they wished it exceedingly, because both he & they were sensible that he would be able to render the most essential services to both countries by remaining in Paris during a crisis of such momentous expectation. No one will deny that the occasion & the place called for the first diplomatic talents and the purest republican virtue that the United States could afford. Jefferson went from Paris on a short leave of absence with a fixed determination to return as soon as possible. But the president ordered it otherwise, and the French believe it was from a disapprobation of Jefferson's attachment to the cause of liberty in France. This opinion may have been too hastily formed; but they were confirmed in it by his naming to the same place Gouverneur Morris, who for two winters past had filled Paris with invectives against every principle of liberty, who was personally detested by all the leaders in the revolution, who was known to be the banker, protector & correspondent of the most obnoxious emigrants.

It is possible that Washington, in not suffering Jefferson to return, might have acted from other motives than those of enmity to the French revolution, though no other motives appear; but his naming Morris is an insult that admits of no paliation. It is in vain to say that he was ignorant of the character that this man bore in Paris. He was a wide-mouth'd bawler, & had been for two years the exaggerating echo of all the abuse in all Burke's pamphlets & the court papers of London.

This man was continued here, to the astonishment of all Europe, for three years. His business was to mislead the president with respect to the principles & probable consequences of what was going on in France,—to insult the french nation, and as far as possible to betray them; for it was universally believed, & I have no doubt of the fact, that, after the Austrian & the English Ambassadors retired from Paris, Morris acted as secret agent & spy for both those cabinets.

A hasty word or action coming from an Ambassador, thought malicious in itself, is not always interpreted to be the language of the government that sent him. But a series of ostentatious abuse continued for three years becomes unequivocal. All Europe, leagued against Liberty, considered America already in the coalition; and France would at that time have grouped you among her enemies had it not been for several circumstances wholly adventitious, or foreign to the conduct of your cabinet. 1st, Some Americans in Paris, of characters far more respectable than that of Morris, endeavored and with a momentary success to convince the leaders here that his conduct when known in America must be disapproved. 2dly, France was in want of the trade and the provisions of the U.S. both for her colonies & herself; it would therefore be inconvenient at that time to have them for Enemies. 3dly, the conduct of Citizen Genêt, a subject of so much triumph to your cabinet & to that of St. James's, was one of the causes that saved you from a war at that time. Genêt had been sent by Brissot. Brissot was now fallen; it was for this reason that the conduct of Genêt was disapproved, and that of the American Government passed over in silence, though a silence mixed with secret resentment & contempt.

When, after long remonstrances, and a formal demand from this

Government, your Executive consented to remove Morris from his ostensible situation in Paris, he *emigrated* (as the french at that time expressed it) that is, he went & joined the emigrants in Germany, and has been ever since among the enemies of France. But this is not all: a letter from president Washington to Morris dated the latter end of the year 1795, intercepted & now in the hands of the Directoire, gives him a commission as a secret agent to the cabinet of London, to transact business so apparently hostile to the interests of France, that I am assured that this letter has sharpened the edge of resentment here more than the whole of Jay's treaty. This and other circumstances have given full credit to the opinion here that a journey which Morris took from London to Berlin in the year 1796 was a mission on the part of the British government to engage the King of Prussia to rejoin the coalition against France.

Another fact, though of less consequence, could not escape the animadversion of the French Executive. John Parish, American consul in Hamburg, was employed by the British Government as their agent for transmitting the subsidies & loans to the emperor & king of Prussia for the war against France, and to freight & fit out vessels for transporting troops to the West Indies. It may be said that the American Government cannot be answerable for a thing of this sort, of which they could have no previous knowledge; but this has not prevented the fact from being reckoned amongst the proofs of an unfriendly disposition on your side. And certainly great allowance ought to be made for the jealousies, even unreasonable ones, of a nation goaded by all Europe, tormented by her own traitors, and standing alone in a cause in which she expected at least a friendly countenance from us, if not an active support. She looked upon the cause of republican liberty as our cause; and though she did not require us to take arms she considered herself as fighting our battles in her own. Much has been said on the subject of national gratitude, and to ascertain how much, & whether any, was due from us to France for the part she took in the American war. I will not add to the observations that have been made on this head; but it is clearly my opinion that she has rendered us more solid service by establishing the principle of representative government in Europe than by aiding us in America.

I shall say very little on the mission of Monroe, because I take it for granted, from what I have heard, that he has already told his own story in print. I will only say that in the midst of all the difficulties created by the madness of his predecessor, the continued folly of your executive, the unfortunate conclusion & ratification of the English treaty, he conducted himself in such a manner as to form by his single character a counterpose to all the weight of resentment from this Government. No body doubts here but that he would have continued so to do to the end of the war, if your cabinet would only have let him alone & confined its blunders to its own continent. What must then have been the astonishment of all our friends & the exultation of the court of London to see him recalled, in the most abrupt censorious manner, for the apparent crime of preventing a war. I shall say nothing of the personal qualities of General Pinckney; because they had nothing or very little, to do with his being refused here as the successor of Monroe. I will excuse him for writing weak & idle letters, but I will not excuse your executive for printing them. Being rejected as ambassador he went to pass the winter in Holland; and all the world knows how many carriage wheels it cost him to make these journies through this frightful republican territory.

Notwithstanding all these injuries both real & imaginary there still remained one more prop to the patience of this very impatient & jealous government. They knew that Washington was in the dotage of his natural life, and near the close of his political career. They indulged the hope that when he should be out of office the American people would come to their senses; or at least they saw that the character of the new president would be a criterion by which the decided friendship or enmity of the United States to France might be clearly seen. The candidates were Adams & Jefferson, one a reputed royalist & enemy to France, the other an eminent republican & friend to the cause of liberty in all countries. The sentiments of these two men were well known; those of the people were not yet known, because it was supposed that the general idolatry for Washington had prevented them being freely uttered. These were the reasons why the Directoire determined to take no decided step in consequence of Monroe's recall till the public voice should declare itself relative to France in the choice it should make between these two candidates. This accounts for the interest that the French seemed to take in the event of that election. Their wishing you to elect Jefferson proves that they did not wish to quarrel with you, & that they still hoped that the people of America were friends to liberty. The Government here waited the event. This was an awful pause in the American affairs in Europe, & it is astonishing to me how you could fail to view it in that light in America and to take the measure that the most moderate share of common sense & the most palpable self interest pointed out.

When the election of Adams was announced here, it produced the order of the 2d of March; which was meant to be little short of a declaration of war, but at the same time so far short of it as to leave room on your side to come forward with a rational project of negotiation, if you wished to avoid that calamity. The enmity of the old president towards France was now considered as nationalized in America; and the government here was determined to fleece you of your property to a sufficient degree to bring you to your feeling in the only point in which it was presumed your sensibility lay, which was your pecuniary interest.

This uncomplying disposition of the Directoire induced Mr. Adams to call an extraordinary meeting of Congress, & consequently to make a speech. To a man who had the least pretensions to prudence there were but two courses to be taken; one was to declare war, if he wished to ruin his country; the other was, if he wished to save it, to offer to negotiate by sending some man or men that he knew would be agreeable to the French; or at least not to play the Bully by forcing a man back who had just been driven out of Paris. The true policy would have been to retrieve the mistake of Washington by sending back Monroe. You cannot imagine the effect produced here by the *name* only of a known friend of Liberty in America. A report prevailed for a few days that Maddison was named to this mission. It almost disarmed the government here of all resentment. Had the news proved true, & Maddison arrived, the business would have been settled in 24 hours. But Adams, to attain his object whatever it might be, found out a third course, which discovered more invention than I had supposed him to possess. He formed a mission of three, to make the people of the United States believe that a negotiation was offered on their part; and then filled it up with names from which there could not be the least expectation of success. The first was a man who had just been refused, & could not be offered again without an insult. Sending him back was undoubtedly intended as an insult, and it was so received. The second was a man whose effigy had been burnt in Virginia for his violent defence of the English treaty; at least it was so reported & believed in this place; the third was a little make-weight man, appointed with the intention that he should have no influence. And yet, to prove to you the facility of this government, after all that had passed, I am able to assure you from the best authority that if Gerry had been sent alone, and not been shackled with the other two, the Directoire would have negotiated with him without any difficulty. At present the three have been here five months, without being either received or rejected; and a new law is lately made by which an additional number of neutral vessels will fall into the hands of the French.

I should hardly gain credit with you were I to state on how small a pivote the fates of nations turn in Paris at this moment. The speech of John Adams at the opening in November was waited for with as much expectation as if peace & war depended upon it. It was hoped that after he had sent his commissioners he would at least avoid the use of insulting language against the nation with which he was pretending to treat. But when we found him borrowing the cant of Edmond Burke, & telling the world that, though he should succeed in treating with the French, there was no dependance to be placed in any of their engagements; that their religion & morality were at an end; that they had turned pirates & plunderers, and that it would be necessary to be perpetually armed against them although you were at peace,—we wondered that the answer of both houses had not been an order to send him to the Mad-house. Instead of this the senate has echoed the speech with more servility than ever George the third experienced from either house of Parliament. Read over again the paragraph that speaks of the negotiation with France. His bringing in the word Europe, under pretense of generalizing, is so flimsy a cover for his attack upon this nation that it only adds to the abuse by attempting to impose on the understanding. He certainly could not mean the English; for he brags in the next paragraph how well they keep their treaty. He certainly can mean no body but the French; for no other nation has overturned religion. Had this speech borne a friendly aspect; or had the paragraph in question been similar to the one inserted on the same subject in the speech of Governor

Miflin it would have facilitated the negotiation, & probably saved millions to the United States.

In enumerating the causes which have brought the two republics to the brink of war, several memorable speechs in the house of representatives ought not to be forgotten. One of your orators calls the French government *a five-headed monster;* another says that Barras when he made his farewell address to Monroe must have been *drunk or mad.* These gentlemen forget that Barras reads their speeches, and that the five-headed monster when it shall have devoured the fry of Europe, may possibly thank them in their turn.

Another subject of complaint, & that not the least, is the scurrility of many of your newspapers against the French republic. Among the most abusive is the United States Gazette, which is considered here (I know not for what reason) as an official paper or printed under the eye & patronage of the Government. The office of Foreign affairs here receives these papers regularly; and you cannot suppose that any of these insults pass unnoticed. It is remarked here, & with great truth, that there is more dirty calumny against the French in the American than in the London papers.

But it is in vain to amuse ourselves in describing the nature of the disorder unless there be a remedy within our reach. In my opinion there is one, but I have scarcely any hope that your wise ones will stumble upon it. Acknowledge your error in sending Pinckney & Marshall to this country; recall them, & perhaps Gerry with them; name and send Maddison or Monroe to take their place; and let the president in his message to the senate accompanying the nomination utter sentiments full of friendship to the French nation, government & cause. Let him acknowledge that the principles of liberty are equally dear to the two countries, and deprecate the idea of gratifying the tyrants of the world by exhibiting the two great republics, whose existence they strove in vain to prevent, now tearing out each other's vitals.

I perceive that much stress is laid by your president & your other royalists on the conduct of this government in refusing to receive your ambassador Pinckney. I wish those gentlemen could somehow or other be made acquainted with the following history. I hope you will not suppose that by inserting it here my intention is to justify the French government. No, my object can be only to serve my country

& to vindicate the honor of all the ardent spirits among you if they should neglect this opportunity of going to war for the three broken wheels of General Pinckney's carriage. In the year 1796 the Swedish ambassador here, Baron de Stahl, obtained leave of absence, & presented his secretary as chargé d'affaires, who had the king's commission for that purpose. This man was refused; on which De Stahl presented a note to the minister of foreign affairs, desiring him to assign the reasons, that the king might know in what he had offended the republic; since he had been the first in Europe to acknowledge it, & the most ardent to deserve its friendship. The answer to this note was an order to the new chargé d'affaires to quit the territory of the republic, and a recall of the French ambassador from Stockholm. As soon as couriers could pass to Sweden & return, the matter was accommodated by the king's renaming the Baron de Stahl, who was agreeable to the Directoire.

About the same time the Ambassador of Tuscany, while in the peaceable exercise of his functions, was ordered by this government to quit Paris in 24 hours & the republic in eight days, without any reason assigned. He obeyed and the Grand Duke very compliantly sent another.

The ambassadors of Portugal and Rome, who were in full credence and activity a few weeks ago, are now imprisoned in Paris. It is true this was in consequence of a rupture between this Government & each of theirs. But the fate of public agents in such cases used to be, to be sent away, & not imprisoned.

The King of Spain lately sent a new ambassador here in great pomp, M. Cabarus, who is refused without reasons publickly assigned, & ordered to quit the republic.

You will remark that in this list the Spanish & Swedish are cases in point for your Pinckney. But their poor kings had not learned the tactique of John Adams, to rename & send back the same men who had been refused. Kings at this day have no notion for a rupture with France.

Another event has lately happened to the Baron de Stahl which makes the Swedish case, taken all together, different from the American. God grant that the American never may come up to it, as long as you have loving couples to send on these missions. The wife of De Stahl is just sent out of the Republic on a suspicion of conspiracy, while the husband remains at his post. What would the Columbian blood say to that? Let me hear some of you wicked batchelors remark that this order to send away the wife may possibly have been solicited by the husband. No such reason is assigned. Indeed it is probable, had this been the case, that when he obtained the order, he would have obtained leave to clamour against it afterwards. Decency seemed to require it, and yet he has not done it. Had it been an American ambassador, & had that American been me, I would have tried hard to get my case inserted in a speech of John Adams or a letter of Timothy Pinckney.

I repeat to you that I am not undertaking the hopeless & useless task of vindicating all the measures that the violent convulsions of the revolution have induced the frenchmen to adopt. But when Mr. Adams shall hear of the second sending away of his ambassador, I would advise him & all those who are concerned in his wounded honour, to club that commodity with the Kings, Princes, & States above mentioned, & to try to bear their part with a patience becoming a government which had merited this sort of chastisement more than all their fellow sufferers put together.

Your three commissioners will doubtless seize this occasion by Mr. Lee to forward their dispatches. These will probably be of a nature to induce the president to take some decisive steps; and I am in trembling expectation of seeing him give another desperate leap into the region of madness. Without knowing precisely the face that the commissioners will put upon the business, I will venture to affirm that their *amour propre* will contribute more than its due share of the colouring. A manly & independent style of acting or writing appears to me not to belong to their characters. Were I to write their letters to the Executive it should be in language like this:—'The French have many reasons to be offended with the American Government. These reasons are exaggerated by their jealousy & other great passions inseparable from the revolution; this is an unfavorable moment, and we are improper persons, to attempt to explain away the imaginary wrongs on which a great part of their resentment is founded. We advise you immediately to recall us three, and at the same time to replace us with one or more persons whose characters are well known & approved by the French, such as Maddison or Monroe.

'If you wish to terminate these disputes by negotiation you must be prepared for considerable sacrifices, such as a loan of money similar to what this nation made to you the last war,—such as a modification of the British treaty, or at least a new treaty with France giving her more advantages than that treaty gives to England. It is possible that on conditions like these you may obtain some indemnification for the spoliations of your commerce, somewhat in the manner provided for with the English in Mr. Jay's treaty. It is scarcely necessary for us to observe that your commission, considering the distance between the two countries, must not be straitened in its powers.—As so much depends on *manner* in this affair, the president will excuse us if we insist on the necessity of his using the utmost precaution in his public speeches relative to this country, and of his expressing the highest respect for the principles of the revolution, the magnanimity of the nation & the sacrifices they have made in the cause of liberty. The French are extremely sensible on this subject.—'

I do not know that a letter of this kind would produce any effect with you; but I beg you to remember the warning I now give you, that if your executive is not accessible to these sentiments, you are very soon at war with the conquerors of Europe. So much depends on the measures to be taken in consequence of the dispatches which I suppose will accompany this letter, that I could not rest easy without communicating my sentiments to some one who would be likely to make some good use of them. I was going to address them to Monroe or Jefferson; but I thought they would be safest in the hands of my oldest & best friend.

You will naturally conclude that some credit is due to my opinions when you reflect that they have been formed from a close observation of every stage of the revolution, & an intimate relation with every succeeding sett of leaders. The present directors are but the successors & sub-successors of my fellow-laborers in the days of my activity. For these political generations have passed away so rapidly, that in every thing but wisdom I am one of the nestors of the present race.

From the manner in which your present commission was composed there is very little doubt in my mind, and there is certainly none in the mind of the Directoire, that the embassy was really intended for Louis XVIII. Your executive did not foresee the 18th of fructidor. When in God's name are we to expect from America just ideas relative to France? Look for a republic in England; but do not, I beseech you, look for a monarchy in France.

12 March

Since writing this letter I reflect that you may be gone to Georgia before it can arrive. Anxious to give it a chance to do some good, I send a copy of the substantial part of it to Jefferson.

With all his knowledge of French politics, even as late as '98, Barlow couldn't foresee what sort of consolidation of power under Bonaparte was brewing, any more than American sympathizers during the twenties with the Soviet experiment could imagine that a new czar was hatching in the Kremlin. Along with the letter to Prom, Barlow wrote to Jefferson:

DEAR SIR—

The extreme mortification with which I view the progress of a misintelligence between two nations that ought to cherish each other with peculiar sympathy has induced me to address to my Brother in law, Mr. Baldwin, my sentiments on that subject. But I am apprehensive that before my letter can arrive, congress may adjourn and Baldwin be gone to Georgia. In that case the chance of its doing any good may be lost, as the present crisis of our affairs cannot last long.

For this reason I enclose a copy of it to you, trusting in your prudence to make such use of it only as may do the most good to the cause of truth & the least mischief to me. The bluntness and severity with which I have delivered some of my sentiments, you will see, are not calculated for your eyes, but for those of a more intimate friend.

Permit me to thank you, as I do sincerely, for accepting the place of *vice president*. I know it must have been a sacrifice of feeling & every personal consideration to the hope of rendering public service, at a time when I was afraid you had become quite discouraged.

I am with great attachment & respect . . .

At the same time he sent along a letter to his old friend Lemuel Hopkins, whose nephew was taking home the packet of despatches, that gives us an idea of how he had learned to be at ease in the world: ". . . Though it is a long time since all communication has ceased between us, I can assure you that my friendship has not abated; and I still love to indulge the hope of once more taking you by the hand, and indeed of passing the evening of life nearer you than you perhaps may imagine. I embrace the opportunity of telling you so by the return of your nephew. You cannot conceive how sensibly I was affected, on my arrival from Africa, to meet with this young man; and to recognize in him the native good sense, the cast of thought, the turn of expression, & even the features of my old friend. I assure you that I have met with very few men of his years possesst of so much information. I have certainly seen none of a superior strength of mind, a more quick & ample comprehension, greater candor, or a better disposition to turn to useful purposes the knowledge he has acquired.

"I restore him to you & to his country, though I have tried to seduce him to stay a little longer, & go with Mrs. B—— and myself this summer to Switzerland, where we promise ourselves an interesting and instructive journey.

"My residence in Europe has been, as you may suppose, much longer than I intended. It has on the whole afforded me as much satisfaction & even tranquility as could be expected, considering the violent convulsions of this great revolution. The mission to Barbary was extremely painful & difficult, but by an energy and perseverance, of which I wish never to be put to the trial again, I succeeded in every object.

"Your nephew & I have contemplated a great scheme of national improvements in the United States, in which you must help us.

"I am glad to learn that your state of health is generally good, and that your prospect of long life is promising. The health of your wife & family, & other circumstances of domestic happiness, give me likewise much pleasure.

"My health is uniformly very perfect. I have grown fleshy, weigh 170 pounds, have contracted no vitious habits, have acquired a moderate but sufficient income, & a pure & undivided taste for tranquility Study & doing good. The health of my precious wife has grown by degrees much better than when you used to mend it so often; & her temper and taste are perfectly conformable to my own. Indeed I rank myself in the rarest class of living creatures. I am a happy man."

Indeed, when they settled down to their common life together in Paris, the Barlows were happy people. Even if their political hopes had guttered out, they couldn't help enjoying having a stake in the booming days of this new imperial Paris that was becoming the capital of Europe. They didn't have the daily worry about how to pay yesterday's bills any more. They were completely happy in each other's company. They were the center of a group of lively friends. In the fall of '97, just when the W X Y Z business was beginning, they had made an addition to their family that opened up for Joel an immense field of new interests.

They had moved out of their apartment on the rue du Bac and were staying for a time at White's while they looked around for a comfortable house that had a garden. At White's they met a lanky curlyheaded young American painter with remarkably deepset bright black eyes whom they both immediately fell in love with. He came from Lancaster, Pennsylvania. He had been on his own since he was seventeen and had started out making his living by painting miniatures in Philadelphia. He had just come over from London, where he had been trying to improve his style by studying under Benjamin West, another Pennsylvanian, an old friend of his family's who was president of the Royal Academy and considered the best painter in England. In England he had traveled round painting portraits in noble families and so had gotten to know the mechanicalminded Earl Stanhope who was ruining himself, his friends said, building canals. Like every other bright young American of his time Robert Fulton was crazy about practical mechanics, and soon began to neglect his portraitpainting for the invention of devices for putting barges through locks. He worked out a system for moving canalboats up and down on inclined planes, which he patented in London. Not finding himself as quickly rich as he expected as a result, he had gone over to Paris to see if he could interest the Directory in his schemes. Besides his canals he had plans for a weaving machine and for a boat to be propelled by steam and for a submarine for the defense of blockaded harbors. Every afternoon he was getting himself drenched trying out on the placid green Seine an underwater torpedo that would blow up enemy warships. He was a lively plausible sanguine fellow, and he and Barlow hit it off immediately.

When Joel and Ruth went to live in their roomy new house with its acre of garden on rue Vaugirard, out near the Invalides, Fulton went to live with them and for the seven years that followed he was a member of the family. For some reason they called him 'Toot.'

Toot was full of ideas on every subject under the sun. He'd never had much education, so with Barlow's help he took to studying languages and higher mathematics and physics. When war between England and France started up again, Toot's canals were laid on the shelf and he began putting all his time in on his submarine. Since Bushnell's attempt on a British battleship in the Hudson River in '76 with a turtleshaped contraption that he propelled with a sort of scull underwater it had been a Yankee notion that something could be done for harbor defense with a submarine boat. With Barlow's help, advice, money, introductions to officials, Toot worked out a submarine that really dived. What eventually stopped him was that there was no really efficient method existing at the time for propelling it. It was built of wood, driven through the water by a screw in the stern which was turned by a crank inside. On the surface it sailed like a catboat. He called it a plunging boat and named it the *Nautilus*. He tried the first seventyfoot model out on the Seine between the bridges in

Paris, and the next year in the basin at Havre managed with his fullsized model to go some hundred yards underwater, to turn around and to return to his startingpoint. The French navy got interested and let him blow up a sloop in the harbor of Brest the following summer with a submarine bomb planted by his plunging boat. The Barlows were as worried as a hen that's hatched out ducklings when Toot blithely entered into a contract with the French to blow up a British manofwar for them. He actually went out hunting for a Britisher along the coast of Brittany, but the *Nautilus* was too slow to catch up with one, probably very fortunately for Toot. When he found he couldn't go further with his submarine he started to work in earnest on drawings and specifications for a boat to be propelled by steam along the surface.

Meanwhile he helped out his friend Barlow with a suggestion of how to use some lots he had acquired an interest in near the boulevard Montmartre. In England, Toot had visited a circular painting of a view of London that people were paying admission to see. Some Scotchman had rigged it up and called it a panorama. So Toot set to work to put up a circular building on Barlow's lot and to paint a view of Paris in it. It was only moderately successful as a moneymaker, but later, with some other enterprising Americans, they added a second panorama, this time of the Battle of Tilsit. The battlepiece was a hit and thereafter panoramas of notable events were one of the typical shows of the Paris boulevards. In his spare time he made sketches for illustrating the edition Barlow had in project of a new version of *The Vision of Columbus* that he was going to call *The Columbiad.*

They all lived comfortably together in the big house on the rue Vaugirard, where Joel had his library and Toot his studio and workshop, growing their own vegetables and their strawberries and raspberries and peaches in the garden, having breakfast parties out under the trees in good weather and big cheerful dinners in the stately diningroom the Barlows never could quite manage to finish furnishing, and watching, without taking part in it, the transformation of France. As Bonaparte's military victories bowled over the ancient regime in one country after another, the Republic One and Indivisible became the broodhen of a nest of subordinate republics. But as the republics multiplied, order and property became the watchword more than the rights of man. After Hoche's death, Bonaparte became more and more the only great French leader and the pillar of order and property. By this time Joel Barlow, watching the astonishing Abbé Sieyès, like a somewhat maladroit magician at a children's party, bringing each time he was asked a new and odder constitution out of his hat, had decided that the republic had never been a republic at all. In a series of lurid transformation scenes, the Convention had given way to the Directory, the Directory to the Consulate, the Consulate to the Empire; and suddenly France was back in the vigorous authoritarian mood of Louis Quatorze and Richelieu. It was a far cry from the Revolution of the World.

The France Barlow and Jefferson and Franklin had fallen in love with, the France of the generousminded talkative nobles, of the Encyclopaedia and the Enlightenment and Lafayette, was turning into something much more like the rigid mercantile authorityminded France of the novels of Balzac. The nineteenth century, with its closed mind in so many departments of life, was coming on in a hurry. Though his heart revolted at the new order, Barlow couldn't help enjoying its benefits. After Bonaparte's whiff of grapeshot, Barlow's investments in French funds rose in value more than enough to make up for the money he lost from so often putting too much goodnatured confidence in other men in his shipping speculations. With Napoleon's every new infringement of the Rights of Man, Barlow's real estate rose in cash value.

He had his own traveling carriage now, with a pair of neat white horses. Ruth, whose illhealth was the only shadow on their happiness in these prosperous years, drove behind them to the various wateringplaces of France. When Joel couldn't go on account of business in Paris, Toot, who lived with them in perfect confidence like a younger brother, was her cavalier. It was when he went with Ruth to Plombières in the summer of 1802 that he finished his experiments in a little stream he dammed up for the purpose with a model run by clockwork of the paddlewheeldriven boat that later became the *Clermont*.

While Ruthy and Toot were taking the waters in their respective ways, Joel, who had a deal on in London, went over to England. He was a little uneasy, but the police didn't bother him. It was the first time Barlow the businessman had gone back to the tight little island, which Barlow the agitator had left under a cloud ten years before. He was amazed at the changes he found. The fissure so much wider than the Channel that had appeared between London and Paris was illustrated by the women's styles. He had left the ladies on the rue de Rivoli and in the Bois showing all their charms in the clinging stuffs of the Attic style that was all that was left of republican simplicity, but on Pall Mall and in St. James' Park he found them all swathed up to the ears in layers of flounces, wearing great frilled hats like lampshades. Mrs. Grundy had come to town.

In spite of the waters Ruth's health wasn't any too good that summer. To cheer her up, Joel wrote her some comical letters about London when he got home to the house in the rue Vaugirard: ". . . it was a gay time, the town full for the season, parliament not yet dissolved, tho midsummer, the weather remarkably fine, except Sunday when I was quite disappointed. I intended to go to Kensington to see the splendor of beauty and fashion, but it rained like the devil & I did not go,—but was several times, gay evenings, in St. James' Park & Green Park. But the ladies dress astonishingly different from what ours do— Why they cover all their bubbies & bosoms & necks & gorges, clear up to the chin. They wear nothing but stays, as long as your arm. And they cover their shoulders & armpits

& elbows. And I am positively assured by those who pretend to be well informed, that they wear petty coats. As to the stays, the milliners' shops & the haberdashers' wearhouses are full of them. I would lay my money that there are ten thousand pounds worth of stays in Bond Street alone, now for sale; long, labored, stiff & armed with ribs of whale. It is a frightful thing to think of. They don't walk so handsome as our ladies do, but they have handsomer streets, finer shops & cleaner houses. London is sensibly increased & filled up. The display of carriages and other signs of wealth is very great . . .

". . . Hub saw the King go to parlement, to *prorogue* the *rogues*. He looks as much like a beef as ever. And hub talked of going once to Ranalah & another time to Vauxhall & another time to the opera, but didn't get to either of them. In fact there is not so much fun in going to these places at London as in Paris, especially the public walks. Here one goes to see infinite quantities of bare bubbies & shape of mootens, but there we see nothing but white chip hats and muslins! Why you may as well look into a bleachfield. Quelle difference! Madame Recamier made a great figure in England, as you must have seen by the newspapers, & it was chiefly owing to the display of the striking features of womanhood above mentioned. It was the reason why London was so remarkably crowded this season & continued so late. She promenaded these in all the great public places. Cuntry gentlemen came from all parts of the kingdom to see & stare & those who were in London for the winter continued there till the end of June. Parlement continued its session uncommonly late, not being able to get through the business. And if Mme. Recamier had not left London, it is supposed the agricultural & manufacturing interests would have suffered very much from this new species of French invasion— When she was to go to the opera or to Ranalah or to walk in Kensington garden of a Sunday it was previously announced in the papers, & the crowd was so immense that the poor woman was in danger of being crushed. One Sunday she attracted such a kingdom of eager starers that Kensington was absolutely chuck'd up full, & there was danger of the loss of many lives. She could not get along half through the garden before a number of gentlemen were forced to make a rampart of their bodies & conduct her back to her carriage, & it was with infinite risk that the carriage could be got back to London, the throng was everywhere so great. So fierce was John to look at the little globes, that every tinker would sooner get his eyes knocked out than not have a glance . . ."

Victoria wasn't born yet, but her island empire was ready for her. Throughout the eighteenth century there had been some sort of unity to Europe. Soldiers, diplomats, scientific philosophers, people who thought and read on both sides of the Channel and of the Rhine and the Alps had a common language. Now that unity was broken never to be mended. The old toast, 'to the Republic of the World' had no meaning any more. Pitt's England was growing up as the grim petticoated Britannia of Threadneedle Street. Out of Napoleon's empire in Europe was to come, not the civilized unity the philosophers dreamed of, but a fragmentary travesty of feudalism in modern dress, a pack of jangling nations, part castle, part bank and part merchant that were to follow at England's heels in the pillage of the exploitable globe. It seems to be almost a rule of human behavior that when a revolution overthrows the rotting debris of an old order, there should appear in the saddle, when the dust clears away, a set of rulers nobody has foreseen. King Status had fallen on his face; all men were equal, but it was Citizen Money, not Citizen Man, that came out on top of the heap.

Meanwhile Jefferson, now President of the sixteen United States of America, was urging Barlow, by letter and through friends, to get to work and write the history of the Revolutionary War before the Federalists cornered the market. A counterweight was needed right away to John Marshall's *Life of Washington*, which Jefferson considered an unfair piece of campaign pleading. Barlow's intentions were the best; but he went on living easy in Paris, collecting material and making notes it is true on the history of both revolutions, but never settling down to the work. His days slipped by, puttering in the garden and playing with his cat named Min and taking Ruthy for drives and seeing company and advising Toot about his inventions, and discussing with him and the new American minister, Robert Livingston, plans for financing the steamboat that they felt was now a thoroughly practicable project.

One piece of work, however, he did do at Jefferson's request. That was a translation of the *Ruines* of their mutual friend Volney. Much as T. S. Eliot's *The Waste Land* set the key to a great deal of the dominant mood of thought in the nineteen twenties, the French traveler and skeptic Volney's meditation on the ruins of Palmyra appealed to people of a philosophical cast of mind during the years when the eighteenth century was dying. Jefferson took a great fancy to the book himself and translated the *Invocation*, then much admired as a prose poem drenched with meaning. He sent his translation to Barlow with the suggestion that he finish the job in order to supersede a miserably bad translation that had come out in Philadelphia and that was the target for the satirical shafts of the Federalists in the American press. Thoroughly beaten at the polls the Federalists were making a last stand in the churches and the schools and newspapers. Jefferson already foresaw and was working to avoid the very thing that happened, which was that they would get hold of the literary and historical mind of America.

Barlow made and published the translation, using Jefferson's invocation, thereby getting himself marked down blacker than ever on the proscription lists of the godly, who thought of Volney as an immoral French atheist and Jacobin whom President Adams had very properly run out of the States. A link clicks into place in the history of the thought of the time when you remember that it was Volney's *Ruines* that so impressed that prodigious English schoolboy Shelley that his first important poem, *Queen Mab*, paraphrased many passages from it. Shelley later married the daughter of the Barlows' illfated friend Mary Wollstonecraft. Though there is no comparison in ability between the two poets, there's some kinship in humane feeling and political attitude and in their obsession with the weather and in the peculiar madeup frame of mythology on which they hung their ideas. I wonder if Shelley ever read *The Columbiad* and if he did, what he thought of it.

For a long time Jefferson had been urging Barlow to come home. He felt that he was the sort of man he needed to help people the desolation of the Federal City with intelligent conversation and good company. Jefferson even went so far as to pick out a house for the Barlows on an estate on a hill overlooking Georgetown and Rock Creek. At last in 1804, when Ruth's health seemed at last to have taken a turn for the better, and after a time spent in London consulting the best physicians about her case, they set sail; and landed, somewhat shattered as always from seasickness, in time for Christmas in New York.

Barlow thought he had shaken off the dust of Europe forever. The time had come, he said, answering a toast at a dinner given to him by the Republicans in New Haven when he went up to Connecticut to take a look at his old stamping grounds, when 'our country must be considered as the depository and guardian of the best interests of mankind.' Certainly there was no freedom anywhere else, and in America the voters were proving every day more forcibly that whoever the hardshell Federalists so smitten with the need for authority were, they weren't the majority of the American people.

Barlow was arriving in America with his portmanteau full of great projects that he and Toot Fulton had been working out in their spare time. The new capital city must have a national university that should be the center of a national educational system. It should include a school of mines, a school of roads and bridges, a conservatory of art, a national library and museum of painting and sculpture, a military school, a mint, a veterinary college, an observatory. Washington must be the center of a network of national highways and canals linking all the rivers. Jefferson was for all these internal improvements, the Quaker Logan tried to get the bill for them through the Senate, but there was no way of interesting Congress in them. At the moment of Republican victory it was as if atrophy had come over the American sense of nationality. Impossible to distract any public man from sectional interests, speculative interests, private interests. The population was doubling, the continent was being opened up along every day richer and vaster reaches into the West. Everything was happening too fast. Hurry. Fill your pockets and the devil take the hindmost. It wasn't for a hundred years that Americans were to think again of their nation in the broad allinclusive terms in which Barlow and Jefferson and their friends thought of it. And now a new means of transportation was just on the edge of coming into use that would immensely speed up and intensify all this scrambling exploitation.

Toot Fulton stayed on in England to sell his torpedo to the British and to superintend the building of an engine for his steamboat. In September 1806, he wrote Joel from London: "My situation now is, my hands are free to burn, sink, and destroy whom I please, and I shall now seriously set about giving liberty to the seas by publishing my system of attack. I have, or will have when Parker sends me my two thousand pounds, 500 sterling a year, with a steam-engine and pictures worth two thousand pounds. Therefore I am not in a state to be pitied. I am now busy winding up everything, and will leave London about the 3rd inst. for Falmouth, from whence I shall sail in the packet the first week in October, and be with you, I hope, in November, perhaps about the 14th, my birthday, so you must have a roast goose ready . . . I have made out a complete set of drawings and descriptions of my whole system of submarine attack, and another set of drawings with description of the steamboat. These, with my will, I shall put in a tin cylinder, sealed, and leave them in the care of General Lyman, not to be opened unless I am lost. Should such an event happen I have left you the means to publish these works, with engravings, in a handsome manner, and to which you will add your own ideas—showing how the liberty of the seas may be gained by such means, and with such liberty, the immense advantages to America and civilization: you will also show the necessity of perfecting and establishing the steamboat and canals on the inclined plane principle. I have sent you three hundred complete sets of prints [of Fulton's drawings for *The Columbiad*] by the Orb directed to Mr. Tolman, New York, value £30 . . . How shall we manage this winter, as you must be in Philadelphia for the printing, and I want to be at New York to build my boat? I am in excellent health, never better, and in good spirits. You know I cannot exist without a project or projects, and I have two or three of the first order of sublimity . . . Mr. West has been retouching my pictures, they are charming."

After considerable difficulty Fulton had gotten the famous firm of Boulton and Watt to build a steamengine that fitted his specifications, and had permission from the government to ship it to America. It was Barlow who doped out the shape of the boiler and who had taken the patent out for it in Paris. Livingston had put in the capital and a certain amount of experience with Nicholas Roosevelt's earlier unsuccessful venture on the Hudson. Toot was certain he would succeed where poor old Fitch in Philadelphia and Rumsey on the Potomac and all the others had failed. He had worked everything out with scale models and could even predict the speed of his steamboat. As soon as he arrived in New York he set to work getting the hull constructed. The boat was to be called the *Clermont* after Livingston's place up the Hudson.

On August 17, 1807, the paddlewheels started churning the water of the North River at a dock near the state's prison, and, after only one false start, the *Clermont* clanking and puffing, with a somewhat worried group of friends on board feeling under their feet the strange vibration of the afterdeck, moved smoothly out into the stream. Toot wrote Barlow, who was settled in Washington at Kalorama: ". . . My steamboat voyage to Albany and back has turned out rather more favorably than I had calculated. The distance from New York to Albany is one hundred and fifty miles. I ran it up in thirty-two hours and down in thirty. I had a light breeze against me the whole way, both going and coming, and the voyage has been performed wholly by the power of the steam-engine. I overtook many sloops and schooners beating to windward and parted with them as if they had been at anchor . . ."

Going through the narrow reaches under Storm King through the mountains the passengers joined in singing *Ye Banks an' Braes o' Bonny Doone*. At another point on the journey Livingston, in the highest spirits, announced Robert Fulton's engagement to his young cousin Harriet. Toot Fulton had made good. Later that fall the *Clermont* was somewhat rebuilt and put into regular service as a packet up the river, and renamed the *North River*. A new and bigger steamboat that had more passenger accommodations and was named the *Paragon* went on the ways immediately. *Neptune's Car* followed and several bluntend steamferries and later, when the war with England began, Fulton designed and built a huge twinhulled floating battery or steam frigate named the *Demologos* or, more popularly, *Fulton the First*. The Fultons settled down to raise a family on a fine estate up the Hudson. Their first boy they named Barlow.

Joel Barlow, at Kalorama, was leading very much the sort of life he'd led in Paris. He cultivated his farm and planted fruittrees and grew in his own garden most of the vegetables he needed for his own table. During Jefferson's and Madison's administrations the Barlows' house, which Latrobe did over for them in his now fashionable Ionic revival style that Jefferson had launched with the Virginia capitol so many years before, became the place to go in the swampy young capital for good company and good talk. Only the more pernickety Federalists smelt unbelief and stayed away. But even for them it was hard to dislike the genial Yankee with his big frame and rather heavy features so easy smiling, and his buoyant interest in everything that went on in the world. Or little Mrs. Barlow with her bright eyes and her long thin nose and the small comical turns of speech and witty cracks that made the guests forget the frail look of pain she often wore.

As soon as the Barlows were established in Washington they began filling up the house with friends and relatives to take the place of the absent Toot. Joel's brother Aaron had died leaving a large family behind. Joel took them over. Some of them he settled out in Ohio on the sections he'd managed to hold on to near Marietta ever since the bad times of the Scioto business. To young Aaron he lent money to venture on a sailing ship. He was particularly interested in the education of his youngest nephew, Tom, who he hoped had brains, and wrote him often and carefully watched his progress.

From his intimacy with three presidents the only political plums Barlow gathered were two postoffices, one for his nephew Stephen at Saugatuck, Connecticut, and another for a Mr. Ellicott whose daughter had married one of the Baldwins. Writing to ask Gideon Granger, the Postmaster General, for the job for Ellicott he said rather ruefully: "I have certainly a great esteem for Mr. Ellicott as a mathematician and astronomer, and would suggest that in all our country there is too little attention paid to men of science, as well as to men of literature. It is really discouraging to all liberal pursuits and proves that the Government is accessory to the great national sin of our country which I fear will overturn its liberties; I mean the inordinate and universal pursuit of wealth as a means of distinction. For example, if I find that writing the Columbiad, with all the moral qualities, literature and science which that work supposes, will not put me on a footing with John Taylor, who is rich, than I'll be rich too; I'll despise my literary labors, which tend to build up our system of free government, and I'll boast of my bank shares, which tend to pull it down, because these and not those procure me the distinction which we all desire. I will teach my young nephews by precept, and all the rising generation by example, that merit consists in oppressing mankind and not in serving them. Excuse, my dear Sir, this dull sermon and make Andrew Ellicott postmaster of Lancaster."

The Columbiad, which he considered his best work, had been printed in its final form in Philadelphia. It was the handsomest job of bookmaking ever done in America, with excellent print and paper and, as illustrations, the engravings from Fulton's paintings that had been made in England;—for some reason the only one he put his name to was the portrait of Barlow in the frontispiece. On the whole the reception the critics gave the poem corresponded exactly with their political prejudices. The Republicans thought it was a great work, and the Federalists damned it. Joel sent a copy to his old friend Noah Webster. The letter he got back expresses the attitude towards him of most of the old Connecticut crowd:

New Haven, Oct. 13 1808

SIR:—I had intended to give to the public a short review of your Columbiad before this time, but two causes have prevented me, first a feeble state of health and much occupation during the summer past, and secondly a doubt whether I can execute this purpose in a manner to satisfy you and my own conscience at the same time. Of the poem, as a poem, I can conscientiously say all, perhaps, which you can expect or desire, but I cannot in a review, omit to pass a severe censure on the atheistical principles it contains. The principles of irreligion which you avow, of which I saw a specimen in a letter you wrote to Royal Flint in 1794 or 1795, form the partition-wall which has separated you from many of your old friends. No man on earth not allied to me by nature or marriage had so large a share in my affections as Joel Barlow until you renounced the religion you once preached and which I believe. But with my view of the principles you have introduced into the Columbiad I apprehend my silence will be most agreeable to you, and most expedient for your old friend and obedient servant

N. WEBSTER.

Breaking with old friends is one of the most painful of the changes in all that piling up of a multitude of small distasteful changes that constitutes growing older, and it was particularly bitter to Barlow who, perhaps because he had no children, felt more dependent on his friends than most men. To tell the truth, these stifflipped backers of the old order in Connecticut had really changed more than Joel. Scared by the swift currents of the new century swirling about them they had grown shells and fastened like oysters for safety on the rocky doctrines of the calvinist churches. As a group they had achieved security and a small measure of power that they felt all these selfgoverning and leveling doctrines jeopardized. They called on the ministers of their smallminded exclusive creed to protect them in their favored positions. What they called atheism in Paine and Jefferson and Barlow was their belief in the perfectibility of man, of all men, not only of the landowning Elect who bossed the small Connecticut towns. Naturally the clergy were against any such liberal idea, because the liberals made it all too apparent that they considered the clergy a fifth wheel to the cart. As they controlled the schools and all the avenues to literacy, between vestrymen and parsons who both felt their privileges and prejudices in danger from free thought, the American mind was tied in a straitjacket, that through the whole nineteenth century it could never quite get free from.

Although Barlow was very much in the councils of the Republican administrations for a long time he wouldn't accept any official position. As he grew older he hated politics and political wrangling more and more. At last in the menacing year 1811 he let Madison talk him into going abroad as ambassador to the Emperor Napoleon. War with England was getting closer every day and it was essential that somebody the administration could thoroughly trust and who knew France and French should be sent over to try to get a treaty of commerce out of the Empire. Between the British Orders in Council and Napoleon's Berlin Decrees, blockade and counterblockade, American shipping which had flourished so all over the world since the Revolution, was being ground to bits. Madison convinced Joel Barlow that he was the man and that it was his duty to go.

Joel was comfortable in Washington and didn't want to move again on account of Ruth's health. Fulton wanted him to stay to advise him about the steamboats he was planning to launch in the Mississippi. Jefferson, who felt that there was the possibility of a firstrate historian in Barlow, wanted him to stay to finish his history. He was ready to furnish him with all the documents and all the advice he needed. There was still time to get the history of the achievements of a generation of Americans, which would be the school of the future, away from the authorityminded Federalists. But in the end they all admitted that nobody but Joel Barlow could fill the bill in Paris and that he had to go.

Anyway Joel Barlow was a man who never turned down a trip if he could help it. There'd be time to do his history when he got home. He'd had pretty good luck with the Dey of Algiers, maybe he could do the same with the Corsican upstart, who after all was a dog of a similar stripe. He packed up Ruth and her sister Clara, and took along young Tom as his secretary, and sailed from Annapolis to France on the *Constitution*. On the last pilotboat came loving messages from the Fultons. From Hampton Roads, Joel wrote a last note back to Toot: ". . . My wife is in excellent spirits, the captain and all the officers very amiable, the most perfect harmony, discipline, cleanliness and comfort prevails. Never was a fairer prospect of a good passage; but my heart is heavy. I have left my country

—possibly and why not probably? forever. But if such should be the result it will not be my fault; that is, the fault of my inclination or wishes. I go with an ardent wish, but without much hope, of doing good, and with the full intention, though with the feeble hope of living to return . . ."

The Barlows arrived in Cherbourg September 8th after a splendid crossing. In Paris they rented their old *hôtel* on the rue Vaugirard which they thought themselves lucky to find vacant. The fruittrees had all grown up. The currants and raspberries were a thicket. All their old friends came around.

The apparatus of the Empire was enormous, stately and cumbersome. During the whole year that Napoleon was planning and organizing his expedition against Russia, Barlow was in Paris drawing up with the foreign office the terms of the treaty between France and the United States. He got some American ships released, he arranged the lifting of some of the restrictions on American trade, but he never could get the treaty itself past the throng of dignitaries in ermine and gold chains that were so thick round the imperial dais. At last when the march to Moscow had started, Napoleon sent back word that he would meet the ambassadors of foreign states who had business with him in October at Vilna. The Duke of Bassano wrote Barlow that if he would come to Vilna the Emperor would be pleased to sign. Napoleon wanted the foreign diplomats to see how he had crushed the last power in Europe that had held out against him.

Joel Barlow was a man who never turned down a trip if he could help it. At the end of October he and Tom set out in Barlow's own carriage swathed in sheepskins and carriage robes, with Robertson's *Charles the Fifth* to read and a copy of *The Iliad* and *The Columbiad* in reserve. Tom read him Robertson as they drove across the Champagne and through Metz to Frankfort-on-Main. They drove day and night with posthorses across Germany to Berlin, crossing on the way the battlefield of Jena where Napoleon had given the Prussians their lesson six years before. Berlin they liked. They rested up there a few hours before driving to Koenigsberg. All the way they never once saw the sun; it wasn't cold but a chilly rain drizzled down from the flat leaden sky clamped down over the leaden plains of North Germany. After Koenigsberg the roads, cut up by the supply wagons of Napoleon's army, were a hopeless ruin. Progress became slow through the mud and the ruts, but the carriage was sound, so Joel wrote his sister-in-law Clara: ". . . These roads have probably never been so cut up since the wars of Wittikind and Charlemagne, and you could not make a set of darker nights, or call out of heaven with all your prayers a more unceasing succession of rain. Eight of these nights we have been on the road, four in succession at one time and three at another. Three other nights we stopped at midnight and were going again as soon as day broke. The worst of it was that the universality and great preponderance of the mud prevented me from getting out of the carriage to walk up hill or down hill. Even the inside of the posthouses, where I got myself hoisted in once a day to eat my boiled milk, was often too muddy for my nice, clean boots, whose habitual position on the long wool of sheepskin on the floor of the carriage rendered it highly proper that they should be kept clean. Thus my position within my nice, strong comfortable carriage (not a pins head of which has started to this day, over these eleven hundred miles of racking, rending, slumping, slouching rocks and mud) was monotonous but tolerable. Tom was all the time sucking in ideas like a calf; his soul seemed to fatten . . . I hope Tom has given you and sister some account of the instructive part of our travels, such as tombs, temples, and monuments, especially those moving monuments of the wisdom of war,—hundreds of wagonloads of invalid soldiers returning from Russia covered with glory, rags, and mud . . ."

Suddenly they found themselves in winter. The frost improved the roads, hundreds of wheels were flattening the frozen ruts. The country was flatter and poorer every day. Instead of houses, low log huts like pigsties. Bearded peasants: filthy bags of muddy rags. Frozen rivers. Bridges down, here and there a hut burned in a clearing in the scraggly forest. Dead horses. As they got near Vilna the road was a heaving steaming mass of wagons, horses and men hopelessly jammed. At last after skirting the worst of the jam, slipping heaving jingling along the sides of the ruined roads, the ambassador's carriage clattered again over pavings in the streets of Vilna.

In Vilna mud, filth, misery, wretchedness, bentbacked Jews in pointed fur caps with long dirty ragged beards. The streets were full of wounded soldiers; men in scabby bandages were dying halfnaked in doorways. Every inn, hotel, billet was jammed with frightened officials, dignitaries of the Empire, officers of the Grand Army. Moscow is burning. The Emperor is skillfully superintending the retreat.

The Americans eventually got themselves a lodging in a hotel that was set apart for ambassadors. They got to be friends with the Danish minister. Snow fell. The weather became pleasanter. Vilna, with its narrow packed streets and its hills bristling with towers and its little black river, looked better for the snow. Joel and Tom began to find it picturesque.

Nothing to do till the Emperor came. On December 4th instead of the Emperor an imperial courier. Beresina has been fought. The Grand Army is no longer in retreat. The Grand Army is in flight; *sauve qui peut.*

The dignitaries, the dukes, the ambassadors, the imperial functionaries are poured out over the frozen roads in a tangled slowly moving mass of carriages, wagons, men on horseback, wounded soldiers on foot. Already the Cossacks are near.

The Americans and the Danes start out together, impossible to get horses strong enough to draw the carriages; the horses are tiny things like rats, anyway, too small and weak from underfeeding to pull the wheels out of the grip of the icy roads. They kick and stumble. They fall down on the frozen puddles. At last the Danish minister moves off with six horses drawing his carriage. It's three in the afternoon before the Americans can start, heading off for Paris by a different road to avoid the army.

On a little hill they find the Danish minister stuck; thirteen horses can't pull him up the hill. Barlow lends him three and finally they are off over the icy tracks that stretch in wide yellow and brown swaths across the flat snowy country.

Delays, difficulties about posthouses, no food in the inns. The broken army is spreading out ahead of them like a stain of blood and pus creeping over the clean snow. The bridge was burned so they crossed the Niemen on the ice.

Somewhere along the road the Emperor passed them behind foamflecked horses traveling at top speed in a small closed chaise with the shades pulled down. He is traveling under the name of Duroc.

Warsaw was in confusion, wagons loaded with wounded frozen in the suburbs, regiments that had lost their officers roaming aimlessly about the streets. No place to find quarters. They picked up a French friend of Joel's named Petry and started west again. Even in Warsaw they were expecting the Cossacks. Outlying villages burning cast a feeble glare across the snow at night.

Joel had a bad cold, he had begun to feel feverish; he was discouraged; all year he'd fretted and fumed over the treaty and now all his work was poured out down the drain.

They rumble out of Warsaw and at last at the little village of Zarnowitch near Cracow they find a decent inn. Joel feels numb and sluggish with fever. He has sharp pains in his chest. Tom and Petry insist on getting him into bed. It's a clean bed, a warm room, the servantgirls bring hot water and towels, hot milk, brandy. They find a doctor. Among the mountainous pillows and the deep feather beds Joel is stifling with fever; it's too hot; he's stifling.

December 24, 1812, he died of 'inflammation of the lungs,' as they called pneumonia in those days.

Tom barely had time to bury him under the snow in the village graveyard, before he had to drive off towards Vienna to keep out of the way of the advancing Russians. The Americans in Paris held a meeting and presented a resolution of condolence to Ruth who was now a thin frailfaced widow with remarkably bright eyes and a long nose under a frilled cap.

She answered them with a stiff little letter in her own handwriting:

GENTLEMEN,

With sentiments of grateful acknowledgment I receive the assurances of esteem and regard which my resident countrymen in Paris bore my dear departed husband. He left his peaceful retreat with no other motive than a desire to be useful to his country. To that ardent desire he sacrificed his life; and devoted me to unceasing sorrow. Yet it will be most soothing to my afflicted heart to know that my countrymen do him justice and will permit his memory to live in their remembrance.

RUTH BARLOW.

In his notes for the trip Tom found an account of Napoleon's interview with the Polish minister of finance at Warsaw in which the Emperor, even in his flight, managed to shake him loose of some cash; and this quatrain:

Yet other Spains in victim smoke shall rise
And other Moskows suffocate the skies,
Till men resume their souls & dare to shed
Earth's total vengeance on oppression's head.

5. Modern Chivalry

FROM the early years of the eighteenth century, settlers had been pushing west through all the easier passes of the Appalachian mountain wall and breaking through the forested valleys beyond into the vast country of rivers and great lakes to the westward. Every year there were more of them, most of them sons of the tough Scotch and Irish protestant families, forced west because there was no livelihood at home. As they advanced they drove the forest Indians before them, shot the game, felled the trees and started clearing the scrub off the deep soil of the riverbottoms. During the Seven Years' War the French trappers and soldiers and furtraders and explorer-priests who had first penetrated the country of the great rivers worked hard to stiffen the Indian tribes and to hold back the onset of Englishspeaking hunters and settlers. But Bourbon France had gone soft and limp at the roots; after Wolfe's capture of Quebec it began to be a certainty that English and not French would be spoken in the new cities that would spring up along the Ohio and the Mississippi and on the shores of the huge lakes stretching endlessly westward. During the Revolutionary War the English, who had inherited the French policy of stirring up the Indians from the Canadian bases, tried to push back the Americans behind the mountain wall. When the new flag with the thirteen stars was hoisted at Fort Pitt, it meant that the level land of the lakes and rivers would be the nursery of a new century of the young republic.

Fort Pitt guarded the entrance to the Western Country. It was an elaborate starshaped fortification with brick moats and counterscarps, placed right at the point where, in a deep valley among steep uneasy hills, the Allegheny poured into the Monongahela to form the Ohio, *la Belle Rivière* that was now lost to the French religious orders and to the British Crown forever. While peace negotiations were dragging along after Yorktown, hampered by the delays of bad Atlantic crossings, settlers again started making their way into the West along every stony trail that climbed steeply into the mountains up the clear loud boulderstrewn streams that scurried down the valleys. On both banks of the Ohio the Indians still had fight in them. Protected by Fort Pitt, a scraggly log town of boatbuilders and outfitters had grown up on the level ground between the ranks of whitetrunked sycamores that flanked the rivers. There were two inns and twenty or thirty cabins. Already they were burning in their fires the soft coal they cut so easily out of the shaly hillsides. Travelers coming to the edge of the ridge above the town and pulling in their reins as they turned into the rough road down to the ferry noticed right away the unfamiliar smell of coalsmoke. Among the first of this new freshet of settlers was a canny young Scotch lawyer out of Samuel Chase's office in Annapolis named Hugh Henry Brackenridge.

He had come to America when he was five years old from Campbellton in Scotland with his parents and had been brought up to poverty, the Presbyterian church, hard work in the fields, and Latin exercises on a stony farm in York County, Pennsylvania. He had early shown that he had a good hard head on his shoulders; by the time he was fifteen he was teaching school. Then he worked his way, tutoring other boys, through Nassau Hall at Princeton, where he was a classmate of Madison's and of restless young Philip Freneau's. Nassau Hall under Dr. Witherspoon was possibly more wholeheartedly patriot than any of the other American colleges. Patriotism and poetry were young Brackenridge's two passions.

With Freneau, who became his closest friend, he composed for the commencement in 1771 a poetic dialogue, *On the Rising*

Glory of America, that they recited together to the great admiration of teachers and scholars. He took orders and founded an academy for boys in Maryland with his friend Freneau as assistant. There he had his scholars declaim two tragedies he wrote in blank verse, one on Bunker Hill and one on Montgomery's death before Quebec, that carry a note of conviction to this day. But Freneau was already restless for the sea and the islands south of the Gulf Stream, and Brackenridge had too little patience and too much bite to his tongue and was too fond of making sarcastic wisecracks to be a success as a schoolteacher. He got an appointment as an army chaplain. In camp he made a hit with officers and men by his riproaring political sermons.

But he was ambitious, he wanted to make a name for himself in the world. He was sensitive about his poverty and his somewhat uncouth manners. He gave up preaching and schoolteaching and put his tough active mind to work on the law in Samuel Chase's office in Annapolis. But there were too many lawyers in the settled East already. When he was admitted to the bar he decided to tack up his shingle somewhere out in the country beyond the mountains. All over the states people were speculating in western lands. Where there were lands there were titles to contest; where there was speculation there was meat for an agile lawyer.

He settled in Pittsburgh and took root there. The little log village was growing fast. Almost immediately Brackenridge became the leading lawyer in the place and one of the chief citizens. His practice had mostly to do with the conflict between squatter rights and proprietary titles derived from the Penns. He helped found the Presbyterian church and the Masonic lodge and induced a pair of young printers to come out to start a newspaper, and organized an academy for the education of the youth, and when he was elected a delegate to the General Assembly, got through the bill that established Allegheny County with Pittsburgh as the county seat. He had even had time to inaugurate the literature of the West by publishing a book. The first volume of his salty and rambling narrative *Modern Chivalry* was printed in Pittsburgh in 1791, the first book to be printed west of the mountains.

He married and built himself a large frame house painted blue and set back behind a picket fence on Market Street. In spite of Indian raids, and the difficulty of the roads that led into the settled country that made transport so expensive and precarious, and agitation among the settlers to form all the Western Country into a new state, even into an independent nation, and the violent harumscarum life along the border of the wilderness, the town was growing. Germans came in with small trades and crafts, stores multiplied, a trickle of bar iron and iron pots and tools began to come in from the forges up the Juniata River. An industry grew up round building keelboats and flatboats for river travel; in 1792 a sloop named the *Western Experiment* was launched which finally made its way, in spite of sandbars and customs barriers, downriver to New Orleans. But in spite of the toil and bustle, ranks of great chestnuts and oaks and beeches still climbed the hills that rimmed the steep valleys. There was plenty deer in the woods. A man could still shoot himself enough squirrels for a pie in a short ramble through the thickets back of Grant's Hill. The river was full of great catfish; there were otter and beaver up the creeks, and at midnight you could hear the strangled scream of wildcats in the narrow scrubby gulches.

In the forest loam of the valleys and the deep silt of the bottomlands the settlers grew fine crops of wheat and barley and rye. As grain was expensive to ship across the long trails and rutted roads into the markets in the settled country, the practice among the farmers was to distill it and to ship it in the form of whiskey. When a farmer couldn't sell his whiskey it was easy to store as it improved with age instead of perishing, and furnished a sort of capital reserve. As currency was scarce whiskey had become virtually the medium of exchange. Hence the great uproar over the excise on spirits that was one of the first measures Hamilton put through when he got control of the Treasury.

The western settlers were suspicious of the new Constitution anyway. They didn't like the funding system because many of them had served in the Continental Army and had sold the paper in which they had been paid at great loss to speculators. Redemption at full value would make these men profit by the soldiers' misfortune. Particularly the newly arrived Scotch and Irish hated excisemen and gaugers. Their tyranny had helped drive them from their old homes in the British Isles. Now that they were getting a little prosperity after all their danger and hard work, Alexander Hamilton's financial system seemed to them the grasping claw of prerogative reaching out after them from beyond the sea.

Back in Philadelphia, Alexander Hamilton, ever since Jefferson had resigned as Secretary of State on the last day of 1793, was virtual prime minister. He had regained over Washington's slow formal mind much of the ascendancy of the old wartime days when he was the prodigious schoolboy secretary to whom nothing could be refused. He had defeated all his enemies. He had had his way with the Treasury and the Bank. Now his restless effervescent mind was reaching out for new realms to conquer. His picture of an empire for America was of the rule of consolidated property interests over a stratified society such as he'd known when he was growing up on Nevis and St. Croix. He was immensely brilliant, immensely ambitious. There'd always been in the back of his head a schoolboy dream of military glory and conquest oddly like Napoleon's. He was passionately in love with the new nation; if it could be kept out of the hands of rustics and levelers it would be made the stage of a career as dazzling as the career his bastard birth had barred him from in England.

Just as the sections of the mighty scheme were falling into place in Philadelphia, from the Western Country began to come rumors of mobs, excise agents tarred and feathered, a

United States marshal fired on, the house of the respectable propertyholder who had been appointed Inspector attacked and burned, Democratic Societies, Liberty poles, Whiskey Boys, Tom the Tinker, insurrection, anarchy and rebellion. This news came at a time when the governing circles in Philadelphia were rigid with horror over the tales from France, the massacres of the aristocrats, the knitting women round the guillotine, the revolutionary armies sweeping away frontiers. From England they heard the deep organnotes of Edmund Burke's lament for the old order in Europe and accounts of the sharp effectiveness of Pitt's repression of the reformers and republicans. The men and women just settling down comfortably into the ritual of authority of the new-established government began to see Jacobin clubs in every waterfront tavern. At once they jumped at the idea that an American carmagnole was beginning in the Western Country. There must be a show of force to consolidate the government. Hamilton's mind, as was its wont, quickly reached the formula; nothing would do but a show of force.

The first thing he had to do was to talk Washington around; the rest of the cabinet was helpless before his persuasive energy. Washington too, great landowner that he was, was horrified by the Jacobin revolution that encouraged the peasantry to burn the landlords out of their mansions. It was decided that fifteen thousand militia must be raised to advance across the mountains and bring the law to the frontier. While the levies were being drilled in Virginia, New Jersey, Pennsylvania and Massachusetts, three commissioners were sent to Pittsburgh to demand the submission of the inhabitants of the four counties involved. The commissioners came back with the report that there had been outrages but that things were quieting down and that gradually the more level heads were coming to the top. With them they brought lists of voters who had signed the submission that would insure them amnesty. But others claimed that they'd never been in insurrection anyway and that to sign a submission would be incriminating themselves. Some men round the administration gave their opinion that it was best to let it go at that, especially as the features of the excise law most repugnant to the western people had been repealed anyway by Congress, and it looked as if the local officials were establishing order, but Hamilton was for going on; not enough had submitted; there must be a show of force.

So General Washington rode out to Carlisle to review the troops, flags were unfurled and bands played. Governor Henry Lee of Virginia was placed in command and the march began. Instead of going back to Philadelphia with the rest of the cabinet, Secretary Hamilton rode west with the army to see for himself that authority was preserved.

There had been so many delays that by the time the march began it was already October and the forested hills flared red and yellow and russet in the frosty air. The militiamen turned out to be not exactly the conquering army Hamilton had dreamed of. Many of them had come for a lark because it seemed to be a good chance to see the Western Country, others were thugs and lowlives who had been hired as substitutes by substantial citizens. They were illtrained and illdisciplined and rowed with the countrypeople and pilfered from the farms along the way. The only thing they had in common was a fanatical hate, generated by the Federalist press in the cities, for Jacobins and Democrats. They saw the insurrection as a great movement led by this mysterious Tom the Tinker who had instigated all the rioting and the burning of barns and houses and the tarring and the feathering. Liberty poles had been set up; that meant the guillotine, atheism, and the butchery of respectable citizens.

As the columns straggled along the rough wagontracks through the mountains, men whacking at the bushes with their swords yelled to one another that that was how they would treat Tom the Tinker when they met him. Rumor, meanwhile, fed by some citizens who had fled from the mobs to take refuge in the settled country, of whom the loudest was

General Neville, Inspector for the Treasury, the most important landowner in Pittsburgh, whose house had been burned by the Whiskey Boys, had it that Tom the Tinker was none other than a rascally Scotch lawyer named Brackenridge.

Great was their indignation when in their last bivouac in the hills before reaching Pittsburgh they found a handbill being passed around in which this man who had been represented as an outlaw ventured to defend himself in print.

Citizens of the Army advancing to the Western Country:

SERIOUS intimations are given me, that I am considered by you as greatly criminal in the late insurrection in this country; and though I may have shielded myself from the law, by taking advantage of the terms of the amnesty proposed by the commissioners, and sanctioned by the proclamation of the President, yet that I shall not escape the resentment of individuals. It would seem to me totally improbable, that republican soldiers would sully the glory of their voluntary rising, by a single intemperate act. Nevertheless, as it would wound me with exquisite sensibility, to be treated with indignity, by words or looks, short of violence, I beg leave to suggest to you, that it is a maxim of reason, that a man 'shall be presumed innocent till the contrary is proved;' and I give you a strong presumption of my innocence, viz. that though having an opportunity of relinquishing the country, I stand firm, and will surrender myself to the closest examination of the judges, and put myself entirely on the merit or demerit of my conduct, through the whole of the unfortunate crisis.

H. H. BRACKENRIDGE

Pittsburgh, October 26, 1794.

Ever since the whiskey troubles began Brackenridge had had a tough row to hoe. Outside of Gallatin, who had settled in Fayette county, he was the smartest and besteducated man in the district. He was a democrat in manners and politics, but he had a scorching sense of humor that often hurt the feelings of stupider men. He had an impatient, somewhat touchy manner, and a canny pokerfaced way of setting traps for people and not hiding his amusement when they stepped into them. He had some warm friends and cronies, but was considered somewhat of an oddity in the region and had made many enemies. Unblushingly independent in his opinions, he'd been for the federal Constitution, but he'd opposed the funding system. He'd been against the excise, but had tried to talk people out of their opposition to it, which in many settlers was so violent it was an obsession, by slow degrees. His situation was complicated by the fact that he was running for Congress in the district and had every intention of representing the interests of his constituents, the small farmers and distillers, there, if he were elected. His enemies, some of whom were running for Congress against him, claimed that this attitude constituted insurrection; his friends, illegal distillers who were mostly, willingly or unwillingly, riding the hills with the Whiskey Boys, on their side took it amiss that he wasn't ready to ride out at their head with a gun in his hand.

His feud with the Neville connection, a group of families headed by the old irascible general who had, out of sheer bravado, accepted the office of Inspector, came from the fact that many of his clients were squatters who claimed the land because they had cleared it and built buildings on it, while the Nevilles and their friends had large holdings which they had bought from the old proprietory of Pennsylvania. In court, Brackenridge, who had a great gift of putting his opponents in a ridiculous position and getting the jury laughing at them, had won many cases and made the 'improvement rights' stick. He'd also had some success defending small distillers whose stills and whiskeybarrels the excisemen were trying to seize. Naturally the defeated contestants and their lawyers would have thought Brackenridge was a scoundrel, even if he hadn't published this book *Modern Chivalry*, which was being so read, that made fun of everything and everybody.

Things had been touch and go all summer. There had been stormy massmeetings at Mingo Creek meetinghouse and out under the trees at Braddock's Fields and campings out of armed men where, what with the violent speech and the whiskey and the shooting off of guns, it had taken nerve for a man to get up, as Gallatin and Brackenridge had done, to try to get some idea of the folly of their proceedings into the heads of the wild frontiersmen. Yet, once the movement against the excise had been organized into meetings, there had been only one fight, and little blood shed. When the soldiers from the fort had tried to protect General Neville's farmhouse from an armed delegation that went there to demand that he give up his commission, there had been shooting and one Whiskey Boy had been killed and several wounded, and in the end the mob had set fire to the barn and the house had caught fire from the barn, so that the soldiers had been forced to show a white flag to avoid being roasted and been allowed to go home and carry off their wounded, unharmed. As a result of the killing there had been great indignation among the insurgents and they had announced that all those who upheld the excise law must leave the country. The Nevilles and their friends had had to run for it, and Kirkpatrick, the officer in command of the fort, and others had slipped out of sight.

Since there were something like seven thousand men up in arms, all wild as hares, and many of them experienced Indian-fighters into the bargain, and since every cabin had its barrel of whiskey, so that everybody was halfdrunk most of the time, the position of a proponent of law and order like Brackenridge was ticklish indeed. Besides, these people were his clients and he hoped they'd elect him to Congress, and he liked them and sympathized with their troubles, to boot. He was constantly attending meetings of the insurgents, going halfway with them in his speeches, but marshaling all the wit and all the funny stories he had to try to laugh them out of the business.

Brackenridge's worst moment came when, at the great meeting in Braddock's Fields, a few miles from Pittsburgh, the crowd decided to go into Pittsburgh and to burn the houses of their opponents there just to teach them a lesson. The Pittsburgh militia and most of the storekeepers and publicans had ridden out to the meeting to try to avert that very suggestion. They very well knew that if one house went their whole town would go up in smoke, and they couldn't trust the Whiskey Boys to keep their hands off their goods and chattels. Pittsburgh had been getting a bad reputation for lukewarmness in the cause anyway. Once the people had made up their minds there was no way of changing them; so Brackenridge made the best of a bad business by inviting the multitude to pay a friendly visit to the town. As he knew the easiest trails and the fords across the river, he offered to lead the march himself.

He had sent people ahead to set out food and drink in an open field to the east of the houses. He tells about it in his narrative of the event: "by order of the committee every possible provision had been made for them on the ground, that the short space of time would allow; and as soon as the Pittsburgh militia, who had marched in the rear, could be dismissed from the ranks, they were employed in carrying water to the plain [back of Brackenridge's house]. Members of the committee set the example, by carrying water and whiskey to these whiskey boys, as they have since been called. I was employed among the rest very busily. I thought it better to be employed extinguishing the fire of their thirst, than of my house." In another place he writes that this day's entertainment had cost him four barrels of his best whiskey. At length to the great relief of the townspeople the horsemen among the Whiskey Boys were induced to cross the ford to the other side of the Monongahela while those on foot were very politely ferried across in boats. A couple of hundred were so drunk they couldn't be gotten rid of, but by a combination of tact and bluff, and the help of the more levelheaded among them, they were kept from doing any damage other than extorting free drinks from the innkeepers. After dark the town and the whole valley was suddenly lit up by the burning of Kirkpatrick's barn, full of hay and his summer's crops, which stood on the height above the opposite bank of the river. Having carefully collected all the available boats on their side of the river, the citizens went to bed with a feeling of relief that nothing worse had happened.

The exiles, mostly members of General Neville's powerful connection, who had escaped a worse fate than having houses and barns burned by the skin of their teeth, went off in great dudgeon across the mountains to seek the authorities in the settled country. For their own safety Brackenridge and the Pittsburgh townmeeting urged them to leave until things quieted down. With them went 'my brother of the bar,' as Brackenridge calls him in his book, a lawyer named Woods who was his great rival before the local courts and who was also running against him for Congress. Brackenridge was no friend of theirs and they got it fixed in their heads that their humiliating exile had been his fault. I don't say that he wasn't a man to enjoy a foe's discomfiture, but at least he was trying to keep them from being tarred and feathered. There was one point on which they thought they had Brackenridge for sure; he had been so busy riding round with the submission list, urging his constituents and clients to sign, that he'd quite forgotten to sign it himself and had only put his name on the day after the time limit had expired.

To go back to his account: "The right wing of the army had now crossed the mountain, and were in the western country. It was like the approach of a tempest to me. I could hear the thunder at a distance; every day new accounts of butchery denounced against me, without judge or jury. I began to hear General Neville raise his voice; 'the damnedest rascal that there ever was on God Almighty's earth.'

"The left wing had also crossed the mountain at a distance of 30 miles to the westward, I could hear Colonel Neville at the table of general Lee, and publickly elsewhere, through that camp, denounce revenge against the 'damned rascal,' meaning me . . .

"My brother of the bar [his opponent Lawyer Woods] had gone to the camp, and had entered into his office of solicitor of testimony against me. The justice of the peace, on whose paper of submission I had put my name, had been called before the judiciary, in order to ascertain the fact, that I was not within the amnesty . . . In the examination of all witnesses the burden of the song was, 'What do you know of Brackenridge?' I knew well that secretary Hamilton would have a predisposition against me. He would rather find the opposition to the law to have originated in the plan of some leading individuals, than with the mass of the people: for the excise law being the result of the funding system, of which the secretary was an advocate, it would save the pride of judgment, to have it thought opposed by the seditious arts of one, or a few, rather than by the feeling or common sense of many. I reflected also, that the secretary would have observed in my letter to Tench Coxe . . . that I was not a friend to the funding system itself. And this even with a man of integrity, would constitute a bias imperceptible to himself; and I was sensible, that the opinion of the secretary, in my case, would have weight with the judiciary . . .

". . . I began to think it would be unsafe to stand it . . . and as before I had mediated to escape from Tom the Tinker, by going to the east, so now I mediated to escape from an equally outrageous banditti, as I began to think them, by going to the west . . . I had thought of a hunter whom I could employ to go to the woods with me . . . I lay upon a couch and thought of it till midnight."

In the end he decided to stay to face the music. He and Gallatin, who had both done the best they could to quiet people down, were considered the chief culprits by the advancing army, where there was daily talk of hanging the big fish and letting the little minnows go. In the election neither Brackenridge nor Woods had been elected, but Albert Gallatin, whose speeches, in spite of his French accent, had greatly struck the settlers by their moderation and good sense. As Woods was thick with the Nevilles and riding in with General Lee's staff, there was only Brackenridge left for a scapegoat. He put his papers in order, wrote out an outline of his proceedings during the summer, and quietly waited at home to see what would happen. The first detachment that rode into Pittsburgh was in command of a corporal who had ordered his men on no account to speak to the dangerous traitor Brackenridge.

"The next detachment that arrived, was an escort of three or four squadrons of horse, conducting, in great pomp, the younger Neville. General Morgan himself was along. They showed themselves on the southern bank of the Monongahela; they crossed the river; the standards were unfurled and the cornets blew their horns; the guns of the garrison were discharged;—it was like a Roman ovation, a species of the lesser triumph.

"General Morgan, in the evening, accompanied by his suite and parading near my house, with a military gait, was heard to say, 'Hang the rascal, hang him.'

"That night I was informed by my servants, that some of the dragoons were occasionally coming and going, and watching the avenues to the house; and that two of them had come into the kitchen and looked into the adjoining rooms. About 9 o'clock, I had further information that two of them had been in the yard, and had gone away. This did not strike me much; I resolved it into curiosity, or an intention of plundering something. They would naturally think it would be no great harm to make free with the property of an insurgent.

"However the danger was greater than I had imagined; that night, at about eleven o'clock I was to have been assassinated. The troops had advanced within 20 yards of my door, when an officer, who had been apprised of their intention, and in vain laboured to dissuade them, having run to General Morgan, who was in the house of Neville the Younger, and not gone to bed, gave him information. The general and the colonel ran out without their hats, the general opposing himself to the fury of the troops, said 'That it must be through him that they would reach me;' and that I had stood my ground; it would be cognizable by the judiciary, and let the law take its course."

The next day Brackenridge found that the Commander-in-Chief General Lee, whom he had known and tutored as a boy at Princeton, was taking his house for his headquarters. The situation made him nervous and uneasy. He didn't know whether to speak to him or not or whether to eat dinner with him or not when he was invited. He fidgeted around in the backroom of the house. In all his distress of mind he couldn't help playing a kind of prank: ". . . I had just before this time, got a large cocked hat, and buff under dress with a coat of military blue; and now and then occasionally shewed myself in the street, imitating, as well as I could, the grave deportment, and stately gait of a general officer. A variety of detachments of horse had come to town, and I found it was a matter of curiosity, to see the leader of the insurgents. I would sometimes hear it said, when not supposed to hear it, 'He has the appearance of a military man.' "

Meanwhile Hamilton had come into town and his inquisition was being set up. The schoolboy dream of conquest was fading fast. This tiny log town, hemmed in by the hills, where the coalsmoke hung low over the loghouses, the deeprutted mud of the streets full of dogs, drays, oxcarts, rooting hogs, dirty-faced children running underfoot, was nothing like the panoply and show of the old days at Yorktown, and Cornwallis so elegantly dressed, and his fine officers so straight and stern. By night parties had ridden all over the country dragging poor devils out of their beds who were supposed to be implicated, and now they were driving them in through the rain and the mud at the breasts of their horses. The town was so small, the houses were so small; everybody was on top of everybody. These were not an Alexander's conquests.

Hamilton had a knack of taking in a situation at a glance like a man who reads page by page instead of word by word.

He had absolutely none of the skill at deluding himself that allows so many men to do dirty things without knowing it. He saw what he saw clear and he saw it fast. He was a vain man, but he was never able to distort his clear view of things to his own advantage. He must have already felt that this stirring up the dead embers of last summer's insurrection was a paltry business. It wasn't worth his time or the expense of fifteen thousand men at arms. For one thing the Democratic Societies had nothing to do with the business. He could see that some of the men round him were crooks and that General Neville was a loudmouthed old fool, and that the whole thing had been overplayed. There was something wrong with the show of force.

Hamilton had enough political acumen to understand, besides, that it would turn out badly for his party in the end. The Pennsylvania state authorities, who were thinking of the voters, had never been for it; now they were more leery than ever. The Federalists would take a licking in the next election: Jefferson and his devilish Jacobins would make the most of it. The cool clearsightedness of his mind never let him take advantage of this sort of situation for his own career. It never seems to have occurred to him that he could do it. He was ambitious, but this was one of the many times in his life when his simple honesty interfered with his ambition. There have not been many men like him in politics.

Possibly he had already decided to resign when he got back to Philadelphia. He was already sick of politics, and dreaming of making a fortune at the bar. But he had started on this business. He had to go through with it. The leading Whiskey Boys had all escaped downriver. An illchosen assortment of poor devils had been arrested and brought in for examination. Most of them were released. Of the score or more marched back across the mountains to Philadelphia by the militia with a label saying *Insurgent* on their hats, now somewhat bedraggled by the late November rains and sleetstorms, all but two were to be acquitted when they were brought to trial. The show of force had been a hopeless fizzle. This was not the scene of military glory Hamilton had been planning for. When a problem was fresh he could examine every side of it with vast impersonal energy, but he tired easily when things were going wrong. He made up his mind to resign.

Meanwhile a subpoena had been served on Brackenridge. He was taken before the Secretary for questioning. "I attended the judge and was referred by him to secretary Hamilton, for examination. I was received by Hamilton with that countenance, which a man will have when he sees a person, with regard to whom his humanity and his sense of justice struggles;—he would have him saved, but is afraid he must be hanged;—he was willing to treat me with civility, but was embarrassed with a sense, that, in a short time, I must probably stand in the predicament of a culprit, and be in irons. He began by asking me some general questions, with regard to any system or plan, within my knowledge, of overthrowing the government. I had known of nothing of the kind . . ."

After a number of general questions about the supposed Jacobin revolution being planned by the Democratic Societies in the Western Country, which Brackenridge couldn't answer very well because no such thing existed, it was decided that Brackenridge must tell what he did know. The Secretary was covering a long sheet of paper with his rapid small handwriting.

"I gave him the outlines of the narrative . . . until I came to the particular, where after the burning of Neville's house, I represented the people calling on Bradford [David Bradford, the rather emptyheaded young man who had ridden round in a new militia uniform and had had the illusion for a while that he was leading the rioters; he had already run off for Louisiana] and Marshall to come forward, and support what was done, under the pain of being treated as Neville himself had been. At this the secretary laid down his pen and addressed himself to me;

" 'Mr. Brackenridge,' said he, 'I observe one leading trait in your account, a disposition to excuse the principal actors; and before we go further, I must be candid and inform you of the delicate situation in which you stand; *you are not within the amnesty; you have not signed upon the day;* a thing we did not know until we came upon this ground, I mean into the western country; and though the government may not be disposed to proceed rigorously, yet it has you in its power, and it will depend upon the candour of your account, what your fate will be.' "

Brackenridge answered that he knew that all too well, but that he was telling the truth and there was nothing else to say. He went on with his account of what had happened until Hamilton was called to dinner. Brackenridge went back home, "but declined dining with General Lee that day, though pressed by several messages. I could not bear to show myself in that company, in the doubtful predicament in which I stood."

Meanwhile a scene had taken place at Hamilton's lodgings that Brackenridge only learned about later: "The general, who has been a subject of the outrages, was there in the light of a private prosecutor; and in the aid of the judiciary was assisting in bringing forward and interrogating witnesses. My brother of the bar [Lawyer Woods, of whom Brackenridge wrote that 'he had all hell in his bosom; and had it not been for the prospect of hanging me, would have struggled hard to have me murdered'] was active in sounding, embracing and marshalling them; and if on examination, anything was omitted by the judiciary, he took the general aside, and gave him a hint of it. The general would then return to the charge with fresh questions. This is the account I have had from witnesses examined, and from gentlemen occasionally present.

"When the matter was thought to be pretty well fixed against me, the great and concluding stroke was to be given. A treasonable letter of mine addressed to a certain Bradford had fallen into the hands of my adversaries. It was dark and mysterious, and respected certain papers, a duplicate of which I wished him to send me, having mislaid the first copy; that these were so essential, I could not go on with the business without them. This letter was now brought forward.

" 'What do you make of that?' said secretary Hamilton to James Ross, who was present: 'you have averred as your opinion, that Brackenridge has had no correspondence with Bradford; look at that, is it not the handwriting of Brackenridge?'

" 'It is the handwriting,' said James Ross, pausing for some time; 'and there is only this small matter observable in the case, that it is addressed to William Bradford, attorney general of the United States, and not to David Bradford.'

"When a blast, transverse, takes a shallop on the river, and throws her on her beam ends, with all her sails set: or when a scud of wind takes the standing corn of the farmer, and on the field bows the stalks to the earth, so languished my brother of the bar. The old general stood motionless and speechless, and to this hour had been standing, had not secretary Hamilton broken the silence;

" 'Gentlemen,' said he, 'you are too fast; this will not do.' "

Brackenridge, who was a nervous man, had been bolting a little food and pacing up and down the backroom of his house. "At three o'clock I returned to my examination; Mr. Hamilton entering the room where I had been waiting for him, appeared to have been reflecting, and said:

" 'Mr. Brackenridge, your conduct has been horribly misrepresented.'

". . . I went on, giving an account of the town meeting of Pittsburgh. I stated it, as moved by me, that we should march and affect to join the people at Braddock's fields. I saw the secretary pause at this and sink into deep reflection. It staggered him.

" 'Was it any more,' said I, 'than what Richard the second

did when a mob of 100,000 men assembled on Blackheath? the young prince addressed them, put himself at their head, and said, What do you want, gentlemen? I will lead you on.'

"My narrative now continued. After some time the secretary observed:

" 'My breast begins to ach, we will stop to night; we will resume it tomorrow morning at 9 o'clock.'

"I withdrew but was struck by his last expression. I was at a loss to know whether his breast ached for my sake, or from his writing; but disposed to construe everything unfavorable, I supposed it was for my sake, and that he saw I must be arrested.

"Next morning general Lee made an aplogy to Mrs. Brackenridge, that for the sake of retirement, and to be in a less central part of the town, he was about to withdraw to other quarters, with some part of his family. I considered this owing to the delicacy of his feelings, that he wished to be out of the way, and not a witness of a circumstance of one, with whom he had been acquainted in juvenile years, sinking into a melancholy situation just under his eye. I had taken it for granted that he had received a hint from Mr. Hamilton, of what was to take place.

"Waiting on the secretary at 9 o'clock, my examination recommenced. In the course of the narrative, his countenance began to brighten and having finished the history there was an end.

" 'Mr. Brackenridge,' said he, 'in the course of yesterday I had uneasy feelings, I was concerned for you as a man of talents; my impressions were unfavorable; you may have observed it. I now think it my duty to inform you, that not a single one remains. Had we listened to some people, I do not know what we might have done. There is a side to your account; your conduct has been horribly misrepresented, owing to misconception. I will announce you in this point of view to governor Lee who represents the executive. You are in no personal danger. You will not be troubled even by a simple inquisition by the judge; what may be due to yourself with the public, is another question.'

"In so delicate a case, where life had been sought by insidious men; and where, what I felt with more sensibility, my hopes of estimation in the world, were likely to be blasted, at least for a time, it may easily be supposed that no word escaped me, or will ever be forgotten.

"My sensibility had been greatly wounded, when I waited on judge Peters with the narrative to sign it, as directed by Mr. Hamilton. It was with difficulty, I could write my name. I cursed the circumstance of having to write it five times, to the five different sheets of paper, of which my narrative consisted. I returned to my house with different feelings from those I had had a long time before."

As the divines of the old days of the Commonwealth would have put it both Hamilton and Brackenridge had 'the root of the matter' in them. Though they were both vain, ambitious, pushing men, each given to moments of irresponsibility, something in their early training had engrained into their behavior the minimum of personal restraint needed to keep the fabric of a selfgoverning society unbroken. Men brought up under Club Law would have behaved differently. It was a commonplace of our fathers' and grandfathers' thought that men of Anglo-Saxon training and tradition knew how to govern themselves better than other men. Even through the shames and hypocrisies of the age of money rule which is now coming to an end it was not entirely an empty boast. Today our lives depend on it. If we can keep the fabric of a selfgoverning republic unbroken at home, we are in no danger from the attacks of the slave states of Europe and Asia; if we can't, everything we as Americans have stood for from the beginning will have been in vain.

Notes on Books to Read

THE only way to find out anything about what kind of lives people led in any given period is to tunnel into their records and to let them speak for themselves. I have noted down a few books that furnished me valuable clews.

To get your bearings in the period of the Commonwealth in England nothing can take the place of David Masson's *Life of John Milton Narrated in Connexion with the History of his Time,* and its useful index volume. William Godwin's *History of the Commonwealth of England* is pretty fair; his *Lives of Edward and John Phillips, Nephews and Pupils of Milton,* very effectively complements Pepys for the Restoration period. Carlyle's lurid presentation of Oliver Cromwell's letters and speeches is valuable and stirring, perhaps the best thing that worthy ever did, but it needs the corrective of some recent scholarly work such as Wilbur C. Abbott's edition, published by the Harvard University Press. Two other useful books on the period are *The Leveller Movement* by Theodore Calvin Pease and L. H. Berens' *The Digger Movement in the Days of the Commonwealth.* Lucy Hutchinson's *Life of Colonel Hutchinson* is a personal document of the time no one should miss.

Although there have been many lives of Roger Williams, none of them is very satisfactory by itself and most of them are extremely inaccurate. The newest and best, and certainly the most careful and scholarly, has just come out: *The Irrepressible Democrat, Roger Williams* by H. S. Brockunier who wrote the excellent article on Williams in the *Dictionary of American Biography.* A good critical edition of Roger Williams' correspondence would make mighty good reading. Something else that's very much needed is a first rate scholarly work on Defoe and his time. In spite of the fact that he completely ignores Defoe's life and many other important matters as being beneath the notice of a brilliant early Victorian, Macaulay's

History of England still offers more leads into the history of the period than anything else I've seen. The Franklin literature in English and French is immense and confusing. Old Parton's life isn't bad. Fortunately Ben did a good deal of writing himself.

On the whole, with all its obvious faults and inaccuracies, I found early American historical writing better than later; Parton and Randall and Tucker, and even Jared Sparks when he's at his best, and Bancroft may have occasionally overcolored or undercolored the picture, but they had an idea of what it was all about. So much later historical writing was merely Federalist apologetics. Beard, of course, granted the aridity of his economic viewpoint, did a great work in clearing the ground for new construction in *The Rise of American Civilization* and *An Economic Interpretation of the Constitution of the United States* and in his corresponding book on Jeffersonian Democracy. The only American work I can think of comparable in imagination and scope to the work of the great British liberal historians is Vernon L. Parrington's tragically unfinished *Main Currents in American Thought.*

Samuel Adams is one of the most difficult characters in history to get at. John C. Miller's *Sam Adams: Pioneer in Propaganda* is full of valuable clews, but for me the book was spoiled by its debunking tone. You feel like asking Mr. Miller on every page: Did Sam Adams do a good job or didn't he? For Jefferson, I think that there are more good leads in Claude Bowers' *Hamilton and Jefferson* and in Hirst's *Life and Letters of Thomas Jefferson* than in any other recent books. Gilbert Chinard's monographs, such as *Jefferson et les Idéologues* and *Volney et l'Amérique* I found immensely useful. A good new critical edition of Jefferson's writings would be a great help to everybody interested in the first fifty years of the history of this republic. The present editions are a national disaster.

There is a very useful little book about Joel Barlow called *The Early Days of Joel Barlow,* by Theodore Albert Zunder which confines itself strictly to documents and seems to me a singularly fresh and entertaining piece of scholarly reconstruction. I also got help from a doctor's thesis by Victor Clyde Miller: *Joel Barlow, Revolutionist: London 1791-92* which presents useful research even if it is, to my way of thinking, based on a complete misconception of Barlow's character and of the political situation at the time.

The British background of the American Revolution is pretty well treated in Lecky's *History of England in the Eighteenth Century*. George Otto Trevelyan's volumes starting with *The Early History of Charles James Fox* were at one time highly thought of, and deserve to be read again. A great deal of excavation remains to be done in the field of the interaction of American and French ideas and personalities at the end of the eighteenth century. Moncure Conway's life of Tom Paine opens up some terrain. In French I found the *Memoirs* of Larévellière-Lépeau very illuminating. Beatrix Cary Davenport's new edition of Gouverneur Morris' diary for 1789 to 1793 is a model of what that sort of editing should be, and an extremely useful and entertaining book. John Adams' letters and comments are always salty and John Quincy Adams' journal is indispensable for the latter part of the period.

H. H. Brackenridge luckily was able to tell his own story and to tell it comically and well. In the literature of the Alexander Hamilton legend, in which I can't pretend to be very expert, I found no book that opened up so many dynamic possibilities as Claude Bowers' *Jefferson and Hamilton*, cited above.

For general reference I found nothing to compare with the British *Dictionary of National Biography*. Its American counterpart contains some good articles, but it has not yet reached the same level of excellence.

Index